REPRESENTATIVE OPINIONS OF JUSTICE ANTONIN SCALIA

REPRESENTATIVE OPINIONS OF JUSTICE ANTONIN SCALIA

Michael H. Hoeflich William Skepnek

CO-EDITORS

TALBOT
PUBLISHING
Clark, New Jersey

ISBN 978-1-61619-572-4

TALBOT PUBLISHING

AN IMPRINT OF

THE LAWBOOK EXCHANGE, LTD.

33 Terminal Avenue
Clark, New Jersey 07066-1321

Please see our website for a selection of our other publications and fine facsimile reprints of classic works of legal history:
www.lawbookexchange.com

Library of Congress Cataloging-in-Publication Data

Names: Scalia, Antonin. | Hoeflich, Michael H., editor. | Skepnek, William, editor.
Title: Representative opinions of Justice Antonin Scalia / Michael H. Hoeflich, William Skepnek, co-editors.
Description: Clark, NJ : Talbot Publishing, an imprint of The Lawbook Exchange, Ltd., [2018] | Includes bibliographical references and index.
Identifiers: LCCN 2018010064 | ISBN 9781616195724 (hardcover : alk. paper)
Subjects: LCSH: Judicial opinions--United States. | Law--United States--Cases. | LCGFT: Court decisions and opinions.
Classification: LCC KF213.S32 H645 2018 | DDC 347.73/26--dc23
LC record available at https://lccn.loc.gov/2018010064

Printed in the United States of America on acid-free paper

Table of Contents

Acknowledgments

Thanks to my research assistants Matthew Beal, KU Law '19 and Shelley Woodard, KU Law '17.

Michael H. Hoeflich

INTRODUCTION

Michael H. Hoeflich[*]

Beginnings

The place of Justice Antonin Scalia in the American judicial firmament is assured. Like Chief Justice Marshall and Justices Story, Harlan, Holmes, Brandeis, and Cardozo, Justice Scalia left an indelible mark on American law. And this was no accident. From his earliest days Justice Scalia was driven to excel and he certainly did. Indeed, it is fair to say, that with a few minor exceptions, Justice Scalia conquered every field of battle on to which he entered until he found himself at the supreme pinnacle of the American legal profession: the Supreme Court of the United States.

Justice Scalia had a profound and wide-ranging intellect coupled with a mastery of literary and judicial style matched by few of his contemporaries or his predecessors. This is not surprising since his father who began his life in the United States as a poor immigrant from Italy was, by the end of his life, one of the most distinguished literary scholars of his time. Justice Scalia was an outstanding student as an undergraduate at Georgetown University where he not only acquired a superb Jesuit education but also learned the art of debate and was confirmed in his lifelong Catholic beliefs. At Harvard Law School Justice Scalia

---

[*] Michael H. Hoeflich is the John H. & John M. Kane Distinguished Professor of Law, University of Kansas School of Law.

discovered the world of jurisprudence and also realized that there were no limits to how high he could rise in the legal profession. Justice Scalia's intellectual brilliance combined with his ambition and his determination to succeed ensured that his early years would provide a base from which he could build a career without limitations.[1]

On Course

After law school Justice Scalia made all the right moves. His first experience in the legal world was an associate at Jones, Day, a nationally prominent Cleveland law firm.[2] For six years he stayed there as an associate honing his legal skills. In 1967 he moved from Jones, Day to accept a faculty position at the University of Virginia, but his stay in Charlottesville was brief. In 1970 he moved to Washington, D.C. where he became the general counsel of the newly formed Office of Telecommunications policy in the Nixon administration. In 1972 he moved on to become Chairman of the U.S. Administrative Conference. Finally, in 1974, nearing the end of the Nixon Presidency he joined the White House Office of Legal Counsel as its head. He remained there through the end of the Nixon and Ford administrations and only left Washington when Jimmy Carter, a Democrat, had won the Presidential election. For a brief time, Scalia then taught at Georgetown Law School and served as a resident scholar at the American Enterprise Institute, a conservative political think tank. In the fall of 1977 Justice Scalia decided to move to the University of Chicago Law School and join a faculty filled with prominent legal scholars such as Rich-

---

[1] In this introduction I have relied heavily upon the excellent biography by Bruce Allen Murphy, *Scalia. A Court of One* (2014).

[2] Biographical details are taken from Murphy, n.1, above.

ard Posner, Frank Easterbrook, and Richard Epstein. For most lawyers, this remarkable professional trajectory that had landed him amongst the most thoughtful and productive legal scholars at Chicago would have been immensely satisfying. But the young Justice Scalia had his eyes set on higher ground: the federal judiciary and the U.S. Supreme Court. Justice Scalia's work as a faculty advisor to the newly formed Federalist Society of Chicago, his growing reputation as a young star in the conservative legal firmament, and the election of Ronald Reagan to the Presidency just a few years after he arrived at Chicago meant that he would achieve his ultimate goal at the age of 47. In 1982 he was appointed to the D.C. Court of Appeals and in 1986 he was nominated, confirmed, and sworn in as an Associate Justice of the United States Supreme Court.

Justice Scalia was not only a prolific author of Supreme Court decisions, both majority and in dissent, but, also, published law review articles, popular journalism, and scholarly legal books throughout his career. He also was one of the Justices who happily travelled from law school to law school throughout the United States and abroad to lecture on the law.[3] Like Justice Holmes before him, Justice Scalia was never shy about explaining his methodologies and his approaches to cases to a wide public. For the purposes of this introduction to his representative majority opinions, I will limit myself to two aspects of Justice Scalia's legal thought: textualism and historicism, both of which were closely tied in his legal writing as both scholar and judge.

---

[3] It is at this point that I must admit that when MHH was a faculty member at the University of Illinois in the early 1980s and when MHH was the dean of the University of Kansas Law School, I invited first Professor and then Justice Scalia to visit and speak at my law schools. Indeed, my invitation to Justice Scalia to come to KU was the subject of some controversy, see, Murphy, n.1, above, at 300.

The Textualist

Although Justice Scalia was recognized as the foremost conservative on the Supreme Court during his tenure there, he did not subscribe to the methodology of "original intent," i.e. the search for the intention of the Framers, that so beguiled some of the conservative jurists of his era, such as Robert Bork and Edwin Meese.[4] Instead, Justice Scalia was an unabashed "textualist" who subscribed to the theory of "original meaning" and, thus, sought to understand the meaning of the words used by the Founders by focusing on the general understanding of these words at the time the Constitution was founded. This is a subtle but crucial difference. While those who deemed themselves to be "original intentionalists" after the theory propounded by Attorney-General Edwin Meese in a now famous speech at Tulane University, sought to understand the Constitution by understanding the Framers' intent through their letters and through accounts of the debate on the adoption of the Constitution, Justice Scalia adopted a more nuanced approach and sought to understand the common meaning of words as they were understood at the time of the ratification of the Constitution.[5] This methodological approach to the text of the Constitution arose, in part, from Justice Scalia's disdain of the use of legislative history and, in part, from Justice Scalia's doubts that legislative history was, in fact, at all reliable. But Justice Scalia did agree with those who sought the "original intent" of the Framers in one major aspect, i.e. that the focus of

---

[4] I wish to thank Prof. Bruce Murphy for drawing the distinction between "original intent" and "original meaning" to my attention.

[5] See, Edwin Meese III, "The Law of the Constitution," [New Orleans, October 10, 1986] repr. *Tulane Law Review* 61 (1987): 979–90; on Meese's role in helping Scalia's career and their disagreements as to method, see, Murphy, n.1 at p. 123–127.

any judicial inquiry into a question of constitutionality should be centered upon the text of the Constitution. In this focus Justice Scalia repudiated the ideas of his more liberal colleagues on the court and in the profession that there was such a thing as a "Living Constitution" that could depart from the actual text in favor of post-constitutional developments in society.

Justice Scalia explained his textualist approach to constitutional interpretation in his "Common-Law Courts in a Civil Law System: The Role of United States Federal Courts in Interpreting the Constitution and Laws" published in 1997.[6] He begins by making it clear that common-law judges, in his opinion play "God" when they use their power of interpretation to make law:

> What intellectual fun all of this is! It explains why first-year law school is so exhilarating: because it consists of playing common-law judge, which in turn consists of playing king—devising out of the brilliance of one's own mind, those laws that ought to govern mankind. How exciting! And no wonder so many law students having drunk at this intoxicating well, aspire for the rest of their lives to be judges![7]

The deep distrust of common law judges and judging displayed in this passage makes it clear that Justice Scalia saw his textualist method and search for the "original meaning" of the Constitution as a means of curbing the excessive activism of the judges he saw all around him. Indeed, Justice Scalia goes on to disparage Justices Holmes and Cardozo for their "broken-

---

[6] A. Scalia, *A Matter of Interpretation. Federal Courts and the Law* (1997); see, also, Antonin Scalia and Bryan A. Garner, *Reading Law: The Interpretation of Legal Texts*, p. 356 (2012). I wish to thank Bryan Garner for this reference.

[7] Ibid., p. 7.

field running" through precedents to reach what they "discerned" as the best rule of law. He said:

> A text should not be construed strictly, and it should not be construed leniently; it should be construed reasonably, to contain all that it fairly means. ... Of all the criticisms leveled against textualism, the most mindless is that it is "formalistic." The answer to that is, *of course it's formalistic*! The law is about form.[8]

Textualism for Justice Scalia was a means by which common law judges could be reined in. It was a methodology which substantially reduced judicial discretion by forcing judges to look at external, objective (or so he argued) sources to determine what a word meant as used by the general, literate public at the time the word was used. And, as he so tellingly stated, the "law is about form," not justice.

In fact, Justice Scalia's textualism was far from a perfect solution to the problems he sought to correct. First, of course, are the difficulties in actually determining what a particular word or phrase meant in the past. Historical linguists have shown that the word meanings differ over time and place and that even in the same time and the same place a word may have quite different meanings depending on how it is used. This was driven home to me quite forcefully when I went to Cambridge University to do graduate work. I found, much to my delight, that I had been assigned a quite luxurious suite consisting of a bedroom and study and that there was a college servant who was assigned to clean my rooms five days each week. She introduced herself as Mrs. Moore and proved to be a delightful woman in her mid-thirties. After she explained what she would

---

[8] Ibid., p.25.

be doing each morning, she asked me at what time I generally awoke. When I replied that I awoke most mornings at 6 am, she cheerfully replied that she would "knock me up" at 6 the next morning. As a product of NYC, when I heard these words I blushed a deep red not realizing that "knock me up" in Cambridge parlance meant "knock on the door" as opposed to the rather more lurid meaning it had back home in N.Y.

Indeed, Justice Scalia often argued for the use of the 1828 edition of Webster's *Dictionary* as being the perfect starting place into researching the meaning of a constitutional word or phrase.[9] In some ways this is a perfect source since it is the first major dictionary published by an American in the United States thus, on that ground, making it a good source for understanding the meaning of contemporary American documents. However, the first edition of the *Dictionary* was not published until 1828 and Noah Webster did not begin work on the volume until 1807 so at the best nearly twenty years separated the drafting of the Constitution from the time that Webster began work on his great book. Indeed, it is far more likely that the Founders and their contemporaries used English dictionaries, such as the great dictionary written by Samuel Johnson.[10]

Flaws or not, Justice Scalia clung to his textualist approach. I would suggest that the reason for this was pragmatic as much as theoretical. While not perfect, the textual approach to judicial interpretation and the search for "original meaning" does significantly limit judicial law-making, if it is done properly.[11] And that was, in fact, Justice Scalia's conservative goal: to slow

---

[9] Noah Webster, *American Dictionary of the English Language* (1828); see, Murphy, n.1, above, pp.143–144.

[10] Samuel Johnson, *A Dictionary of the English Language* (1755).

[11] Murphy, n. 1, above, at p. 144 re *Thompson v. Oklahoma* and Scalia's explicit statements against the notion of an "evolving" or "living" Constitution.

judicial law-making and to repudiate the idea of a living Constitution and all that this entailed. In this sense, Justice Scalia was the "perfect" judicial conservative, conserving the meaning and force of statutes, including the Constitution, no matter how old they might be, no matter how much the social context in which the law operates had changed.[12]

The Historian

The textualist approach as it was espoused by Justice Scalia was, of its very nature, historical in essence. A judge who would follow the textualist approach when confronted by a question of constitutional authority must, of necessity, delve into historical sources in order to determine the proper meaning of a word or phrase. The variety of such sources includes not only legal documents, but also a wide array of literary and practical documents drawn from the daily life of the late eighteenth century. Fortunately or unfortunately, there are thousands upon thousands upon thousands of such documents available in print, manuscript, and on the Web and the number increases every year. Thus, a judge who is a textualist also becomes a historical researcher. But there is a difficulty.

A historian when he approaches historical material, be it in print or manuscript, will generally approach the material with a series of questions, but not, generally, with the answers to those questions already formulated.[13] The purpose of "pure"

---

[12] And, see, Scalia and Garner, above, at p. 336. I wish to thank Bryan Garner for this reference.

[13] I am indebted to the late Sir Geoffrey Elton, Regius Professor of Modern History at Cambridge University, my teacher and mentor, for my understanding, however imperfect, of how a professional historian approaches historical sources; see, G. Elton, *The Practice of History* (1967).

historical research is to gain greater insight into the lives and thoughts of those who have come before us. Historians may well have theories about the past and then turn to the sources to discover whether those theories are supported by the sources. But a good historian, when confronted by the actuality of the sources and what they say will not reject them or any part of them simply because they do not support the conclusions which he hopes will be proved. In short, an historian is not an advocate. A lawyer, on the other hand, is an advocate and when a lawyer approaches historical sources he is generally doing so because there is a point he wishes to make in support of an argument. Since a lawyer's job is advocacy, a lawyer will not approach the sources neutrally, but, instead, will deal with the sources as he would any other text: he will seek to find historical texts which bolster his argument, attempt to interpret and construe ambiguous historical texts in a manner that makes them support his argument, and will attempt to distinguish away or otherwise neutralize texts that harm his argument. This approach is generally referred to as "law office history."

Judge Frank Easterbrook, a former academic colleague of Justice Scalia, has spoken of this practice in quite negative terms:

> Law office history is an oxymoron. I don't pay much attention to purported history in legal briefs because people are always taking things out of context. Not that the lawyers generally know enough to understand the original context. They may not even know which particular kind of mistake they're making when they take statements out of context. [14]

---

[14] "Dialogue with Federal Judges on the Role of History in Interpretation," 80 *George Washington Law Review* 1889 (2012) (with Diane P. Wood & Jeffrey S. Sutton & Reena Raggi).

One core question when evaluating the utility of the textual approach in a case is whether the judge employing this approach acts more like a professional historian who treats the sources neutrally or whether the judge acts more like an advocate who treats the sources as the raw material from which to construct an argument for supporting an a priori conclusion.

How one uses the textualist approach propounded by Justice Scalia will determine whether it is actually a valid approach to constitutional interpretation from a historical perspective. This is a very different question from asking whether a judge should recognize the existence of a "Living Constitution." Fundamentally, if a textualist judge approaches the historical sources that underlie his interpretation of a constitutional word or phrase as an advocate, if he "cherry picks" the sources for only those words and phrases that support the conclusion he has already decided is correct, if he deliberately misinterprets sources that are adverse to that conclusion, then he may call himself a textualist, but he is not a true textualist who must, by necessity, respect the historical sources and treat them as a professional historian would.[15] He is simply an advocate using historical sources without any respect for historical methodology.

It is this criticism that has been leveled at a number of Justice Scalia's decisions, such as his opinion in *District of Columbia v. Heller*.[16] Here, the bottom line is not that Justice

---

[15] See, J. Harvie Wilkinson, "Of Guns, Abortions and the Unraveling Rule of Law, Virginia Law Review, vol. 95, p.p. 253–323 (April, 2009). See, also, Justice Scalia's response to this criticism in his speech on the "Methodology of Originalism," I want to thank Prof. Bruce Murphy for this reference. See, also, Scalia and Garner, n. 7, above, at p. 399.

[16] 554 U.S. 570 (2008); see, the scathing attack of Justice Scalia's opinion in *Heller* by his former colleague at Chicago, Richard Posner, "In Defense of Looseness," *New Republic* (August 26, 2008), on the web at https://newrepub

Scalia used a textualist approach; it is that he *misused a textualist* approach. Of course, so long as he could gather the votes of four other Justices, such criticisms had no practical impact.

A related problem for the judge who uses historical sources as a basis for a textualist approach is the vast quantity of sources of questionable reliability that are available for use in many cases. Justice Scalia was not at all worried by this, however:

> Properly done, the task requires the consideration of an enormous mass of material—in the case of the Constitution and its Amendments, for example, to mention only one element, the records of the ratifying debates in all the states. Even beyond that, it requires an evaluation of the reliability of the material—many of the reports of the ratifying debates, for example, are thought to be quite unreliable. And further still it requires immersing oneself in the political and intellectual atmosphere of the time—somehow placing out of mind knowledge that we have which an earlier age did not, and putting on beliefs, attitudes, philosophies, prejudices and loyalties that are not those of our day.[17]

Justice Scalia was well aware of the dangers inherent in using historical sources upon which to base critical constitutional decisions. Indeed, he commented that, perhaps, this was a job for an "American historian" rather than a judge.[18] Nevertheless, this awareness did not stop him from using historical research in his textualist analyses leaving him wide open to the

---

lic.com/article/62124/defense-looseness, cited by Murphy, Scalia, n. 1, above, at p. 391.

[17] A. Scalia, "Originalism: The Lesser Evil," in *University of Cincinnati Law. Review,* vol. 57 (1989) quoted and commented upon in Murphy, n.1, above, p. 165.

[18] Murphy, n.1, above, p. 165.

challenge that some of his decisions were merely examples of "law office history."[19]

The "Shin-Kicker"[20]

There can be no doubt in the mind of anyone who has read even a small number of Justice Scalia's opinions that he was a master of judicial style. Further, he was also a master of invective and remarks *ad hominem*. Unlike Holmes who certainly was not afraid of using a *bon mot* or expressing a legal point in a cutting maxim ("three generations of idiots is enough") but did not generally attack his colleagues on the Bench in public, Justice Scalia seems to have felt no hesitation in turning his formidable intellect and powerful literary style against his colleagues in his opinions, especially his dissents. Many of his colleagues were the targets of invective that most lawyers would deem to be more appropriate for a college debate than a Supreme Court opinion [and, since Justice Scalia had been a champion collegiate debater, there may well be a connection].

For the general reader who encounters the sting of Justice Scalia's words in so many of his opinions, this may result only in a bit of *Schadenfreude* or, in our polarized society today, perhaps a bit of amusement or even pleasure to see more liberal Justices skewered. But to lawyers and scholars who study these opinions the acerbity of the language can be quite revealing. First, of course, they may well mark Justice Scalia's isolation from other

---

[19] See, the comments of the distinguished American historian Gordon S. Wood, that follow Justice Scalia's essays in Scalia, *A Matter of Interpretation*, n. 5, above, pp. 49–63.

[20] On Justice Scalia's fondness for this phrase, see *The New York Times* (Feb. 14, 2016) on the web at https://www.nytimes.com/2016/02/15/nyregion/in-queens-antonin-scalia-took-pride-in-melting-pot-and-confrontation.html.

members of the Court, an isolation also demonstrated by his frequent dissents and by his willingness to openly criticize his colleagues in speeches, articles, and even the popular media. At the very simplest level, such isolation may harm the legitimacy of the Court's opinions. It is one thing to oppose one's colleague on the Bench in a polite dissent; it is quite another to do so in a scathing dissent or majority opinion coupled with an onslaught of additional criticism off the Bench.

A second danger that presented itself in Justice Scalia's often stinging attacks upon his colleagues is that these often-made compromises among the Justices far more difficult. Time and time again Justice Scalia found himself as a lonely dissenter rather than a member of the majority or even in position to write a concurrence. [21] This meant, of course, that his actual impact on the law as it was developed by the Court on which he sat became less. Of course, since he believed fervently that he was right and his colleagues wrong, he knew that someday many of his dissents, like those of Justice Holmes before him, would guide future members of the Supreme Court in charting a different path. Only a man with the greatest confidence in his ideas could have been content to be in dissent so much of his career on the Bench.

The Choice and Editing of the Opinions in this Volume

This volume (and its companion volume of dissenting opinions) is based upon the model of Alfred Lief, *Representative Opinions of Mr. Justice Holmes* (1931). The criteria by which opinions were selected are as follows:

---

[21] For a collection of Justice Scalia's dissenting opinions, see, M.H. Hoeflich & C. Stegall, *Dissenting Opinions of Justice Antonin Scalia* (2018).

1. **Date.** We attempted to include opinions from Justice Scalia's full time on the Supreme Court to show the development of his judicial thought and methodology;
2. **Subject.** We attempted to choose opinions that covered a wide subject range representative of the Court's work;
3. **Significance.** We chose opinions that were, for the most part, of some general significance to American legal development during Justice Scalia's tenure on the Court.
4. **Style & Methodology.** We chose opinions that we believed were noteworthy examples either of Justice Scalia's judicial style and/or methodology of textualism;
5. **Personal Preference.** As lawyers and legal scholars we have personal likes and dislikes about both Justices and Supreme Court opinions. No doubt this, too, influenced the selection of opinions to be included in this volume.

We have not intended to be comprehensive. Hence the title includes the phrase "representative cases." It is our aim that this book should make Justice Scalia's Supreme Court opinions available to a wide audience. Thus, we have not edited his language or opinions. But in the interest of space, we have deleted the footnotes. The typical editing of opinions included in law school casebooks is brutal and often leads to gross misunderstanding of what was actually written. In addition, Justice Scalia was a masterly writer whose judicial style is among the best of any American judge, living or dead. It would be an immense disservice to him and those who read the opinions contained in this volume to do anything that would harm his prose. Thus, we have chosen to exercise a very light editorial touch.

REPRESENTATIVE OPINIONS OF JUSTICE ANTONIN SCALIA

1

Constitutional Structure

The Rights of Soldiers under the Federal Tort Claims Act
United States v. Stanley, 483 U.S. 669 (1987)

On the Power to Bestow Citizenship
INS v. Pangilinan, 486 U.S. 875 (1988)

Federal Preemption of State Law
Riegel v. Medtronic, Inc., 552 U.S. 312 (2008)

On Voting Rights and Preemption
Arizona v. Inter Tribal Council of Ariz., Inc., 133 S. Ct. 2247 (2013)

Interpreting the Clean Air Act
Michigan v. E.P.A., 135 S.Ct. 2699 (2015)

There is no subject closer to the core function of the United States Supreme Court than the proper structure of the Union under the Constitution. These majority decisions represent instances in which Justice Scalia's constitutional vision and sense of the proper structure of American governance won enough of his colleagues' support to put him into the majority. These decisions set forth Justice Scalia's vision of the proper balance between the authority of the federal government, the individual states, and individuals, and of the allocation of authority among the three branches of the federal government. The decisions range over a number of critical constitutional topics including pre-emption of voting rights, standards for federal agency regulations, and the allocation of power between Congress and the Judiciary in determining citizenship. One case, *U.S. v. Stanley*, deals with one of the most shameful episodes in American military history, in which soldiers "volunteered" to be given drugs to evaluate their utility for chemical warfare. The court barred their claims under the *Federal Tort Claims Act*.

The Rights of Soldiers under the Federal Tort Claims Act

United States v. Stanley, 483 U.S. 669 (1987)

Justice Scalia delivered the opinion of the Court.

In February 1958, James B. Stanley, a master sergeant in the Army stationed at Fort Knox, Kentucky, volunteered to participate in a program ostensibly designed to test the effectiveness of protective clothing and equipment as defenses against chemical warfare. He was released from his then-current duties and went to the Army's Chemical Warfare Laboratories at the Aberdeen Proving Grounds in Maryland. Four times that month, Stanley was secretly administered doses of lysergic acid diethylamide (LSD), pursuant to an Army plan to study the effects of the drug on human subjects. According to his Second Amended Complaint (the allegations of which we accept for purposes of this decision), as a result of the LSD exposure, Stanley has suffered from hallucinations and periods of incoherence and memory loss, was impaired in his military performance, and would on occasion "awake from sleep at night and, without reason, violently beat his wife and children, later being unable to recall the entire incident." App. 5. He was discharged from the Army in 1969. One year later, his marriage dissolved because of the personality changes wrought by the LSD.

On December 10, 1975, the Army sent Stanley a letter soliciting his cooperation in a study of the long-term effects of LSD on "volunteers who participated" in the 1958 tests. This was the Government's first notification to Stanley that he had been given LSD during his time in Maryland. After an administrative claim for compensation was denied by the

Army, Stanley filed suit under the Federal Tort Claims Act (FTCA), 28 U.S.C. § 2671 *et seq.*, alleging negligence in the administration, supervision, and subsequent monitoring of the drug testing program.

The District Court granted the Government's motion for summary judgment, finding that Stanley "was at all times on active duty and participating in a bona fide Army program during the time the alleged negligence occurred," No. 78-8141-Civ-CF, p. 2 (SD Fla., May 14, 1979), and that his FTCA suit was therefore barred by the doctrine of *Feres v. United States,* 340 U.S. 135, 71 S.Ct. 153, 95 L.Ed. 152 (1950), which determined that "the Government is not liable under the Federal Tort Claims Act for injuries to servicemen where the injuries arise out of or are in the course of activity incident to service." *Id.,* at 146, 71 S.Ct., at 159. The Court of Appeals for the Fifth Circuit agreed that the *Feres* doctrine barred Stanley's FTCA suit against the United States, but held that the District Court should have dismissed for lack of subject-matter jurisdiction rather than disposing of the case on the merits. *Stanley v. CIA,* 639 F.2d 1146 (1981). The Government contended that a remand would be futile, because *Feres* would bar any claims that Stanley could raise either under the FTCA or directly under the Constitution against individual officers under *Bivens v. Six Unknown Fed. Narcotics Agents,* 403 U.S. 388, 91 S.Ct. 1999, 29 L.Ed.2d 619 (1971). The court concluded, however, that Stanley "has at least a colorable constitutional claim based on *Bivens,*" 639 F.2d, at 1159, and remanded "for the consideration of the trial court of any amendment which the appellant may offer, seeking to cure the jurisdictional defect." *Id.,* at 1159–1160.

Stanley then amended his complaint to add claims against unknown individual federal officers for violation of his constitutional rights. He also specifically alleged that the United States' failure to warn, monitor, or treat him after he was discharged constituted a separate tort which, because occurring subsequent to his discharge, was not "incident to service" within the *Feres* exception to the FTCA. See *United States v. Brown,* 348 U.S. 110, 75 S.Ct. 141, 99 L.Ed. 139 (1954). The District Court dismissed the FTCA claim because the alleged negligence was not "separate and distinct from any acts occurring before discharge, so as to give rise to a separate actionable tort not barred by the *Feres* doctrine." 549 F.Supp. 327, 329 (SD Fla.1982). It refused, however, to dismiss the *Bivens* claims. The court rejected, *inter alia,* the Government's argument that the same considerations giving rise to the *Feres* exception to the FTCA should constitute "special factors" of the sort alluded to in *Bivens, supra,* 403 U.S., at 396, 91 S.Ct., at 2005, and other cases as bars to a *Bivens* action. It cited as sole authority for that rejection the Court of Appeals for the Ninth Circuit's decision in *Wallace v. Chappell,* 661 F.2d 729 (1981). *Sua sponte,* the court certified its order for interlocutory appeal under 28 U.S.C. § 1292(b).

Following issuance of the order, the Government moved for partial final judgment pursuant to Federal Rule of Civil Procedure 54(b) on behalf of itself and three federal agencies that had (improperly) been named as FTCA defendants throughout the proceedings. The Government also argued that because no individual defendants had been named or served, and thus had neither appeared as parties nor sought representation from the Department of Justice, there was no one to seek interlocutory review of the court's refusal to dismiss the *Bivens* actions. The court concluded that the Government's contentions were "well taken," *Stanley v. CIA,* 552 F.Supp. 619 (SD Fla.1982), and on November 9, 1982, it granted the motion for partial final judgment, ordered the Clerk to "enter final judgment in favor of the United States forthwith," *ibid.,* and vacated the portion of its prior order ruling on the *Bivens* claims against the individual defendants, giving Stanley 90 days to serve at least one individual defendant. The docket sheet for the case reflects the terms of that order ("The clerk to enter final judgment in favor of USA," App. to Brief in Opposition A4), but does not indicate that an additional "separate document," Fed.Rule Civ.Proc. 58, containing the judgment was entered. See Fed.Rule Civ.Proc. 79(a).

Stanley then filed his Second Amended Complaint, naming as defendants nine individuals (seven of whom are before us as petitioners) and the Board of Regents of the University of Maryland, and asserting civil rights claims under 42 U.S.C. §§ 1983 and 1985. Motions to dismiss for lack of personal jurisdiction and improper venue were filed on behalf of some of the defendants (it was alleged that proper service had not been made on the others), but before those motions were ruled on, we issued our decision in *Chappell v. Wallace*, 462 U.S. 296, 103 S.Ct. 2362, 76 L.Ed.2d 586 (1983), holding that "enlisted military personnel may not maintain a suit to recover damages from a superior officer for alleged constitutional violations," *id.*, at 305, 103 S.Ct., at 2368, and reversing the sole authority cited by the District Court in its prior order refusing to dismiss Stanley's *Bivens* claims. Stanley's counsel brought the *Chappell* decision to the attention of the District Court, which, apparently treating the filing of the Second Amended Complaint as automatically reinstating its previously vacated order concerning the *Bivens* claims, *sua sponte* reconsidered and reaffirmed its prior decision. It concluded that, despite the broadly stated holding of the case, *Chappell* did not "totally ba[r] *Bivens* actions by servicemen for torts committed against them during their term of service." 574 F.Supp. 474, 478 (1983). Rather, it said, *Chappell* only bars *Bivens* actions when "a member of the military brings a suit against a superior officer for wrongs which involve direct orders in the performance of military duty and the discipline and order necessary thereto," 574

F.Supp., at 479, factors that in its view were not involved in Stanley's claim. Nor could the court find in congressionally prescribed remedies, such as the Veterans Benefits' Act, 38 U.S.C. § 301 *et seq.*, any expression of exclusivity of the sort *Bivens* contemplated would preclude recovery. See 403 U.S., at 397, 91 S.Ct., at 2005. The court again certified its order for interlocutory appeal under § 1292(b), which petitioners sought and the Court of Appeals for the Eleventh Circuit granted.

The Court of Appeals affirmed the conclusion that *Chappell* does not require dismissal of Stanley's *Bivens* claims, on essentially the grounds relied upon by the District Court. 786 F.2d 1490 (1986). The court did not think that Congress' activity in the military justice field was a "special facto[r]" precluding Stanley's claim, as "[t]hose intramilitary administrative procedures which the Court found adequate to redress the servicemen's racial discrimination complaints in *Chappell* are clearly inadequate to compensate Stanley for the violations complained of here." *Id.*, at 1496.

Although the issue had not been addressed in the order from which the interlocutory appeal was taken, the Court of Appeals further determined that recent precedent in the Eleventh Circuit, including *Johnson v. United States,* 749 F.2d 1530 (1985), rev'd, 481 U.S. 681, 107 S.Ct. 2063, 95 L.Ed.2d 648 (1987), indicated that Stanley might have a viable FTCA claim against the United States, and that law-of-the-case principles therefore did not require adherence to the 1982 holding that Stanley's FTCA claim was barred by *Feres.* It remanded with instructions to the District Court to "allow Stanley the opportunity to amend to plead consistent with recent precedent." 786 F.2d, at 1499.

Because the Courts of Appeals have not been uniform in their interpretation of the holding in *Chappell,* and because the Court of Appeals' reinstatement of Stanley's FTCA claims seems at odds with sound judicial practice, we granted certiorari. 479 U.S. 1005, 107 S.Ct. 642, 93 L.Ed.2d 699 (1986).

I

We first address the Court of Appeals' instruction to the District Court to allow Stanley to replead his FTCA claim. While petitioners advance several reasons why that action was improper, and additional reasons can perhaps be found in our recent decision in *United States v. Johnson,* 481 U.S. 681, 107 S.Ct. 2063, 95 L.Ed.2d 648 (1987), we find it necessary to discuss only one. The case did not come before the Court of Appeals on appeal from a final decision of the District Court under 28 U.S.C. § 1291. Rather, the Court of Appeals had jurisdiction pursuant to § 1292(b), which provides:

> "When a district judge in making in a civil action an order not otherwise appealable under this section, shall be of the opinion that *such order* involves a controlling question of law as to which there is substantial ground for difference of opinion and that an immediate appeal *from the order* may materially advance the ultimate termination of the litigation, he shall so state in writing in such order. The Court of Appeals may thereupon, in its discretion, permit an appeal to be taken *from such order....*" (Emphasis added.)

An appeal under this statute is from the *certified order,* not from any other orders that may have been entered in the case. Even if the Court of Appeals' jurisdiction is not confined to the precise question certified by the lower court (because the statute brings the "order," not the question, before the court), that jurisdiction *is* confined to the particular order appealed from. Commentators and courts have consistently observed that "the scope of the issues open to the court of appeals is closely limited to the order appealed from [and] [t]he court of appeals will not consider matters that were ruled upon in other orders." 16 C. Wright, A. Miller, E. Cooper, & E. *Gressman, Federal Practice and Procedure* § 3929, p. 143 (1977). See *Pritchard-Keang Nam Corp. v. Jaworski,* 751 F.2d 277, 281, n. 3 (CA8 1984), cert. dism'd, 472 U.S. 1022, 105 S.Ct. 3491, 87 L.Ed.2d 625 (1985); *United States v. Bear Marine Services,* 696 F.2d 1117, 1119, n. 1 (CA5 1983); *Time, Inc. v. Ragano,* 427 F.2d 219, 221 (CA5 1970).

Here, the "order appealed from" was an order refusing to dismiss Stanley's *Bivens* claims on the basis of our holding in *Chappell.* The Court of Appeals therefore had no jurisdiction to enter orders relating to Stanley's long-dismissed FTCA claims, whether or not, as Stanley argues, "the issues involved in the *Bivens* claim and the alleged immunity of the individual defendants closely parallels [sic] the government's immunity due to the *Feres* doctrine ... [and] that is what all parties were arguing about in the interlocutory appeal." Brief for Respondent 17–18. The Court of Appeals' action is particularly astonishing in light of the fact that the United States was not even a party to the appeal, which involved only Stanley and the individual *Bivens* defendants (Stanley's *Bivens* claim against the United States having been dismissed by the District Court in 1982). We vacate that portion of the Court of Appeals' judgment.

II

That leaves the Court of Appeals' ruling that Stanley can proceed with his *Bivens* claims notwithstanding the decision in *Chappell.* In our view, the court took an unduly narrow view of the circumstances in which courts should decline to permit nonstatutory damages actions for injuries arising out of military service.

In *Bivens,* we held that a search and seizure that violates the Fourth Amendment can give rise to an action for damages against the offending federal officials even in the absence of a statute authorizing such relief. We suggested in dictum that inferring such an action directly from the Constitution might not be appropriate when there are "special factors counselling hesitation in the absence of affirmative action by Congress," 403 U.S., at 396, 91 S.Ct., at 2005, or where there is an "explicit congressional declaration that persons injured by a federal officer's violation of the Fourth Amendment may not recover money damages from the agents, but must instead be remitted to another remedy, equally effective in the view of Congress." *Id.*, at 397, 91 S.Ct., at 2005. We subsequently held that actions for damages could be brought directly under the Due Process Clause of the Fifth Amendment, *Davis v. Passman,* 442 U.S. 228, 99 S.Ct. 2264, 60 L.Ed.2d 846 (1979), and under the Eighth Amendment's proscription against cruel and unusual punishment, *Carlson v. Green,* 446 U.S. 14, 100 S.Ct. 1468, 64 L.Ed.2d 15 (1980), repeating each time the dictum that "special factors counselling hesitation" or an "explicit congressional declaration" that another remedy is exclusive would bar such an action. 442 U.S., at 246–247, 99 S.Ct., at 2277–2278, 446 U.S., at 18–19, 100 S.Ct., at 1471–1472. In *Chappell* (and in *Bush v. Lucas,* 462 U.S. 367, 103 S.Ct. 2404, 76 L.Ed.2d 648 1983), decided the same day), that dictum became holding. *Chappell* reversed a determination that no "special factors" barred a constitutional damages remedy on behalf of minority servicemen who alleged that because of their race their superior officers "failed to assign them desirable duties, threatened them, gave them low performance evaluations, and imposed penalties of unusual severity." 462 U.S., at 297, 103 S.Ct., at 2364. We found "factors counselling hesitation" in "[t]he need for special regulations in relation to military discipline, and the consequent need and justification for a special and exclusive system of military justice...." *Id.,* at 300, 103 S.Ct., at 2365. We observed that the Constitution explicitly conferred upon Congress the power, *inter alia,* "[t]o make Rules for the Government and Regulation of the land and naval Forces," U.S. Const. Art. I, § 8, cl. 14, thus showing that "the Constitution contemplated that the Legislative Branch have plenary control over rights, duties, and responsibilities in the framework of the Military Establishment...." 462 U.S., at 301, 103 S.Ct., at 2366. Congress, we noted, had exercised that authority to "establis[h] a comprehensive internal system of justice to regulate military life, taking into account the special patterns that define the military structure." *Id.,* at 302, 103 S.Ct., at 2367. We concluded that "[t]aken together, the unique disciplinary structure of the Military Establishment and Congress' activity in the field constitute 'special factors' which dictate that it would be inappropriate to provide enlisted military personnel a *Bivens*-type remedy against their superior officers." *Id.,* at 304, 103 S.Ct., at 2368.

Stanley seeks to distance himself from this holding in several ways. First, he argues that the defendants in this case were not Stanley's superior military officers, and indeed may well have been civilian personnel, and that the chain-of-command concerns at the heart of *Chappell* and cases such as *Gaspard v. United States,* 713 F.2d 1097, 1103–1104 (CA5 1983) (plaintiff was ordered to expose himself to radiation from nuclear test), cert. denied, *sub nom. Sheehan v. United States,* 466 U.S. 975, 104 S.Ct. 2354, 80 L.Ed.2d 826 (1984), are thus not implicated. Second, Stanley argues that there is no evidence that this injury was "incident to service," because we do not know the precise character of the drug testing program, the titles and roles of the various individual defendants, or Stanley's duty status when he was at the Maryland testing grounds. If that argument is sound, then even if *Feres* principles apply fully to *Bivens* actions, further proceedings are necessary to determine whether they apply to this case.

The second argument, however, is not available to Stanley here. The issue of service incidence, as that term is used in *Feres*, was decided adversely to him by the Court of Appeals in 1981, 639 F.2d, at 1150–1153, and there is no warrant for reexamining that ruling here. See *Allen v. McCurry*, 449 U.S. 90, 94, 101 S.Ct. 411, 414, 66 L.Ed.2d 308 (1980). As for his first argument, Stanley and the lower courts may well be correct that *Chappell* implicated military chain-of-command concerns more directly than do the facts alleged here; in the posture of this case, one must assume that at least some of the defendants were not Stanley's superior officers, and that he was not acting under orders from superior officers when he was administered LSD. It is therefore true that *Chappell* is not strictly controlling, in the sense that no holding can be broader than the facts before the court. It is even true that some of the language of *Chappell*, explicitly focusing on the officer-subordinate relationship that existed in the case at hand, would not be applicable here. To give controlling weight to those facts, however, is to ignore our plain statement in *Chappell* that "[t]he 'special factors' that bear on the propriety of respondents' *Bivens* action also formed the basis of this Court's decision in *Feres v. United States*," 462 U.S., at 298, 103 S.Ct., at 2365, and that "[a]lthough this case concerns the limitations on the type of nonstatutory damages remedy recognized in *Bivens*, rather than Congress' intent in enacting the Federal Tort Claims Act, the Court's analysis in *Feres* guides our analysis in this case." *Id.*, at 299, 103 S.Ct., at 2365. Since *Feres* did not consider the officer-subordinate relationship crucial, but established instead an "incident to service" test, it is plain that our reasoning in *Chappell* does not support the distinction Stanley would rely on.

As we implicitly recognized in *Chappell*, there are varying levels of generality at which one may apply "special factors" analysis. Most narrowly, one might require reason to believe that in the particular case the disciplinary structure of the military would be affected—thus not even excluding *all* officer-subordinate suits, but allowing, for example, suits for officer conduct so egregious that no responsible officer would feel exposed to suit in the performance of his duties. Somewhat more broadly, one might disallow *Bivens* actions whenever an officer-subordinate relationship underlies the suit. More broadly still, one might disallow them in the officer-subordinate situation and also beyond that situation when it affirmatively appears that military discipline would be affected. (This seems to be the position urged by Stanley.) Fourth, as we think appropriate, one might disallow *Bivens* actions whenever the injury arises out of activity "incident to service." And finally, one might conceivably disallow them by servicemen entirely. Where one locates the rule along this spectrum depends upon how prophylactic one thinks the prohibition should be (*i.e.*, how much occasional, unintended impairment of military discipline one is willing to tolerate), which in turn depends upon how harmful and inappropriate judicial intrusion upon military discipline is thought to be. This is essentially a policy judgment, and there is no scientific or analytic demonstration of the right answer. Today, no more than when we wrote *Chappell*, do we see any reason why our judgment in the *Bivens* context should be any less protective of military concerns than it has been with respect to FTCA suits, where we adopted an "incident to service" rule. In fact, if anything we might have felt freer to compromise military concerns in the latter context, since we were confronted with an explicit congressional authorization for judicial involvement that was, on its face, unqualified; whereas here we are confronted with an explicit constitutional authorization for *Congress* "[t]o make Rules for the Government and Regulation of the land and naval Forces," U.S. Const. Art. I, § 8, cl. 14, and rely upon inference for our own authority to allow money damages. This is not to say, as Justice Brennan's dissent characterizes it, *post,* at 3076, that all matters within congressional power are exempt from *Bivens.* What is distinctive here is the specificity of that technically superfluous grant of power, and the insistence (evident from the number of Clauses devoted to the subject) with which the Constitution confers authority over the Army, Navy, and militia upon the political branches. All this counsels hesitation in our creation of damages remedies in this field.

The other major factor determining at which point, along the spectrum of generality, one should apply *Chappell*'s "special factors" analysis consists of the degree of disruption which each of them will in fact produce. This is an analytic rather than a policy judgment—but once again we see no reason why it should differ in the *Bivens* and the *Feres* contexts. Stanley underestimates the degree of disruption that would be caused by the rule he proposes. A test for liability that depends on the extent to which particular suits would call into question military discipline and decisionmaking would itself require judicial inquiry into, and hence intrusion upon, military matters. Whether a case implicates those concerns would often be problematic, raising the prospect of compelled depositions and trial testimony by military officers concerning the details of their military commands. Even putting aside the risk of erroneous judicial conclusions (which would becloud military decisionmaking), the mere process of arriving at correct conclusions would disrupt the military regime. The "incident to service" test, by contrast, provides a line that is relatively clear and that can be discerned with less extensive inquiry into military matters.

Contrary to the view of the Court of Appeals, 786 F.2d, at 1496, it is irrelevant to a "special factors" analysis whether the laws currently on the books afford Stanley, or any other particular serviceman, an "adequate" federal remedy for his injuries. The "special facto[r]" that "counsel[s] hesitation" is not the fact that Congress has chosen to afford some manner of relief in the particular case, but the fact that congressionally uninvited intrusion into military affairs by the judiciary is inappropriate. Similarly irrelevant is the statement in *Chappell,* erroneously relied upon by Stanley and the lower courts, that we have "never held, nor do we now hold, that military personnel are barred from all redress in civilian courts for constitutional wrongs suffered in the course of military service." 462 U.S., at 304, 103 S.Ct., at 2368. As the citations immediately following that statement suggest, it referred to redress designed to halt or prevent the constitutional violation rather than the award of money damages. See *Brown v. Glines,* 444 U.S. 348, 100 S.Ct. 594, 62 L.Ed.2d 540 (1980); *Parker v. Levy,* 417 U.S. 733, 94 S.Ct. 2547, 41 L.Ed.2d 439 (1974); *Frontiero v. Richardson,* 411 U.S. 677, 93 S.Ct. 1764, 36 L.Ed.2d 583 (1973). Such suits, like the case of *Wilkes v. Dinsman,* 7 How. 89, 12 L.Ed. 618 (1849), distinguished in *Chappell,* 462 U.S., at 305, n. 2, 103 S.Ct., at 2368, n. 2, sought traditional forms of relief, and "did not ask the Court to imply a new kind of cause of action." *Ibid.*

We therefore reaffirm the reasoning of *Chappell* that the "special factors counselling hesitation"—"the unique disciplinary structure of the Military Establishment and Congress' activity in the field," *id.,* at 304, 103 S.Ct., at 2368—extend beyond the situation in which an officer-subordinate relationship exists, and require abstention in the inferring of *Bivens* actions as extensive as the exception to the FTCA established by *Feres* and *United States v. Johnson.* We hold that no *Bivens* remedy is available for injuries that "arise out of or are in the course of activity incident to service." 340 U.S., at 146, 71 S.Ct., at 159.

Part II of Justice Brennan's opinion argues in essence that because the refusal to entertain a *Bivens* action has the same effect as a grant of unqualified immunity, we should find "special factors" sufficient to preclude a *Bivens* action only when our immunity decisions would absolutely foreclose a money judgment against the defendant officials. The short answer to this argument is that *Chappell* made no reference to immunity principles, and *Bivens* itself explicitly distinguished the question of immunity from the question whether the Constitution directly provides the basis for a damages action against individual officers. 403 U.S., at 397, 91 S.Ct., at 2005. The analytic answer is that the availability of a damages action under the Constitution for particular *injuries* (those incurred in the course of military service) is a question logically distinct from immunity to such an action on the part of particular *defendants.* When liability is asserted under a statute, for example, no one would suggest that whether a cause of action exists should be determined by consulting the scope of common-law immunity enjoyed by actors in the area to which the statute pertains. Rather, one applies that immunity (unless the statute says otherwise) *to* whatever actions and remedies the terms of the statute are found to provide. Similarly, the *Bivens* inquiry in this case—whether a damages action for injury in the course of military service can be founded directly upon the Constitution—is analytically distinct from the question of official immunity from *Bivens* liability.

We do not understand Justice Brennan to dispute this. Rather, he argues that the answer to the former inquiry should be such that it produces a result coextensive with the answer to the latter. That is of course quite possible to achieve, since one can adjust the definition of a cause of action to produce precisely the same results as a given definition of immunity. For example, if a State wanted to eliminate driver liability for automobile accidents, it could *either* prescribe that all automobile drivers are immune from suit for injuries caused by their negligent driving *or* prescribe that no cause of action exists for injuries caused by negligent driving. But what Justice Brennan fails to produce is any *reason* for creating such an equivalency in the present case (and, presumably, in all *Bivens* actions). In the sole case he relies upon for his novel analysis, *Davis v. Passman*, 442 U.S. 228, 99 S.Ct. 2264, 60 L.Ed.2d 846 (1979), there was a reason. There the Constitution itself contained an applicable immunity provision—the Speech or Debate Clause, Art. I, § 6, cl. 1—which rendered Members of Congress immune from suit for their legislative activity. The Court held that the "special concerns counseling hesitation" in the inference of *Bivens* actions in that area "are coextensive with the protections afforded by the Speech or Debate Clause." 442 U.S., at 246, 99 S.Ct., at 2277. That is to say, the Framers addressed the special concerns in that field through an immunity provision—and had they believed further protection was necessary they would have expanded that immunity provision. It would therefore have distorted their plan to achieve the same effect as more expansive immunity by the device of denying a cause of action for injuries caused by Members of Congress where the constitutionally prescribed immunity does not apply.

Thus, *Davis v. Passman* would be relevant here if the Constitution contained a grant of immunity to military personnel similar to the Speech or Debate Clause. It does not, of course, and so we are compelled in the military field, as in others, to make our own assessment of whether, given the "special concerns counseling hesitation," *Bivens* actions will lie. There is no more reason why court-created rules of immunity (as opposed to immunity specifically prescribed in the Constitution) should be held *a priori* to describe the limit of those concerns here than in any other field. Thus, the rule Justice Brennan proposes is not an application but a repudiation of the "special factors" limitation upon the inference of *Bivens* actions. That limitation is quite hollow if it does nothing but duplicate pre-existing immunity from suit.

For the foregoing reasons, we vacate the Court of Appeals' judgment that Stanley can assert an FTCA claim on remand to the District Court and reverse its judgment refusing to dismiss the *Bivens* claims against petitioners. The judgment of the Court of Appeals is reversed in part and vacated in part, and the case is remanded for further proceedings consistent with this opinion.

It is so ordered.

Justice O'Connor, concurring in part and dissenting in part.

Justice Brennan, with whom Justice Marshall joins, and with whom Justice Stevens joins as to Part III, concurring in part and dissenting in part.

On the Power to Bestow Citizenship

INS v. Pangilinan,

486 U.S. 875 (1988)

Justice Scalia delivered the opinion of the Court.

The respondents, 16 Filipino nationals who served with the United States Armed Forces during World War II, claim they are entitled to apply for and receive American citizenship under a special immigration statute that expired over 40 years ago, §§ 701 to 705 of the Nationality Act of 1940, Ch. 876, 54 Stat. 1137, as amended by the Second War Powers Act of 1942, § 1001, Ch. 199, 56 Stat. 182, 8 U.S.C. §§ 1001 to 1005 (1940 ed., Supp. V) (1940 Act). In the decisions below the Ninth Circuit has, for the third time, ordered naturalization under that expired provision. See *Mendoza v. United States,* 672 F.2d 1320 (CA9 1982), rev'd, 464 U.S. 154, 104 S.Ct. 568, 78 L.Ed.2d 379 (1984); *INS v. Hibi,* 475 F.2d 7 (CA9), rev'd, 414 U.S. 5, 94 S.Ct. 19, 38 L.Ed.2d 7 (1973). In part because the decision below was in direct conflict with the Second Circuit's decision in *Olegario v. United States,* 629 F.2d 204 (CA2 1980), cert. denied, 450 U.S. 980, 101 S.Ct. 1513, 67 L.Ed.2d 814 (1981), we granted certiorari, 484 U.S. 814, 108 S.Ct. 66, 98 L.Ed.2d 30.

I

A

In March 1942, Congress amended the immigration laws to make American citizenship more readily available to aliens who served honorably in the United States Armed Forces during World War II. As amended at that time, § 701 of the 1940 Nationality Act exempted those aliens from such naturalization requirements as five years of residency in the United States and proficiency in the English language. Section 702 authorized representatives designated by the Commissioner of Immigration and Naturalization to receive petitions, conduct hearings, and grant naturalization outside the United States. And § 705 authorized the Commissioner, with the approval of the Attorney General, to make such rules and regulations as were necessary to carry into effect the provisions of §§ 701 and 702.

Over the next three years, approximately 7,000 Filipino soldiers were naturalized as American citizens in places outside the Philippine Islands (which were occupied during that entire period by Japan). Most of these were naturalized by courts in this country, but at least 1,000 others were naturalized by immigration officials appointed under § 702, traveling from post to post on rotation throughout England, Iceland, North Africa, and the islands of the Pacific. See *Hibi,* 414 U.S., at 10, 94 S.Ct., at 22–23 (Douglas, J., dissenting). After the Philippines were liberated from Japanese occupation in August 1945, George Ennis, the American Vice Consul in Manila, was designated to naturalize aliens pursuant to the 1940 Act. Almost immediately after that, the Philippine Government began to express its concern that a mass migration of newly naturalized veterans would drain the country of essential manpower, undermining postwar reconstruction efforts in the soon-to-be independent country. Accordingly, on September 13, 1945, the Commissioner recommended to Attorney General Clark that Vice Consul Ennis' naturalization authority be revoked. On October 26, 1945, Ennis was informedof that revocation. For the next nine months no official with § 702 authority to receive and act upon petitions for naturalization was present in the Philippines, the Immigration and Naturalization Service (INS) apparently taking the position that appointment of such an official was authorized but not mandated. Not until August 1946 did the INS designate a new § 702 official for the Philippines, who naturalized approximately 4,000 Filipinos before the December 31, 1946, expiration date of the 1940 Act.

B

Attorney General Clark's revocation of Vice Consul Ennis' naturalization authority during those nine months of 1945 and 1946 has led to a stream of litigation involving efforts by Filipino veterans to obtain naturalization under the expired 1940 Act. In the suits we have before us here, all of the respondents except Mario Valderrama Litonjua and Bonifacio Lorenzana Manzano filed their petitions in the United States District Court for the Northern District of California. The INS has stipulated that all of these 14 respondents (the *Pangilinan* respondents) were eligible for naturalization under the 1940 Act and were present in the Philippines during the period from October 1945 to August 1946, though they had not taken affirmative steps to be naturalized before the cutoff date. The naturalization examiner who handled these cases recommended against naturalization, and the District Court decided against naturalization, relying on the Second Circuit's decision in *Olegario.* The naturalization petitions were consolidated for purposes of appeal to the Ninth Circuit.

Respondent Litonjua's petition for naturalization was filed in the United States District Court for the Southern District of California. Litonjua had served as a member of the United States Navy from May 1941 to April 1946, but had made no effort to apply for naturalization while on active duty. He made preliminary efforts to obtain citizenship while working as a civilian employee of the United States Army in Seattle, Washington, after his discharge, but he did not complete the petition process before the December 31, 1946, cutoff date. The naturalization examiner recommended against naturalization, and the District Court concurred, for reasons similar to those adopted by the District Court in *Pangilinan.*

Respondent Manzano also petitioned for naturalization in the Southern District of California. His situation was the same as that of the *Pangilinan* respondents, except that he claims that in July 1946, after completing his military service, he specifically inquired at the American Embassy in the Philippines about the possibility of obtaining citizenship but was told there was no longer anyone there to assist him. The District Court, following the recommendation of the naturalization examiner, denied the petition for reasons similar to those adopted by the District Courts in *Pangilinan* and *Litonjua.*

The appeals of the *Pangilinan* respondents and Litonjua were filed in 1980 and 1981 and were consolidated by the Court of Appeals (No. 86–1992). Manzano's appeal (No. 86–2019) was filed later and assigned to a different panel. The Ninth Circuit initially decided the *Pangilinan-Litonjua* consolidated cases by relying on the collateral-estoppel theory of its *Mendoza* decision, which had not yet been reversed by this Court. We vacated that judgment in light of our ruling in *Mendoza. INS v. Litonjua,* 465 U.S. 1001, 104 S.Ct. 990, 79 L.Ed.2d 224 (1984), vacating and remanding *Barretto v. United States,* 694 F.2d 603 (CA9 1982). On remand, the Ninth Circuit held that the revocation of Vice Consul Ennis' naturalization authority violated what it characterized as the mandatory language of §§ 702 and 705 of the 1940 Act, and that the naturalization of the respondents was an appropriate equitable remedy. *Pangilinan v. INS,* 796 F.2d 1091 (CA9 1986). After this decision was announced, the panel in No. 86–2019 reversed and remanded to the District Court for reconsideration in light of the *Pangilinan* decision, characterizing the two cases as nearly identical. In 86–1992, the

INS' petition for rehearing with suggestion for rehearing en banc was denied, with Judge Kozinski (writing for himself and seven others) dissenting. *Pangilinan v. INS,* 809 F.2d 1449 (CA9 1987). We granted the INS' petition for a writ of certiorari. 484 U.S. 814, 108 S.Ct. 66, 98 L.Ed.2d 30 (1987).

II

A

Article I, § 8, cl. 4, of the Constitution provides: "The Congress shall have Power ... [t]o establish an uniform Rule of Naturalization...." Sections 701, 702, and 705 of the amended 1940 Act, set forth in the margin above, constitute a complete description of the extent of the liberalized naturalization rights conferred under that exclusive constitutional authority in 1942. Section 701 explicitly limits the benefits to those who filed petitions no later than December 31, 1946. Moreover, Congress has again exercised its exclusive constitutional power to provide that any petition for naturalization filed on or after September 26, 1961, will be heard and determined under the 1952 Nationality Act, as amended. See § 310(e), 75 Stat. 656, 8 U.S.C. § 1421(e). Respondents concede that they are not entitled to be naturalized under that law. Brief for Respondent Pangilinan in Opposition 12–13. Since all the petitions for naturalization in this case were filed after December 31, 1946, and even after September 26, 1961, it is incontestable (and uncontested) that respondents have no statutory right to citizenship.

In *INS v. Hibi,* 414 U.S. 5, 94 S.Ct. 19, 38 L.Ed.2d 7 (1973), we summarily reversed the holding of the Ninth Circuit that the same official acts alleged here gave rise to an estoppel that prevented the Government from invoking the December 31, 1946, cutoff in the 1940 Act. We said that normal estoppel rules applicable to private litigants did not apply to the INS since, "in enforcing the cutoff date established by Congress, as well as in recognizing claims for the benefits conferred by the Act, [the INS] is enforcing the public policy established by Congress." *Id.*, at 8, 94 S.Ct., at 21–22.

Although the Ninth Circuit's holding in the present cases rests upon a somewhat different theory—not that estoppel eliminates the effectiveness of the December 31, 1946, cutoff, but that equitable authority to craft a remedy enables the conferral of citizenship despite that cutoff—we think our reasoning in *Hibi* quite clearly produces the same result. The reason we expressed why estoppel could not be applied, viz., that that doctrine could not override a "public policy established by Congress," surely applies as well to the invocation of equitable remedies. Even assuming the truth of the Ninth Circuit's unsupported assertion that "[i]n reviewing naturalization petitions, federal courts sit as courts of equity," 796 F.2d, at 1102, it is well established that "[c]ourts of equity can no more disregard statutory and constitutional requirements and provisions than can courts of law." *Hedges v. Dixon County,* 150 U.S. 182, 192, 14 S.Ct. 71, 74–75, 37 L.Ed. 1044 (1893). "A Court of equity cannot, by avowing that there is a right but no remedy known to the law, create a remedy in violation of law...." *Rees v. Watertown,* 86 U.S. [19 Wall.] 107, 122, 22 L.Ed. 72 (1874). See also, *e.g., Thompson v. Allen County,* 115 U.S. 550, 555, 6 S.Ct. 140, 142, 29 L.Ed. 472 (1885); 1 J. Story, *Equity Jurisprudence* § 19 (W. Lyon ed. 1918).

More fundamentally, however, the power to make someone a citizen of the United States has not been conferred upon the federal courts, like mandamus or injunction, as one of their generally applicable equitable powers. See, *e.g.,* 28 U.S.C. § 1361; 28 U.S.C. § 1651. Rather, it has been given them as a specific function to be performed in strict compliance with the terms of an authorizing statute which says that "[a] person may be naturalized ... in the manner and under the conditions prescribed in this subchapter, *and not otherwise.*" 8 U.S.C. § 1421(d) (emphasis added).

> "An alien who seeks political rights as a member of this Nation can rightfully obtain them only upon terms and conditions specified by Congress. Courts are without authority to sanction changes or modifications; their duty is rigidly to enforce the legislative will in respect of a matter so vital to the public welfare." *United States v. Ginsberg,* 243 U.S. 472, 474, 37 S.Ct. 422, 425, 61 L.Ed. 853 (1917).

Or as we have more recently said:

> "'Once it has been determined that a person does not qualify for citizenship, ... the district court has no discretion to ignore the defect and grant citizenship.'" *Fedorenko v. United States,* 449 U.S. 490, 517, 101 S.Ct. 737, 752–753, 66 L.Ed.2d 686 (1981) (citation omitted).

The congressional command here could not be more manifest. Besides the explicit cutoff date in the 1940 Act, Congress in 1948, adopted a new liberalized citizenship program that excluded Filipino servicemen, and specifically provided that even applications timely filed under the 1940 Act and still pending would be adjudged under the new provisions. Act of June 1, 1948, Ch. 360, 62 Stat. 281. These provisions were carried forward into the 1952 Nationality Act see, 66 Stat. 250, 8 U.S.C. § 1440. (It is particularly absurd to contemplate that Filipinos who actually filed their applications before the 1946 cutoff were denied citizenship by reason of this provision, whereas the present respondents, who filed more than 30 years after the deadline, were awarded it by the Ninth Circuit.) Finally, in 1961, Congress amended the 1952 Act by adding § 310(e), 8 U.S.C. § 1421(e), which specifies that "any" petition thereafter filed will be adjudged under the requirements of the

1952 Act. Neither by application of the doctrine of estoppel, nor by invocation of equitable powers, nor by any other means does a court have the power to confer citizenship in violation of these limitations.

B

Respondents advance as an alternative ground for affirmance the claim that Attorney General Clark's revocation of Vice Consul Ennis' naturalization authority deprived them of their rights under the Due Process Clause of the Fifth Amendment and under its equal protection component. See *Hampton v. Mow Sun Wong,* 426 U.S. 88, 100, 96 S.Ct. 1895, 1903–1904, 48 L.Ed.2d 495 (1976). Assuming that these respondents can properly invoke the protections of the United States Constitution, and granting that they are members of a special class that Congress intended to favor with statutory entitlements to naturalization, they were not deprived of those entitlements without due process. First, it did not violate due process for Congress to impose a reasonable limitations period upon the filing of naturalization petitions. Cf. *Logan v. Zimmerman Brush Co.,* 455 U.S. 422, 437, 102 S.Ct. 1148, 1158–1159, 71 L.Ed.2d 265 (1982). Second, even assuming that a reasonable opportunity to file for naturalization was required, respondents were accorded at least that. Unlike noncitizen servicemen in other parts of the world, they had the continuous presence of a § 702 naturalization officer in the Philippines from August 1945 through October 1945, and from August 1946 to the end of that year. In this last period, the officer naturalized approximately 4,000 Filipinos. In addition, approximately another 7,000 Filipinos were naturalized either in this country or by naturalization officers traveling post to post around the world. We do not agree with respondents' contention that in addition to these ample opportunities, respondents were entitled as a matter of due process to individualized notice of any statutory rights and to the continuous presence of a naturalization officer in the Philippines from October 1945 until July 1946.

We also reject the possibility of a violation of the equal protection component of the Fifth Amendment's Due Process Clause. The approximately 7-month presence of a naturalization officer in the Philippines not only met the applicable standard of equal protection, but indeed compared favorably with the merely periodic presence of such officers elsewhere in the world. See generally *Fiallo v. Bell,* 430 U.S. 787, 792, 97 S.Ct. 1473, 1477–1478, 52 L.Ed.2d 50 (1977); *Mathews v. Diaz,* 426 U.S. 67, 79–83, 96 S.Ct. 1883, 1891–1893, 48 L.Ed.2d 478 (1976). Moreover, beyond the absence of any unequal treatment, the historical record lends no support whatever to the contention that the actions at issue here were motivated by any racial animus. Indeed, it is fair to assume that the Filipino soldiers who fought so valiantly during the early months of World War II were regarded with especial esteem when this legislation was enacted and implemented. Every court to consider this matter has observed that Attorney General Clark's and Commissioner Carusi's decisions were taken in response to the concerns of Philippine officials that their nation would suffer a manpower drain, and not because of hostility towards Filipinos. See n. 5, *supra.* Thousands of Filipinos were naturalized outside the Philippines during the period in question, and approximately 4,000 more in the Philippines after a successor to Ennis was appointed in August 1946.

C

Respondents Litonjua and Manzano argue that the Government cannot prevail in their cases even if it prevails with respect to the 14 *Pangilinan* respondents because it did not introduce any evidence in their cases concerning the historical events at issue. This argument fails, since "it has been universally accepted that the burden is on the alien applicant to show his eligibility for citizenship in every respect," *Berenyi v. District Director, INS,* 385 U.S. 630, 637, 87 S.Ct. 666, 670–671, 17 L.Ed.2d 656 (1967). We also reject respondent Litonjua's assertion that his claim should be treated differently because he is within that category of veterans ("Category I" as described in *Matter of Naturalization of 68 Filipino War Veterans,* 406 F.Supp. 931, 937–940 (ND Cal.1975)) whose petitions it has been the policy of the Government not to oppose. That category includes only veterans who had taken some affirmative steps to obtain naturalization both before the December 31, 1946, cutoff date and while they were still on active duty. *Ibid.* Litonjua made his first efforts after he was no longer on active duty with the Armed Forces.

We have considered Litonjua's and Manzano's other separate claims and have found none that is meritorious.

* * *

For the reasons stated, the judgments of the Court of Appeals are reversed.

It is so ordered.

Justice Blackmun concurs in the result.

Justice Kennedy took no part in the consideration or decision of these cases.

Federal Preemption of State Law

Riegel v. Medtronic, Inc.,

552 U.S. 312 (2008)

Justice Scalia delivered the opinion of the Court.

We consider whether the pre-emption clause enacted in the Medical Device Amendments of 1976, 21 U.S.C. § 360k, bars common-law claims challenging the safety and effectiveness of a medical device given premarket approval by the Food and Drug Administration (FDA).

I

A

The Federal Food, Drug, and Cosmetic Act (FDCA), 52 Stat. 1040, as amended, 21 U.S.C. § 301 *et seq.*, has long required FDA approval for the introduction of new drugs into the market. Until the statutory enactment at issue here, however, the introduction of new medical devices was left largely for the States to supervise as they saw fit. See *Medtronic, Inc. v. Lohr,* 518 U.S. 470, 475–476, 116 S.Ct. 2240, 135 L.Ed.2d 700 (1996).

The regulatory landscape changed in the 1960's and 1970's, as complex devices proliferated and some failed. Most notably, the Dalkon Shield intrauterine device, introduced in 1970, was linked to serious infections and several deaths, not to mention a large number of pregnancies. Thousands of tort claims followed. R. Bacigal, *The Limits of Litigation: The Dalkon Shield Controversy* 3 (1990). In the view of many, the Dalkon Shield failure and its aftermath demonstrated the inability of the common-law tort system to manage the risks associated with dangerous devices. See, *e.g.*, S. Foote, *Managing the Medical Arms Race* 151–152 (1992). Several States adopted regulatory measures, including California, which in 1970 enacted a law requiring premarket approval of medical devices. 1970 Cal. Stats. ch. 1573, §§ 26670–26693; see also Leflar & Adler, "The Preemption Pentad: Federal Preemption of Products Liability Claims After *Medtronic*," 64 *Tenn. L.Rev.* 691, 703, n. 66 (1997) (identifying 13 state statutes governing medical devices as of 1976).

Congress stepped in with passage of the Medical Device Amendments of 1976(MDA), 21 U.S.C. § 360c *et seq.*, which swept back some state obligations and imposed a regime of detailed federal oversight. The MDA includes an express pre-emption provision that states:

> "Except as provided in subsection (b) of this section, no State or political subdivision of a State may establish or continue in effect with respect to a device intended for human use any requirement—
>
> "(1) which is different from, or in addition to, any requirement applicable under this chapter to the device, and
>
> "(2) which relates to the safety or effectiveness of the device or to any other matter included in a requirement applicable to the device under this chapter." § 360k(a).

The exception contained in subsection (b) permits the FDA to exempt some state and local requirements from pre-emption.

The new regulatory regime established various levels of oversight for medical devices, depending on the risks they present. Class I, which includes such devices as elastic bandages and examination gloves, is subject to the lowest level of oversight: "general controls," such as labeling requirements. § 360c(a)(1)(A); FDA, Device Advice: Device Classes, http://www.fda. gov/cdrh/devadvice/3132.html (all Internet materials as visited Feb. 14, 2008, and available in Clerk of Court's case file). Class II, which includes such devices as powered wheelchairs and surgical drapes, *ibid.*, is subject in addition to "special controls" such as performance standards and postmarket surveillance measures, § 360c(a)(1)(B).

The devices receiving the most federal oversight are those in Class III, which include replacement heart valves, implanted cerebella stimulators, and pacemaker pulse generators, FDA, Device Advice: Device Classes, *supra*. In general, a device is assigned to Class III if it cannot be established that a less stringent classification would provide reasonable assurance of safety and effectiveness, and the device is "purported or represented to be for a use in supporting or sustaining human life or for a use which is of substantial importance in preventing impairment of human health," or "presents a potential unreasonable risk of illness or injury." § 360c(a)(1)(C)(ii).

Although the MDA established a rigorous regime of premarket approval for new Class III devices, it grandfathered many that were already on the market. Devices sold before the MDA's effective date may remain on the market until the FDA promulgates, after notice and comment, a regulation requiring premarket approval. §§ 360c(f)(1), 360e(b)(1). A related provision seeks to limit the competitive advantage grandfathered devices receive. A new device need not undergo premarket approval if the FDA finds it is "substantially equivalent" to another device exempt from premarket approval. § 360c(f) (1)(A). The agency's review of devices for substantial equivalence is known as the § 510(k) process, named after the statutory provision describing the review. Most new Class III devices enter the market through § 510(k). In 2005, for example, the FDA authorized the marketing of 3,148 devices under § 510(k) and granted premarket approval to just 32 devices. P. Hutt, R. Merrill, & L. Grossman, *Food and Drug Law* 992 (3d ed.2007).

Premarket approval is a "rigorous" process. *Lohr, supra,* at 477, 116 S.Ct. 2240. A manufacturer must submit what is typically a multivolume application. FDA, Device Advice–Premarket Approval (PMA) 18, http://www.fda.gov/cdrh/dev advice/pma/printer.html. It includes, among other things, full reports of all studies and investigations of the device's safety and effectiveness that have been published or should reasonably be known to the applicant; a "full statement" of the device's "components, ingredients, and properties and of the principle or principles of operation"; "a full description of the methods used in, and the facilities and controls used for, the manufacture, processing, and, when relevant, packing and installation of, such device"; samples or device components required by the FDA; and a specimen of the proposed labeling. § 360e(c)(1). Before deciding whether to approve the application, the agency may refer it to a panel of outside experts, 21 CFR § 814.44(a) (2007), and may request additional data from the manufacturer, § 360e(c)(1)(G).
The FDA spends an average of 1,200 hours reviewing each application, *Lohr,* 518 U.S., at 477, 116 S.Ct. 2240, and grants premarket approval only if it finds there is a "reasonable assurance" of the device's "safety and effectiveness," § 360e(d). The agency must "weig[h] any probable benefit to health from the use of the device against any probable risk of injury or illness from such use." § 360c(a)(2)(C). It may thus approve devices that present great risks if they nonetheless offer great benefits in light of available alternatives. It approved, for example, under its Humanitarian Device Exemption procedures, a ventricular assist device for children with failing hearts, even though the survival rate of children using the device was less than 50 percent. FDA, Center for Devices and Radiological Health, Debakey VAD Child Left Ventricular

Assist System-H030003, Summary of Safety and Probable Benefit 20 (2004), http://www.fda.gov/cdrh/pdf3/H030003b.pdf.

The premarket approval process includes review of the device's proposed labeling. The FDA evaluates safety and effectiveness under the conditions of use set forth on the label, § 360c(a)(2)(B), and must determine that the proposed labeling is neither false nor misleading, § 360e(d)(1)(A).

After completing its review, the FDA may grant or deny premarket approval. § 360e(d). It may also condition approval on adherence to performance standards, 21 CFR § 861.1(b)(3), restrictions upon sale or distribution, or compliance with other requirements, § 814.82. The agency is also free to impose device-specific restrictions by regulation. § 360j(e)(1).

If the FDA is unable to approve a new device in its proposed form, it may send an "approvable letter" indicating that the device could be approved if the applicant submitted specified information or agreed to certain conditions or restrictions. 21 CFR § 814.44(e). Alternatively, the agency may send a "not approvable" letter, listing the grounds that justify denial and, where practical, measures that the applicant could undertake to make the device approvable. § 814.44(f).

Once a device has received premarket approval, the MDA forbids the manufacturer to make, without FDA permission, changes in design specifications, manufacturing processes, labeling, or any other attribute, that would affect safety or effectiveness. § 360e(d)(6)(A)(i). If the applicant wishes to make such a change, it must submit, and the FDA must approve, an application for supplemental premarket approval, to be evaluated under largely the same criteria as an initial application. § 360e(d)(6); 21 CFR § 814.39(c).

After premarket approval, the devices are subject to reporting requirements. § 360i. These include the obligation to inform the FDA of new clinical investigations or scientific studies concerning the device which the applicant knows of or reasonably should know of, 21 CFR § 814.84(b)(2), and to report incidents in which the device may have caused or contributed to death or serious injury, or malfunctioned in a manner that would likely cause or contribute to death or serious injury if it recurred, § 803.50(a). The FDA has the power to withdraw premarket approval based on newly reported data or existing information and must withdraw approval if it determines that a device is unsafe or ineffective under the conditions in its labeling. § 360e(e)(1); see also § 360h(e) (recall authority).

B

Except as otherwise indicated, the facts set forth in this section appear in the opinion of the Court of Appeals. The device at issue is an Evergreen Balloon Catheter marketed by defendant-respondent Medtronic, Inc. It is a Class III device that received premarket approval from the FDA in 1994; changes to its label received supplemental approvals in 1995 and 1996.

Charles Riegel underwent coronary angioplasty in 1996, shortly after suffering a myocardial infarction. App. to Pet. for Cert. 56a. His right coronary artery was diffusely diseased and heavily calcified. Riegel's doctor inserted the Evergreen Balloon Catheter into his patient's coronary artery in an attempt to dilate the artery, although the device's labeling stated that use was contraindicated for patients with diffuse or calcified stenoses. The label also warned that the catheter should not be inflated beyond its rated burst pressure of eight atmospheres. Riegel's doctor inflated the catheter five times, to a pressure of 10 atmospheres; on its fifth inflation, the catheter ruptured. Complaint 3. Riegel developed a heart block, was placed on life support, and underwent emergency coronary bypass surgery.

Riegel and his wife Donna brought this lawsuit in April 1999, in the United States District Court for the Northern District of New York. Their complaint alleged that Medtronic's catheter was designed, labeled, and manufactured in a manner that violated New York common law, and that these defects caused Riegel to suffer severe and permanent injuries. The complaint raised a number of common-law claims. The District Court held that the MDA pre-empted Riegel's claims of strict liability; breach of implied warranty; and negligence in the design, testing, inspection, distribution, labeling, marketing, and sale of the catheter. App. to Pet. for Cert. 68a; Complaint 3–4. It also held that the MDA pre-empted a negligent manufacturing claim insofar as it was not premised on the theory that Medtronic violated federal law. App. to Pet. for Cert. 71a. Finally, the court concluded that the MDA pre-empted Donna Riegel's claim for loss of consortium to the extent it was derivative of the pre-empted claims. *Id.,* at 68a; see also *id.,* at 75a.

The United States Court of Appeals for the Second Circuit affirmed these dismissals. 451 F.3d 104 (2006). The court concluded that Medtronic was "clearly subject to the federal, device-specific requirement of adhering to the standards contained in its individual, federally approved" premarket approval application. *Id.,* at 118. The Riegels' claims were pre-empted because they "would, if successful, impose state requirements that differed from, or added to," the device-specific federal requirements. *Id.,* at 121. We granted certiorari. 551 U.S. 1144, 127 S.Ct. 3000, 168 L.Ed.2d 725 (2007).

II

Since the MDA expressly pre-empts only state requirements "different from, or in addition to, any requirement applicable ... to the device" under federal law, §

360k(a)(1), we must determine whether the Federal Government has established requirements applicable to Medtronic's catheter. If so, we must then determine whether the Riegels' common-law claims are based upon New York requirements with respect to the device that are "different from, or in addition to," the federal ones, and that relate to safety and effectiveness. § 360k(a).

We turn to the first question. In *Lohr,* a majority of this Court interpreted the MDA's pre-emption provision in a manner "substantially informed" by the FDA regulation set forth at 21 CFR § 808.1(d). 518 U.S., at 495, 116 S.Ct. 2240; see also *id.,* at 500–501, 116 S.Ct. 2240. That regulation says that state requirements are pre-empted "only when the Food and Drug Administration has established specific counterpart regulations or there are other specific requirements applicable to a particular device...." 21 CFR § 808.1(d). Informed by the regulation, we concluded that federal manufacturing and labeling requirements applicable across the board to almost all medical devices did not pre-empt the common-law claims of negligence and strict liability at issue in *Lohr.* The federal requirements, we said, were not requirements specific to the device in question—they reflected "entirely generic concerns about device regulation generally." 518 U.S., at 501, 116 S.Ct. 2240. While we disclaimed a conclusion that general federal requirements could never pre-empt, or general state duties never be pre-empted, we held that no pre-emption occurred in the case at hand based on a careful comparison between the state and federal duties at issue. *Id.,* at 500–501, 116 S.Ct. 2240.

Even though substantial-equivalence review under § 510(k) is device specific, *Lohr* also rejected the manufacturer's contention that § 510(k) approval imposed device-specific "requirements." We regarded the fact that products entering the market through § 510(k) may be marketed only so long as they remain substantial equivalents of the relevant pre–1976 devices as a qualification for an exemption rather than a requirement. *Id.*, at 493–494, 116 S.Ct. 2240; see also *id.*, at 513, 116 S.Ct. 2240 (O'Connor, J., concurring in part and dissenting in part).

Premarket approval, in contrast, imposes "requirements" under the MDA as we interpreted it in *Lohr*. Unlike general labeling duties, premarket approval is specific to individual devices. And it is in no sense an exemption from federal safety review—it *is* federal safety review. Thus, the attributes that *Lohr* found lacking in § 510(k) review are present here. While § 510(k) is "'focused on *equivalence*, not safety,'" *id.*, at 493, 116 S.Ct. 2240 (opinion of the Court), premarket approval is focused on safety, not equivalence. While devices that enter the market through § 510(k) have "never been formally reviewed under the MDA for safety or efficacy," *ibid.*, the FDA may grant premarket approval only after it determines that a device offers a reasonable assurance of safety and effectiveness, § 360e(d). And while the FDA does not "'require'" that a device allowed to enter the market as a substantial equivalent "take any particular form for any particular reason," 518 U.S., at 493, 116 S.Ct. 2240, the FDA requires a device that has received premarket approval to be made with almost no deviations from the specifications in its approval application, for the reason that the FDA has determined that the approved form provides a reasonable assurance of safety and effectiveness.

III

We turn, then, to the second question: whether the Riegels' common-law claims rely upon "any requirement" of New York law applicable to the catheter that is "different from, or in addition to," federal requirements and that "relates to the safety or effectiveness of the device or to any other matter included in a requirement applicable to the device." § 360k(a).

Safety and effectiveness are the very subjects of the Riegels' common-law claims, so the critical issue is whether New York's tort duties constitute "requirements" under the MDA.

A

In *Lohr,* five Justices concluded that common-law causes of action for negligence and strict liability do impose "requirement[s]" and would be pre-empted by federal requirements specific to a medical device. See 518 U.S., at 512, 116 S.Ct. 2240 (opinion of O'Connor, J., joined by Rehnquist, C. J., and Scalia and Thomas, JJ.); *id.,* at 503–505, 116 S.Ct. 2240 (Breyer, J., concurring in part and concurring in judgment). We adhere to that view. In interpreting two other statutes we have likewise held that a provision pre-empting state "requirements" pre-empted common-law duties. *Bates v. Dow Agrosciences LLC,* 544 U.S. 431, 125 S.Ct. 1788, 161 L.Ed.2d 687 (2005), found common-law actions to be pre-empted by a provision of the Federal Insecticide, Fungicide, and Rodenticide Act that said certain States "'shall not impose or continue in effect *any requirements* for labeling or packaging in addition to or different from those required under this subchapter.'" *Id.,* at 443, 125 S.Ct. 1788 (discussing 7 U.S.C. § 136v(b); emphasis added). *Cipollone v. Liggett Group, Inc.,* 505 U.S. 504, 112 S.Ct. 2608, 120 L.Ed.2d 407 (1992), held common-law actions pre-empted by a provision of the Public Health Cigarette Smoking Act of 1969, 15 U.S.C. § 1334(b), which said that "[n]o requirement or prohibition based on smoking and health shall be imposed under State law with respect to the advertising or promotion of any cigarettes" whose packages were labeled in accordance with federal law. See 505 U.S., at 523, 112 S.Ct. 2608 (plurality opinion); *id.,* at 548–549, 112 S.Ct. 2608 (Scalia, J., concurring in judgment in part and dissenting in part).

Congress is entitled to know what meaning this Court will assign to terms regularly used in its enactments. Absent other indication, reference to a State's "requirements" includes its common-law duties. As the plurality opinion said in *Cipollone,* common-law liability is "premised on the existence of a legal duty," and a tort judgment therefore establishes that the defendant has violated a state-law obligation. *Id.*, at 522, 112 S.Ct. 2608. And while the common-law remedy is limited to damages, a liability award "'can be, indeed is designed to be, a potent method of governing conduct and controlling policy.'" *Id.,* at 521, 112 S.Ct. 2608.

In the present case, there is nothing to contradict this normal meaning. To the contrary, in the context of this legislation excluding common-law duties from the scope of pre-emption would make little sense. State tort law that requires a manufacturer's catheters to be safer, but hence less effective, than the model the FDA has approved disrupts the federal scheme no less than state regulatory law to the same effect. Indeed, one would think that tort law, applied by juries under a negligence or strict-liability standard, is less deserving of preservation. A state statute, or a regulation adopted by a state agency, could at least be expected to apply cost-benefit analysis similar to that applied by the experts at the FDA: How many more lives will be saved by a device which, along with its greater effectiveness, brings a greater risk of harm? A jury, on the other hand, sees only the cost of a more dangerous design, and is not concerned with its benefits; the patients who reaped those benefits are not represented in court. As Justice Breyer explained in *Lohr,* it is implausible that the MDA was meant to "grant greater power (to set state standards 'different from, or in addition to,' federal standards) to a single state jury than to state officials acting through state administrative or legislative lawmaking processes." 518 U.S., at 504, 116 S.Ct. 2240. That perverse distinction is not required or even suggested by the broad language Congress chose in the MDA, and we will not turn somersaults to create it.

B

The dissent would narrow the pre-emptive scope of the term "requirement" on the grounds that it is "difficult to believe that Congress would, without comment, remove all means of judicial recourse" for consumers injured by FDA-approved devices. *Post,* at 1015 (opinion of Ginsburg, J.) (internal quotation marks omitted). But, as we have explained, this is exactly what a pre-emption clause for medical devices does by its terms. The operation of a law enacted by Congress need not be seconded by a committee report on pain of judicial nullification. See, *e.g., Connecticut Nat. Bank v. Germain,* 503 U.S. 249, 253–254, 112 S.Ct. 1146, 117 L.Ed.2d 391 (1992) . It is not our job to speculate upon congressional motives. If we were to do so, however, the only indication available—the text of the statute—suggests that the solicitude for those injured by FDA-approved devices, which the dissent finds controlling, was overcome in Congress's estimation by solicitude for those who would suffer without new medical devices if juries were allowed to apply the tort law of 50 States to all innovations.

In the case before us, the FDA has supported the position taken by our opinion with regard to the meaning of the statute. We have found it unnecessary to rely upon that agency view because we think the statute itself speaks clearly to the point at issue. If, however, we had found the statute ambiguous and had accorded the agency's current position deference, the dissent is correct, see *post,* at 1016, n. 8, that—inasmuch as mere *Skidmore* deference would seemingly be at issue—the degree of deference might be reduced by the fact that the agency's earlier position was different. See *Skidmore v. Swift & Co.,* 323 U.S. 134, 65 S.Ct. 161, 89 L.Ed. 124 (1944); *United*

States v. Mead Corp., 533 U.S. 218, 121 S.Ct. 2164, 150 L.Ed.2d 292 (2001); *Good Samaritan Hospital v. Shalala,* 508 U.S. 402, 417, 113 S.Ct. 2151, 124 L.Ed.2d 368 (1993). But of course the agency's earlier position (which the dissent describes at some length, *post,* at 1015–1016, and finds preferable) is even more compromised, indeed deprived of all claim to deference, by the fact that it is no longer the agency's position.

The dissent also describes at great length the experience under the FDCA with respect to drugs and food and color additives. *Post,* at 1016–1018. Two points render the conclusion the dissent seeks to draw from that experience—that the pre-emption clause permits tort suits—unreliable. (1) It has not been established (as the dissent assumes) that no tort lawsuits are pre-empted by drug or additive approval under the FDCA. (2) If, as the dissent believes, the pre-emption clause permits tort lawsuits for medical devices just as they are (by hypothesis) permitted for drugs and additives; and if, as the dissent believes, Congress wanted the two regimes to be alike; Congress could have applied the pre-emption clause to the entire FDCA. It did not do so, but instead wrote a pre-emption clause that applies only to medical devices.

C

The Riegels contend that the duties underlying negligence, strict-liability, and implied-warranty claims are not pre-empted even if they impose "requirements," because general common-law duties are not requirements maintained "'with respect to devices.'" Brief for Petitioner 34–36. Again, a majority of this Court suggested otherwise in *Lohr.* See 518 U.S., at 504–505, 116 S.Ct. 2240 (opinion of Breyer, J.); *id.*, at 514, 116 S.Ct. 2240 (opinion of O'Connor, J., joined by Rehnquist, C. J., and Scalia and Thomas, JJ.). And with good reason. The language of the statute does not bear the Riegels' reading. The MDA provides that no State "may establish or continue in effect *with respect to a device ... any requirement*" relating to safety or effectiveness that is different from, or in addition to, federal requirements. § 360k(a) (emphasis added). The Riegels' suit depends upon New York's "continu[ing] in effect" general tort duties "with respect to" Medtronic's catheter. Nothing in the statutory text suggests that the pre-empted state requirement must apply *only* to the relevant device, or only to medical devices and not to all products and all actions in general.

The Riegels' argument to the contrary rests on the text of an FDA regulation which states that the MDA's pre-emption clause does not extend to certain duties, including "[s]tate or local requirements of general applicability where the purpose of the requirement relates either to other products in addition to devices (*e.g.*, requirements such as general electrical codes, and the Uniform Commercial Code (warranty of fitness)), or to unfair trade practices in which the requirements are not limited to devices." 21 CFR § 808.1(d)(1). Even assuming that this regulation could play a role in defining the MDA's pre-emptive scope, it does not provide unambiguous support for the Riegels' position. The agency's reading of its own rule is entitled to substantial deference, see *Auer v. Robbins,* 519 U.S. 452, 461, 117 S.Ct. 905, 137 L.Ed.2d 79 (1997), and the FDA's view put forward in this case is that the regulation does not refer to general tort duties of care, such as those underlying the claims in this case that a device was designed, labeled, or manufactured in an unsafe or ineffective manner, Brief for United States as *Amicus Curiae* 27–28. That is so, according to the FDA, because the regulation excludes from pre-emption requirements that relate only incidentally to medical devices, but not other requirements. General tort duties of care, unlike fire codes or restrictions on trade practices, "directly regulate" the device itself, including its design. *Id.,* at 28. We find the agency's explanation less than compelling, since the same could be said of general requirements imposed by electrical codes, the Uniform Commercial Code, or unfair-trade-practice law, which the regulation specifically excludes from pre-emption.

Other portions of 21 CFR § 808.1, however, support the agency's view that § 808.1(d)(1) has no application to this case (though still failing to explain why electrical codes, the Uniform Commercial Code, or unfair-trade-practice requirements are different). Section 808.1(b) states that the MDA sets forth a "general rule" pre-empting state duties "having the force and effect of law (whether established by statute, ordinance, regulation, *or court decision*)...." (Emphasis added.) This sentence is far more comprehensible under the FDA's view that § 808.1(d)(1) has no application here than under the Riegels' view. We are aware of no duties established by court decision other than common-law duties, and we are aware of no common-law duties that relate solely to medical devices.

The Riegels' reading is also in tension with the regulation's statement that adulteration and misbranding claims are pre-empted when they "ha [ve] the effect of establishing a substantive requirement for a specific device, *e.g.*, a specific labeling requirement" that is "different from, or in addition to," a federal requirement. § 808.1(d)(6)(ii). Surely this means that the MDA would pre-empt a jury determination that the FDA-approved labeling for a pacemaker violated a state common-law requirement for additional warnings. The Riegels' reading of § 808.1(d)(1), however, would allow a claim for tortious mislabeling to escape pre-emption so long as such a claim could also be brought against objects other than medical devices.

All in all, we think that § 808.1(d)(1) can add nothing to our analysis but confusion. Neither accepting nor rejecting the proposition that this regulation can properly be consulted to determine the statute's meaning; and neither accepting nor rejecting the FDA's distinction between general requirements that directly regulate and those that regulate only incidentally; the regulation fails to alter our interpretation of the text insofar as the outcome of this case is concerned.

IV

State requirements are pre-empted under the MDA only to the extent that they are "different from, or in addition to" the requirements imposed by federal law. § 360k(a)(1). Thus, § 360k does not prevent a State from providing a damages remedy for claims premised on a violation of FDA regulations; the state duties in such a case "parallel," rather than add to, federal requirements. *Lohr*, 518 U.S., at 495, 116 S.Ct. 2240; see also *id.*, at 513, 116 S.Ct. 2240 (O'Connor, J., concurring in part and dissenting in part). The District Court in this case recognized that parallel claims would not be pre-empted, see App. to Pet. for Cert. 70a–71a, but it interpreted the claims here to assert that Medtronic's device violated state tort law notwithstanding compliance with the relevant federal requirements, see *id.*, at 68a. Although the Riegels now argue that their lawsuit raises parallel claims, they made no such contention in their briefs before the Second Circuit, nor did they raise this argument in their petition for certiorari. We decline to address that argument in the first instance here.

* * *

For the foregoing reasons, the judgment of the Court of Appeals is

Affirmed.

Justice Stevens, concurring in part and concurring in the judgment.

Justice Ginsburg, dissenting.

On Voting Rights and Preemption

Arizona v. Inter Tribal Council of Ariz., Inc.,

133 S. Ct. 2247 (2013)

Justice Scalia delivered the opinion of the Court.

The National Voter Registration Act requires States to "accept and use" a uniform federal form to register voters for federal elections. The contents of that form (colloquially known as the Federal Form) are prescribed by a federal agency, the Election Assistance Commission. The Federal Form developed by the EAC does not require documentary evidence of citizenship; rather, it requires only that an applicant aver, under penalty of perjury, that he is a citizen. Arizona law requires voter-registration officials to "reject" any application for registration, including a Federal Form, that is not accompanied by concrete evidence of citizenship. The question is whether Arizona's evidence-of-citizenship requirement, as applied to Federal Form applicants, is pre-empted by the Act's mandate that States "accept and use" the Federal Form.

I

Over the past two decades, Congress has erected a complex superstructure of federal regulation atop state voter-registration systems. The National Voter Registration Act of 1993 (NVRA), 107 Stat. 77, as amended, 42 U.S.C. § 1973gg *et seq.*, "requires States to provide simplified systems for registering to vote in *federal* elections." *Young v. Fordice*, 520 U.S. 273, 275, 117 S.Ct. 1228, 137 L.Ed.2d 448 (1997). The Act requires each State to permit prospective voters to "register to vote in elections for Federal office" by any of three methods: simultaneously with a driver's license application, in person, or by mail. § 1973gg-2(a).

This case concerns registration by mail. Section 1973gg-2(a)(2) of the Act requires a State to establish procedures for registering to vote in federal elections "by mail application pursuant to section 1973gg-4 of this title." Section 1973gg-4, in turn, requires States to "accept and use" a standard federal registration form. § 1973gg-4(a)(1). The Election Assistance Commission is invested with rulemaking authority to prescribe the contents of that Federal Form. § 1973gg-7(a)(1); see § 15329. The EAC is explicitly instructed, however, to develop the Federal Form "in consultation with the chief election officers of the States." § 1973gg-7(a)(2). The Federal Form thus contains a number of state-specific instructions, which tell residents of each State what additional information they must provide and where they must submit the form. See National Mail Voter Registration Form, pp. 3–20, online at http://www.eac.gov (all Internet materials as visited June 11, 2013, and available in Clerk of Court's case file); 11 CFR § 9428.3 (2012). Each state-specific instruction must be approved by the EAC before it is included on the Federal Form.

To be eligible to vote under Arizona law, a person must be a citizen of the United States. Ariz. Const., Art. VII, § 2; Ariz.Rev.Stat. Ann. § 16-101(A) (West 2006). This case concerns Arizona's efforts to enforce that qualification. In 2004, Arizona voters adopted Proposition 200, a ballot initiative designed in part "to combat voter fraud by requiring voters to present proof of citizenship when they register to vote and to present identification when they vote on election day." *Purcell v. Gonzalez,* 549 U.S. 1, 2, 127 S.Ct. 5, 166 L.Ed.2d 1 (2006) (*per curiam*). Proposition 200 amended the State's election code to require county recorders to "reject any application for registration that is not accompanied by satisfactory evidence of United States citizenship." Ariz.Rev.Stat. Ann. § 16–166(F) (West Supp.2012). The proof-of-citizenship requirement is satisfied by (1) a photocopy of the applicant's passport or birth certificate, (2) a driver's license number, if the license states that the issuing authority verified the holder's U.S. citizenship, (3) evidence of naturalization, (4) tribal identification, or (5) "[o]ther documents or methods of proof ... established pursuant to the Immigration Reform and Control Act of 1986." *Ibid.* The EAC did not grant Arizona's request to include this new requirement among the state-specific instructions for Arizona on the Federal Form. App. 225. Consequently, the Federal Form includes a statutorily required attestation, subscribed to under penalty of perjury, that an Arizona applicant meets the State's voting requirements (including the citizenship requirement), see § 1973gg-7(b)(2), but does not require concrete evidence of citizenship.

The two groups of plaintiffs represented here—a group of individual Arizona residents (dubbed the Gonzalez plaintiffs, after lead plaintiff Jesus Gonzalez) and a group of nonprofit organizations led by the Inter Tribal Council of Arizona (ITCA)—filed separate suits seeking to enjoin the voting provisions of Proposition 200. The District Court consolidated the cases and denied the plaintiffs' motions for a preliminary injunction. App. to Pet. for Cert. 1g. A two-judge motions panel of the Court of Appeals for the Ninth Circuit then enjoined Proposition 200 pending appeal. *Purcell,* 549 U.S., at 3, 127 S.Ct. 5. We vacated that order and allowed the impending 2006 election to proceed with the new rules in place. *Id.,* at 5–6, 127 S.Ct. 5. On remand, the Court of Appeals affirmed the District Court's initial denial of a preliminary injunction as to respondents' claim that the NVRA pre-empts Proposition 200's registration rules. *Gonzalez v. Arizona,* 485 F.3d 1041, 1050–1051 (2007). The District Court then granted Arizona's motion for summary judgment as to that claim. App. to Pet. for Cert. 1e, 3e. A panel of the Ninth Circuit affirmed in part but reversed as relevant here, holding that "Proposition 200's documentary proof of citizenship requirement conflicts with the NVRA's text, structure, and purpose." *Gonzalez v. Arizona,* 624 F.3d 1162, 1181 (2010). The en banc Court of Appeals agreed. *Gonzalez v. Arizona,* 677 F.3d 383, 403 (2012). We granted certiorari. 568 U.S. ---, 133 S.Ct. 476, 184 L.Ed.2d 296 (2012).

II

The Elections Clause, Art. I, § 4, cl. 1, provides:

> "The Times, Places and Manner of holding Elections for Senators and Representatives, shall be prescribed in each State by the Legislature thereof; but the Congress may at any time by Law make or alter such Regulations, except as to the places of chusing Senators."

The Clause empowers Congress to pre-empt state regulations governing the "Times, Places and Manner" of holding congressional elections. The question here is whether the federal statutory requirement that States "accept and use" the Federal Form pre-empts Arizona's state-law requirement that officials "reject" the application of a prospective voter who submits a completed Federal Form unaccompanied by documentary evidence of citizenship.

A

The Elections Clause has two functions. Upon the States it imposes the duty ("*shall* be prescribed") to prescribe the time, place, and manner of electing Representatives and Senators; upon Congress it confers the power to alter those regulations or supplant them altogether. See *U.S. Term Limits, Inc. v. Thornton,* 514 U.S. 779, 804–805, 115 S.Ct. 1842, 131 L.Ed.2d 881 (1995); *id.,* at 862, 115 S.Ct. 1842 (Thomas, J., dissenting). This grant of congressional power was the Framers' insurance against the possibility that a State would refuse to provide for the election of representatives to the Federal Congress. "[E]very government ought to contain in itself the means of its own preservation," and "an exclusive power of regulating elections for the national government, in the hands of the State legislatures, would leave the existence of the Union entirely at their mercy. They could at any moment annihilate it by neglecting to provide for the choice of persons to administer its affairs." *The Federalist* No. 59, pp. 362–363 (C. Rossiter ed. 1961) (A. Hamilton) (emphasis deleted). That prospect seems fanciful today, but the widespread, vociferous opposition to the proposed Constitution made it a very real concern in the founding era.

The Clause's substantive scope is broad. "Times, Places, and Manner," we have written, are "comprehensive words," which "embrace authority to provide a complete code for congressional elections," including, as relevant here and as petitioners do not contest, regulations relating to "registration." *Smiley v. Holm,* 285 U.S. 355, 366, 52 S.Ct. 397, 76 L.Ed. 795 (1932); see also *Roudebush v. Hartke,* 405 U.S. 15, 24–25, 92 S.Ct. 804, 31 L.Ed.2d 1 (1972) (recounts); *United States v. Classic,* 313 U.S. 299, 320, 61 S.Ct. 1031, 85 L.Ed. 1368 (1941) (primaries). In practice, the Clause functions as "a default provision; it invests the States with responsibility for the mechanics of congressional elections, but only so far as Congress declines to pre-empt state legislative choices." *Foster v. Love,* 522 U.S. 67, 69, 118 S.Ct. 464, 139 L.Ed.2d 369 (1997) (citation omitted). The power of Congress over the "Times, Places and Manner" of congressional elections "is paramount, and may be exercised at any time, and to any extent which it deems expedient; and so far as it is exercised, and no farther, the regulations effected supersede those of the State which are inconsistent therewith." *Ex parte Siebold,* 100 U.S. 371, 392, 25 L.Ed. 717 (1880).

B

The straightforward textual question here is whether Ariz.Rev.Stat. Ann. § 16-166(F), which requires state officials to "reject" a Federal Form unaccompanied by documentary evidence of citizenship, conflicts with the NVRA's mandate that Arizona "accept and use" the Federal Form. If so, the state law, "so far as the conflict extends, ceases to be operative." *Siebold, supra,* at 384. In Arizona's view, these seemingly incompatible obligations can be read to operate harmoniously: The NVRA, it contends, requires merely that a State receive the Federal Form willingly and use that form as one element in its (perhaps lengthy) transaction with a prospective voter.

Taken in isolation, the mandate that a State "accept and use" the Federal Form is fairly susceptible of two interpretations. It might mean that a State must accept the Federal Form as a complete and sufficient registration application; or it might mean that the State is merely required to receive the form willingly and use it *somehow* in its voter registration process. Both readings—"receive willingly" and "accept as sufficient"—are compatible with the plain meaning of the word "accept." See 1 *Oxford English Dictionary* 70 (2d ed. 1989) ("To take or receive (a thing offered) willingly"; "To receive as sufficient or adequate"); *Webster's New International Dictionary* 14 (2d ed. 1954) ("To receive (a thing offered to or thrust upon one) with a consenting mind"; "To receive with favor; to approve"). And we take it as self-evident that the "elastic" verb "use," read in isolation, is broad enough to encompass Arizona's preferred construction. *Smith v. United States,* 508 U.S. 223, 241, 113 S.Ct. 2050, 124 L.Ed.2d 138 (1993) (Scalia, J., dissenting). In common parlance, one might say that a restaurant accepts and uses credit cards even though it requires customers to show matching identification when making a purchase. See also Brief for State Petitioners 40 ("An airline may advertise that it 'accepts and uses' e-tickets ..., yet may still require photo identification before one could board the airplane").

"Words that can have more than one meaning are given content, however, by their surroundings." *Whitman v. American Trucking Assns., Inc.,* 531 U.S. 457, 466, 121 S.Ct. 903, 149 L.Ed.2d 1 (2001); see also *Smith, supra,* at 241, 113 S.Ct. 2050 (Scalia, J., dissenting). And reading "accept" merely to denote willing receipt seems out of place in the context of an official mandate to accept and use something for a given purpose. The implication of such a mandate is that its object is to be accepted *as sufficient* for the requirement it is meant to satisfy. For example, a government *diktat* that "civil servants shall accept government IOUs for payment of salaries" does not invite the response, "sure, we'll accept IOUs—if you pay us a ten percent down payment in cash." Many federal statutes contain similarly phrased commands, and they contemplate more than mere willing receipt. See, *e.g.*, 5 U.S.C. § 8332(b), (m)(3) ("The Office [of Personnel Management] shall accept the certification of various officials concerning creditable service toward civilian-employee retirement); 12 U.S.C.A. § 2605(*l*) (2) (Supp.2013) ("A servicer of a federally related mortgage shall accept any reasonable form of written confirmation from a borrower of existing insurance coverage"); 16 U.S.C. § 1536(p) (Endangered Species Committee "shall accept the determinations of the President" with respect to whether a major disaster warrants an exception to the Endangered Species Act's requirements); § 4026(b)(2), 118 Stat. 3725, note following 22 U.S.C. § 2751, p. 925 (FAA Administrator "shall accept the certification of the Department of Homeland Security that a missile defense system is effective and functional to defend commercial aircraft against" man-portable surface-to-air missiles); 25 U.S.C. § 1300h-6(a) ("For the purpose of proceeding with the per capita distribution" of certain funds, "the Secretary of the Interior shall accept the tribe's certification of enrolled membership"); 30

U.S.C. § 923(b) (the Secretary of Labor "shall accept a board certified or board eligible radiologist's interpretation" of a chest X ray used to diagnose black lung disease); 42 U.S.C. § 1395w-21(e)(6)(A) ("[A] Medi-care+Choice organization ... shall accept elections or changes to elections during" specified periods).

Arizona's reading is also difficult to reconcile with neighboring provisions of the NVRA. Section 1973gg-6(a)(1)(B) provides that a State shall "ensure that any eligible applicant is registered to vote in an election ... if the *valid voter registration form* of the applicant is postmarked" not later than a specified number of days before the election. (Emphasis added.) Yet Arizona reads the phrase "accept and use" in § 1973gg-4(a)(1) as permitting it to *reject* a completed Federal Form if the applicant does not submit additional information required by state law. That reading can be squared with Arizona's obligation under § 1973gg-6(a)(1) only if a completed Federal Form is not a "valid voter registration form," which seems unlikely. The statute empowers the EAC to create the Federal Form, § 1973gg-7(a), requires the EAC to prescribe its contents within specified limits, § 1973gg-7(b), and requires States to "accept and use" it, § 1973gg-4(a)(1). It is improbable that the statute envisions a completed copy of the form it takes such pains to create as being anything less than "valid."

The Act also authorizes States, "[*i*]*n addition to* accepting and using the" Federal Form, to create their own, state-specific voter-registration forms, which can be used to register voters in both state and federal elections. § 1973gg-4(a)(2) (emphasis added). These state-developed forms may require information the Federal Form does not. (For example, unlike the Federal Form, Arizona's registration form includes Proposition 200's proof-of-citizenship requirement. See Arizona Voter Registration Form, p. 1, online at http://www.azsos.gov.) This permission works in tandem with the requirement that States "accept and use" the Federal Form. States retain the flexibility to design and use their own registration forms, but the Federal Form provides a backstop: No matter what procedural hurdles a State's own form imposes, the Federal Form guarantees that a simple means of registering to vote in federal elections will be available. Arizona's reading would permit a State to demand of Federal Form applicants every additional piece of information the State requires on its state-specific form. If that is so, the Federal Form ceases to perform any meaningful function, and would be a feeble means of "increas[ing] the number of eligible citizens who register to vote in elections for Federal office." § 1973gg(b).

Finally, Arizona appeals to the presumption against pre-emption sometimes invoked in our Supremacy Clause cases. See, *e.g., Gregory v. Ashcroft,* 501 U.S. 452, 460–461, 111 S.Ct. 2395, 115 L.Ed.2d 410 (1991). Where it applies, "we start with the assumption that the historic police powers of the States were not to be superseded by the Federal Act unless that was the clear and manifest purpose of Congress." *Rice v. Santa Fe Elevator Corp.,* 331 U.S. 218, 230, 67 S.Ct. 1146, 91 L.Ed. 1447 (1947). That rule of construction rests on an assumption about congressional intent: that "Congress does not exercise lightly" the "extraordinary power" to "legislate in areas traditionally regulated by the States." *Gregory, supra,* at 460, 111 S.Ct. 2395. We have never mentioned such a principle in our Elections Clause cases. *Siebold,* for example, simply said that Elections Clause legislation, "so far as it extends and conflicts with the regulations of the State, necessarily supersedes them." 100 U.S., at 384. There is good reason for treating Elections Clause legislation differently: The assumption that Congress is reluctant to pre-empt does not hold when Congress acts under that constitutional provision, which empowers Congress to "make or alter" state election regulations. Art. I, § 4, cl. 1. When Congress legislates with respect to the "Times, Places and Manner" of holding congressional elections, it *necessarily* displaces some element of a pre-existing legal regime erected by the States. Because the power the Elections Clause confers is none other than the power to pre-empt, the reasonable assumption is that the statutory text accurately communicates the scope of Congress's pre-emptive intent. Moreover, the federalism concerns underlying the presumption in the Supremacy Clause context are somewhat weaker here. Unlike the States' "historic police powers," *Rice, supra,* at 230, 67 S.Ct. 1146, the States' role in regulating congressional elections—while weighty and worthy of respect—has always existed subject to the express qualification that it "terminates according to federal law." *Buckman Co. v. Plaintiffs' Legal Comm.,* 531 U.S. 341, 347, 121 S.Ct. 1012, 148 L.Ed.2d 854 (2001). In sum, there is no compelling reason not to read Elections Clause legislation simply to mean what it says.

We conclude that the fairest reading of the statute is that a state-imposed requirement of evidence of citizenship not required by the Federal Form is "inconsistent with" the NVRA's mandate that States "accept and use" the Federal Form. *Siebold, supra,* at 397. If this reading prevails, the Elections Clause requires that Arizona's rule give way.

We note, however, that while the NVRA forbids States to demand that an applicant submit additional information beyond that required by the Federal Form, it does not preclude States from "deny[ing] registration based on information in their possession establishing the applicant's ineligibility." Brief for United States as *Amicus Curiae* 24. The NVRA clearly contemplates that not every submitted Federal Form will result in registration. See § 1973gg-7(b)(1) (Federal Form "may require only" information "necessary to enable the appropriate State election official to *assess the eligibility of the applicant*" (emphasis added)); § 1973gg-6(a)(2) (States must require election officials to "send notice to each applicant of the disposition of the application").

III

Arizona contends, however, that its construction of the phrase "accept and use" is necessary to avoid a conflict between the NVRA and Arizona's constitutional authority to establish qualifications (such as citizenship) for voting. Arizona is correct that the Elections Clause empowers Congress to regulate *how* federal elections are held, but not *who* may vote in them. The Constitution prescribes a straightforward rule for the composition of the federal electorate. Article I, § 2, cl. 1, provides that electors in each State for the House of Representatives "shall have the Qualifications requisite for Electors of the most numerous Branch of the State Legislature," and the Seventeenth Amendment adopts the same criterion for senatorial elections. Cf. also Art. II, § 1, cl. 2 ("Each State shall appoint, in such Manner as the Legislature thereof may direct," presidential electors). One cannot read the Elections Clause as treating implicitly what these other constitutional provisions regulate explicitly. "It is difficult to see how words could be clearer in stating what Congress can control and what it cannot control. Surely nothing in these provisions lends itself to the view that voting qualifications in federal elections are to be set by Congress." *Oregon v. Mitchell,* 400 U.S. 112, 210, 91 S.Ct. 260, 27 L.Ed.2d 272 (1970) (Harlan, J., concurring in part and dissenting in part); see also *U.S. Term Limits,* 514 U.S., at 833–834, 115 S.Ct. 1842; *Tashjian v. Republican Party of Conn.,* 479 U.S. 208, 231–232, 107 S.Ct. 544, 93 L.Ed.2d 514 (1986) (Stevens, J., dissenting).

Prescribing voting qualifications, therefore, "forms no part of the power to be conferred upon the national government" by the Elections Clause, which is "expressly restricted to the regulation of the *times,* the *places,* and the *manner* of elections." *The Federalist* No. 60, at 371 (A. Hamilton); see also *id.,* No. 52, at 326 (J. Madison). This allocation of authority sprang from the

Framers' aversion to concentrated power. A Congress empowered to regulate the qualifications of its own electorate, Madison warned, could "by degrees subvert the Constitution." 2 *Records of the Federal Convention of 1787*, p. 250 (M. Farrand rev. 1966). At the same time, by tying the federal franchise to the state franchise instead of simply placing it within the unfettered discretion of state legislatures, the Framers avoided "render[ing] too dependent on the State governments that branch of the federal government which ought to be dependent on the people alone." *The Federalist* No. 52, at 326 (J. Madison).

Since the power to establish voting requirements is of little value without the power to enforce those requirements, Arizona is correct that it would raise serious constitutional doubts if a federal statute precluded a State from obtaining the information necessary to enforce its voter qualifications. If, but for Arizona's interpretation of the "accept and use" provision, the State would be precluded from obtaining information necessary for enforcement, we would have to determine whether Arizona's interpretation, though plainly not the best reading, is at least a possible one. Cf. *Crowell v. Benson,* 285 U.S. 22, 62, 52 S.Ct. 285, 76 L.Ed. 598 (1932) (the Court will "ascertain whether a construction of the statute *is fairly possible* by which the [constitutional] question may be avoided" (emphasis added)). Happily, we are spared that necessity, since the statute provides another means by which Arizona may obtain information needed for enforcement.

Section 1973gg-7(b)(1) of the Act provides that the Federal Form "may require only such identifying information (including the signature of the applicant) and other information (including data relating to previous registration by the applicant), as is necessary to enable the appropriate State election official to assess the eligibility of the applicant and to administer voter registration and other parts of the election process." At oral argument, the United States expressed the view that the phrase "may require only" in § 1973gg-7(b)(1) means that the EAC "*shall require* information that's necessary, but may only require that information." Tr. of Oral Arg. 52 (emphasis added); see also Brief for ITCA Respondents 46; Tr. of Oral Arg. 37–39 (ITCA Respondents' counsel). That is to say, § 1973gg-7(b)(1) acts as both a ceiling and a floor with respect to the contents of the Federal Form. We need not consider the Government's contention that despite the statute's statement that the EAC "may" require on the Federal Form information "necessary to enable the appropriate State election official to assess the eligibility of the applicant," other provisions of the Act indicate that such action is statutorily required. That is because we think that—by analogy to the rule of statutory interpretation that avoids questionable constitutionality—validly conferred discretionary executive authority is properly exercised (as the Government has proposed) to avoid serious constitutional doubt. That is to say, it is surely permissible if not requisite for the Government to say that necessary information which *may* be required *will* be required.

Since, pursuant to the Government's concession, a State may request that the EAC alter the Federal Form to include information the State deems necessary to determine eligibility, see § 1973gg-7(a)(2); Tr. of Oral Arg. 55 (United States), and may challenge the EAC's rejection of that request in a suit under the Administrative Procedure Act, see 5 U.S.C. §§ 701–706, no constitutional doubt is raised by giving the "accept and use" provision of the NVRA its fairest reading. That alternative means of enforcing its constitutional power to determine voting qualifications remains open to Arizona here. In 2005, the EAC divided 2-to-2 on the request by Arizona to include the evidence-of-citizenship requirement among the state-specific instructions on the Federal Form, App. 225, which meant that no action could be taken, see 42 U.S.C. § 15328 ("Any action which the Commission is authorized to carry out under this chapter may be carried out only with the approval of at least three of its members"). Arizona did not challenge that agency action (or rather inaction) by seeking APA review in federal court, see Tr. of Oral Arg. 11–12 (Arizona), but we are aware of nothing that prevents Arizona from renewing its request. Should the EAC's inaction persist, Arizona would have the opportunity to establish in a reviewing court that a mere oath will not suffice to effectuate its citizenship requirement and that the EAC is therefore under a nondiscretionary duty to include Arizona's concrete evidence requirement on the Federal Form. See 5 U.S.C. § 706(1). Arizona might also assert (as it has argued here) that it would be arbitrary for the EAC to refuse to include Arizona's instruction when it has accepted a similar instruction requested by Louisiana.

We hold that 42 U.S.C. § 1973gg-4 precludes Arizona from requiring a Federal Form applicant to submit information beyond that required by the form itself. Arizona may, however, request anew that the EAC include such a requirement among the Federal Form's state-specific instructions, and may seek judicial review of the EAC's decision under the Administrative Procedure Act.

The judgment of the Court of Appeals is affirmed.

It is so ordered.

Justice Kennedy, concurring in part and concurring in the judgment.

Justice Thomas, dissenting.

Justice Alito, dissenting.

Interpreting the Clean Air Act
Michigan v. E.P.A.,
135 S.Ct. 2699 (2015)

Justice Scalia delivered the opinion of the Court.

The Clean Air Act directs the Environmental Protection Agency to regulate emissions of hazardous air pollutants from power plants if the Agency finds regulation "appropriate and necessary." We must decide whether it was reasonable for EPA to refuse to consider cost when making this finding.

I

The Clean Air Act establishes a series of regulatory programs to control air pollution from stationary sources (such as refineries and factories) and moving sources (such as cars and airplanes). 69 Stat. 322, as amended, 42 U.S.C. §§ 7401–7671q. One of these is the National Emissions Standards for Hazardous Air Pollutants Program—the hazardous-air-pollutants program, for short. Established in its current form by the Clean Air Act Amendments of 1990, 104 Stat. 2531, this program targets for regulation stationary-source emissions of more than 180 specified "hazardous air pollutants." § 7412(b).

For stationary sources in general, the applicability of the program depends in part on how much pollution the source emits. A source that emits more than 10 tons of a single pollutant or more than 25 tons of a combination of pollutants per year is called a major source. § 7412(a)(1). EPA is required to regulate all major sources under the program. § 7412(c)(1)-(2). A source whose emissions do not cross the just-mentioned thresholds is called an area source. § 7412(a)(2). The Agency is required to regulate an area source under the program if it "presents a threat of adverse effects to human health or the environment ... warranting regulation." § 7412(c)(3).

At the same time, Congress established a unique procedure to determine the applicability of the program to fossil-fuel-fired power plants. The Act refers to these plants as electric utility steam generating units, but we will simply call them power plants. Quite apart from the hazardous-air-pollutants program, the Clean Air Act Amendments of 1990 subjected power plants to various regulatory requirements. The parties agree that these requirements were expected to have the collateral effect of reducing power plants' emissions of hazardous air pollutants, although the extent of the reduction was unclear. Congress directed the Agency to "perform a study of the hazards to public health reasonably anticipated to occur as a result of emissions by [power plants] of [hazardous air pollutants] after imposition of the requirements of this chapter." § 7412(n)(1)(A). If the Agency "finds ... regulation is appropriate and necessary after considering the results of the study," it "shall regulate [power plants] under [§ 7412]." *Ibid.* EPA has interpreted the Act to mean that power plants become subject to regulation on the same terms as ordinary major and area sources, see 77 Fed.Reg. 9330 (2012), and we assume without deciding that it was correct to do so.

And what are those terms? EPA must first divide sources covered by the program into categories and subcategories in accordance with statutory criteria. § 7412(c)(1). For each category or subcategory, the Agency must promulgate certain minimum emission regulations, known as floor standards. § 7412(d)(1), (3). The statute generally calibrates the floor standards to reflect the emissions limitations already achieved by the best-performing 12% of sources within the category or subcategory. § 7412(d)(3). In some circumstances, the Agency may also impose more stringent emission regulations, known as beyond-the-floor standards. The statute expressly requires the Agency to consider cost (alongside other specified factors) when imposing beyond-the-floor standards. § 7412(d)(2).

EPA completed the study required by § 7412(n)(1)(A) in 1998, 65 Fed.Reg. 79826 (2000), and concluded that regulation of coal- and oil-fired power plants was "appropriate and necessary" in 2000, *id.*, at 79830. In 2012, it reaffirmed the appropriate-and-necessary finding, divided power plants into subcategories, and promulgated floor standards. The Agency found regulation "appropriate" because (1) power plants' emissions of mercury and other hazardous air pollutants posed risks to human health and the environment and (2) controls were available to reduce these emissions. 77 Fed.Reg. 9363. It found regulation "necessary" because the imposition of the Act's other requirements did not eliminate these risks. *Ibid.* EPA concluded that "costs should not be considered" when deciding whether power plants should be regulated under § 7412. *Id.*, at 9326.

In accordance with Executive Order, the Agency issued a "Regulatory Impact Analysis" alongside its regulation. This analysis estimated that the regulation would force power plants to bear costs of $9.6 billion per year. *Id.*, at 9306. The Agency could not fully quantify the benefits of reducing power plants' emissions of hazardous air pollutants; to the extent it could, it estimated that these benefits were worth $4 to $6 million per year. *Ibid.* The costs to power plants were thus between 1,600 and 2,400 times as great as the quantifiable benefits from reduced emissions of hazardous air pollutants. The Agency continued that its regulations would have ancillary benefits—including cutting power plants' emissions of particulate matter and sulfur dioxide, substances that are not covered by the hazardous-air-pollutants program. Although the Agency's appropriate-and-necessary finding did not rest on these ancillary effects, *id.*, at 9320, the regulatory impact analysis took them into account, increasing the Agency's estimate of the quantifiable benefits of its regulation to $37 to $90 billion per year, *id.*, at 9306. EPA concedes that the regulatory impact analysis "played no role" in its appropriate-and-necessary finding. Brief for Federal Respondents 14.

Petitioners (who include 23 States) sought review of EPA's rule in the Court of Appeals for the D.C. Circuit. As relevant here, they challenged the Agency's refusal to consider cost when deciding whether to regulate power plants. The Court of Appeals upheld the Agency's decision not to consider cost, with Judge Kavanaugh concurring in part and dissenting in part. *White Stallion Energy Center, LLC v. EPA*, 748 F.3d 1222 (2014) (*per curiam*). We granted certiorari. 574 U.S. ----, 135 S.Ct. 702, 703, 190 L.Ed.2d 434 (2014).

II

Federal administrative agencies are required to engage in "reasoned decisionmaking." *Allentown Mack Sales and Service, Inc. v. NLRB*, 522 U.S. 359, 374, 118 S.Ct. 818, 139 L.Ed.2d 797 (1998) (internal quotation marks omitted). "Not only must an agency's decreed result be within the scope of its lawful authority, but the process by which it reaches that result must be logical and rational." *Ibid.* It follows that agency action is lawful only if it rests "on a consideration of the relevant factors." *Motor Vehicle Mfrs. Assn. of United States, Inc. v. State Farm Mut. Automobile Ins. Co.*, 463 U.S. 29, 43, 103 S.Ct. 2856, 77 L.Ed.2d 443 (1983) (internal quotation marks omitted).

EPA's decision to regulate power plants under § 7412 allowed the Agency to reduce power plants' emissions of hazardous air pollutants and thus to improve public health and the environment. But the decision also ultimately cost power plants, according to the Agency's own estimate, nearly $10 billion a year. EPA refused to consider whether the costs of its decision outweighed the benefits. The Agency gave cost no thought *at all*, because it considered cost irrelevant to its initial decision to regulate.

EPA's disregard of cost rested on its interpretation of § 7412(n)(1)(A), which, to repeat, directs the Agency to regulate power plants if it "finds such regulation is appropriate and necessary." The Agency accepts that it *could* have interpreted this provision to mean that cost is relevant to the decision to add power plants to the program. Tr. of Oral Arg. 44. But it chose to read the statute to mean that cost makes no difference to the initial decision to regulate. See 76 Fed.Reg. 24988 (2011) ("We further interpret the term 'appropriate' to not allow for the consideration of costs"); 77 Fed.Reg. 9327 ("Cost does not have to be read into the definition of 'appropriate'").

We review this interpretation under the standard set out in *Chevron U.S.A. Inc. v. Natural Resources Defense Council, Inc.*, 467 U.S. 837, 104 S.Ct. 2778, 81 L.Ed.2d 694 (1984). *Chevron* directs courts to accept an agency's reasonable resolution of an ambiguity in a statute that the agency administers. *Id.*, at 842–843, 104 S.Ct. 2778. Even under this deferential standard, however, "agencies must operate within the bounds of reasonable interpretation." *Utility Air Regulatory Group v. EPA*, 573 U.S. ––––, ––––, 134 S.Ct. 2427, 2442, 189 L.Ed.2d 372 (2014) (internal quotation marks omitted). EPA strayed far beyond those bounds when it read § 7412(n)(1) to mean that it could ignore cost when deciding whether to regulate power plants.

A

The Clean Air Act treats power plants differently from other sources for purposes of the hazardous-air-pollutants program. Elsewhere in § 7412, Congress established cabined criteria for EPA to apply when deciding whether to include sources in the program. It required the Agency to regulate sources whose emissions exceed specified numerical thresholds (major sources). It also required the Agency to regulate sources whose emissions fall short of these thresholds (area sources) if they "presen[t] a threat of adverse effects to human health or the environment ... warranting regulation." § 7412(c)(3). In stark contrast, Congress instructed EPA to add power plants to the program if (but only if) the Agency finds regulation "appropriate and necessary." § 7412(n)(1)(A). One does not need to open up a dictionary in order to realize the capaciousness of this phrase. In particular, "appropriate" is "the classic broad and all-encompassing term that naturally and traditionally includes consideration of all the relevant factors." 748 F.3d, at 1266 (opinion of Kavanaugh, J.). Although this term leaves agencies with flexibility, an agency may not "entirely fai[l] to consider an important aspect of the problem" when deciding whether regulation is appropriate. *State Farm, supra,* at 43, 103 S.Ct. 2856.

Read naturally in the present context, the phrase "appropriate and necessary" requires at least some attention to cost. One would not say that it is even rational, never mind "appropriate," to impose billions of dollars in economic costs in return for a few dollars in health or environmental benefits. In addition, "cost" includes more than the expense of complying with regulations; any disadvantage could be termed a cost. EPA's interpretation precludes the Agency from considering *any* type of cost—including, for instance, harms that regulation might do to human health or the environment. The Government concedes that if the Agency were to find that emissions from power plants do damage to human health, but that the technologies needed to eliminate these emissions do even more damage to human health, it would *still* deem regulation appropriate. See Tr. of Oral Arg. 70. No regulation is "appropriate" if it does significantly more harm than good.

There are undoubtedly settings in which the phrase "appropriate and necessary" does not encompass cost. But this is not one of them. Section 7412(n)(1)(A) directs EPA to determine whether "*regulation* is appropriate and necessary." (Emphasis added.) Agencies have long treated cost as a centrally relevant factor when deciding whether to regulate. Consideration of cost reflects the understanding that reasonable regulation ordinarily requires paying attention to the advantages *and* the disadvantages of agency decisions. It also reflects the reality that "too much wasteful expenditure devoted to one problem may well mean considerably fewer resources available to deal effectively with other (perhaps more serious) problems." *Entergy Corp. v. Riverkeeper, Inc.*, 556 U.S. 208, 233, 129 S.Ct. 1498, 173 L.Ed.2d 369 (2009) (Breyer, J., concurring in part and dissenting in part). Against the backdrop of this established administrative practice, it is unreasonable to read an instruction to an administrative agency to determine whether "regulation is appropriate and necessary" as an invitation to ignore cost.

Statutory context reinforces the relevance of cost. The procedures governing power plants that we consider today appear in § 7412(n)(1), which bears the caption "Electric utility steam generating units." In subparagraph (A), the part of the law that has occupied our attention so far, Congress required EPA to study the hazards to public health posed by power plants and to determine whether regulation is appropriate and necessary. But in subparagraphs (B) and (C), Congress called for two additional studies. One of them, a study into mercury emissions from power plants and other sources, must consider "the health and environmental effects of such emissions, technologies which are available to control such emissions, *and the costs of such technologies.*" § 7412(n)(1)(B) (emphasis added). This directive to EPA to study cost is a further indication of the relevance of cost to the decision to regulate.

In an effort to minimize this express reference to cost, EPA now argues that § 7412(n)(1)(A) requires it to consider only the study mandated by that provision, not the separate mercury study, before deciding whether to regulate power plants. But when adopting the regulations before us, the Agency insisted that the provisions concerning all three studies "provide a framework for [EPA's] determination of whether to regulate [power plants]." 76 Fed.Reg. 24987. It therefore decided "to interpret the scope of the appropriate and necessary finding *in the context of all three studies.*" 77 Fed.Reg. 9325 (emphasis added). For example:

> EPA considered environmental effects relevant to the appropriate-and-necessary finding. It deemed the mercury study's reference to this factor "direct evidence that Congress was concerned with environmental effects." 76 Fed.Reg. 24987.
>
> EPA considered availability of controls relevant to the appropriate-and-necessary finding. It thought that doing so was "consistent with" the mercury study's reference to availability of controls. *Id.*, at 24989.
>
> EPA concluded that regulation of power plants would be appropriate and necessary even if a single pollutant emitted by them posed a hazard to health or the environment. It believed that "Congress' focus" on a single pollutant in the mercury study "support[ed]" this interpretation. *Ibid.*
>
> EPA has not explained why § 7412(n)(1)(B)'s reference to "environmental effects ... and ... costs" provides "direct evidence that Congress was concerned with environmental effects," but not "direct evidence" that it was concerned with cost. *Chevron* allows agencies to choose among competing reasonable interpretations of a statute; it does not license interpretive gerrymanders under which an agency keeps parts of statutory context it likes while throwing away parts it does not.

B

EPA identifies a handful of reasons to interpret § 7412(n)(1)(A) to mean that cost is irrelevant to the initial decision to regulate. We find those reasons unpersuasive.

EPA points out that other parts of the Clean Air Act expressly mention cost, while § 7412(n)(1)(A) does not. But this observation shows only that § 7412(n)(1)(A)'s broad reference to appropriateness encompasses *multiple* relevant factors (which include but are not limited to cost); other provisions' specific references to cost encompass just cost. It is unreasonable to infer that, by expressly making cost relevant to other decisions, the Act implicitly makes cost irrelevant to the appropriateness of regulating power plants. (By way of analogy, the Fourth Amendment's Reasonableness Clause requires searches to be "[r]easonable," while its Warrant Clause requires warrants to be supported by "probable cause." Nobody would argue that, by expressly making level of suspicion relevant to the validity of a warrant, the Fourth Amendment implicitly makes level of suspicion categorically *irrelevant* to the reasonableness of a search. To the contrary, all would agree that the expansive word "reasonable" encompasses degree of suspicion alongside other relevant circumstances.) Other parts of the Clean Air Act also expressly mention environmental effects, while § 7412(n)(1)(A) does not. Yet that did not stop EPA from deeming environmental effects relevant to the appropriateness of regulating power plants.

Along similar lines, EPA seeks support in this Court's decision in *Whitman v. American Trucking Assns., Inc.*, 531 U.S. 457, 121 S.Ct. 903, 149 L.Ed.2d 1 (2001). There, the Court addressed a provision of the Clean Air Act requiring EPA to set ambient air quality standards at levels "requisite to protect the public health" with an "adequate margin of safety." 42 U.S.C. § 7409(b). Read naturally, that discrete criterion does not encompass cost; it encompasses health and safety. The Court refused to read that provision as carrying with it an implicit authorization to consider cost, in part because authority to consider cost had "elsewhere, and so often, been expressly granted." 531 U.S., at 467, 121 S.Ct. 903. *American Trucking* thus establishes the modest principle that where the Clean Air Act expressly directs EPA to regulate on the basis of a factor that on its face does not include cost, the Act normally should not be read as implicitly allowing the Agency to consider cost anyway. That principle has no application here. "Appropriate and necessary" is a far more comprehensive criterion than "requisite to protect the public health"; read fairly and in context, as we have explained, the term plainly subsumes consideration of cost.

Turning to the mechanics of the hazardous-air-pollutants program, EPA argues that it need not consider cost when first deciding *whether* to regulate power plants because it can consider cost later when deciding *how much* to regulate them. The question before us, however, is the meaning of the "appropriate and necessary" standard that governs the initial decision to regulate. And as we have discussed, context establishes that this expansive standard encompasses cost. Cost may become relevant again at a later stage of the regulatory process, but that possibility does not establish its irrelevance at *this* stage. In addition, once the Agency decides to regulate power plants, it must promulgate certain minimum or floor standards no matter the cost (here, nearly $10 billion a year); the Agency may consider cost only when imposing regulations *beyond* these minimum standards. By EPA's logic, someone could decide whether it is "appropriate" to buy a Ferrari without thinking about cost, because he plans to think about cost later when deciding whether to upgrade the sound system.

EPA argues that the Clean Air Act makes cost irrelevant to the initial decision to regulate sources other than power plants. The Agency claims that it is reasonable to interpret §

7412(n)(1)(A) in a way that "harmonizes" the program's treatment of power plants with its treatment of other sources. This line of reasoning overlooks the whole point of having a separate provision about power plants: treating power plants *differently* from other stationary sources. Congress crafted narrow standards for EPA to apply when deciding whether to regulate other sources; in general, these standards concern the volume of pollution emitted by the source, § 7412(c)(1), and the threat posed by the source "to human health or the environment," § 7412(c)(3). But Congress wrote the provision before us more expansively, directing the Agency to regulate power plants if "appropriate and necessary." "That congressional election settles this case. [The Agency's] preference for symmetry cannot trump an asymmetrical statute." *CSX Transp., Inc. v. Alabama Dept. of Revenue,* 562 U.S. 277, 296, 131 S.Ct. 1101, 179 L.Ed.2d 37 (2011).

EPA persists that Congress treated power plants differently from other sources because of uncertainty about whether regulation of power plants would still be needed after the application of the rest of the Act's requirements. That is undoubtedly *one* of the reasons Congress treated power plants differently; hence § 7412(n)(1)(A)'s requirement to study hazards posed by power plants' emissions "after imposition of the requirements of [the rest of the Act]." But if uncertainty about the need for regulation were the *only* reason to treat power plants differently, Congress would have required the Agency to decide only whether regulation remains "necessary," not whether regulation is "appropriate *and* necessary." In any event, EPA stated when it adopted the rule that "Congress did not limit [the] appropriate and necessary inquiry to [the study mentioned in § 7412(n)(1)(A)]." 77 Fed.Reg. 9325. The Agency instead decided that the appropriate-and-necessary finding should be understood in light of all three studies required by §

7412(n)(1), and as we have discussed, one of those three studies reflects concern about cost.

C

The dissent does not embrace EPA's far-reaching claim that Congress made costs altogether irrelevant to the decision to regulate power plants. Instead, it maintains that EPA need not "explicitly analyze costs" before deeming regulation appropriate, because other features of the regulatory program will on their own ensure the cost-effectiveness of regulation. *Post,* at 2714 (opinion of Kagan, J.). This line of reasoning contradicts the foundational principle of administrative law that a court may uphold agency action only on the grounds that the agency invoked when it took the action. *SEC v. Chenery Corp.,* 318 U.S. 80, 87, 63 S.Ct. 454, 87 L.Ed. 626 (1943). When it deemed regulation of power plants appropriate, EPA said that cost was *irrelevant* to that determination—not that cost-benefit analysis would be deferred until later. Much *less* did it say (what the dissent now concludes) that the consideration of cost at subsequent stages will ensure that the costs are not disproportionate to the benefits. What it said is that cost is irrelevant to the decision to regulate.

That is enough to decide these cases. But for what it is worth, the dissent vastly overstates the influence of cost at later stages of the regulatory process. For example, the dissent claims that the floor standards—which the Act calibrates to reflect emissions limitations already achieved by the best-performing sources in the industry—reflect cost considerations, because the best-performing power plants "must have considered costs in arriving at their emissions outputs." *Post,* at 2719. EPA did not rely on this argument, and it is not obvious that it is correct. Because power plants are regulated under other federal and state laws, the best-performing power plants' emissions limitations might reflect cost-blind regulation rather than cost-conscious decisions. Similarly, the dissent suggests that EPA may consider cost when dividing sources into categories and subcategories. *Post,* at 2720. Yet according to EPA, "it is *not* appropriate to premise subcategorization on costs." 77 Fed.Reg. 9395 (emphasis added). That statement presumably explains the dissent's carefully worded observation that EPA considered "technological, geographic, and other factors" when drawing categories, *post,* at 2720, n. 4, which factors were in turn "related to costs" in some way, *post,* at 2719. Attenuated connections such as these hardly support the assertion that EPA's regulatory process featured "exhaustive consideration of costs," *post,* at 2714.

All in all, the dissent has at most shown that some elements of the regulatory scheme mitigate cost in limited ways; it has not shown that these elements ensure cost-effectiveness. If (to take a hypothetical example) regulating power plants would yield $5 million in benefits, the prospect of mitigating cost from $11 billion to $10 billion at later stages of the program would not by itself make regulation appropriate. In all events, we need not pursue these points, because EPA did not say that the parts of the regulatory program mentioned by the dissent prevent the imposition of costs far in excess of benefits. "[EPA's] action must be measured by what [it] did, not by what it might have done." *Chenery, supra,* at 93–94, 63 S.Ct. 454.

D

Our reasoning so far establishes that it was unreasonable for EPA to read § 7412(n)(1)(A) to mean that cost is irrelevant to the initial decision to regulate power plants. The Agency must consider cost—including, most importantly, cost of compliance—before deciding whether regulation is appropriate and necessary. We need not and do not hold that the law unambiguously required the Agency, when making this preliminary estimate, to conduct a formal cost-benefit analysis in which each advantage and disadvantage is assigned a monetary value. It will be up to the Agency to decide (as always, within the limits of reasonable interpretation) how to account for cost.

Some of the respondents supporting EPA ask us to uphold EPA's action because the accompanying regulatory impact analysis shows that, once the rule's ancillary benefits are considered, benefits plainly outweigh costs. The dissent similarly relies on these ancillary benefits when insisting that "the outcome here [was] a rule whose benefits exceed its costs." *Post,* at 2722. As we have just explained, however, we may uphold agency action only upon the grounds on which the agency acted. Even if the Agency *could* have considered ancillary benefits when deciding whether regulation is appropriate and necessary—a point we need not address—it plainly did not do so here. In the Agency's own words, the administrative record "utterly refutes [the] assertion that [ancillary benefits] form the basis for the appropriate and necessary finding." 77 Fed.Reg. 9323. The Government concedes, moreover, that "EPA did not rely on the [regulatory impact analysis] when deciding to regulate power plants," and that "[e]ven if EPA had considered costs, it would not necessarily have adopted ... the approach set forth in [that analysis]." Brief for Federal Respondents 53–54.

* * *

We hold that EPA interpreted § 7412(n)(1)(A) unreasonably when it deemed cost irrelevant to the decision to regulate power plants. We reverse the judgment of the Court of Appeals for the D.C. Circuit and remand the cases for further proceedings consistent with this opinion.

It is so ordered.

Justice Thomas, concurring.

Justice Kagan, with whom Justice Ginsburg, Justice Breyer, and

Justice Sotomayor join, dissenting.

2

Structure and Procedures of the Judiciary

Interpreting the Endangered Species Act
Lujan v. Defenders of Wildlife, 504 U.S. 555 (1992)

On the Power of Tribal Courts
Nevada v. Hicks, 533 U.S. 353 (2001)

The "State Secrets" Doctrine in Court
General Dynamics Corp. v. U.S., 563 U.S. 478 (2011)

On the Limits to Class Actions
Wal-Mart Stores, Inc. v. Dukes, 131 S. Ct. 2541 (2011)

The federal judiciary is a hierarchy of courts and of judges culminating at its peak in the Supreme Court. One of the important roles played by the Supreme Court is to act as final arbiter on all matters relating to the organization, structure, and powers of the entire federal judiciary. The decisions reprinted in this section range from the proper allocation of jurisdiction between tribal courts and state and federal courts to what limits should be placed on the ability of class action plaintiffs to sue as a class in federal courts. These decisions show Justice Scalia's ability to analyze the complex constitutional and statutory provisions that underlie the federal judiciary and show, as well, his mastery of the intricacies of federal judicial procedure.

Interpreting the Endangered Species Act
Lujan v. Defenders of Wildlife,
504 U.S. 555 (1992)

Justice Scalia delivered the opinion of the Court with respect to Parts I, II, III-A, and IV, and an opinion with respect to Part III-B, in which the Chief Justice, Justice White, and Justice Thomas join.

This case involves a challenge to a rule promulgated by the Secretary of the Interior interpreting § 7 of the Endangered Species Act of 1973 (ESA), 87 Stat. 884, 892, as amended, 16 U.S.C. § 1536, in such fashion as to render it applicable only to actions within the United States or on the high seas. The preliminary issue, and the only one we reach, is whether respondents here, plaintiffs below, have standing to seek judicial review of the rule.

I

The ESA, 87 Stat. 884, as amended, 16 U.S.C. § 1531 *et seq.*, seeks to protect species of animals against threats to their continuing existence caused by man. See generally *TVA v. Hill,* 437 U.S. 153, 98 S.Ct. 2279, 57 L.Ed.2d 117 (1978). The ESA instructs the Secretary of the Interior to promulgate by regulation a list of those species which are either endangered or threatened under enumerated criteria, and to define the critical habitat of these species. 16 U.S.C. §§ 1533, 1536. Section 7(a)(2) of the Act then provides, in pertinent part:

> "Each Federal agency shall, in consultation with and with the assistance of the Secretary [of the Interior], insure that any action authorized, funded, or carried out by such agency ... is not likely to jeopardize the continued existence of any

> endangered species or threatened species or result in the destruction or adverse modification of habitat of such species which is determined by the Secretary, after consultation as appropriate with affected States, to be critical." 16 U.S.C. § 1536(a)(2).

In 1978, the Fish and Wildlife Service (FWS) and the National Marine Fisheries Service (NMFS), on behalf of the Secretary of the Interior and the Secretary of Commerce respectively, promulgated a joint regulation stating that the obligations imposed by § 7(a)(2) extend to actions taken in foreign nations. 43 Fed.Reg. 874 (1978). The next year, however, the Interior Department began to reexamine its position. Letter from Leo Kuliz, Solicitor, Department of the Interior, to Assistant Secretary, Fish and Wildlife and Parks, Aug. 8, 1979. A revised joint regulation, reinterpreting § 7(a)(2) to require consultation only for actions taken in the United States or on the high seas, was proposed in 1983, 48 Fed.Reg. 29990, and promulgated in 1986, 51 Fed.Reg. 19926; 50 CFR 402.01 (1991).

Shortly thereafter, respondents, organizations dedicated to wildlife conservation and other environmental causes, filed this action against the Secretary of the Interior, seeking a declaratory judgment that the new regulation is in error as to the geographic scope of § 7(a)(2) and an injunction requiring the Secretary to promulgate a new regulation restoring the initial interpretation. The District Court granted the Secretary's motion to dismiss for lack of standing. *Defenders of Wildlife v. Hodel,* 658 F.Supp. 43, 47–48 (Minn.1987). The Court of Appeals for the Eighth Circuit reversed by a divided vote. *Defenders of Wildlife v. Hodel,* 851 F.2d 1035 (1988). On remand, the Secretary moved for summary judgment on the standing issue, and respondents moved for summary judgment on the merits. The District Court denied the Secretary's motion, on the ground that the Eighth Circuit had already determined the standing question in this case; it granted respondents' merits motion, and ordered the Secretary to publish a revised regulation. *Defenders of Wildlife v. Hodel,* 707 F.Supp. 1082 (Minn.1989). The Eighth Circuit affirmed. 911 F.2d 117 (1990). We granted certiorari, 500 U.S. 915, 111 S.Ct. 2008, 114 L.Ed.2d 97 (1991).

II

While the Constitution of the United States divides all power conferred upon the Federal Government into "legislative Powers," Art. I, § 1, "[t]he executive Power," Art. II, § 1, and "[t]he judicial Power," Art. III, § 1, it does not attempt to define those terms. To be sure, it limits the jurisdiction of federal courts to "Cases" and "Controversies," but an executive inquiry can bear the name "case" (the Hoffa case) and a legislative dispute can bear the name "controversy" (the Smoot-Hawley controversy). Obviously, then, the Constitution's central mechanism of separation of powers depends largely upon common understanding of what activities are appropriate to legislatures, to executives, and to courts. In *The Federalist* No. 48, Madison expressed the view that "[i]t is not infrequently a question of real nicety in legislative bodies whether the operation of a particular measure will, or will not, extend beyond the legislative sphere," whereas "the executive power [is] restrained within a narrower compass and ... more simple in its nature," and "the judiciary [is] described by landmarks still less uncertain." *The Federalist* No. 48, p. 256 (Carey and McClellan eds. 1990). One of those landmarks, setting apart the "Cases" and "Controversies" that are of the justiciable sort referred to in Article III—"serv[ing] to identify those disputes which are appropriately resolved through the judicial process," *Whitmore v. Arkansas,* 495 U.S. 149, 155, 110

S.Ct. 1717, 1722, 109 L.Ed.2d 135 (1990)—is the doctrine of standing. Though some of its elements express merely prudential considerations that are part of judicial self-government, the core component of standing is an essential and unchanging part of the case-or-controversy requirement of Article III. See, *e.g., Allen v. Wright,* 468 U.S. 737, 751, 104 S.Ct. 3315, 3324, 82 L.Ed.2d 556 (1984).

Over the years, our cases have established that the irreducible constitutional minimum of standing contains three elements. First, the plaintiff must have suffered an "injury in fact"—an invasion of a legally protected interest which is (a) concrete and particularized, see *id.,* at 756, 104 S.Ct., at 3327; *Warth v. Seldin,* 422 U.S. 490, 508, 95 S.Ct. 2197, 2210, 45 L.Ed.2d 343 (1975); *Sierra Club v. Morton,* 405 U.S. 727, 740–741, n. 16, 92 S.Ct. 1361, 1368–1369, n. 16, 31 L.Ed.2d 636 (1972); and (b) "actual or imminent, not 'conjectural' or 'hypothetical,'" *Whitmore, supra,* 495 U.S., at 155, 110 S.Ct., at 1723 (quoting *Los Angeles v. Lyons,* 461 U.S. 95, 102, 103 S.Ct. 1660, 1665, 75 L.Ed.2d 675 (1983)). Second, there must be a causal connection between the injury and the conduct complained of—the injury has to be "fairly ... trace[able] to the challenged action of the defendant, and not ... th[e] result [of] the independent action of some third party not before the court." *Simon v. Eastern Ky. Welfare Rights Organization,* 426 U.S. 26, 41–42, 96 S.Ct. 1917, 1926, 48 L.Ed.2d 450 (1976). Third, it must be "likely," as opposed to merely "speculative," that the injury will be "redressed by a favorable decision." *Id.,* at 38, 43, 96 S.Ct., at 1924, 1926.

The party invoking federal jurisdiction bears the burden of establishing these elements. See *FW/PBS, Inc. v. Dallas,* 493 U.S. 215, 231, 110 S.Ct. 596, 608, 107 L.Ed.2d 603 (1990); *Warth, supra,* 422 U.S., at 508, 95 S.Ct., at 2210. Since they are not mere pleading requirements but rather an indispensable part of the plaintiff's case, each element must be supported in the same way as any other matter on which the plaintiff bears the burden of proof, *i.e.,* with the manner and degree of evidence required at the successive stages of the litigation. See *Lujan v. National Wildlife Federation,* 497 U.S. 871, 883–889, 110 S.Ct. 3177, 3185–3189, 111 L.Ed.2d 695 (1990); *Gladstone, Realtors v. Village of Bellwood,* 441 U.S. 91, 114–115, and n. 31, 99 S.Ct. 1601, 1614–1615, and n. 31, 60 L.Ed.2d 66 (1979); *Simon, supra,* 426 U.S., at 45, n. 25, 96 S.Ct., at 1927, and n. 25; *Warth, supra,* 422 U.S., at 527, and n. 6, 95 S.Ct., at 2219, and n. 6 (Brennan, J., dissenting). At the pleading stage, general factual allegations of injury resulting from the defendant's conduct may suffice, for on a motion to dismiss we "presum[e] that general allegations embrace those specific facts that are necessary to support the claim." *National Wildlife Federation, supra,* 497 U.S., at 889, 110 S.Ct., at 3189. In response to a summary judgment motion, however, the plaintiff can no longer rest on such "mere allegations," but must "set forth" by affidavit or other evidence "specific facts," Fed.Rule Civ.Proc. 56(e), which for purposes of the summary judgment motion will be taken to be true. And at the final stage, those facts (if controverted) must be "supported adequately by the evidence adduced at trial." *Gladstone, supra,* 441 U.S., at 115, n. 31, 99 S.Ct., at 1616, n. 31.

When the suit is one challenging the legality of government action or inaction, the nature and extent of facts that must be averred (at the summary judgment stage) or proved (at the trial stage) in order to establish standing depends considerably upon whether the plaintiff is himself an object of the action (or forgone action) at issue. If he is, there is ordinarily little question that the action or inaction has caused him injury, and that a judgment preventing or requiring the action will redress it. When, however, as in this case, a plaintiff's asserted injury arises from the government's allegedly unlawful regulation (or lack of regulation) of *someone else,* much more is needed. In that circumstance, causation and redressability ordinarily hinge on the response of the regulated (or regulable) third party to the government action or inaction—and perhaps on the response of others as well. The existence of one or more of the essential elements of standing "depends on the unfettered choices made by independent actors not before the courts and whose exercise of broad and legitimate discretion the courts cannot presume either to control or to predict," *ASARCO Inc. v. Kadish,* 490 U.S. 605, 615, 109 S.Ct. 2037, 2044, 104 L.Ed.2d 696 (1989) (opinion of KENNEDY, J.); see also *Simon, supra,* 426 U.S., at 41–42, 96 S.Ct., at 1925, 1926; and it becomes the burden of the plaintiff to adduce facts showing that those choices have been or will be made in such manner as to produce causation and permit redressability of injury. *E.g., Warth, supra,* 422 U.S., at 505, 95 S.Ct., at 2208. Thus, when the plaintiff is not himself the object of the government action or inaction he challenges, standing is not precluded, but it is ordinarily "substantially more difficult" to establish. *Allen, supra,* 468 U.S., at 758, 104 S.Ct., at 3328; *Simon, supra,* 426 U.S., at 44–45, 96 S.Ct., at 1927; *Warth, supra,* 422 U.S., at 505, 95 S.Ct., at 2208.

III

We think the Court of Appeals failed to apply the foregoing principles in denying the Secretary's motion for summary judgment. Respondents had not made the requisite demonstration of (at least) injury and redressability.

A

Respondents' claim to injury is that the lack of consultation with respect to certain funded activities abroad "increas[es] the rate of extinction of endangered and threatened species." Complaint ¶ 5, App. 13. Of course, the desire to use or observe an animal species, even for purely esthetic purposes, is undeniably a cognizable interest for purpose of standing. See, *e.g., Sierra Club v. Morton,* 405 U.S., at 734, 92 S.Ct., at 1366. "But the 'injury in fact' test requires more than an injury to a cognizable interest. It requires that the party seeking review be himself among the injured." *Id.,* at 734–735, 92 S.Ct., at 1366. To survive the Secretary's summary judgment motion, respondents had to submit affidavits or other evidence showing, through specific facts, not only that listed species were in fact being threatened by funded activities abroad, but also that one or more of respondents' members would thereby be "directly" affected apart from their "'special interest' in th[e] subject." *Id.,* at 735, 739, 92 S.Ct., at 1366, 1368. See generally *Hunt v. Washington State Apple Advertising Comm'n,* 432 U.S. 333, 343, 97 S.Ct. 2434, 2441, 53 L.Ed.2d 383 (1977).

With respect to this aspect of the case, the Court of Appeals focused on the affidavits of two Defenders' members—Joyce Kelly and Amy Skilbred. Ms. Kelly stated that she traveled to Egypt in 1986 and "observed the traditional habitat of the endangered nile crocodile there and intend[s] to do so again, and hope[s] to observe the crocodile directly," and that she "will suffer harm in fact as the result of [the] American ... role ... in overseeing the rehabilitation of the Aswan High Dam on the Nile ... and [in] develop [ing] ... Egypt's ... Master Water Plan." App. 101. Ms. Skilbred averred that she traveled to Sri Lanka in 1981 and "observed th[e] habitat" of "endangered species such as the Asian elephant and the leopard" at what is now the site of the Mahaweli project funded by the Agency for International Development (AID), although she "was unable to see any of the endangered species"; "this development project," she continued, "will seriously reduce endangered, threatened, and endemic species habitat including areas that I visited ... [, which] may severely shorten the future of these species"; that threat, she concluded, harmed her because she "intend[s] to return to Sri Lanka in the future and hope[s] to be more fortunate in spotting at least the endangered elephant and leopard." *Id.*, at 145–146. When Ms. Skilbred was asked at a subsequent deposition if and when she had any plans to return to Sri Lanka, she reiterated that "I intend to go back to Sri Lanka," but confessed that she had no current plans: "I don't know [when]. There is a civil war going on right now. I don't know. Not next year, I will say. In the future." *Id.*, at 318.

We shall assume for the sake of argument that these affidavits contain facts showing that certain agency-funded projects threaten listed species—though that is questionable. They plainly contain no facts, however, showing how damage to the species will produce "imminent" injury to Mses. Kelly and Skilbred. That the women "had visited" the areas of the projects before the projects commenced proves nothing. As we have said in a related context, "'Past exposure to illegal conduct does not in itself show a present case or controversy regarding injunctive relief ... if unaccompanied by any continuing, present adverse effects.'" *Lyons,* 461 U.S., at 102, 103 S.Ct., at 1665 (quoting *O'Shea v. Littleton,* 414 U.S. 488, 495–496, 94 S.Ct. 669, 676, 38 L.Ed.2d 674 (1974)). And the affiants' profession of an "inten[t]" to return to the places they had visited before—where they will presumably, this time, be deprived of the opportunity to observe animals of the endangered species—is simply not enough. Such "some day" intentions—without any description of concrete plans, or indeed even any specification of *when* the some day will be—do not support a finding of the "actual or imminent" injury that our cases require. See *supra,* at 2136.

Besides relying upon the Kelly and Skilbred affidavits, respondents propose a series of novel standing theories. The first, inelegantly styled "ecosystem nexus," proposes that any person who uses *any part* of a "contiguous ecosystem" adversely affected by a funded activity has standing even if the activity is located a great distance away. This approach, as the Court of Appeals correctly observed, is inconsistent with our opinion in *National Wildlife Federation,* which held that a plaintiff claiming injury from environmental damage must use the area affected by the challenged activity and not an area roughly "in the vicinity" of it. 497 U.S., at 887–889, 110 S.Ct., at 3188–3189; see also *Sierra Club,* 405 U.S., at 735, 92 S.Ct., at 1366. It makes no difference that the general-purpose section of the ESA states that the Act was intended in part "to provide a means whereby the ecosystems upon which endangered species and threatened species depend may be conserved," 16 U.S.C. § 1531(b). To say that the Act protects ecosystems is not to say that the Act creates (if it were possible) rights of action in persons who have not been injured in fact, that is, persons who use portions of an ecosystem not perceptibly affected by the unlawful action in question.

Respondents' other theories are called, alas, the "animal nexus" approach, whereby anyone who has an interest in studying or seeing the endangered animals anywhere on the globe has standing; and the "vocational nexus" approach, under which anyone with a professional interest in such animals can sue. Under these theories, anyone who goes to see Asian elephants in the Bronx Zoo, and anyone who is a keeper of Asian elephants in the Bronx Zoo, has standing to sue because the Director of the Agency for International Development (AID) did not consult with the Secretary regarding the AID-funded project in Sri Lanka. This is beyond all reason. Standing is not "an ingenious academic exercise in the conceivable," *United States v. Students Challenging Regulatory Agency Procedures (SCRAP),* 412 U.S. 669, 688, 93 S.Ct. 2405, 2416, 37 L.Ed.2d 254 (1973), but as we have said requires, at the summary judgment stage, a factual showing of perceptible harm. It is clear that the person who observes or works with a particular animal threatened by a federal decision is facing perceptible harm, since the very subject of his interest will no longer exist. It is even plausible—though it goes to the outermost limit of plausibility—to think that a person who observes or works with animals of a particular species in the very area of the world where that species is threatened by a federal decision is facing such harm, since some animals that might have been the subject of his interest will no longer exist, see *Japan Whaling Assn. v. American Cetacean Society,* 478 U.S. 221, 231, n. 4, 106 S.Ct. 2860, 2866, n. 4, 92 L.Ed.2d 166 (1986). It goes beyond the limit, however, and into pure speculation and fantasy, to say that anyone who observes or works with an endangered species, anywhere in the world, is appreciably harmed by a single project affecting some portion of that species with which he has no more specific connection.

B

Besides failing to show injury, respondents failed to demonstrate redressability. Instead of attacking the separate decisions to fund particular projects allegedly causing them harm, respondents chose to challenge a more generalized level of Government action (rules regarding consultation), the invalidation of which would affect all overseas projects. This programmatic approach has obvious practical advantages, but also obvious difficulties insofar as proof of causation or redressability is concerned. As we have said in another context, "suits challenging, not specifically identifiable Government violations of law, but the particular programs agencies establish to carry out their legal obligations ... [are], even when premised on allegations of several instances of violations of law, ... rarely if ever appropriate for federal-court adjudication." *Allen,* 468 U.S., at 759–760, 104 S.Ct., at 3329.

The most obvious problem in the present case is redressability. Since the agencies funding the projects were not parties to the case, the District Court could accord relief only against the Secretary: He could be ordered to revise his regulation to require consultation for foreign projects. But this would not remedy respondents' alleged injury unless the funding agencies were bound by the Secretary's regulation, which is very much an open question. Whereas in other contexts the ESA is quite explicit as to the Secretary's controlling authority, see, *e.g.,* 16 U.S.C. § 1533(a)(1) ("The Secretary shall" promulgate regulations determining endangered species); § 1535(d)(1) ("The Secretary is authorized to provide financial assistance to any State"), with respect to consultation the initiative, and hence arguably the initial responsibility for determining statutory necessity, lies with the agencies, see § 1536(a)(2) ("*Each Federal agency shall,* in consultation with and with the assistance of the Secretary, insure that any" funded action is not likely to jeopardize endangered or threatened species) (emphasis added). When the Secretary promulgated the regulation at issue here, he thought it was binding on the agencies, see 51 Fed.Reg. 19928 (1986). The Solicitor General, however, has repudiated that position here, and the agencies themselves apparently deny the Secretary's authority. (During the period when the Secretary took the view that § 7(a)(2) did apply abroad, AID and FWS engaged in a running controversy over whether consultation was required with respect to the Mahaweli project, AID insisting that consultation applied only to domestic actions.)

Respondents assert that this legal uncertainty did not affect redressability (and hence standing) because the District Court itself could resolve the issue of the Secretary's authority as a necessary part of its standing inquiry. Assuming that it is appropriate to resolve an issue of law such as this in connection with a threshold standing inquiry, resolution by the District Court would not have remedied respondents' alleged injury anyway, because it would not have been binding upon the agencies. They were not parties to the suit, and there is no reason they should be obliged to honor an incidental legal determination the suit produced. The Court of Appeals tried to finesse this problem by simply proclaiming that "[w]e are satisfied that an injunction requiring the Secretary to publish [respondents' desired] regulatio[n] ... would result in consultation." *Defenders of Wildlife,* 851 F.2d, at 1042, 1043–1044. We do not know what would justify that confidence, particularly when the Justice Department (presumably after consultation with the agencies) has taken the position that the regulation is not binding. The short of the matter is that redress of the only injury in fact respondents complain of requires action (termination of funding until consultation) by the individual funding agencies; and any relief the District Court could have provided in this suit against the Secretary was not likely to produce that action.

A further impediment to redressability is the fact that the agencies generally supply only a fraction of the funding for a foreign project. AID, for example, has provided less than 10% of the funding for the Mahaweli project. Respondents have produced nothing to indicate that the projects they have named will either be suspended, or do less harm to listed species, if that fraction is eliminated. As in *Simon,* 426 U.S., at 43–44, 96 S.Ct., at 1926–1927, it is entirely conjectural whether the nonagency activity that affects respondents will be altered or affected by the agency activity they seek to achieve. There is no standing.

IV

The Court of Appeals found that respondents had standing for an additional reason: because they had suffered a "procedural injury." The so-called "citizen-suit" provision of the ESA provides, in pertinent part, that "any person may commence a civil suit on his own behalf (A) to enjoin any person, including the United States and any other governmental instrumentality or agency ... who is alleged to be in violation of any provision of this chapter." 16 U.S.C. § 1540(g). The court held that, because § 7(a)(2) requires interagency consultation, the citizen-suit provision creates a "procedural righ[t]" to consultation in all "persons"—so that *anyone* can file suit in federal court to challenge the Secretary's (or presumably any other official's) failure to follow the assertedly correct consultative procedure, notwithstanding his or her inability to allege any discrete injury flowing from that failure. 911 F.2d, at 121–122. To understand the remarkable nature of this holding one must be clear about what it does *not* rest upon: This is not a case where plaintiffs are seeking to enforce a procedural requirement the disregard of which could impair a separate concrete interest of theirs (*e.g.*, the procedural requirement for a hearing prior to denial of their license application, or the procedural requirement for an environmental impact statement before a federal facility is constructed next door to them). Nor is it simply a case where concrete injury has been suffered by many persons, as in mass fraud or mass tort situations. Nor, finally, is it the unusual case in which Congress has created a concrete private interest in the outcome of a suit against a private party for the government's benefit, by providing a cash bounty for the victorious plaintiff. Rather, the court held that the injury-in-fact requirement had been satisfied by congressional conferral upon *all* persons of an abstract, self-contained, noninstrumental "right" to have the

Executive observe the procedures required by law. We reject this view.

We have consistently held that a plaintiff raising only a generally available grievance about government—claiming only harm to his and every citizen's interest in proper application of the Constitution and laws, and seeking relief that no more directly and tangibly benefits him than it does the public at large—does not state an Article III case or controversy. For example, in *Fairchild v. Hughes,* 258 U.S. 126, 129–130, 42 S.Ct. 274, 275, 66 L.Ed. 499 (1922), we dismissed a suit challenging the propriety of the process by which the Nineteenth Amendment was ratified. Justice Brandeis wrote for the Court:

> "[This is] not a case within the meaning of ... Article III.... Plaintiff has [asserted] only the right, possessed by every citizen, to require that the Government be administered according to law and that the public moneys be not wasted. Obviously this general right does not entitle a private citizen to institute in the federal courts a suit...." *Ibid.*

In *Massachusetts v. Mellon,* 262 U.S. 447, 43 S.Ct. 597, 67 L.Ed. 1078 (1923), we dismissed for lack of Article III standing a taxpayer suit challenging the propriety of certain federal expenditures. We said:

> "The party who invokes the power [of judicial review] must be able to show not only that the statute is invalid but that he has sustained or is immediately in danger of sustaining some direct injury as the result of its enforcement, and not merely that he suffers in some indefinite way in common with people generally.... Here the parties plaintiff have no such case.... [T]heir complaint ... is merely that officials of the executive department of the government are executing and will execute an act of Congress asserted to be

> unconstitutional; and this we are asked to prevent. To do so would be not to decide a judicial controversy, but to assume a position of authority over the governmental acts of another and co-equal department, an authority which plainly we do not possess." *Id.*, at 488–489, 43 S.Ct., at 601.

In *Ex parte Lévitt,* 302 U.S. 633, 58 S.Ct. 1, 82 L.Ed. 493 (1937), we dismissed a suit contending that Justice Black's appointment to this Court violated the Ineligibility Clause, Art. I, § 6, cl. 2. "It is an established principle," we said, "that to entitle a private individual to invoke the judicial power to determine the validity of executive or legislative action he must show that he has sustained or is immediately in danger of sustaining a direct injury as the result of that action and it is not sufficient that he has merely a general interest common to all members of the public." 302 U.S., at 634, 58 S.Ct., at 1. See also *Doremus v. Board of Ed. of Hawthorne,* 342 U.S. 429, 433–434, 72 S.Ct. 394, 396–397, 96 L.Ed. 475 (1952) (dismissing taxpayer action on the basis of *Mellon*).

More recent cases are to the same effect. In *United States v. Richardson,* 418 U.S. 166, 94 S.Ct. 2940, 41 L.Ed.2d 678 (1974), we dismissed for lack of standing a taxpayer suit challenging the Government's failure to disclose the expenditures of the Central Intelligence Agency, in alleged violation of the constitutional requirement, Art. I, § 9, cl. 7, that "a regular Statement and Account of the Receipts and Expenditures of all public Money shall be published from time to time." We held that such a suit rested upon an impermissible "generalized grievance," and was inconsistent with "the framework of Article III" because "the impact on [plaintiff] is plainly undifferentiated and 'common to all members of the public.'" *Richardson, supra,* at 171, 176–177, 94 S.Ct., at 2944, 2946. And in *Schlesinger v. Reservists Comm. to Stop the War,* 418 U.S. 208, 94 S.Ct. 2925, 41 L.Ed.2d 706 (1974), we dismissed for the same reasons a citizen-taxpayer suit contending that it was a violation of the Incompatibility Clause, Art. I, § 6, cl. 2, for Members of Congress to hold commissions in the military Reserves. We said that the challenged action, "standing alone, would adversely affect only the generalized interest of all citizens in constitutional governance.... We reaffirm *Levitt* in holding that standing to sue may not be predicated upon an interest of th[is] kind...." *Schlesinger, supra,* at 217, 220, 94 S.Ct., at 2930, 2932. Since *Schlesinger* we have on two occasions held that an injury amounting only to the alleged violation of a right to have the Government act in accordance with law was not judicially cognizable because "'assertion of a right to a particular kind of Government conduct, which the Government has violated by acting differently, cannot alone satisfy the requirements of Art. III without draining those requirements of meaning.'" *Allen,* 468 U.S., at 754, 104 S.Ct., at 3326; *Valley Forge Christian College v. Americans United for Separation of Church and State, Inc.,* 454 U.S. 464, 483, 102 S.Ct. 752, 764, 70 L.Ed.2d 700 (1982). And only two Terms ago, we rejected the notion that Article III permits a citizen suit to prevent a condemned criminal's execution on the basis of "'the public interest protections of the Eighth Amendment'"; once again, "[t]his allegation raise [d] only the 'generalized interest of all citizens in constitutional governance' ... and [was] an inadequate basis on which to grant ... standing." *Whitmore,* 495 U.S., at 160, 110 S.Ct., at 1725.

To be sure, our generalized-grievance cases have typically involved Government violation of procedures assertedly ordained by the Constitution rather than the Congress. But there is absolutely no basis for making the Article III inquiry turn on the source of the asserted right. Whether the courts were to act on their own, or at the invitation of Congress, in ignoring the concrete injury requirement described in our cases, they would be discarding a principle fundamental to the separate and distinct constitutional role of the Third Branch—one of the essential elements that identifies those "Cases" and "Controversies" that are the business of the courts rather than of the political branches. "The province of the court," as Chief Justice Marshall said in *Marbury v. Madison,* 5 U.S. (1 Cranch) 137, 170, 2 L.Ed. 60 (1803), "is, solely, to decide on the rights of individuals." Vindicating the *public* interest (including the public interest in Government observance of the Constitution and laws) is the function of Congress and the Chief Executive. The question presented here is whether the public interest in proper administration of the laws (specifically, in agencies' observance of a particular, statutorily prescribed procedure) can be converted into an individual right by a statute that denominates it as such, and that permits all citizens (or, for that matter, a subclass of citizens who suffer no distinctive concrete harm) to sue. If the concrete injury requirement has the separation-of-powers significance we have always said, the answer must be obvious: To permit Congress to convert the undifferentiated public interest in executive officers' compliance with the law into an "individual right" vindicable in the courts is to permit Congress to transfer from the President to the courts the Chief Executive's most important constitutional duty, to "take Care that the Laws be faithfully executed," Art. II, § 3. It would enable the courts, with the permission of Congress, "to assume a position of authority over the governmental acts of another and co-equal department," *Massachusetts v. Mellon,* 262 U.S., at 489, 43 S.Ct., at 601, and to become "'virtually continuing monitors of the wisdom and soundness of Executive action.'" *Allen, supra,* 468 U.S., at 760, 104 S.Ct., at 3329 (quoting *Laird v. Tatum,* 408 U.S. 1, 15, 92 S.Ct. 2318, 2326, 33 L.Ed.2d 154 (1972)). We have always rejected that vision of our role:

> "When Congress passes an Act empowering administrative agencies to carry on governmental activities, the power of those agencies is circumscribed by the authority granted. This permits the courts to participate in law enforcement entrusted to administrative bodies only to the extent necessary to protect justiciable individual rights against administrative action fairly beyond the granted powers.... This is very far from assuming that the courts are charged more than administrators or legislators with the protection of the rights of the people. Congress and the Executive supervise the acts of administrative agents.... But under Article III, Congress established courts to adjudicate cases and controversies as to claims of infringement of individual rights whether by unlawful action of private persons or by the exertion of unauthorized administrative power." *Stark v. Wickard,* 321 U.S. 288, 309–310, 64 S.Ct. 559, 571, 88 L.Ed. 733 (1944) (footnote omitted).

"Individual rights," within the meaning of this passage, do not mean public rights that have been legislatively pronounced to belong to each individual who forms part of the public. See also *Sierra Club,* 405 U.S., at 740–741, n. 16, 92 S.Ct., at 1369, n. 16.

Nothing in this contradicts the principle that "[t]he ... injury required by Art. III may exist solely by virtue of 'statutes creating legal rights, the invasion of which creates standing.'" *Warth,* 422 U.S., at 500, 95 S.Ct., at 2206 (quoting *Linda R. S. v. Richard D.,* 410 U.S. 614, 617, n. 3, 93 S.Ct. 1146, 1148, n. 3, 35 L.Ed.2d 536 (1973)). Both of the cases used by *Linda R. S.* as an illustration of that principle involved Congress' elevating to the status of legally cognizable injuries concrete, *de facto* injuries that were previously inadequate in law (namely, injury to an individual's personal interest in living in a racially integrated community, see *Trafficante v. Metropolitan Life Ins. Co.,* 409 U.S. 205, 208–212, 93 S.Ct. 364, 366–368, 34 L.Ed.2d

415 (1972), and injury to a company's interest in marketing its product free from competition, see *Hardin v. Kentucky Utilities Co.*, 390 U.S. 1, 6, 88 S.Ct. 651, 654, 19 L.Ed.2d 787 (1968)). As we said in *Sierra Club*, "[Statutory] broadening [of] the categories of injury that may be alleged in support of standing is a different matter from abandoning the requirement that the party seeking review must himself have suffered an injury." 405 U.S., at 738, 92 S.Ct., at 1368. Whether or not the principle set forth in *Warth* can be extended beyond that distinction, it is clear that in suits against the Government, at least, the concrete injury requirement must remain.

* * *

We hold that respondents lack standing to bring this action and that the Court of Appeals erred in denying the summary judgment motion filed by the United States. The opinion of the Court of Appeals is hereby reversed, and the cause is remanded for proceedings consistent with this opinion.

It is so ordered.

Justice Kennedy, with whom Justice Souter joins, concurring in part and concurring in the judgment.

Justice Stevens, concurring in the judgment.

Justice Blackmun, with whom Justice O'Connor joins, dissenting.

On the Power of Tribal Courts
Nevada v. Hicks,
533 U.S. 353 (2001)

Justice Scalia delivered the opinion of the Court.

This case presents the question whether a tribal court may assert jurisdiction over civil claims against state officials who entered tribal land to execute a search warrant against a tribe member suspected of having violated state law outside the reservation.

I

Respondent Hicks is one of about 900 members of the Fallon Paiute-Shoshone Tribes of western Nevada. He resides on the Tribes' reservation of approximately 8,000 acres, established by federal statute in 1908, ch. 53, 35 Stat. 85. In 1990 Hicks came under suspicion of having killed, off the reservation, a California bighorn sheep, a gross misdemeanor under Nevada law, see Nev.Rev.Stat. § 501.376 (1999). A state game warden obtained from state court a search warrant "SUBJECT TO OBTAINING APPROVAL FROM THE FALLON TRIBAL COURT IN AND FOR THE FALLON PAIUTE-SHOSHONE TRIBES." According to the issuing judge, this tribal-court authorization was necessary because "[t]his Court has no jurisdiction on the Fallon Paiute-Shoshone Indian Reservation." App. G to Pet. for Cert. 1. A search warrant was obtained from the tribal court, and the warden, accompanied by a tribal police officer, searched respondent's yard, uncovering only the head of a Rocky Mountain bighorn, a different (and unprotected) species of sheep.

Approximately one year later, a tribal police officer reported to the warden that he had observed two mounted bighorn sheep heads in respondent's home. The warden again obtained a search warrant from state court; though this warrant did not explicitly require permission from the Tribes, see App. F to Pet. for Cert. 2, a tribal-court warrant was nonetheless secured, and respondent's home was again (unsuccessfully) searched by three wardens and additional tribal officers.

Respondent, claiming that his sheep heads had been damaged, and that the second search exceeded the bounds of the warrant, brought suit against the Tribal Judge, the tribal officers, the state wardens in their individual and official capacities, and the State of Nevada in the Tribal Court in and for the Fallon Paiute-Shoshone Tribes. (His claims against all defendants except the state wardens and the State of Nevada were dismissed by directed verdict and are not at issue here.) Respondent's causes of action included trespass to land and chattels, abuse of process, and violation of civil rights—specifically, denial of equal protection, denial of due process, and unreasonable search and seizure, each remediable under Rev.Stat. § 1979, 42 U.S.C. § 1983. See App. 8–21, 25–29. Respondent later voluntarily dismissed his case against the State and against the state officials in their official capacities, leaving only his suit against those officials in their individual capacities. See *id.*, at 32–35.

The Tribal Court held that it had jurisdiction over the claims, a holding affirmed by the Tribal Appeals Court. The state officials and Nevada then filed an action in Federal District Court seeking a declaratory judgment that the Tribal Court lacked jurisdiction. The District Court granted summary judgment to respondent on the issue of jurisdiction, and also held that the state officials would have to exhaust any claims of qualified immunity in the tribal court. The Ninth Circuit affirmed, concluding that the fact that respondent's home is located on tribe-owned land within the reservation is sufficient to support tribal jurisdiction over civil claims against nonmembers arising from their activities on that land. 196 F.3d 1020 (1999). We granted certiorari, 531 U.S. 923, 121 S.Ct. 296, 148 L.Ed.2d 238 (2000).

II

In this case, which involves claims brought under both tribal and federal law, it is necessary to determine, as to the former, whether the Tribal Court in and for the Fallon Paiute-Shoshone Tribes has jurisdiction to adjudicate the alleged tortious conduct of state wardens executing a search warrant for evidence of an off-reservation crime; and, as to the latter, whether the Tribal Court has jurisdiction over claims brought under 42 U.S.C. § 1983. We address the former question first.

A

The principle of Indian law central to this aspect of the case is our holding in *Strate v. A-1 Contractors,* 520 U.S. 438, 453, 117 S.Ct. 1404, 137 L.Ed.2d 661 (1997):

> "As to nonmembers ... a tribe's adjudicative jurisdiction does not exceed its legislative jurisdiction...." That formulation leaves open the question whether a tribe's adjudicative jurisdiction over nonmember defendants *equals* its legislative jurisdiction. We will not have to answer that open question if we determine that the Tribes in any event lack legislative jurisdiction in this case. We first inquire, therefore, whether the Fallon Paiute-Shoshone Tribes-either as an exercise of their inherent sovereignty, or under grant of federal authority-can regulate state wardens executing a search warrant for evidence of an off-reservation crime.
>
> Indian tribes' regulatory authority over nonmembers is governed by the principles set forth in *Montana v. United States,* 450 U.S. 544, 101 S.Ct. 1245, 67 L.Ed.2d 493 (1981),

> which we have called the "pathmarking case" on the subject, *Strate, supra,* at 445, 117 S.Ct. 1404. In deciding whether the Crow Tribe could regulate hunting and fishing by nonmembers on land held in fee simple by nonmembers, *Montana* observed that, under our decision in *Oliphant v. Suquamish Tribe,* 435 U.S. 191, 98 S.Ct. 1011, 55 L.Ed.2d 209 (1978), tribes lack criminal jurisdiction over nonmembers. Although, it continued, "*Oliphant* only determined inherent tribal authority in criminal matters, the principles on which it relied support the general proposition that the inherent sovereign powers of an Indian tribe do not extend to the activities of nonmembers of the tribe." 450 U.S., at 565, 101 S.Ct. 1245 (footnote omitted). Where nonmembers are concerned, the "exercise of tribal power *beyond what is necessary to protect tribal self-government or to control internal relations* is inconsistent with the dependent status of the tribes, and so cannot survive without express congressional delegation." *Id.,* at 564, 101 S.Ct. 1245 (emphasis added).

Both *Montana* and *Strate* rejected tribal authority to regulate nonmembers' activities on land over which the tribe could not "assert a landowner's right to occupy and exclude," *Strate, supra,* at 456, 117 S.Ct. 1404; *Montana, supra,* at 557, 564, 101 S.Ct. 1245. Respondents and the United States argue that since Hicks's home and yard *are* on tribe-owned land within the reservation, the Tribe may make its exercise of regulatory authority over nonmembers a condition of nonmembers' entry. Not necessarily. While it is certainly true that the non-Indian ownership status of the land was central to the analysis in both *Montana* and *Strate,* the reason that was so was *not* that Indian ownership suspends the "general proposition" derived from *Oliphant* that "the inherent sovereign powers of an Indian tribe do not extend to the activities of nonmembers of the tribe" except to the extent "necessary to protect tribal self-government or to control internal relations." 450 U.S., at 564–565, 101 S.Ct. 1245. *Oliphant* itself drew no distinctions based on the status of land. And *Montana*, after announcing the general rule of no jurisdiction over nonmembers,cautioned that "[t]o be sure, Indian tribes retain inherent sovereign power to exercise some forms of civil jurisdiction over non-Indians on their reservations, even on non-Indian fee lands," 450 U.S., at 565, 101 S.Ct. 1245-clearly implying that the general rule of *Montana* applies to both Indian and non-Indian land. The ownership status of land, in other words, is only one factor to consider in determining whether regulation of the activities of nonmembers is "necessary to protect tribal self-government or to control internal relations." It may sometimes be a dispositive factor. Hitherto, the absence of tribal ownership has been virtually conclusive of the absence of tribal civil jurisdiction; with one minor exception, we have never upheld under *Montana* the extension of tribal civil authority over nonmembers on non-Indian land. Compare, *e.g.*, *Merrion v. Jicarilla Apache Tribe*, 455 U.S. 130, 137, 142, 102 S.Ct. 894, 71 L.Ed.2d 21 (1982) (tribe has taxing authority over tribal lands leased by nonmembers), with *Atkinson Trading Co. v. Shirley*, 532 U.S. 645, 659, 121 S.Ct. 1825, 149 L.Ed.2d 889 (2001) (tribe has no taxing authority over nonmembers' activities on land held by nonmembers in fee); but see *Brendale v. Confederated Tribes and Bands of Yakima Nation*, 492 U.S. 408, 443–444, 458–459, 109 S.Ct. 2994, 106 L.Ed.2d 343 (1989) (opinions of Stevens, J., and Blackmun, J.) (tribe can impose zoning regulation on that 3.1% of land within reservation area closed to public entry that was not owned by the tribe). But the existence of tribal ownership is not alone enough to support regulatory jurisdiction over nonmembers.

We proceed to consider, successively, the following questions: whether regulatory jurisdiction over state officers in the present context is "necessary to protect tribal self-government or to control internal relations," and, if not, whether such regulatory jurisdiction has been congressionally conferred.

B

In *Strate,* we explained that what is necessary to protect tribal self-government and control internal relations can be understood by looking at the examples of tribal power to which *Montana* referred: tribes have authority "[to punish tribal offenders,] to determine tribal membership, to regulate domestic relations among members, and to prescribe rules of inheritance for members," 520 U.S., at 459, 117 S.Ct. 1404 (brackets in original), quoting *Montana, supra,* at 564, 101 S.Ct. 1245. These examples show, we said, that Indians have "'the right ... to make their own laws and be ruled by them,'" 520 U.S., at 459, 117 S.Ct. 1404, quoting *Williams v. Lee,* 358 U.S. 217, 220, 79 S.Ct. 269, 3 L.Ed.2d 251 (1959). See also *Fisher v. District Court of Sixteenth Judicial Dist. of Mont.,* 424 U.S. 382, 386, 96 S.Ct. 943, 47 L.Ed.2d 106 (1976) *(per curiam)* ("In litigation between Indians and non-Indians arising out of conduct on an Indian reservation, resolution of conflicts between the jurisdiction of state and tribal courts has depended, absent a governing Act of Congress, on whether the state action infringed on the right of reservation Indians to make their own laws and be ruled by them" (internal quotation marks and citation omitted)). Tribal assertion of regulatory authority over nonmembers must be connected to that right of the Indians to make their own laws and be governed by them. See *Merrion, supra,* at 137, 142, 102 S.Ct. 894 ("The power to tax is an essential attribute of Indian sovereignty because it is a necessary instrument of self-government," at least as to "tribal lands" on which the tribe "has ... authority over a nonmember").

Our cases make clear that the Indians' right to make their own laws and be governed by them does not exclude all state regulatory authority on the reservation. State sovereignty does not end at a reservation's border. Though tribes are often referred to as "sovereign" entities, it was "long ago" that "the Court departed from Chief Justice Marshall's view that 'the laws of [a State] can have no force' within reservation boundaries. *Worcester v. Georgia,* 6 Pet. 515, 561, 8 L.Ed. 483 (1832)," *White Mountain Apache Tribe v. Bracker,* 448 U.S. 136, 141, 100 S.Ct. 2578, 65 L.Ed.2d 665 (1980). "Ordinarily," it is now clear, "an Indian reservation is considered part of the territory of the State." U.S. Dept. of Interior, Federal Indian Law 510, and n. 1 (1958), citing *Utah & Northern R. Co. v. Fisher,* 116 U.S. 28, 6 S.Ct. 246, 29 L.Ed. 542 (1885); see also *Organized Village of Kake v. Egan,* 369 U.S. 60, 72, 82 S.Ct. 562, 7 L.Ed.2d 573 (1962).

That is not to say that States may exert the same degree of regulatory authority within a reservation as they do without. To the contrary, the principle that Indians have the right to make their own laws and be governed by them requires "an accommodation between the interests of the Tribes and the Federal Government, on the one hand, and those of the State, on the other." *Washington v. Confederated Tribes of Colville Reservation,* 447 U.S. 134, 156, 100 S.Ct. 2069, 65 L.Ed.2d 10 (1980); see also *id.,* at 181, 100 S.Ct. 2069 (opinion of Rehnquist, J.). "When on-reservation conduct involving only Indians is at issue, state law is generally inapplicable, for the State's regulatory interest is likely to be minimal and the federal interest in encouraging tribal self-government is at its strongest." *Bracker, supra,* at 144, 100 S.Ct. 2578. When, however, state interests outside the reservation are implicated, States may regulate the activities even of tribe members on tribal land, as exemplified by our decision in *Confederated Tribes.* In that case, Indians were selling cigarettes on their reservation to nonmembers from off reservation, without collecting the state cigarette tax. We held that the State could require the Tribes to collect the tax from nonmembers, and could "impose at least 'minimal' burdens on the Indian retailer to aid in enforcing and collecting the tax," 447 U.S., at 151, 100 S.Ct. 2069. It is also well established in our precedent that States have criminal jurisdiction over reservation Indians for crimes committed (as was the alleged poaching in this case) off the reservation. See *Mescalero Apache Tribe v. Jones,* 411 U.S. 145, 148–149, 93 S.Ct. 1267, 36 L.Ed.2d 114 (1973).

While it is not entirely clear from our precedent whether the last mentioned authority entails the corollary right to enter a reservation (including Indian-fee lands) for enforcement purposes, several of our opinions point in that direction. In *Confederated Tribes,* we explicitly reserved the question whether state officials could seize cigarettes held for sale to nonmembers in order to recover the taxes due. See 447 U.S., at 162, 100 S.Ct. 2069. In *Utah & Northern R. Co.,* however, we observed that "[i]t has ... been held that process of [state] courts may run into an Indian reservation of this kind, where the subject-matter or controversy is otherwise within their cognizance," 116 U.S., at 31, 6 S.Ct. 246. Shortly thereafter, we considered, in *United States v. Kagama,* 118 U.S. 375, 6 S.Ct. 1109, 30 L.Ed. 228 (1886), whether Congress could enact a law giving federal courts jurisdiction over various common-law, violent crimes committed by Indians on a reservation within a State. We expressed skepticism that the Indian Commerce Clause could justify this assertion of authority in derogation of state jurisdiction, but ultimately accepted the argument that the law

> "does not interfere with the process of the State courts within the reservation, nor with the operation of State laws upon white people found there. Its effect is confined to the

> acts of an Indian of some tribe, of a criminal character, committed within the limits of the reservation.
>
> "It seems to us that this is within the competency of Congress." *Id.,* at 383, 6 S.Ct. 1109.

The Court's references to "process" in *Utah & Northern R. Co.* and *Kagama,* and the Court's concern in *Kagama* over possible federal encroachment on state prerogatives, suggest state authority to issue search warrants in cases such as the one before us. ("Process" is defined as "any means used by a court to acquire or exercise its jurisdiction over a person or over specific property," *Black's Law Dictionary* 1084 (5th ed.1979), and is equated in criminal cases with a warrant, *id.,* at 1085.) It is noteworthy that *Kagama* recognized the right of state *laws* to "operat[e] ... upon [non-Indians] found" within a reservation, but did not similarly limit to non-Indians or the property of non-Indians the scope of the *process* of state courts. This makes perfect sense, since, as we explained in the context of federal enclaves, the reservation of state authority to serve process is necessary to "prevent [such areas] from becoming an asylum for fugitives from justice." *Fort Leavenworth R. Co. v. Lowe,* 114 U.S. 525, 533, 5 S.Ct. 995, 29 L.Ed. 264 (1885).

We conclude today, in accordance with these prior statements, that tribal authority to regulate state officers in executing process related to the violation, off reservation, of state laws is not essential to tribal self-government or internal relations—to "the right to make laws and be ruled by them." The State's interest in execution of process is considerable, and even when it relates to Indian-fee lands it no more impairs the tribe's self-government than federal enforcement of federal law impairs state government. Respondents argue that, even conceding the State's general interest in enforcing its off-reservation poaching law on the reservation, Nevada's interest in *this suit* is minimal, because it is a suit against state officials in their *individual* capacities. We think, however, that the distinction between individual and official capacity suits is irrelevant. To paraphrase our opinion in *Tennessee v. Davis,* 100 U.S. 257, 263, 25 L.Ed. 648 (1879), which upheld a federal statute permitting federal officers to remove to federal court state criminal proceedings brought against them for their official actions, a State "can act only through its officers and agents," and if a tribe can "affix penalties to acts done under the immediate direction of the [state] government, and in obedience to its laws," "the operations of the [state] government may at any time be arrested at the will of the [tribe]." Cf. *Anderson v. Creighton,* 483 U.S. 635, 638, 107 S.Ct. 3034, 97 L.Ed.2d 523 (1987) ("[P]ermitting damages suits against government officials can entail substantial social costs, including the risk that fear of personal monetary liability and harassing litigation will unduly inhibit officials in the discharge of their duties").

C

The States' inherent jurisdiction on reservations can of course be stripped by Congress, see *Draper v. United States,* 164 U.S. 240, 242–243, 17 S.Ct. 107, 41 L.Ed. 419 (1896). But with regard to the jurisdiction at issue here that has not occurred. The Government's assertion that "[a]s a general matter, although state officials have jurisdiction to investigate and prosecute crimes on a reservation that exclusively involve non-Indians, ... they do not have jurisdiction with respect to crimes involving Indian perpetrators or Indian victims," Brief for United States as *Amicus Curiae* 12–13, n. 7, is misleading. The statutes upon which it relies, see *id.,* at 18–19, show that the last half of the statement, like the first, is limited to "crimes *on a reservation.*" Sections 1152 and 1153 of Title 18, which give United States and tribal criminal law generally exclusive application, apply only to crimes committed *in Indian country;* Public Law 280, codified at 18 U.S.C. § 1162, which permits some state jurisdiction as an exception to this rule, is similarly limited. And 25 U.S.C. § 2804, which permits federal-state agreements enabling state law enforcement agents to act on reservations, applies only to deputizing them for the enforcement of federal or tribal criminal law. Nothing in the federal statutory scheme prescribes, or even remotely suggests, that state officers cannot enter a reservation (including Indian-fee land) to investigate or prosecute violations of state law occurring off the reservation. To the contrary, 25 U.S.C. § 2806 affirms that "the provisions of this chapter alter neither ... the law enforcement, investigative, or judicial authority of any ... State, or political subdivision or agency thereof...."

III

We turn next to the contention of respondent and the Government that the tribal court, as a court of general jurisdiction, has authority to entertain federal claims under § 1983. It is certainly true that state courts of "general jurisdiction" can adjudicate cases invoking federal statutes, such as § 1983, absent congressional specification to the contrary. "Under [our] system of dual sovereignty, we have consistently held that state courts have inherent authority, and are thus presumptively competent, to adjudicate claims arising under the laws of the United States," *Tafflin v. Levitt,* 493 U.S. 455, 458, 110 S.Ct. 792, 107 L.Ed.2d 887 (1990). That this would be the case was assumed by the Framers, see *The Federalist* No. 82, pp. 492–493 (C. Rossiter ed.1961). Indeed, that state courts could enforce federal law is presumed by Article III of the Constitution, which leaves to Congress the decision whether to create lower federal courts at all. This historical and constitutional assumption of concurrent state-court jurisdiction over federal-law cases is completely missing with respect to tribal courts.

Respondents' contention that tribal courts are courts of "general jurisdiction" is also quite wrong. A state court's jurisdiction is general, in that it "lays hold of all subjects of litigation between parties within its jurisdiction, though the causes of dispute are relative to the laws of the most distant part of the globe." *Id.*, at 493. Tribal courts, it should be clear, cannot be courts of general jurisdiction in this sense, for a tribe's inherent adjudicative jurisdiction over nonmembers is at most only as broad as its legislative jurisdiction. See *supra*, at 2308–2310. It is true that some statutes proclaim tribal-court jurisdiction over certain questions of federal law. See, *e.g.*, 25 U.S.C. § 1911(a) (authority to adjudicate child custody disputes under the Indian Child Welfare Act of 1978); 12 U.S.C. § 1715z-13(g)(5) (jurisdiction over mortgage foreclosure actions brought by the Secretary of Housing and Urban Development against reservation homeowners). But no provision in federal law provides for tribal-court jurisdiction over § 1983 actions.

Furthermore, tribal-court jurisdiction would create serious anomalies, as the Government recognizes, because the general federal-question removal statute refers only to removal from *state* court, see 28 U.S.C. § 1441. Were § 1983 claims cognizable in tribal court, defendants would inexplicably lack the right available to state-court § 1983 defendants to seek a federal forum. The Government thinks the omission of reference to tribal courts in § 1441 unproblematic. Since, it argues, "[i]t is doubtful ... that Congress intended to deny tribal court defendants the right given state court defendants to elect a federal forum for the adjudication of causes of action under federal law," we should feel free to create that right by permitting the tribal-court defendant to obtain a federal-court injunction against the action, effectively forcing it to be refiled in federal court. Brief for United States as *Amicus Curiae* 25–26. The sole support for devising this extraordinary remedy is *El Paso Natural Gas Co. v. Neztsosie,* 526 U.S. 473, 119 S.Ct. 1430, 143 L.Ed.2d 635 (1999), where we approved a similar procedure with regard to claims under the Price-Anderson Act brought in tribal court. In *Neztsosie,* however, the claims were not initially federal claims, but Navajo tort claims that the Price-Anderson Act provided "shall be deemed to be ... action[s] arising under" 42 U.S.C. § 2210; there was little doubt that the tribal court had jurisdiction over such tort claims, see 526 U.S., at 482, n. 4, 119 S.Ct. 1430. And for the propriety of the injunction in *Neztsosie,* we relied not on § 1441, but on the removal provision of the Price-Anderson Act, 42 U.S.C. § 2210(n)(2). Although, like § 1441, that provision referred only to removal from state courts, in light of the Act's detailed and distinctive provisions for the handling of "nuclear incident" cases in federal court, see 526 U.S., at 486, 119 S.Ct. 1430, we thought it clear Congress envisioned the defendant's ability to get into federal court in all instances. Not only are there missing here any distinctive federal-court procedures, but in order even to *confront* the question whether an unspecified removal power exists, we must first attribute to tribal courts jurisdiction that is not apparent. Surely the simpler way to avoid the removal problem is to conclude (as other indications suggest anyway) that tribal courts cannot entertain § 1983 suits.

IV

The last question before us is whether petitioners were required to exhaust their jurisdictional claims in Tribal Court before bringing them in Federal District Court. See *National Farmers Union Ins. Cos. v. Crow Tribe,* 471 U.S. 845, 856–857, 105 S.Ct. 2447, 85 L.Ed.2d 818 (1985). In *National Farmers*

Union we recognized exceptions to the exhaustion requirement, where "an assertion of tribal jurisdiction is motivated by a desire to harass or is conducted in bad faith, ... or where the action is patently violative of express jurisdictional prohibitions, or where exhaustion would be futile because of the lack of an adequate opportunity to challenge the court's jurisdiction," *id.*, at 856, n. 21, 105 S.Ct. 2447 (internal quotation marks omitted). None of these exceptions seems applicable to this case, but we added a broader exception in *Strate:* "[w]hen ... it is plain that no federal grant provides for tribal governance of nonmembers' conduct on land covered by *Montana's* main rule," so the exhaustion requirement "would serve no purpose other than delay." 520 U.S., at 459–460, and n. 14, 117 S.Ct. 1404. Though this exception too is technically inapplicable, the reasoning behind it is not. Since it is clear, as we have discussed, that tribal courts lack jurisdiction over state officials for causes of action relating to their performance of official duties, adherence to the tribal exhaustion requirement in such cases "would serve no purpose other than delay," and is therefore unnecessary.

V

Finally, a few words in response to the concurrence of Justice O'Connor, which is in large part a dissent from the views expressed in this opinion.

The principal point of the concurrence is that our reasoning "gives only passing consideration to the fact that the state officials' activities in this case occurred on land owned and controlled by the Tribes," *post*, at 2327. According to Justice O'Connor, "that factor is not prominent in the Court's analysis," *post*, at 2329. Even a cursory reading of our opinion demonstrates that this is not so. To the contrary, we acknowledge that tribal ownership is a factor in the *Montana* analysis, and a factor significant enough that it "may sometimes be ... dispositive," *supra,* at 2310. We simply do not find it dispositive in the present case, when weighed against the State's interest in pursuing off-reservation violations of its laws. See *supra,* at 2312 (concluding that "[t]he State's interest in execution of process is considerable" enough to outweigh the tribal interest in self-government "even when it relates to Indian-fee lands").

The concurrence is of course free to disagree with this judgment; but to say that failure to give tribal ownership determinative effect "fails to consider adequately the Tribe's inherent sovereign interests in activities on their land," *post,* at 2332 (opinion of O'Connor, J.), is an exaggeration.

The concurrence marshals no authority and scant reasoning to support its judgment that tribal authority over state officers pursuing, on tribe-owned land, off-reservation violations of state law may be "necessary to protect tribal self-government or to control internal relations." *Montana,* 450 U.S., at 564–565, 101 S.Ct. 1245. *Self*-government and *internal* relations are not directly at issue here, since the issue is whether the Tribes' law will apply, not to their own members, but to a narrow category of outsiders. And the concurrence does not try to explain how allowing state officers to pursue off-reservation violation of state law "threatens or has some direct effect on the political integrity, the economic security, or the health or welfare of the tribe," *id.,* at 566, 101 S.Ct. 1245. That the actions of these state officers cannot threaten or affect those interests is guaranteed by the limitations of federal constitutional and statutory law to which the officers are fully subject.

The concurrence exaggerates and distorts the consequences of our conclusion, *supra,* at 2310, n. 3, that the term "other arrangements" in a passage from *Montana* referred to other "*private consensual*" arrangements—so that it did not include the state officials' obtaining of tribal warrants in the present case. That conclusion is correct, as a fuller exposition of the passage from *Montana* makes clear:

> "To be sure, Indian tribes retain inherent sovereign power to exercise some forms of civil jurisdiction over non-Indians on their reservations, even on non-Indian fee lands. A tribe may regulate, through taxation, licensing, or other means, the activities of nonmembers who enter consensual relationships with the tribe or its members, through commercial dealing, contracts, leases, or other arrangements." 450 U.S., at 565, 101 S.Ct. 1245.

The Court (this is an opinion, bear in mind, not a statute) obviously did not have in mind States or state officers acting in their governmental capacity; it was referring to private individuals who voluntarily submitted themselves to tribal regulatory jurisdiction by the arrangements that they (or their employers) entered into. This is confirmed by the fact that all four of the cases in the immediately following citation involved private commercial actors. See *Confederated Tribes,* 447 U.S., at 152, 100 S.Ct. 2069 (nonmember purchasers of cigarettes from tribal outlet); *Williams v. Lee,* 358 U.S., at 217, 79 S.Ct. 269 (general store on the Navajo reservation); *Morris v. Hitchcock,* 194 U.S. 384, 24 S.Ct. 712, 48 L.Ed. 1030 (1904) (ranchers grazing livestock and horses on Indian lands "under contracts with individual members of said tribes"); *Buster v. Wright,* 135 F. 947, 950 (C.A.8 1905) (challenge to the "permit tax" charged by a tribe to nonmembers for "the privilege ... of trading within the borders").

The concurrence concludes from this brief footnote discussion that we would invalidate express or implied cessions of regulatory authority over nonmembers contained in state-tribal cooperative agreements, including those pertaining to mutual law enforcement assistance, tax administration assistance, and child support and paternity matters. See *post,* at 2328. This is a great overreaching. The footnote does not assert that "a consensual relationship [between a tribe and a State] could never exist," *ibid.* (opinion of O'Connor, J.). It merely asserts that "other arrangements" in the passage from *Montana* does not include state officers' obtaining of an (unnecessary) tribal warrant. Whether contractual relations between State and tribe can expressly or impliedly confer tribal regulatory jurisdiction over nonmembers—and whether such conferral can be effective to confer adjudicative jurisdiction as well—are questions that may arise in another case, but are not at issue here.

Another exaggeration is the concurrence's contention that we "give nonmembers freedom to act with impunity on tribal land based solely on their status as state law enforcement officials," *post,* at 2332 (opinion of O'Connor, J.). We do not say state officers cannot be regulated; we say they cannot be regulated in the performance of their law enforcement duties. Action unrelated to that is potentially subject to tribal control depending on the outcome of *Montana* analysis. Moreover, even where the issue is whether the officer has acted unlawfully in the performance of his duties, the tribe and tribe members are of course able to invoke the authority of the Federal Government and federal courts (or the state government and state courts) to vindicate constitutional or other federal- and state-law rights.

We must comment upon the final paragraphs of Part II of the concurrence's opinion-which bring on stage, in classic fashion, a *deus ex machina* to extract, from the seemingly insoluble difficulties that the prior writing has created, a happy ending. The concurrence manages to have its cake and eat it too—to hand over state law enforcement officers to the jurisdiction of tribal courts and yet still assure that the officers' traditional immunity (and hence the State's law enforcement interest) will be protected—by simply announcing "that in order to protect government officials, immunity claims should be considered in reviewing tribal court jurisdiction." *Post,* at 2332 (opinion of O'Connor, J.). What wonderful magic. Without so much as a citation (none is available) the concurrence declares the qualified immunity inquiry to be part of the jurisdictional inquiry, thus bringing it within the ken of the federal court at the outset of the case. There are two problems with this declaration. The first is that it is not true. There is no authority whatever for the proposition that absolute- and qualified-immunity defenses pertain to the court's jurisdiction—much less to the tribe's *regulatory* jurisdiction, which is what is at issue here. (If they did pertain to the court's jurisdiction, they would presumably be nonwaivable. Cf. *Idaho v. Coeur d'Alene Tribe of Idaho,* 521 U.S. 261, 267, 117 S.Ct. 2028, 138 L.Ed.2d 438 (1997).) And the second problem is that without *first* determining whether the tribe has regulatory jurisdiction, it is impossible to know which "immunity defenses" the federal court is supposed to consider. The tribe's law on this subject need not be the same as the State's; indeed, the tribe may decide (as did the common law until relatively recently) that there is no immunity defense whatever without a warrant. See *California v. Acevedo,* 500 U.S. 565, 581, 111 S.Ct. 1982, 114 L.Ed.2d 619 (1991) (Scalia, J., concurring in judgment). One wonders whether, deprived of its *deus ex machina,* the concurrence would not alter the conclusion it reached in Part I of its opinion, and agree with us that a proper balancing of state and tribal interests would give the Tribes no jurisdiction over state officers pursuing off-reservation violations of state law.

Finally, it is worth observing that the concurrence's resolution would, for the first time, hold a non-Indian subject to the jurisdiction of a tribal court. The question (which we have avoided) whether tribal regulatory and adjudicatory jurisdiction are coextensive is simply answered by the concurrence in the affirmative. As Justice Souter's separate opinion demonstrates, it surely deserves more considered analysis.

* * *

Because the Fallon Paiute-Shoshone Tribes lacked legislative authority to restrict, condition, or otherwise regulate the ability of state officials to investigate off-reservation violations of state law, they also lacked adjudicative authority to hear respondent's claim that those officials violated tribal law in the performance of their duties. Nor can the Tribes identify any authority to adjudicate respondent's § 1983 claim. And since the lack of authority is clear, there is no need to exhaust the jurisdictional dispute in tribal court. State officials operating on a reservation to investigate off-reservation violations of state law are properly held accountable for tortious conduct and civil rights violations in either state or federal court, but not in tribal court.

The judgment of the Court of Appeals is reversed, and the case remanded for further proceedings consistent with our opinion.

It is so ordered.

Justice Souter, with whom Justice Kennedy and Justice Thomas join, concurring.

Justice Ginsburg, concurring.

Justice O'Connor, with whom Justice Stevens and Justice Breyer join, concurring in part and concurring in the judgment.

Justice Stevens, with whom Justice Breyer joins, concurring in the judgment.

The "State Secrets" Doctrine in Court
General Dynamics Corp. v. U.S.,
563 U.S. 478 (2011)

Justice Scalia delivered the opinion of the Court.

We consider what remedy is proper when, to protect state secrets, a court dismisses a Government contractor's prima facie valid affirmative defense to the Government's allegations of contractual breach.

I

In 1988, the Navy awarded petitioners a $4.8 billion fixed-price contract to research and develop the A–12 Avenger carrier-based, stealth aircraft. The A-12 proved unexpectedly difficult to design and manufacture, and by December 1990, petitioners were almost two years behind schedule and spending $120 to $150 million each month to develop the A-12.

Petitioners informed the Government that the cost of completing the contract would exceed the contract price by an "'unacceptable'" amount. *McDonnell Douglas Corp. v. United States,* 567 F.3d 1340, 1343 (C.A.Fed.2009); see *McDonnell Douglas Corp. v. United States,* 182 F.3d 1319, 1323 (C.A.Fed.1999). They proposed restructuring the contract as a cost-reimbursement agreement and offered to absorb a $1.5 billion loss. The Department of Defense had lost faith in the project, however, and Rear Admiral William Morris, the Navy's contracting officer for the A-12 agreement, terminated the contract for default on January 7, 1991.

By that point, petitioners had spent $3.88 billion attempting to develop the A-12, and the Government had provided $2.68 billion in progress payments. A few weeks after terminating the contract, the Navy sent petitioners a letter demanding the return of approximately $1.35 billion in progress payments for work never accepted by the Government. The parties later entered into a deferred payment agreement covering this amount.

Petitioners filed suit in the Court of Federal Claims (CFC) to challenge Admiral Morris's termination decision under the Contract Disputes Act of 1978, 92 Stat. 2388, as amended, 41 U.S.C. § 609(a)(1). The Federal Circuit has recognized a governmental obligation not to mislead contractors about, or silently withhold, its "superior knowledge" of difficult-to-discover information "vital" to contractual performance. *GAF Corp. v. United States,* 932 F.2d 947, 949 (1991). Petitioners asserted that the Government's failure to share its "superior knowledge" about how to design and manufacture stealth aircraft excused their default (and also asserted other claims not relevant here).

Uncovering the extent of the Government's prior experience with stealth technology proved difficult. The design, materials, and manufacturing process for two prior stealth aircraft operated by the Air Force—the B-2 and the F-117A—are some of the Government's most closely guarded military secrets. "'[N]eed-to-know' or [special] access controls beyond those normally provided for access to Confidential, Secret, or Top Secret information" apply. 32 CFR § 154.3(x) (2010); see App. 384–385. The Government nevertheless granted 10 members of petitioners' litigation team "access to the Secret/Special Access level of the B-2 and F-117A programs." *Id.,* at 385. Four of those ten individuals received access to even the most sensitive aspects of the programs. See *ibid.*

That neither satisfied petitioners' thirst for discovery nor prevented the unauthorized disclosure of military secrets. In March 1993, Acting Secretary of the Air Force Michael Donley asserted the state-secrets privilege to bar discovery into certain aspects of stealth technology beyond petitioners' "need-to-know" authorizations. At a deposition that month, a former Navy official's responses to questions by petitioners and the Government revealed military secrets neither side's litigation team was authorized to know. Copies of the unclassified deposition were widely distributed and quoted in unsealed court filings until Government security officials discovered the breach a month later. A July 1993 deposition caused further unauthorized disclosures of military secrets.

These disclosures led Acting Secretary of the Air Force Merrill McPeak to file a declaration with the CFC. He warned that further discovery into the extent of the Government's superior knowledge "would present a continuing threat of disclosure of ... military and state secrets" surrounding the "weight, profile or signature, and materials involved in the design and construction of 'stealt[h]' ... aircraft and weapons systems." *Id.*, at 633, 635. Even relatively straightforward and innocuous questions, in his opinion, "would pose unacceptable risks of disclosure of classified, special access information," *id.*, at 636, including the potential disclosure of covert Government programs, *id.*, at 637.

The CFC took Secretary McPeak's concerns seriously and terminated discovery relating to superior knowledge. It later decided that the extent of the Government's superior knowledge was a nonjusticiable question. Both sides had enough evidence to "present a persuasive case" on the superior-knowledge issue, but the CFC worried that, "wit[h] numerous layers of potentially dispositive facts" hidden by the privilege, its superior-knowledge rulings "would be a sham," *McDonnell Douglas Corp. v. United States,* 37 Fed.Cl. 270, 280, 284–285 (1996), and one that would threaten national security, see *id.*, at 281–282.

In 1996, for reasons not relevant here, the CFC converted the termination into a less-Government-friendly termination for convenience and awarded petitioners $1.2 billion.

McDonnell Douglas Corp. v. United States, 35 Fed.Cl. 358 (1996). The Federal Circuit reversed, 182 F.3d, at 1332, and left it for the CFC to reconsider on remand whether the need to protect military secrets precluded discovery into the superior-knowledge issue, *id.*, at 1329–1330.

After a 6-week trial, the CFC sustained the default termination, *McDonnell Douglas Corp. v. United States,* 50 Fed.Cl. 311, 326 (2001), and reaffirmed that the parties could not safely litigate whether the Government's superior knowledge excused petitioners' default, *id.*, at 325. The Court of Appeals reversed the default termination, but agreed that the state-secrets privilege prevented adjudicating whether the Government's superior knowledge excused the default. See *McDonnell Douglas Corp. v. United States,* 323 F.3d 1006, 1024 (C.A.Fed.2003). It rejected petitioners' assertion that the Government could not pursue a claim against a party and then use the state-secrets privilege to completely preempt defenses to that claim; the Court of Appeals believed *United States v. Reynolds,* 345 U.S. 1, 12, 73 S.Ct. 528, 97 L.Ed. 727 (1953), had already "rejected" this "very argument." 323 F.3d, at 1023. Litigants cannot complain, the Court of Appeals held, when the state-secrets privilege trumps a defense "in [a] purely civil matter, suing the sovereign on the limited terms to which it has consented." *Ibid.*

On remand, the CFC again found petitioners had defaulted. *McDonnell Douglas Corp. v. United States,* 76 Fed.Cl. 385, 430 (2007). The Court of Appeals affirmed, see 567 F.3d, at 1356, and we granted certiorari to review its state-secrets holding. 561 U.S. ––––, 131 S.Ct. 62, 177 L.Ed.2d 1151 (2010).

II

Many of the Government's efforts to protect our national security are well known. It publicly acknowledges the size of our military, the location of our military bases, and the names of our ambassadors to Moscow and Peking. But protecting our national security sometimes requires keeping information about our military, intelligence, and diplomatic efforts secret. See *Haig v. Agee,* 453 U.S. 280, 307, 101 S.Ct. 2766, 69 L.Ed.2d 640 (1981); *Martin v. Mott,* 12 Wheat. 19, 30–31, 6 L.Ed. 537 (1827). We have recognized the sometimes-compelling necessity of governmental secrecy by acknowl-edging a Government privilege against court-ordered disclosure of state and military secrets.

In *Reynolds,* three civilian contractors died during a test flight of a B–29 bomber. Their widows filed wrongful-death suits against the Government and sought discovery of the Air Force's accident-investigation report. Federal discovery rules, then as now, did not require production of documents protected by an evidentiary privilege. See 345 U.S., at 6, 73 S.Ct. 528; Fed. Rule Civ. Proc. 26(b)(1). We held that documents that would disclose state secrets enjoyed such a privilege; the state-secrets privilege, we said, had a "well established" pedigree "in the law of evidence." 345 U.S., at 6–7, 73 S.Ct. 528.

The penultimate paragraph of *Reynolds* rejected the widows' assertion that if the Government invoked the state-secrets privilege it had to abandon the claim to which the thereby privileged evidence was relevant. That was, the widows observed, the price paid in criminal cases. If the Government refuses to provide state-secret information that the accused reasonably asserts is necessary to his defense, the prosecution must be dismissed. See *id.,* at 12, 73 S.Ct. 528; *Jencks v. United States,* 353 U.S. 657, 672, 77 S.Ct. 1007, 1 L.Ed.2d 1103 (1957). The penultimate paragraph of *Reynolds* said that this was a false analogy. A like abandonment of the Government's claim is not the consequence "in a civil forum where the Government is not the moving party, but is a defendant only on terms to which it has consented." 345 U.S., at 12, 73 S.Ct. 528. Both petitioners and the Court of Appeals rely upon this statement to support their differing positions.

We think that *Reynolds* has less to do with these cases than the parties believe—and its dictum (of course), less still. *Reynolds* was about the admission of evidence. It decided a purely evidentiary dispute by applying evidentiary rules: The privileged information is excluded and the trial goes on without it. That was to the detriment, of course, of the widows, whom the evidence would have favored. But the Court did not order judgment in favor of the Government. Here, by contrast, the CFC decreed the substantive result that since invocation of the state-secrets privilege obscured too many of the facts relevant to the superior-knowledge defense, the issue of that defense was nonjusticiable, and the defense thus not available. See 37 Fed.Cl., at 284–285. And that was so even though petitioners had brought forward enough unprivileged evidence to "make a *prima facie* showing." *Id.*, at 280.

While we disagree, for reasons set forth below, with the CFC's disposition of the remainder of the case, its perception that in the present context the state-secrets issue raises something quite different from a mere evidentiary point seems to us sound. What we are called upon to exercise is not our power to determine the procedural rules of evidence, but our common-law authority to fashion contractual remedies in Government-contracting disputes. See *Priebe & Sons, Inc. v. United States,* 332 U.S. 407, 411, 68 S.Ct. 123, 92 L.Ed. 32 (1947). And our state-secrets jurisprudence bearing upon that authority is not *Reynolds,* but two cases dealing with alleged contracts to spy.

In *Totten v. United States,* 92 U.S. 105, 23 L.Ed. 605 (1876), the administrator of a self-styled Civil War spy's estate brought a breach-of-contract suit against the United States. He alleged that his testator had entered into a contract with President Lincoln to spy on the Confederacy in exchange for $200 a month. After the war ended, the United States reimbursed expenses but did not pay the monthly salary. We recognized that the estate had a potentially valid breach-of-contract claim but dismissed the suit. The contract was for "a secret service," and litigating the details of that service would risk exposing secret operations and other clandestine operatives "to the serious detriment of the public." *Id.,* at 106–107. "[P]ublic policy," we held, "forbids the maintenance of any suit ... the trial of which would inevitably lead to the disclosure of matters which the law itself regards as confidential, and respecting which it will not allow the confidence to be violated." *Id.,* at 107.

Six years ago, we reaffirmed that "public policy forb[ids]" suits "based on covert espionage agreements." *Tenet v. Doe,* 544 U.S. 1, 3, 125 S.Ct. 1230, 161 L.Ed.2d 82 (2005). Such suits threaten to undermine ongoing intelligence-gathering and covert operations—two vital aspects of national security—through inadvertent exposure of espionage relationships. *Id.,* at 11, 125 S.Ct. 1230. Rather than tempt fate, we leave the parties to an espionage agreement where we found them the day they filed suit.

We think a similar situation obtains here, and that the same consequence should follow. Where liability depends upon the validity of a plausible superior-knowledge defense, and when full litigation of that defense "would inevitably lead to the disclosure of" state secrets, *Totten, supra,* at 107, neither party can obtain judicial relief. As the CFC concluded, that is the situation here. Disclosure of state secrets occurred twice before the CFC terminated discovery. See 37 Fed.Cl., at 277–278. Every document request or question to a witness would risk further disclosure, since both sides have an incentive to probe up to the boundaries of state secrets. State secrets can also be indirectly disclosed. Each assertion of the privilege can provide another clue about the Government's covert programs or capabilities. See *Fitzgerald v. Penthouse International, Ltd.*, 776 F.2d 1236, 1243, and n. 10 (C.A.4 1985). For instance, the fact that the Government had to continue asserting the privilege after granting petitioners access to B–2 and F–117A program information suggests it had other, possibly covert stealth programs in the 1980's and early 1990's.

It seems to us unrealistic to separate, as the CFC did, the claim from the defense, and to allow the former to proceed while the latter is barred. It is claims and defenses *together* that establish the justification, or lack of justification, for judicial relief; and when public policy precludes judicial intervention for the one it should preclude judicial intervention for the other as well. If, in *Totten*, it had been the Government seeking return of funds that the estate claimed had been received in payment for espionage activities, it would have been the height of injustice to deny the defense because of the Government's invocation of state-secret protection, but to maintain jurisdiction over the Government's claim and award it judgment. Judicial refusal to enforce promises contrary to public policy (here, the Government's alleged promise to provide superior knowledge, which we could not determine was breached without penetrating several layers of state secrets) is not unknown to the common law, and the traditional course is to leave the parties where they stood when they knocked on the courthouse door.

"In general, if a court will not, on grounds of public policy, aid a promisee by enforcing the promise, it will not aid him by granting him restitution for performance that he has rendered in return for the unenforceable promise. Neither will it aid the promisor by allowing a claim in restitution for performance that he has rendered under the unenforceable promise. It will simply leave both parties as it finds them, even though this may result in one of them retaining a benefit that he has received as a result of the transaction." 2 Restatement (Second) of Contracts § 197, Comment *a,* p. 71 (1979); see, *e.g., Worlton v. Davis,* 73 Idaho 217, 222–223, 249 P.2d 810, 814 (1952).

These cases differ from the common-law cases that we know, in that the unenforceability did not exist at the time the contract was formed, See 2 Restatement (Second) of Contracts § 179, Comment *d,* at 18, but arose because of the Government's assertion of the state-secrets privilege that rendered the promise of superior knowledge unadjudicable. We do not see why that should affect the remedy. Suit on the contract, or for performance rendered or funds paid under the contract, will not lie, and the parties will be left where they are.

The law of contracts contains another doctrine that relates to the CFC's concern about the reliability of its judgment "without numerous layers of potentially dispositive facts," 37 Fed.Cl., at 284–285. The Statute of Frauds, which has been with us since the 17th century, reflects concerns about the reliability of oral evidence. See *Valdez Fisheries Development Assn., Inc. v. Alyeska Pipeline Serv. Co.,* 45 P.3d 657, 669 (Alaska 2002); 9 R. Lord, *Williston on Contracts* § 21:1, pp. 170–172 (4th ed.1999 and 2010 Supp.). It assumes a valid, enforceable agreement between the parties but nevertheless leaves them without a remedy absent reliable evidence—a writing. See 1 *id.,* § 1:21, at 82 (4th ed.2007 and 2010 Supp.); 9 *id.,* § 21:5, at 192. So also here, it is preferable to leave the parties without a remedy rather than risk the "potential injustice," *Valdez Fisheries, supra,* at 669, of misjudging the superior-knowledge issue based on a distorted evidentiary record.

The Government suggested at oral argument that where the parties stood at the time of suit was that petitioners had been held in default, liable for the ensuing consequences. See Tr. of Oral Arg. 48–49; see also Brief for United States 32, n. 9, 34–35. That had been the declaration of the contracting officer, pursuant to Chapter 9 (entitled "Contract Disputes") of Title 41 (entitled "Public Contracts"). See 41 U.S.C. § 605. It was "final and conclusive ... unless an appeal or suit is timely commenced." § 605(b). We regard that, however, as merely one step in the contractual regime to which the parties had agreed. It has no more bearing upon the question we are discussing than would a provision in a private contract that declaration of default by one of the parties is final unless contested in court. The "position of the parties" in which we will leave them is not their position with regard to legal burdens and the legal consequences of contract-related determinations, but with regard to possession of funds and property.

III

Neither side will be entirely happy with the resolution we reach today. General Dynamics (but not Boeing) wants us to convert the termination into one for convenience and reinstate the CFC's $1.2 billion damages award. See Brief for Petitioner in No. 09–1298, pp. 58–61. The language of the A-12 agreement does not give us that option. It authorizes a court to convert a default termination into a termination for convenience only if it "determine[s] that the Contractor was not in default, or that the default was excusable." 48 CFR § 52.249-9(g) (2010). Our opinion does not express a view on those issues. It holds them nonjusticiable.

Moreover, state secrets would make it impossible to calculate petitioners' damages. A termination for convenience ordinarily entitles a contractor to recover its incurred costs of performance, reasonable termination expenses, and a reasonable profit on the work performed (or an offset to account for the contractor's expected losses had the contract been performed to completion). See § 52.249–2(g). The CFC's $1.2 billion award to petitioners in 1996 simply reflected their actual costs incurred minus progress payments received. The CFC decided it could not calculate petitioners' expected losses (or profits) without deciding the extent to which the Government's alleged failure to share its superior knowledge contributed to petitioners' cost overruns—a nonjusticiable question. See 37 Fed.Cl., at 285. Absent proof of the Government's superior knowledge, and of how the sharing of that would have made this a profitable contract, the $1.2 billion award might represent an undeserved windfall.

The Government, for its part, wants a return of the $1.35 billion it paid petitioners in progress payments for work which it says it never approved. But the validity of that claim depends upon whether petitioners are in default on their contract. If they are not, termination for convenience of the Government would entitle them to retain those progress payments (unless, of course, they would have incurred a loss on the entire contract). Neither the question whether they are in default nor the question whether performance of the entire contract would have left them with a loss can be judicially determined because of the valid assertion of the state-secret privilege.

We leave the parties where they are. As in *Totten,* see 92 U.S., at 106, our refusal to enforce this contract captures what the *ex ante* expectations of the parties were or reasonably ought to have been. Both parties "must have understood," *ibid.,* that state secrets would prevent courts from resolving many possible disputes under the A–12 agreement. The Government asked petitioners to develop an aircraft the design, materials, and manufacturing process for which would be closely guarded military secrets. See Contract Schedule H-1, App. 73–75; Contract Security Classified Specification, *id.,* at 129–135. The contract itself was a classified document at one point. See Contract Schedule H-1, ¶ 8, *id.,* at 75. Both parties—the Government no less than petitioners—must have assumed the risk that state secrets would prevent the adjudication of claims of inadequate performance.

We believe, moreover, that the impact of our ruling on these particular cases (which we think produces rough, very rough, equity) is probably much more significant than its impact in future cases, except to the extent that it renders the law more predictable and hence more subject to accommodation by contracting parties. They can negotiate, for example, the timing and amount of progress payments to account for the possibility that state secrets may ultimately render the contract unenforceable. The Government's concern that contractors will raise frivolous superior-knowledge defenses designed to goad the Government into asserting the state-secrets privilege is misplaced. To begin with, the rule we announce today applies only when the superior-knowledge defense is supported by enough evidence to make out a prima facie case. Moreover, Government contractors—especially cutting-edge defense contractors of the sort likely to operate in the state-secrets field—are repeat players. Even apart from the judicial sanctions available to punish bad conduct, see Fed. Rules Civ. Proc. 11, 26(g), they have strong incentive to behave rather than risk missing out on the next multibillion-dollar defense contract. And finally, while we anticipate that the rule we set forth will ordinarily control Government-contract disputes that become nonjusticiable because of state secrets, what we promulgate today is not a statute but a common-law opinion, which, after the fashion of the common law, is subject to further refinement where relevant factors significantly different from those before us here counsel a different outcome.

The foregoing analysis assumes that the Government generally has an obligation to share its superior knowledge, see *GAF Corp.*, 932 F.2d, at 949; the parties have not challenged that assumption. The Government argued below, however, that it does not have that obligation with respect to "highly classified information," and does not have it when (as was the case here) the agreement specifically identifies information that must be shared. Brief for United States 52. The Court of Appeals did not address those questions (it had no reason to, given its disposition of petitioners' appeal), and we did not grant certiorari to decide them. Those issues (and whether they can safely be litigated without endangering state secrets) therefore remain for the Court of Appeals to address on remand.

* * *

In *Reynolds,* we warned that the state-secrets evidentiary privilege "is not to be lightly invoked." 345 U.S., at 7, 73 S.Ct. 528. Courts should be even more hesitant to declare a Government contract unenforceable because of state secrets. It is the option of last resort, available in a very narrow set of circumstances. Our decision today clarifies the consequences of its use only where it precludes a valid defense in Government-contracting disputes, and only where both sides have enough evidence to survive summary judgment but too many of the relevant facts remain obscured by the state-secrets privilege to enable a reliable judgment.

We vacate the judgment of the Court of Appeals and remand the cases for further proceedings consistent with this opinion.

It is so ordered.

On the Limits to Class Actions
Wal-Mart Stores, Inc. v. Dukes,
131 S. Ct. 2541 (2011)

Justice Scalia delivered the opinion of the Court.

We are presented with one of the most expansive class actions ever. The District Court and the Court of Appeals approved the certification of a class comprising about one and a half million plaintiffs, current and former female employees of petitioner Wal-Mart who allege that the discretion exercised by their local supervisors over pay and promotion matters violates Title VII by discriminating against women. In addition to injunctive and declaratory relief, the plaintiffs seek an award of backpay. We consider whether the certification of the plaintiff class was consistent with Federal Rules of Civil Procedure 23(a) and (b)(2).

I

A

Petitioner Wal-Mart is the Nation's largest private employer. It operates four types of retail stores throughout the country: Discount Stores, Supercenters, Neighborhood Markets, and Sam's Clubs. Those stores are divided into seven nationwide divisions, which in turn comprise 41 regions of 80 to 85 stores apiece. Each store has between 40 and 53 separate departments and 80 to 500 staff positions. In all, Wal-Mart operates approximately 3,400 stores and employs more than one million people.

Pay and promotion decisions at Wal-Mart are generally committed to local managers' broad discretion, which is exercised "in a largely subjective manner." 222 F.R.D. 137, 145

(N.D.Cal.2004). Local store managers may increase the wages of hourly employees (within limits) with only limited corporate oversight. As for salaried employees, such as store managers and their deputies, higher corporate authorities have discretion to set their pay within preestablished ranges.

Promotions work in a similar fashion. Wal-Mart permits store managers to apply their own subjective criteria when selecting candidates as "support managers," which is the first step on the path to management. Admission to Wal-Mart's management training program, however, does require that a candidate meet certain objective criteria, including an above-average performance rating, at least one year's tenure in the applicant's current position, and a willingness to relocate. But except for those requirements, regional and district managers have discretion to use their own judgment when selecting candidates for management training. Promotion to higher office—*e.g.*, assistant manager, co-manager, or store manager—is similarly at the discretion of the employee's superiors after prescribed objective factors are satisfied.

B

The named plaintiffs in this lawsuit, representing the 1.5 million members of the certified class, are three current or former Wal-Mart employees who allege that the company discriminated against them on the basis of their sex by denying them equal pay or promotions, in violation of Title VII of the Civil Rights Act of 1964, 78 Stat. 253, as amended, 42 U.S.C. § 2000e-1 *et seq.*

Betty Dukes began working at a Pittsburgh, California, Wal-Mart in 1994. She started as a cashier, but later sought and received a promotion to customer service manager. After a series of disciplinary violations, however, Dukes was demoted back to cashier and then to greeter. Dukes concedes she violated company policy, but contends that the disciplinary actions were in fact retaliation for invoking internal complaint procedures and that male employees have not been disciplined for similar infractions. Dukes also claims two male greeters in the Pittsburgh store are paid more than she is.

Christine Kwapnoski has worked at Sam's Club stores in Missouri and California for most of her adult life. She has held a number of positions, including a supervisory position. She claims that a male manager yelled at her frequently and screamed at female employees, but not at men. The manager in question "told her to "doll up," to wear some makeup, and to dress a little better." App. 1003a.

The final named plaintiff, Edith Arana, worked at a Wal-Mart store in Duarte, California, from 1995 to 2001. In 2000, she approached the store manager on more than one occasion about management training, but was brushed off. Arana concluded she was being denied opportunity for advancement because of her sex. She initiated internal complaint procedures, whereupon she was told to apply directly to the district manager if she thought her store manager was being unfair. Arana, however, decided against that and never applied for management training again. In 2001, she was fired for failure to comply with Wal-Mart's timekeeping policy.

These plaintiffs, respondents here, do not allege that Wal-Mart has any express corporate policy against the advancement of women. Rather, they claim that their local managers' discretion over pay and promotions is exercised disproportionately in favor of men, leading to an unlawful disparate impact on female employees, see 42 U.S.C. § 2000e-2(k). And, respondents say, because Wal-Mart is aware of this effect, its refusal to cabin its managers' authority amounts to disparate treatment, see § 2000e-2(a). Their complaint seeks injunctive and declaratory relief, punitive damages, and backpay. It does not ask for compensatory damages.

Importantly for our purposes, respondents claim that the discrimination to which they have been subjected is common to *all* Wal-Mart's female employees. The basic theory of their case is that a strong and uniform "corporate culture" permits bias against women to infect, perhaps subconsciously, the discretionary decisionmaking of each one of Wal-Mart's thousands of managers—thereby making every woman at the company the victim of one common discriminatory practice. Respondents therefore wish to litigate the Title VII claims of all female employees at Wal-Mart's stores in a nationwide class action.

C

Class certification is governed by Federal Rule of Civil Procedure 23. Under Rule 23(a), the party seeking certification must demonstrate, first, that:

> "(1) the class is so numerous that joinder of all members is impracticable,
>
> "(2) there are questions of law or fact common to the class,
>
> "(3) the claims or defenses of the representative parties are typical of the claims or defenses of the class, and
>
> "(4) the representative parties will fairly and adequately protect the interests of the class" (paragraph breaks added).

Second, the proposed class must satisfy at least one of the three requirements listed in Rule 23(b). Respondents rely on Rule 23(b)(2), which applies when "the party opposing the class has acted or refused to act on grounds that apply generally to the class, so that final injunctive relief or corresponding declaratory relief is appropriate respecting the class as a whole."

Invoking these provisions, respondents moved the District Court to certify a plaintiff class consisting of "[a]ll women employed at any Wal-Mart domestic retail store at any time since December 26, 1998, who have been or may be subjected to Wal-Mart's challenged pay and management track promotions policies and practices." 222 F.R.D., at 141–142 (quoting Plaintiff's Motion for Class Certification in case No. 3:01-cv-02252-CRB (ND Cal.), Doc. 99, p. 37). As evidence that there were indeed "questions of law or fact common to" all the women of Wal-Mart, as Rule 23(a)(2) requires, respondents relied chiefly on three forms of proof: statistical evidence about pay and promotion disparities between men and women at the company, anecdotal reports of discrimination from about 120 of Wal-Mart's female employees, and the testimony of a sociologist, Dr. William Bielby, who conducted a "social framework analysis" of Wal-Mart's "culture" and personnel practices, and concluded that the company was "vulnerable" to gender discrimination. 603 F.3d 571, 601 (C.A.9 2010) (en banc).

Wal-Mart unsuccessfully moved to strike much of this evidence. It also offered its own countervailing statistical and other proof in an effort to defeat Rule 23(a)'s requirements of commonality, typicality, and adequate representation. Wal-Mart further contended that respondents' monetary claims for backpay could not be certified under Rule 23(b)(2), first because that Rule refers only to injunctive and declaratory relief, and second because the backpay claims could not be manageably tried as a class without depriving Wal-Mart of its right to present certain statutory defenses. With one limitation not relevant here, the District Court granted respondents' motion and certified their proposed class.

D

A divided en banc Court of Appeals substantially affirmed the District Court's certification order. 603 F.3d 571. The majority concluded that respondents' evidence of commonality was sufficient to "raise the common question whether Wal-Mart's female employees nationwide were subjected to a single set of corporate policies (not merely a number of independent discriminatory acts) that may have worked to unlawfully discriminate against them in violation of Title VII." *Id.*, at 612 (emphasis deleted). It also agreed with the District Court that the named plaintiffs' claims were sufficiently typical of the class as a whole to satisfy Rule 23(a)(3), and that they could serve as adequate class representatives, see Rule 23(a)(4). *Id.*, at 614–615. With respect to the Rule 23(b)(2) question, the Ninth Circuit held that respondents' backpay claims could be certified as part of a (b)(2) class because they did not "predominat[e]" over the requests for declaratory and injunctive relief, meaning they were not "superior in strength, influence, or authority" to the nonmonetary claims. *Id.*, at 616 (internal quotation marks omitted).

Finally, the Court of Appeals determined that the action could be manageably tried as a class action because the District Court could adopt the approach the Ninth Circuit approved in *Hilao v. Estate of Marcos*, 103 F.3d 767, 782–787 (1996). There compensatory damages for some 9,541 class members were calculated by selecting 137 claims at random, referring those claims to a special master for valuation, and then extrapolating the validity and value of the untested claims from the sample set. See 603 F.3d, at 625–626. The Court of Appeals "s[aw] no reason why a similar procedure to that used in *Hilao* could not be employed in this case." *Id.*, at 627. It would allow Wal-Mart "to present individual defenses in the randomly selected "sample cases," thus revealing the approximate percentage of class members whose unequal pay or nonpromotion was due to something other than gender discrimination." *Ibid.*, n. 56 (emphasis deleted).

We granted certiorari. 562 U.S. ----, 131 S.Ct. 795, 178 L.Ed.2d 530 (2010).

II

The class action is "an exception to the usual rule that litigation is conducted by and on behalf of the individual named parties only." *Califano v. Yamasaki*, 442 U.S. 682, 700–701, 99 S.Ct. 2545, 61 L.Ed.2d 176 (1979). In order to justify a departure from that rule, "a class representative must be part of the class and "possess the same interest and suffer the same injury" as the class members." *East Tex. Motor Freight System, Inc. v. Rodriguez*, 431 U.S. 395, 403, 97 S.Ct. 1891, 52 L.Ed.2d 453 (1977) (quoting *Schlesinger v. Reservists Comm. to Stop the War*, 418 U.S. 208, 216, 94 S.Ct. 2925, 41 L.Ed.2d 706 (1974)). Rule 23(a) ensures that the named plaintiffs are appropriate representatives of the class whose claims they wish to litigate. The Rule's four requirements—numerosity, commonality, typicality, and adequate representation— "effectively 'limit the class claims to those fairly encompassed by the named plaintiff's claims.'" *General Telephone Co. of Southwest v. Falcon*, 457 U.S. 147, 156, 102 S.Ct. 2364, 72 L.Ed.2d 740 (1982) (quoting *General Telephone Co. of Northwest v. EEOC*, 446 U.S. 318, 330, 100 S.Ct. 1698, 64 L.Ed.2d 319 (1980)).

A

The crux of this case is commonality—the rule requiring a plaintiff to show that "there are questions of law or fact common to the class." Rule 23(a)(2). That language is easy to misread, since "[a]ny competently crafted class complaint literally raises common "questions." "Nagareda, Class Certification in the Age of Aggregate Proof," 84 *N.Y.U.L.Rev.* 97, 131–132 (2009). For example: Do all of us plaintiffs indeed work for Wal-Mart? Do our managers have discretion over pay? Is that an unlawful employment practice? What remedies should we get? Reciting these questions is not sufficient to obtain class certification. Commonality requires the plaintiff to demonstrate that the class members "have suffered the same injury," *Falcon, supra,* at 157, 102 S.Ct. 2364. This does not mean merely that they have all suffered a violation of the same provision of law. Title VII, for example, can be violated in many ways—by intentional discrimination, or by hiring and promotion criteria that result in disparate impact, and by the use of these practices on the part of many different superiors in a single company. Quite obviously, the mere claim by employees of the same company that they have suffered a Title VII injury, or even a disparate-impact Title VII injury, gives no cause to believe that all their claims can productively be litigated at once. Their claims must depend upon a common contention—for example, the assertion of discriminatory bias on the part of the same supervisor. That common contention, moreover, must be of such a nature that it is capable of classwide resolution—which means that determination of its truth or falsity will resolve an issue that is central to the validity of each one of the claims in one stroke.

> "What matters to class certification ... is not the raising of common "questions"—even in droves—but, rather the capacity of a classwide proceeding to generate common *answers* apt to drive the resolution of the litigation. Dissimilarities within the proposed class are what have the potential to impede the generation of common answers." Nagareda, *supra,* at 132.

Rule 23 does not set forth a mere pleading standard. A party seeking class certification must affirmatively demonstrate his compliance with the Rule—that is, he must be prepared to prove that there are *in fact* sufficiently numerous parties, common questions of law or fact, etc. We recognized in *Falcon* that "sometimes it may be necessary for the court to probe behind the pleadings before coming to rest on the certification question," 457 U.S., at 160, 102 S.Ct. 2364, and that certification is proper only if "the trial court is satisfied, after a rigorous analysis, that the prerequisites of Rule 23(a) have been satisfied," *id.*, at 161, 102 S.Ct. 2364; see *id.*, at 160, 102 S.Ct. 2364 ("[A]ctual, not presumed, conformance with Rule 23(a) remains ... indispensable"). Frequently that "rigorous analysis" will entail some overlap with the merits of the plaintiff's underlying claim. That cannot be helped. "'[T]he class determination generally involves considerations that are enmeshed in the factual and legal issues comprising the plaintiff's cause of action.'" *Falcon, supra,* at 160, 102 S.Ct. 2364 (quoting *Coopers & Lybrand v. Livesay,* 437 U.S. 463, 469, 98 S.Ct. 2454, 57 L.Ed.2d 351 (1978); some internal quotation marks omitted). Nor is there anything unusual about that consequence: The necessity of touching aspects of the merits in order to resolve preliminary matters, *e.g.*, jurisdiction and venue, is a familiar feature of litigation. See *Szabo v. Bridgeport Machines, Inc.,* 249 F.3d 672, 676–677 (C.A.7 2001) (Easterbrook, J.).

In this case, proof of commonality necessarily overlaps with respondents' merits contention that Wal-Mart engages in a *pattern or practice* of discrimination. That is so because, in resolving an individual's Title VII claim, the crux of the inquiry is "the reason for a particular employment decision," *Cooper v. Federal Reserve Bank of Richmond,* 467 U.S. 867, 876, 104 S.Ct. 2794, 81 L.Ed.2d 718 (1984). Here respondents wish to sue about literally millions of employment decisions at once.

Without some glue holding the alleged *reasons* for all those decisions together, it will be impossible to say that examination of all the class members' claims for relief will produce a common answer to the crucial question *why was I disfavored.*

B

This Court's opinion in *Falcon* describes how the commonality issue must be approached. There an employee who claimed that he was deliberately denied a promotion on account of race obtained certification of a class comprising all employees wrongfully denied promotions and all applicants wrongfully denied jobs. 457 U.S., at 152, 102 S.Ct. 2364. We rejected that composite class for lack of commonality and typicality, explaining:

> "Conceptually, there is a wide gap between (a) an individual's claim that he has been denied a promotion [or higher pay] on discriminatory grounds, and his otherwise unsupported allegation that the company has a policy of discrimination, and (b) the existence of a class of persons who have suffered the same injury as that individual, such that the individual's claim and the class claim will share common questions of law or fact and that the individual's claim will be typical of the class claims." *Id.,* at 157–158, 102 S.Ct. 2364.

Falcon suggested two ways in which that conceptual gap might be bridged. First, if the employer "used a biased testing procedure to evaluate both applicants for employment and incumbent employees, a class action on behalf of every applicant or employee who might have been prejudiced by the test clearly would satisfy the commonality and typicality requirements of Rule 23(a)." *Id.,* at 159, n. 15, 102 S.Ct. 2364. Second, "[s]ignificant proof that an employer operated under a general policy of discrimination conceivably could justify a class of both applicants and employees if the discrimination manifested itself in hiring and promotion practices in the same general fashion, such as through entirely subjective decisionmaking processes." *Ibid.* We think that statement precisely describes respondents' burden in this case. The first manner of bridging the gap obviously has no application here; Wal-Mart has no testing procedure or other companywide evaluation method that can be charged with bias. The whole point of permitting discretionary decisionmaking is to avoid evaluating employees under a common standard.

The second manner of bridging the gap requires "significant proof" that Wal-Mart "operated under a general policy of discrimination." That is entirely absent here. Wal-Mart's announced policy forbids sex discrimination, see App. 1567a–1596a, and as the District Court recognized the company imposes penalties for denials of equal employment opportunity, 222 F.R.D., at 154. The only evidence of a "general policy of discrimination" respondents produced was the testimony of Dr. William Bielby, their sociological expert. Relying on "social framework" analysis, Bielby testified that Wal-Mart has a "strong corporate culture," that makes it "'vulnerable'" to "gender bias." *Id.*, at 152. He could not, however, "determine with any specificity how regularly stereotypes play a meaningful role in employment decisions at Wal-Mart. At his deposition ... Dr. Bielby conceded that he could not calculate whether 0.5 percent or 95 percent of the employment decisions at Wal-Mart might be determined by stereotyped thinking." 222 F.R.D. 189, 192 (N.D.Cal.2004). The parties dispute whether Bielby's testimony even met the standards for the admission of expert testimony under Federal Rule of Evidence 702 and our *Daubert* case, see *Daubert v. Merrell Dow Pharmaceuticals, Inc.*, 509 U.S. 579, 113 S.Ct. 2786, 125 L.Ed.2d 469 (1993). The district court concluded that

Daubert did not apply to expert testimony at the certification stage of class-action proceedings. 222 F.R.D., at 191. We doubt that is so, but even if properly considered, Bielby's testimony does nothing to advance respondents' case. "[W]hether 0.5 percent or 95 percent of the employment decisions at Wal-Mart might be determined by stereotyped thinking" is the essential question on which respondents' theory of commonality depends. If Bielby admittedly has no answer to that question, we can safely disregard what he has to say. It is worlds away from "significant proof" that Wal-Mart "operated under a general policy of discrimination."

C

The only corporate policy that the plaintiffs' evidence convincingly establishes is Wal-Mart's "policy" of *allowing discretion* by local supervisors over employment matters. On its face, of course, that is just the opposite of a uniform employment practice that would provide the commonality needed for a class action; it is a policy *against having* uniform employment practices. It is also a very common and presumptively reasonable way of doing business—one that we have said "should itself raise no inference of discriminatory conduct," *Watson v. Fort Worth Bank & Trust,* 487 U.S. 977, 990, 108 S.Ct. 2777, 101 L.Ed.2d 827 (1988).

To be sure, we have recognized that, "in appropriate cases," giving discretion to lower-level supervisors can be the basis of Title VII liability under a disparate-impact theory—since "an employer's undisciplined system of subjective decisionmaking [can have] precisely the same effects as a system pervaded by impermissible intentional discrimination." *Id.,* at 990–991, 108 S.Ct. 2777. But the recognition that this type of Title VII claim "can" exist does not lead to the conclusion that every employee in a company using a system of discretion has such a claim in common. To the contrary, left to their own devices most managers in any corporation—and surely most managers in a corporation that forbids sex discrimination—would select sex-neutral, performance-based criteria for hiring and promotion that produce no actionable disparity at all. Others may choose to reward various attributes that produce disparate impact—such as scores on general aptitude tests or educational achievements, see *Griggs v. Duke Power Co.,* 401 U.S. 424, 431–432, 91 S.Ct. 849, 28 L.Ed.2d 158 (1971). And still other managers may be guilty of intentional discrimination that produces a sex-based disparity. In such a company, demonstrating the invalidity of one manager's use of discretion will do nothing to demonstrate the invalidity of another's. A party seeking to certify a nationwide class will be unable to show that all the employees' Title VII claims will in fact depend on the answers to common questions.

Respondents have not identified a common mode of exercising discretion that pervades the entire company—aside from their reliance on Dr. Bielby's social frameworks analysis that we have rejected. In a company of Wal-Mart's size and geographical scope, it is quite unbelievable that all managers would exercise their discretion in a common way without some common direction. Respondents attempt to make that showing by means of statistical and anecdotal evidence, but their evidence falls well short.

The statistical evidence consists primarily of regression analyses performed by Dr. Richard Drogin, a statistician, and Dr. Marc Bendick, a labor economist. Drogin conducted his analysis region-by-region, comparing the number of women promoted into management positions with the percentage of women in the available pool of hourly workers. After considering regional and national data, Drogin concluded that "there are statistically significant disparities between men and women at Wal-Mart ... [and] these disparities ... can be explained only by gender discrimination." 603 F.3d, at 604 (internal quotation marks omitted). Bendick compared workforce data from Wal-Mart and competitive retailers and concluded that Wal-Mart "promotes a lower percentage of women than its competitors." *Ibid.*

Even if they are taken at face value, these studies are insufficient to establish that respondents' theory can be proved on a classwide basis. In *Falcon,* we held that one named plaintiff's experience of discrimination was insufficient to infer that "discriminatory treatment is typical of [the employer's employment] practices." 457 U.S., at 158, 102 S.Ct. 2364. A similar failure of inference arises here. As Judge Ikuta observed in her dissent, "[i]nformation about disparities at the regional and national level does not establish the existence of disparities at individual stores, let alone raise the inference that a company-wide policy of discrimination is implemented by discretionary decisions at the store and district level." 603 F.3d, at 637. A regional pay disparity, for example, may be attributable to only a small set of Wal-Mart stores, and cannot by itself establish the uniform, store-by-store disparity upon which the plaintiffs' theory of commonality depends.

There is another, more fundamental, respect in which respondents' statistical proof fails. Even if it established (as it does not) a pay or promotion pattern that differs from the nationwide figures or the regional figures in *all* of Wal-Mart's 3,400 stores, that would still not demonstrate that commonality of issue exists. Some managers will claim that the availability of women, or qualified women, or interested women, in their stores' area does not mirror the national or regional statistics. And almost all of them will claim to have been applying some sex-neutral, performance-based criteria—whose nature and effects will differ from store to store. In the landmark case of ours which held that giving discretion to lower-level supervisors can be the basis of Title VII liability under a disparate-impact theory, the plurality opinion *conditioned* that holding on the corollary that merely proving that the discretionary system has produced a racial or sexual disparity *is not enough.* "[T]he plaintiff must begin by identifying the specific employment practice that is challenged." *Watson,* 487 U.S., at 994, 108 S.Ct. 2777; accord, *Wards Cove Packing Co. v. Atonio,* 490 U.S. 642, 656, 109 S.Ct. 2115, 104 L.Ed.2d 733 (1989) (approving that statement), superseded by statute on other grounds, 42 U.S.C. § 2000e–2(k). That is all the more necessary when a class of plaintiffs is sought to be certified. Other than the bare existence of delegated discretion, respondents have identified no "specific employment practice"—much less one that ties all their 1.5 million claims together. Merely showing that Wal-Mart's policy of discretion has produced an overall sex-based disparity does not suffice.

Respondents' anecdotal evidence suffers from the same defects, and in addition is too weak to raise any inference that all the individual, discretionary personnel decisions are discriminatory. In *Teamsters v. United States,* 431 U.S. 324, 97 S.Ct. 1843, 52 L.Ed.2d 396 (1977), in addition to substantial statistical evidence of company-wide discrimination, the Government (as plaintiff) produced about 40 specific accounts of racial discrimination from particular individuals. See *id.,* at 338, 97 S.Ct. 1843. That number was significant because the company involved had only 6,472 employees, of whom 571 were minorities, *id.,* at 337, 97 S.Ct. 1843, and the class itself consisted of around 334 persons, *United States v. T.I.M.E.-D.C., Inc.,* 517 F.2d 299, 308 (C.A.5 1975), overruled on other grounds, *Teamsters, supra.* The 40 anecdotes thus represented roughly one account for every eight members of the class. Moreover, the Court of Appeals noted that the anecdotes came from individuals "spread throughout" the company who "for the most part" worked at the company's operational centers that employed the largest numbers of the class members. 517 F.2d, at 315, and n. 30. Here, by contrast, respondents filed some 120 affidavits reporting experiences of discrimination—about 1 for every 12,500 class members—relating to only some 235 out of Wal-Mart's 3,400 stores. 603 F.3d, at 634 (Ikuta, J., dissenting). More than half of these reports are concentrated in only six States (Alabama, California, Florida, Missouri, Texas, and Wisconsin); half of all States have only one or two anecdotes; and 14 States have no anecdotes about Wal-Mart's operations at all. *Id.*, at 634–635, and n. 10. Even if every single one of these accounts is true, that would not demonstrate that the entire company "operate[s] under a general policy of discrimination," *Falcon, supra,* at 159, n. 15, 102 S.Ct. 2364, which is what respondents must show to certify a companywide class.

The dissent misunderstands the nature of the foregoing analysis. It criticizes our focus on the dissimilarities between the putative class members on the ground that we have "blend[ed]" Rule 23(a)(2)'s commonality requirement with Rule 23(b)(3)'s inquiry into whether common questions "predominate" over individual ones. See *post,* at 2550–2552 (GINSBURG, J., concurring in part and dissenting in part). That is not so. We quite agree that for purposes of Rule 23(a)(2) "'[e]ven a single [common] question'" will do, *post,* at 2566, n. 9 (quoting Nagareda, "The Preexistence Principle and the Structure of the Class Action," 103 *Colum. L.Rev.* 149, 176, n. 110 (2003)). We consider dissimilarities not in order to determine (as Rule 23(b)(3) requires) whether common questions *predominate,* but in order to determine (as Rule 23(a)(2) requires) whether there *is* "[e]ven a single [common] question." And there is not here. Because respondents provide no convincing proof of a companywide discriminatory pay and promotion policy, we have concluded that they have not established the existence of any common question.

In sum, we agree with Chief Judge Kozinski that the members of the class:

> "held a multitude of different jobs, at different levels of Wal-Mart's hierarchy, for variable lengths of time, in 3,400 stores, sprinkled across 50 states, with a kaleidoscope of supervisors (male and female), subject to a variety of regional policies that all differed.... Some thrived while others did poorly. They have little in common but their sex and this lawsuit." 603 F.3d, at 652 (dissenting opinion).

III

We also conclude that respondents' claims for backpay were improperly certified under Federal Rule of Civil Procedure 23(b)(2). Our opinion in *Ticor Title Ins. Co. v. Brown,* 511 U.S. 117, 121, 114 S.Ct. 1359, 128 L.Ed.2d 33 (1994) (*per curiam*) expressed serious doubt about whether claims for monetary relief may be certified under that provision. We now hold that they may not, at least where (as here) the monetary relief is not incidental to the injunctive or declaratory relief.

A

Rule 23(b)(2) allows class treatment when "the party opposing the class has acted or refused to act on grounds that apply generally to the class, so that final injunctive relief or corresponding declaratory relief is appropriate respecting the class as a whole." One possible reading of this provision is that it applies *only* to requests for such injunctive or declaratory relief and does not authorize the class certification of monetary claims at all. We need not reach that broader question in this case, because we think that, at a minimum, claims for *individualized* relief (like the backpay at issue here) do not satisfy the Rule. The key to the (b)(2) class is "the indivisible nature of the injunctive or declaratory remedy warranted—the notion that the conduct is such that it can be enjoined or declared unlawful only as to all of the class members or as to none of them." Nagareda, 84 *N.Y.U.L.Rev.*, at 132. In other words, Rule 23(b)(2) applies only when a single injunction or declaratory judgment would provide relief to each member of the class. It does not authorize class certification when each individual class member would be entitled to a *different* injunction or declaratory judgment against the defendant. Similarly, it does not authorize class certification when each class member would be entitled to an individualized award of monetary damages.

That interpretation accords with the history of the Rule. Because Rule 23 "stems from equity practice" that predated its codification, *Amchem Products, Inc. v. Windsor,* 521 U.S. 591, 613, 117 S.Ct. 2231, 138 L.Ed.2d 689 (1997), in determining its meaning we have previously looked to the historical models on which the Rule was based, *Ortiz v. Fibreboard Corp.*, 527 U.S. 815, 841–845, 119 S.Ct. 2295, 144 L.Ed.2d 715 (1999). As we observed in *Amchem,* "[c]ivil rights cases against parties charged with unlawful, class-based discrimination are prime examples" of what (b)(2) is meant to capture. 521 U.S., at 614, 117 S.Ct. 2231. In particular, the Rule reflects a series of decisions involving challenges to racial segregation—conduct that was remedied by a single classwide order. In none of the cases cited by the Advisory Committee as examples of (b)(2)'s antecedents did the plaintiffs combine any claim for individualized relief with their classwide injunction. See Advisory Committee's Note, 39 F.R.D. 69, 102 (1966) (citing cases); *e.g., Potts v. Flax,* 313 F.2d 284, 289, n. 5 (C.A.5 1963); *Brunson v. Board of Trustees of Univ. of School Dist. No. 1, Clarendon Cty.*, 311 F.2d 107, 109 (C.A.4 1962) (*per curiam*); *Frasier v. Board of Trustees of N.C.*, 134 F. Supp. 589, 593 (NC

1955) (three-judge court), aff'd, 350 U.S. 979, 76 S.Ct. 467, 100 L.Ed. 848 (1956).

Permitting the combination of individualized and classwide relief in a (b)(2) class is also inconsistent with the structure of Rule 23(b). Classes certified under (b)(1) and (b)(2) share the most traditional justifications for class treatment—that individual adjudications would be impossible or unworkable, as in a(b)(1) class, or that the relief sought must perforce affect the entire class at once, as in a (b)(2) class. For that reason these are also mandatory classes: The Rule provides no opportunity for (b)(1) or (b)(2) class members to opt out, and does not even oblige the District Court to afford them notice of the action. Rule 23(b)(3), by contrast, is an "adventuresome innovation" of the 1966 amendments, *Amchem,* 521 U.S., at 614, 117 S.Ct. 2231 (internal quotation marks omitted), framed for situations "in which 'class-action treatment is not as clearly called for'," *id.,* at 615, 117 S.Ct. 2231 (quoting Advisory Committee's Notes, 28 U.S.C.App., p. 697 (1994 ed.)). It allows class certification in a much wider set of circumstances but with greater procedural protections. Its only prerequisites are that "the questions of law or fact common to class members predominate over any questions affecting only individual members, and that a class action is superior to other available methods for fairly and efficiently adjudicating the controversy." Rule 23(b)(3). And unlike (b)(1) and (b)(2) classes, the (b)(3) class is not mandatory; class members are entitled to receive "the best notice that is practicable under the circumstances" and to withdraw from the class at their option. See Rule 23(c)(2)(B).

Given that structure, we think it clear that individualized monetary claims belong in Rule 23(b)(3). The procedural protections attending the (b)(3) class—predominance, superiority, mandatory notice, and the right to opt out—are missing from (b)(2) not because the Rule considers them unnecessary, but because it considers them unnecessary *to a (b)(2) class.* When a class seeks an indivisible injunction benefitting all its members at once, there is no reason to undertake a case-specific inquiry into whether class issues predominate or whether class action is a superior method of adjudicating the dispute. Predominance and superiority are self-evident. But with respect to each class member's individualized claim for money, that is not so—which is precisely why (b)(3) requires the judge to make findings about predominance and superiority before allowing the class. Similarly, (b)(2) does not require that class members be given notice and opt-out rights, presumably because it is thought (rightly or wrongly) that notice has no purpose when the class is mandatory, and that depriving people of their right to sue in this manner complies with the Due Process Clause. In the context of a class action predominantly for money damages we have held that absence of notice and opt-out violates due process. See *Phillips Petroleum Co. v. Shutts,* 472 U.S. 797, 812, 105 S.Ct. 2965, 86 L.Ed.2d 628 (1985). While we have never held that to be so where the monetary claims do not predominate, the serious possibility that it may be so provides an additional reason not to read Rule 23(b)(2) to include the monetary claims here.

B

Against that conclusion, respondents argue that their claims for backpay were appropriately certified as part of a class under Rule 23(b)(2) because those claims do not "predominate" over their requests for injunctive and declaratory relief. They rely upon the Advisory Committee's statement that Rule 23(b)(2) "does not extend to cases in which the appropriate final relief relates *exclusively or predominantly* to money damages." 39 F.R.D., at 102 (emphasis added). The negative implication, they argue, is that it *does* extend to cases in which the appropriate final relief relates only partially and nonpredominantly to money damages. Of course it is the Rule itself, not the Advisory Committee's description of it, that governs. And a mere negative inference does not in our view suffice to establish a disposition that has no basis in the Rule's text, and that does obvious violence to the Rule's structural features. The mere "predominance" of a proper (b)(2) injunctive claim does nothing to justify elimination of Rule 23(b)(3)'s procedural protections: It neither establishes the superiority of *class* adjudication over *individual* adjudication nor cures the notice and opt-out problems. We fail to see why the Rule should be read to nullify these protections whenever a plaintiff class, at its option, combines its monetary claims with a request—even a "predominating request"—for an injunction.

Respondents' predominance test, moreover, creates perverse incentives for class representatives to place at risk potentially valid claims for monetary relief. In this case, for example, the named plaintiffs declined to include employees' claims for compensatory damages in their complaint. That strategy of including only backpay claims made it more likely that monetary relief would not "predominate." But it also created the possibility (if the predominance test were correct) that individual class members' compensatory-damages claims would be *precluded* by litigation they had no power to hold themselves apart from. If it were determined, for example, that a particular class member is not entitled to backpay because her denial of increased pay or a promotion was *not* the product of discrimination, that employee might be collaterally estopped from independently seeking compensatory damages based on that same denial. That possibility underscores the need for plaintiffs with individual monetary claims to decide *for themselves* whether to tie their fates to the class representatives" or go it alone—a choice Rule 23(b)(2) does not ensure that they have.

The predominance test would also require the District Court to reevaluate the roster of class members continually. The Ninth Circuit recognized the necessity for this when it concluded that those plaintiffs no longer employed by Wal-Mart lack standing to seek injunctive or declaratory relief against its employment practices. The Court of Appeals' response to that difficulty, however, was not to eliminate *all* former employees from the certified class, but to eliminate only those who had left the company's employ by the date the complaint was filed. That solution has no logical connection to the problem, since those who have left their Wal-Mart jobs *since* the complaint was filed have no more need for prospective relief than those who left beforehand. As a consequence, even though the validity of a (b)(2) class depends on whether "final injunctive relief or corresponding declaratory relief is appropriate respecting the class *as a whole,*" Rule 23(b)(2) (emphasis added), about half the members of the class approved by the Ninth Circuit have no claim for injunctive or declaratory relief at all. Of course, the alternative (and logical) solution of excising plaintiffs from the class as they leave their employment may have struck the Court of Appeals as wasteful of the District Court's time. Which indeed it is, since if a backpay action were properly certified for class treatment under (*b*)(*3*), the ability to litigate a plaintiff's backpay claim as part of the class would not turn on the irrelevant question whether she is still employed at Wal-Mart. What follows from this, however, is not that some arbitrary limitation on class membership should be imposed but that the backpay claims should not be certified under Rule 23(b)(2) at all.

Finally, respondents argue that their backpay claims are appropriate for a (b)(2) class action because a backpay award is equitable in nature. The latter may be true, but it is irrelevant. The Rule does not speak of "equitable" remedies generally but of injunctions and declaratory judgments. As Title VII itself makes pellucidly clear, backpay is neither. See 42 U.S.C. § 2000e-5(g)(2)(B)(i) and (ii) (distinguishing between declaratory and injunctive relief and the payment of "backpay," see § 2000e-5(g)(2)(A)).

C

In *Allison v. Citgo Petroleum Corp.*, 151 F.3d 402, 415 (C.A.5 1998), the Fifth Circuit held that a (b)(2) class would permit the certification of monetary relief that is "incidental to requested injunctive or declaratory relief," which it defined as "damages that flow directly from liability to the class *as a whole* on the claims forming the basis of the injunctive or declaratory relief." In that court's view, such "incidental damage should not require additional hearings to resolve the disparate merits of each individual's case; it should neither introduce new substantial legal or factual issues, nor entail complex individualized determinations." *Ibid.* We need not decide in this case whether there are any forms of "incidental" monetary relief that are consistent with the interpretation of Rule 23(b)(2) we have announced and that comply with the Due Process Clause. Respondents do not argue that they can satisfy this standard, and in any event they cannot.

Contrary to the Ninth Circuit's view, Wal-Mart is entitled to individualized determinations of each employee's eligibility for backpay. Title VII includes a detailed remedial scheme. If a plaintiff prevails in showing that an employer has discriminated against him in violation of the statute, the court "may enjoin the respondent from engaging in such unlawful employment practice, and order such affirmative action as may be appropriate, [including] reinstatement or hiring of employees, with or without backpay ... or any other equitable relief as the court deems appropriate." § 2000e-5(g)(1). But if the employer can show that it took an adverse employment action against an employee for any reason other than discrimination, the court cannot order the "hiring, reinstatement, or promotion of an individual as an employee, or the payment to him of any backpay." § 2000e-5(g)(2)(A).

We have established a procedure for trying pattern-or-practice cases that gives effect to these statutory requirements. When the plaintiff seeks individual relief such as reinstatement or backpay after establishing a pattern or practice of discrimination, "a district court must usually conduct additional proceedings ... to determine the scope of individual relief." *Teamsters,* 431 U.S., at 361, 97 S.Ct. 1843. At this phase, the burden of proof will shift to the company, but it will have the right to raise any individual affirmative defenses it may have, and to "demonstrate that the individual applicant was denied an employment opportunity for lawful reasons." *Id.,* at 362, 97 S.Ct. 1843.

The Court of Appeals believed that it was possible to replace such proceedings with Trial by Formula. A sample set of the class members would be selected, as to whom liability for sex discrimination and the backpay owing as a result would be determined in depositions supervised by a master. The percentage of claims determined to be valid would then be applied to the entire remaining class, and the number of (presumptively) valid claims thus derived would be multiplied by the average backpay award in the sample set to arrive at the entire class recovery—without further individualized proceedings. 603 F.3d, at 625–627. We disapprove that novel project. Because the Rules Enabling Act forbids interpreting Rule 23 to "abridge, enlarge or modify any substantive right," 28 U.S.C. §

2072(b); see *Ortiz,* 527 U.S., at 845, 119 S.Ct. 2295, a class cannot be certified on the premise that Wal-Mart will not be entitled to litigate its statutory defenses to individual claims. And because the necessity of that litigation will prevent backpay from being "incidental" to the classwide injunction, respondents' class could not be certified even assuming, *arguendo,* that "incidental" monetary relief can be awarded to a 23(b)(2) class.

* * *

The judgment of the Court of Appeals is *Reversed.*

Justice Ginsburg, with whom Justice Breyer, Justice Sotomayor, and Justice Kagan join, concurring in part and dissenting in part.

3

FUNDAMENTAL RIGHTS AND FREEDOMS

"Takings," Due Process, and the Fifth Amendment
Nollan v. California Coastal Comm'n., 483 U.S. 825 (1987)

On Peyote and the "Free Exercise Clause"
Employment Division, Department of Human Resources of Oregon v. Smith, 494 U.S. 872 (1990)

"Takings" and the Destruction of Property Value
Lucas v. South Carolina Coastal Council, 505 U.S. 1003 (1992)

Background Checks, Gun Control, and State Rights
Printz v. United States, 521 U.S. 898 (1997)

Limits on Gun Ownership and the Fourth Amendment
District of Columbia v. Heller, 554 U.S. 570 (2008)

Of Religious Freedom, Headscarves and Employment Rights
EEOC v. Abercrombie & Fitch Stores, Inc., 135 S. Ct. 2028 (2015)

Visa Rights and the Fifth Amendment
Kerry v. Din, 135 S. Ct. 2128 (2015)

The Constitution and the Bill of Rights establish the basic, unalterable rights and freedoms of every American. The Supreme Court as the ultimate arbiter of Constitutional meaning thus plays one of the most critical roles possible in our democracy. In the decisions presented in this chapter, fundamental rights, such as the right to gun ownership, to the "free exercise" of religion, to the right to be secure on the ownership of property as against state interference are all discussed. Writing for the majority in these cases, Justice Scalia shows his strong passion for individual rights as against encroachment of those rights by government.

"Takings," Due Process, and the Fifth Amendment

Nollan v. California Coastal Comm'n., 483 U.S. 825 (1987)

Justice Scalia delivered the opinion of the Court.

James and Marilyn Nollan appeal from a decision of the California Court of Appeal ruling that the California Coastal Commission could condition its grant of permission to rebuild their house on their transfer to the public of an easement across their beachfront property. 177 Cal.App.3d 719, 223 Cal.Rptr. 28 (1986). The California court rejected their claim that imposition of that condition violates the Takings Clause of the Fifth Amendment, as incorporated against the States by the Fourteenth Amendment. *Ibid.* We noted probable jurisdiction. 479 U.S. 913, 107 S.Ct. 312, 93 L.Ed.2d 286 (1986).

I

The Nollans own a beachfront lot in Ventura County, California. A quarter-mile north of their property is Faria County Park, an oceanside public park with a public beach and recreation area. Another public beach area, known locally as "the Cove," lies 1,800 feet south of their lot. A concrete seawall approximately eight feet high separates the beach portion of the Nollans' property from the rest of the lot. The historic mean high tide line determines the lot's oceanside boundary.

The Nollans originally leased their property with an option to buy. The building on the lot was a small bungalow, totaling 504 square feet, which for a time they rented to summer vacationers. After years of rental use, however, the building had fallen into disrepair, and could no longer be rented out.

The Nollans' option to purchase was conditioned on their promise to demolish the bungalow and replace it. In order to do so, under Cal.Pub.Res. Code Ann. §§ 30106, 30212, and 30600 (West 1986), they were required to obtain a coastal development permit from the California Coastal Com-mission. On February 25, 1982, they submitted a permit application to the Commission in which they proposed to demolish the existing structure and replace it with a three-bedroom house in keeping with the rest of the neighborhood.

The Nollans were informed that their application had been placed on the administrative calendar, and that the Commission staff had recommended that the permit be granted subject to the condition that they allow the public an easement to pass across a portion of their property bounded by the mean high tide line on one side, and their seawall on the other side. This would make it easier for the public to get to Faria County Park and the Cove. The Nollans protested imposition of the condition, but the Commission overruled their objections and granted the permit subject to their recordation of a deed restriction granting the easement. App. 31, 34.

On June 3, 1982, the Nollans filed a petition for writ of administrative mandamus asking the Ventura County Superior Court to invalidate the access condition. They argued that the condition could not be imposed absent evidence that their proposed development would have a direct adverse impact on public access to the beach. The court agreed, and remanded the case to the Commission for a full evidentiary hearing on that issue. *Id.*, at 36.

On remand, the Commission held a public hearing, after which it made further factual findings and reaffirmed its imposition of the condition. It found that the new house would increase blockage of the view of the ocean, thus contributing to the development of "a 'wall' of residential structures" that would prevent the public "psychologically ... from realizing a stretch of coastline exists nearby that they have every right to visit." *Id.*, at 58. The new house would also increase private use of the shorefront. *Id.*, at 59. These effects of construction of the house, along with other area development, would cumulatively "burden the public's ability to traverse to and along the shorefront." *Id.*, at 65–66. Therefore the Commission could properly require the Nollans to offset that burden by providing additional lateral access to the public beaches in the form of an easement across their property. The Commission also noted that it had similarly conditioned 43 out of 60 coastal development permits along the same tract of land, and that of the 17 not so conditioned, 14 had been approved when the Commission did not have administrative regulations in place allowing imposition of the condition, and the remaining 3 had not involved shorefront property. *Id.*, at 47–48.

The Nollans filed a supplemental petition for a writ of administrative mandamus with the Superior Court, in which they argued that imposition of the access condition violated the Takings Clause of the Fifth Amendment, as incorporated against the States by the Fourteenth Amendment. The Superior Court ruled in their favor on statutory grounds, finding, in part to avoid "issues of constitutionality," that the California Coastal Act of 1976, Cal.Pub.Res.Code Ann. § 30000 *et seq.* (West 1986), authorized the Commission to impose public access conditions on coastal development permits for the replacement of an existing single-family home with a new one only where the proposed development would have an adverse impact on public access to the sea. App. 419. In the court's view, the administrative record did not provide an adequate factual basis for concluding that replacement of the bungalow with the house would create a direct or cumulative burden on public access to the sea. *Id.*, at 416–417. Accordingly, the

Superior Court granted the writ of mandamus and directed that the permit condition be struck.

The Commission appealed to the California Court of Appeal. While that appeal was pending, the Nollans satisfied the condition on their option to purchase by tearing down the bungalow and building the new house, and bought the property. They did not notify the Commission that they were taking that action.

The Court of Appeal reversed the Superior Court. 177 Cal.App.3d 719, 223 Cal.Rptr. 28 (1986). It disagreed with the Superior Court's interpretation of the Coastal Act, finding that it required that a coastal permit for the construction of a new house whose floor area, height or bulk was more than 10% larger than that of the house it was replacing be conditioned on a grant of access. *Id.*, at 723–724, 223 Cal.Rptr., at 31; see Cal.Pub.Res.Code Ann. § 30212. It also ruled that the requirement did not violate the Constitution under the reasoning of an earlier case of the Court of Appeal, *Grupe v. California Coastal Comm'n*, 166 Cal.App.3d 148, 212 Cal.Rptr. 578 (1985). In that case, the court had found that so long as a project contributed to the need for public access, even if the project standing alone had not created the need for access, and even if there was only an indirect relationship between the access exacted and the need to which the project contributed, imposition of an access condition on a development permit was sufficiently related to burdens created by the project to be constitutional. 177 Cal.App.3d, at 723, 223 Cal.Rptr., at 30–31; see *Grupe, supra*, 166 Cal.App.3d, at 165–168, 212 Cal.Rptr., at 587–590; see also *Remmenga v. California Coastal Comm'n*, 163 Cal.App.3d 623, 628, 209 Cal.Rptr. 628, 631, appeal dism'd, 474 U.S. 915, 106 S.Ct. 241, 88 L.Ed.2d 250 (1985). The Court of Appeal ruled that the record established that that was the situation with respect to the Nollans' house. 177

Cal.App.3d, at 722–723, 223 Cal.Rptr., at 30–31. It ruled that the Nollans' taking claim also failed because, although the condition diminished the value of the Nollans' lot, it did not deprive them of all reasonable use of their property. *Id.*, at 723, 223 Cal.Rptr., at 30; see *Grupe, supra,* 166 Cal.App.3d, at 175–176, 212 Cal.Rptr., at 595–596. Since, in the Court of Appeal's view, there was no statutory or constitutional obstacle to imposition of the access condition, the Superior Court erred in granting the writ of mandamus. The Nollans appealed to this Court, raising only the constitutional question.

II

Had California simply required the Nollans to make an easement across their beachfront available to the public on a permanent basis in order to increase public access to the beach, rather than conditioning their permit to rebuild their house on their agreeing to do so, we have no doubt there would have been a taking. To say that the appropriation of a public easement across a landowner's premises does not constitute the taking of a property interest but rather (as Justice Brennan contends) "a mere restriction on its use," *post,* at 3154, n. 3, is to use words in a manner that deprives them of all their ordinary meaning. Indeed, one of the principal uses of the eminent domain power is to assure that the government be able to require conveyance of just such interests, so long as it pays for them. J. Sackman, 1 *Nichols on Eminent Domain* § 2.1[1] (Rev. 3d ed. 1985), 2 *id.*, § 5.01[5]; see 1 *id.*, § 1.42 [9], 2 *id.*, § 6.14. Perhaps because the point is so obvious, we have never been confronted with a controversy that required us to rule upon it, but our cases' analysis of the effect of other governmental action leads to the same conclusion. We have repeatedly held that, as to property reserved by its owner for private use, "the right to exclude [others is] 'one of the most essential sticks in the bundle of rights that are commonly characterized as property.'" *Loretto v. Teleprompter Manhattan CATV Corp.,* 458 U.S. 419, 433, 102 S.Ct. 3164, 3175, 73 L.Ed.2d 868 (1982), quoting *Kaiser Aetna v. United States,* 444 U.S. 164, 176, 100 S.Ct. 383, 391, 62 L.Ed.2d 332 (1979). In *Loretto* we observed that where governmental action results in "[a] permanent physical occupation" of the property, by the government itself or by others, see 458 U.S., at 432–433, n. 9, 102 S.Ct., at 3174–3175, n. 9, "our cases uniformly have found a taking to the extent of the occupation, without regard to whether the action achieves an important public benefit or has only minimal economic impact on the owner," *id.,* at 434–435, 102 S.Ct., at 3175–3176. We think a "permanent physical occupation" has occurred, for purposes of that rule, where individuals are given a permanent and continuous right to pass to and fro, so that the real property may continuously be traversed, even though no particular individual is permitted to station himself permanently upon the premises.

Justice Brennan argues that while this might ordinarily be the case, the California Constitution's prohibition on any individual's "exclu[ding] the right of way to [any navigable] water whenever it is required for any public purpose," Art. X, § 4, produces a different result here. *Post,* at 3153–3154; see also *post,* at 3157, 3158–3159. There are a number of difficulties with that argument. Most obviously, the right of way sought here is not naturally described as one *to* navigable water (from the street to the sea) but *along* it; it is at least highly questionable whether the text of the California Constitution has any prima facie application to the situation before us. Even if it does, however, several California cases suggest that Justice Brennan's interpretation of the effect of the clause is erroneous, and that to obtain easements of access across private property the State must proceed through its eminent domain power. See *Bolsa Land Co. v. Burdick,* 151 Cal. 254, 260, 90 P. 532, 534–535 (1907); *Oakland v. Oakland Water Front Co.,* 118 Cal. 160, 185, 50 P. 277, 286 (1897); *Heist v. County of Colusa,* 163 Cal.App.3d 841, 851, 213 Cal.Rptr. 278, 285 (1984); *Aptos Seascape Corp. v. Santa Cruz,* 138 Cal.App.3d 484, 505–506, 188 Cal.Rptr. 191, 204–205 (1982). (None of these cases specifically addressed the argument that Art. X, § 4 allowed the public to cross private property to get to navigable water, but if that provision meant what Justice Brennan believes, it is hard to see why it was not invoked.) See also 41 Op.Cal.Atty.Gen. 39, 41 (1963) ("In spite of the sweeping provisions of [Art. X, § 4], and the injunction therein to the Legislature to give its provisions the most liberal interpretation, the few reported cases in California have adopted the general rule that one may not trespass on private land to get to navigable tidewaters for the purpose of commerce, navigation or fishing"). In light of these uncertainties, and given the fact that, as Justice Blackmun notes, the Court of Appeal did not rest its decision on Art. X, § 4, *post,* at 3162, we should assuredly not take it upon ourselves to resolve this question of California constitutional law in the first instance. See, *e.g., Jenkins v. Anderson,* 447 U.S. 231, 234, n. 1, 100 S.Ct. 2124, 2127, n. 1, 65 L.Ed.2d 86 (1980). That would be doubly inappropriate since the Commission did not advance this argument in the Court of Appeal, and the Nollans argued in the Superior Court that any claim that there was a pre-existing public right of access had to be asserted through a quiet title action, see Points and Authorities in Support of Motion for Writ of Administrative Mandamus, No. SP50805 (Super.Ct.Cal.), p. 20, which the Commission, possessing no claim to the easement itself, probably would not have had standing under California law to bring. See Cal.Code Civ.Proc.Ann. § 738 (West 1980).

Given, then, that requiring uncompensated conveyance of the easement outright would violate the Fourteenth Amendment, the question becomes whether requiring it to be conveyed as a condition for issuing a land-use permit alters the outcome. We have long recognized that land-use regulation does not effect a taking if it "substantially advance[s] legitimate state interests" and does not "den[y] an owner economically viable use of his land," *Agins v. Tiburon,* 447 U.S. 255, 260, 100 S.Ct. 2138, 2141, 65 L.Ed.2d 106 (1980). See also *Penn Central Transportation Co. v. New York City,* 438 U.S. 104, 127, 98 S.Ct. 2646, 2660, 57 L.Ed.2d 631 (1978) ("[A] use restriction may constitute a 'taking' if not reasonably necessary to the effectuation of a substantial government purpose"). Our cases have not elaborated on the standards for determining what constitutes a "legitimate state interest" or what type of connection between the regulation and the state interest satisfies the requirement that the former "substantially advance" the latter. They have made clear, however, that a broad range of governmental purposes and regulations satisfies these requirements. See *Agins v. Tiburon, supra,* 447 U.S., at 260–262, 100 S.Ct., at 2141–2142 (scenic zoning); *Penn Central Transportation Co. v. New York City, supra* (landmark preservation); *Euclid v. Ambler Realty Co.,* 272 U.S. 365, 47 S.Ct. 114, 71 L.Ed. 303 (1926) (residential zoning); Laitos & Westfall, "Government Interference with Private Interests in Public Resources," 11 *Harv.Envtl.L.Rev.* 1, 66 (1987). The Commission argues that among these permissible purposes are protecting the public's ability to see the beach, assisting the public in overcoming the "psychological barrier" to using the beach created by a developed shorefront, and preventing congestion on the public beaches. We assume, without deciding, that this is so—in which case the Commission unquestionably would be able to deny the Nollans their permit outright if their new house (alone, or by reason of the cumulative impact produced in conjunction with other construction) would substantially impede these purposes, unless the denial would interfere so drastically with the Nollans' use of their property as to constitute a taking. See *Penn Central Transportation Co. v. New York City, supra.*

The Commission argues that a permit condition that serves the same legitimate police-power purpose as a refusal to issue the permit should not be found to be a taking if the refusal to issue the permit would not constitute a taking. We agree. Thus, if the Commission attached to the permit some condition that would have protected the public's ability to see the beach notwithstanding construction of the new house-for example, a height limitation, a width restriction, or a ban on fences—so long as the Commission could have exercised its police power (as we have assumed it could) to forbid construction of the house altogether, imposition of the condition would also be constitutional. Moreover (and here we come closer to the facts of the present case), the condition would be constitutional even if it consisted of the requirement that the Nollans provide a viewing spot on their property for passersby with whose sighting of the ocean their new house would interfere. Although such a requirement, constituting a permanent grant of continuous access to the property, would have to be considered a taking if it were not attached to a development permit, the Commission's assumed power to forbid construction of the house in order to protect the public's view of the beach must surely include the power to condition construction upon some concession by the owner, even a concession of property rights, that serves the same end. If a prohibition designed to accomplish that purpose would be a legitimate exercise of the police power rather than a taking, it would be strange to conclude that providing the owner an alternative to that prohibition which accomplishes the same purpose is not.

The evident constitutional propriety disappears, however, if the condition substituted for the prohibition utterly fails to further the end advanced as the justification for the prohibition. When that essential nexus is eliminated, the situation becomes the same as if California law forbade shouting fire in a crowded theater, but granted dispensations to those willing to contribute $100 to the state treasury. While a ban on shouting fire can be a core exercise of the State's police power to protect the public safety, and can thus meet even our stringent standards for regulation of speech, adding the unrelated condition alters the purpose to one which, while it may be legitimate, is inadequate to sustain the ban. Therefore, even though, in a sense, requiring a $100 tax contribution in order to shout fire is a lesser restriction on speech than an outright ban, it would not pass constitutional muster. Similarly here, the lack of nexus between the condition and the original purpose of the building restriction converts that purpose to something other than what it was. The purpose then becomes, quite simply, the obtaining of an easement to serve some valid governmental purpose, but without payment of compensation. Whatever may be the outer limits of "legitimate state interests" in the takings and land-use context, this is not one of them. In short, unless the permit condition serves the same governmental purpose as the development ban, the building restriction is not a valid regulation of land use but "an out-and-out plan of extortion." *J.E.D. Associates, Inc. v. Atkinson,* 121 N.H. 581, 584, 432 A.2d 12, 14–15 (1981); see Brief for United States as *Amicus Curiae* 22, and n. 20. See also *Loretto v. Teleprompter Manhattan CATV Corp.*, 458 U.S., at 439, n. 17, 102 S.Ct., at 3178, n. 17.

III

The Commission claims that it concedes as much, and that we may sustain the condition at issue here by finding that it is reasonably related to the public need or burden that the Nollans' new house creates or to which it contributes. We can accept, for purposes of discussion, the Commission's proposed test as to how close a "fit" between the condition and the burden is required, because we find that this case does not meet even the most untailored standards. The Commission's principal contention to the contrary essentially turns on a play on the word "access." The Nollans' new house, the Commission found, will interfere with "visual access" to the beach. That in turn (along with other shorefront development) will interfere with the desire of people who drive past the Nollans' house to use the beach, thus creating a "psychological barrier" to "access." The Nollans' new house will also, by a process not altogether clear from the Commission's opinion but presumably potent enough to more than offset the effects of the psychological barrier, increase the use of the public beaches, thus creating the need for more "access." These burdens on "access" would be alleviated by a requirement that the Nollans provide "lateral access" to the beach.

Rewriting the argument to eliminate the play on words makes clear that there is nothing to it. It is quite impossible to understand how a requirement that people already on the public beaches be able to walk across the Nollans' property reduces any obstacles to viewing the beach created by the new house. It is also impossible to understand how it lowers any "psychological barrier" to using the public beaches, or how it helps to remedy any additional congestion on them caused by construction of the Nollans' new house. We therefore find that the Commission's imposition of the permit condition cannot be treated as an exercise of its land-use power for any of these purposes. Our conclusion on this point is consistent with the approach taken by every other court that has considered the question, with the exception of the California state courts. See *Parks v. Watson,* 716 F.2d 646, 651–653 (CA9 1983); *Bethlehem Evangelical Lutheran Church v. Lakewood,* 626 P.2d 668, 671–674 (Colo.1981); *Aunt Hack Ridge Estates, Inc. v. Planning Comm'n,* 160 Conn. 109, 117–120, 273 A.2d 880, 885 (1970); *Longboat Key v. Lands End, Ltd.,* 433 So.2d 574 (Fla.App.1983); *Pioneer Trust & Savings Bank v. Mount Prospect,* 22 Ill.2d 375, 380, 176 N.E.2d 799, 802 (1961); *Lampton v. Pinaire,* 610 S.W.2d 915, 918–919 (Ky.App.1980); *Schwing v. Baton Rouge,* 249 So.2d 304 (La.App.), application denied, 259 La. 770, 252 So.2d 667 (1971); *Howard County v. JJM, Inc.,* 301 Md. 256, 280–282, 482 A.2d 908, 920–921 (1984); *Collis v. Bloomington,* 310 Minn. 5, 246 N.W.2d 19 (1976); *State ex rel. Noland v. St. Louis County,* 478 S.W.2d 363 (Mo.1972); *Billings Properties, Inc. v. Yellowstone County,* 144 Mont. 25, 33–36, 394 P.2d 182, 187–188 (1964); *Simpson v. North Platte,* 206 Neb. 240, 292 N.W.2d 297 (1980); *Briar West, Inc. v. Lincoln,* 206 Neb. 172, 291 N.W.2d 730 (1980); *J.E.D. Associates v. Atkinson,* 121 N.H. 581, 432 A.2d 12 (1981); *Longridge Builders, Inc. v. Planning Bd. of Princeton,* 52 N.J. 348, 350–351, 245 A.2d 336, 337–338 (1968); *Jenad, Inc. v. Scarsdale,* 18 N.Y.2d 78, 271 N.Y.S.2d 955, 218 N.E.2d 673 (1966); *MacKall v. White,* 85 App.Div.2d 696, 445 N.Y.S.2d 486 (1981), appeal denied, 56 N.Y.2d 503, 450 N.Y.S.2d 1025, 435 N.E.2d 1100 (1982); *Frank Ansuini, Inc. v. Cranston,* 107 R.I. 63, 68–69, 71, 264 A.2d 910, 913, 914 (1970); *College Station v. Turtle Rock Corp.,* 680 S.W.2d 802, 807 (Tex.1984); *Call v. West Jordan,* 614 P.2d 1257, 1258–1259 (Utah 1980);

Board of Supervisors of James City County v. Rowe, 216 Va. 128, 136–139, 216 S.E.2d 199, 207–209 (1975); *Jordan v. Menomonee Falls,* 28 Wis.2d 608, 617–618, 137 N.W.2d 442, 447–449 (1965), appeal dism'd, 385 U.S. 4, 87 S.Ct. 36, 17 L.Ed.2d 3 (1966). See also *Littlefield v. Afton,* 785 F.2d 596, 607 (CA8 1986); Brief for National Association of Home Builders et al. as *Amici Curiae* 9–16.

Justice Brennan argues that imposition of the access requirement is not irrational. In his version of the Commission's argument, the reason for the requirement is that in its absence, a person looking toward the beach from the road will see a street of residential structures including the Nollans' new home and conclude that there is no public beach nearby. If, however, that person sees people passing and repassing along the dry sand behind the Nollans' home, he will realize that there is a public beach somewhere in the vicinity. *Post,* at 3154–3155. The Commission's action, however, was based on the opposite factual finding that the wall of houses completely blocked the view of the beach and that a person looking from the road would not be able to see it at all. App. 57–59.

Even if the Commission had made the finding that Justice Brennan proposes, however, it is not certain that it would suffice. We do not share Justice Brennan's confidence that the Commission "should have little difficulty in the future in utilizing its expertise to demonstrate a specific connection between provisions for access and burdens on access," *post,* at 3161, that will avoid the effect of today's decision. We view the Fifth Amendment's Property Clause to be more than a pleading requirement, and compliance with it to be more than an exercise in cleverness and imagination. As indicated earlier, our cases describe the condition for abridgement of property rights through the police power as a "*substantial* advanc[ing]" of a legitimate state interest. We are inclined to be particularly careful about the adjective where the actual conveyance of property is made a condition to the lifting of a land-use restriction, since in that context there is heightened risk that the purpose is avoidance of the compensation requirement, rather than the stated police-power objective.

We are left, then, with the Commission's justification for the access requirement unrelated to land-use regulation:

> "Finally, the Commission notes that there are several existing provisions of pass and repass lateral access benefits already given by past Faria Beach Tract applicants as a result of prior coastal permit decisions. The access required as a condition of this permit is part of a comprehensive program to provide continuous public access along Faria Beach as the lots undergo development or redevelopment." App. 68.

That is simply an expression of the Commission's belief that the public interest will be served by a continuous strip of publicly accessible beach along the coast. The Commission may well be right that it is a good idea, but that does not establish that the Nollans (and other coastal residents) alone can be compelled to contribute to its realization. Rather, California is free to advance its "comprehensive program," if it wishes, by using its power of eminent domain for this "public purpose," see U.S. Const., Amdt. 5; but if it wants an easement across the Nollans' property, it must pay for it.

Reversed.

Justice Brennan, with whom Justice Marshall joins, dissenting.

Justice Blackmun, dissenting.

Justice Stevens, with whom Justice Blackmun joins, dissenting.

On Peyote and the "Free Exercise Clause"
Employment Division, Department of Human Resources of Oregon v. Smith,
494 U.S. 872 (1990)

Justice Scalia delivered the opinion of the Court.

This case requires us to decide whether the Free Exercise Clause of the First Amendment permits the State of Oregon to include religiously inspired peyote use within the reach of its general criminal prohibition on use of that drug, and thus permits the State to deny unemployment benefits to persons dismissed from their jobs because of such religiously inspired use.

I

Oregon law prohibits the knowing or intentional possession of a "controlled substance" unless the substance has been prescribed by a medical practitioner. Ore.Rev.Stat. § 475.992(4) (1987). The law defines "controlled substance" as a drug classified in Schedules I through V of the Federal Controlled Substances Act, 21 U.S.C. §§ 811–812, as modified by the State Board of Pharmacy. Ore.Rev.Stat. § 475.005(6) (1987). Persons who violate this provision by possessing a controlled substance listed on Schedule I are "guilty of a Class B felony." § 475.992(4)(a). As compiled by the State Board of Pharmacy under its statutory authority, see, § 475.035, Schedule I contains the drug peyote, a hallucinogen derived from the plant *Lophophora williamsii Lemaire.* Ore.Admin.Rule 855-80-021(3)(s) (1988).

Respondents Alfred Smith and Galen Black (hereinafter respondents) were fired from their jobs with a private drug rehabilitation organization because they ingested peyote for sacramental purposes at a ceremony of the Native American Church, of which both are members. When respondents applied to petitioner Employment Division (hereinafter petitioner) for unemployment compensation, they were determined to be ineligible for benefits because they had been discharged for work-related "misconduct." The Oregon Court of Appeals reversed that determination, holding that the denial of benefits violated respondents' free exercise rights under the First Amendment.

On appeal to the Oregon Supreme Court, petitioner argued that the denial of benefits was permissible because respondents' consumption of peyote was a crime under Oregon law. The Oregon Supreme Court reasoned, however, that the criminality of respondents' peyote use was irrelevant to resolution of their constitutional claim-since the purpose of the "misconduct" provision under which respondents had been disqualified was not to enforce the State's criminal laws but to preserve the financial integrity of the compensation fund, and since that purpose was inadequate to justify the burden that disqualification imposed on respondents' religious practice. Citing our decisions in *Sherbert v. Verner,* 374 U.S. 398, 83 S.Ct. 1790, 10 L.Ed.2d 965 (1963), and *Thomas v. Review Bd., Indiana Employment Security Div.,* 450 U.S. 707, 101 S.Ct. 1425, 67 L.Ed.2d 624 (1981), the court concluded that respondents were entitled to payment of unemployment benefits. *Smith v. Employment Div., Dept. of Human Resources,* 301 Or. 209, 217–219, 721 P.2d 445, 449–450 (1986). We granted certiorari. 480 U.S. 916, 107 S.Ct. 1368, 94 L.Ed.2d 684 (1987).

Before this Court in 1987, petitioner continued to maintain that the illegality of respondents' peyote consumption was relevant to their constitutional claim. We agreed, concluding that "if a State has prohibited through its criminal laws certain kinds of religiously motivated conduct without violating the First Amendment, it certainly follows that it may impose the lesser burden of denying unemployment compensation benefits to persons who engage in that conduct." *Employment Div., Dept. of Human Resources of Oregon v. Smith,* 485 U.S. 660, 670, 108 S.Ct. 1444, 1450, 99 L.Ed.2d 753 (1988) (*Smith I*). We noted, however, that the Oregon Supreme Court had not decided whether respondents' sacramental use of peyote was in fact proscribed by Oregon's controlled substance law, and that this issue was a matter of dispute between the parties. Being "uncertain about the legality of the religious use of peyote in Oregon," we determined that it would not be "appropriate for us to decide whether the practice is protected by the Federal Constitution." *Id.,* at 673, 108 S.Ct., at 1452. Accordingly, we vacated the judgment of the Oregon Supreme Court and remanded for further proceedings. *Id.,* at 674, 108 S.Ct., at 1452.

On remand, the Oregon Supreme Court held that respondents' religiously inspired use of peyote fell within the prohibition of the Oregon statute, which "makes no exception for the sacramental use" of the drug. 307 Or. 68, 72–73, 763 P.2d 146, 148 (1988). It then considered whether that prohibition was valid under the Free Exercise Clause, and concluded that it was not. The court therefore reaffirmed its previous ruling that the State could not deny unemployment benefits to respondents for having engaged in that practice.

We again granted certiorari. 489 U.S. 1077, 109 S.Ct. 1526, 103 L.Ed.2d 832 (1989).

II

Respondents' claim for relief rests on our decisions in *Sherbert v. Verner, supra, Thomas v. Review Bd. of Indiana*

Employment Security Div., *supra*, and *Hobbie v. Unemployment Appeals Comm'n of Florida*, 480 U.S. 136, 107 S.Ct. 1046, 94 L.Ed.2d 190 (1987), in which we held that a State could not condition the availability of unemployment insurance on an individual's willingness to forgo conduct required by his religion. As we observed in Smith I, however, the conduct at issue in those cases was not prohibited by law. We held that distinction to be critical, for "if Oregon does prohibit the religious use of peyote, and if that prohibition is consistent with the Federal Constitution, there is no federal right to engage in that conduct in Oregon," and "the State is free to withhold unemployment compensation from respondents for engaging in work-related misconduct, despite its religious motivation." 485 U.S., at 672, 108 S.Ct., at 1451. Now that the Oregon Supreme Court has confirmed that Oregon does prohibit the religious use of peyote, we proceed to consider whether that prohibition is permissible under the Free Exercise Clause.

A

The Free Exercise Clause of the First Amendment, which has been made applicable to the States by incorporation into the Fourteenth Amendment, see *Cantwell v. Connecticut,* 310 U.S. 296, 303, 60 S.Ct. 900, 903, 84 L.Ed. 1213 (1940), provides that "Congress shall make no law respecting an establishment of religion, or *prohibiting the free exercise thereof....* " U.S. Const., Amdt. 1 (emphasis added.) The free exercise of religion means, first and foremost, the right to believe and profess whatever religious doctrine one desires. Thus, the First Amendment obviously excludes all "governmental regulation of religious *beliefs* as such." *Sherbert v. Verner, supra,* 374 U.S., at 402, 83 S.Ct., at 1793. The government may not compel affirmation of religious belief, see *Torcaso v. Watkins,* 367 U.S.

488, 81 S.Ct. 1680, 6 L.Ed.2d 982 (1961), punish the expression of religious doctrines it believes to be false, *United States v. Ballard,* 322 U.S. 78, 86–88, 64 S.Ct. 882, 886–87, 88 L.Ed. 1148 (1944), impose special disabilities on the basis of religious views or religious status, see *McDaniel v. Paty,* 435 U.S. 618, 98 S.Ct. 1322, 55 L.Ed.2d 593 (1978); *Fowler v. Rhode Island,* 345 U.S. 67, 69, 73 S.Ct. 526, 527, 97 L.Ed. 828 (1953); cf. *Larson v. Valente,* 456 U.S. 228, 245, 102 S.Ct. 1673, 1683–84, 72 L.Ed.2d 33 (1982), or lend its power to one or the other side in controversies over religious authority or dogma, see *Presbyterian Church in U.S. v. Mary Elizabeth Blue Hull Memorial Presbyterian Church,* 393 U.S. 440, 445 452, 89 S.Ct. 601, 604–608, 21 L.Ed.2d 658 (1969); *Kedroff v. St. Nicholas Cathedral,* 344 U.S. 94, 95–119, 73 S.Ct. 143, 143–56, 97 L.Ed. 120 (1952); *Serbian Eastern Orthodox Diocese v. Milivojevich,* 426 U.S. 696, 708–725, 96 S.Ct. 2372, 2380–2388, 49 L.Ed.2d 151 (1976).

But the "exercise of religion" often involves not only belief and profession but the performance of (or abstention from) physical acts: assembling with others for a worship service, participating in sacramental use of bread and wine, proselytizing, abstaining from certain foods or certain modes of transportation. It would be true, we think (though no case of ours has involved the point), that a State would be "prohibiting the free exercise [of religion]" if it sought to ban such acts or abstentions only when they are engaged in for religious reasons, or only because of the religious belief that they display. It would doubtless be unconstitutional, for example, to ban the casting of "statues that are to be used for worship purposes," or to prohibit bowing down before a golden calf.

Respondents in the present case, however, seek to carry the meaning of "prohibiting the free exercise [of religion]" one large step further. They contend that their religious motivation for using peyote places them beyond the reach of a criminal law that is not specifically directed at their religious practice, and that is concededly constitutional as applied to those who use the drug for other reasons. They assert, in other words, that "prohibiting the free exercise [of religion]" includes requiring any individual to observe a generally applicable law that requires (or forbids) the performance of an act that his religious belief forbids (or requires). As a textual matter, we do not think the words must be given that meaning. It is no more necessary to regard the collection of a general tax, for example, as "prohibiting the free exercise [of religion]" by those citizens who believe support of organized government to be sinful, than it is to regard the same tax as "abridging the freedom ... of the press" of those publishing companies that must pay the tax as a condition of staying in business. It is a permissible reading of the text, in the one case as in the other, to say that if prohibiting the exercise of religion (or burdening the activity of printing) is not the object of the tax but merely the incidental effect of a generally applicable and otherwise valid provision, the First Amendment has not been offended. Compare *Citizen Publishing Co. v. United States,* 394 U.S. 131, 139, 89 S.Ct. 927, 931–32, 22 L.Ed.2d 148 (1969) (upholding application of antitrust laws to press), with *Grosjean v. American Press Co.,* 297 U.S. 233, 250–251, 56 S.Ct. 444, 449, 80 L.Ed. 660 (1936) (striking down license tax applied only to newspapers with weekly circulation above a specified level); see generally *Minneapolis Star & Tribune Co. v. Minnesota Comm'r of Revenue,* 460 U.S. 575, 581, 103 S.Ct. 1365, 1369–70, 75 L.Ed.2d 295 (1983).

Our decisions reveal that the latter reading is the correct one. We have never held that an individual's religious beliefs excuse him from compliance with an otherwise valid law prohibiting conduct that the State is free to regulate. On the contrary, the record of more than a century of our free exercise jurisprudence contradicts that proposition. As described succinctly by Justice Frankfurter in *Minersville School Dist. Bd. of Ed. v. Gobitis,* 310 U.S. 586, 594–595, 60 S.Ct. 1010, 1012–1013, 84 L.Ed. 1375 (1940): "Conscientious scruples have not, in the course of the long struggle for religious toleration, relieved the individual from obedience to a general law not aimed at the promotion or restriction of religious beliefs. The mere possession of religious convictions which contradict the relevant concerns of a political society does not relieve the citizen from the discharge of political responsibilities (footnote omitted)." We first had occasion to assert that principle in *Reynolds v. United States,* 98 U.S. 145, 25 L.Ed. 244 (1878), where we rejected the claim that criminal laws against polygamy could not be constitutionally applied to those whose religion commanded the practice. "Laws," we said, "are made for the government of actions, and while they cannot interfere with mere religious belief and opinions, they may with practices.... Can a man excuse his practices to the contrary because of his religious belief? To permit this would be to make the professed doctrines of religious belief superior to the law of the land, and in effect to permit every citizen to become a law unto himself." *Id.,* at 166–167.

Subsequent decisions have consistently held that the right of free exercise does not relieve an individual of the obligation to comply with a "valid and neutral law of general applicability on the ground that the law proscribes (or prescribes) conduct that his religion prescribes (or proscribes)." *United States v. Lee,* 455 U.S. 252, 263, n. 3, 102 S.Ct. 1051, 1058, n. 3, 71 L.Ed.2d 127 (1982) (Stevens, J., concurring in judgment); see *Minersville School Dist. Bd. of Ed. v. Gobitis, supra,* 310 U.S., at 595, 60 S.Ct., at 1013 (collecting cases). In *Prince v. Massachusetts,* 321 U.S. 158, 64 S.Ct. 438, 88 L.Ed. 645 (1944), we held that a mother could be prosecuted under the child labor laws for using her children to dispense literature in the streets, her religious motivation notwithstanding. We found no constitutional infirmity in "excluding [these children] from doing there what no other children may do." *Id.*, at 171, 64 S.Ct., at 444. In *Braunfeld v. Brown,* 366 U.S. 599, 81 S.Ct. 1144, 6 L.Ed.2d 563 (1961) (plurality opinion), we upheld Sunday-closing laws against the claim that they burdened the religious practices of persons whose religions compelled them to refrain from work on other days. In *Gillette v. United States,* 401 U.S. 437, 461, 91 S.Ct. 828, 842, 28 L.Ed.2d 168 (1971), we sustained the military Selective Service System against the claim that it violated free exercise by conscripting persons who opposed a particular war on religious grounds.

Our most recent decision involving a neutral, generally applicable regulatory law that compelled activity forbidden by an individual's religion was *United States v. Lee,* 455 U.S., at 258–261, 102 S.Ct., at 1055–1057. There, an Amish employer, on behalf of himself and his employees, sought exemption from collection and payment of Social Security taxes on the ground that the Amish faith prohibited participation in governmental support programs. We rejected the claim that an exemption was constitutionally required. There would be no way, we observed, to distinguish the Amish believer's objection to Social Security taxes from the religious objections that others might have to the collection or use of other taxes. "If, for example, a religious adherent believes war is a sin, and if a certain percentage of the federal budget can be identified as devoted to war-related activities, such individuals would have a similarly valid claim to be exempt from paying that percentage of the income tax. The tax system could not function if denominations were allowed to challenge the tax system because tax payments were spent in a manner that violates their religious belief." *Id.*, at 260, 102 S.Ct., at 1056–57. Cf. *Hernandez v. Commissioner,* 490 U.S. 680, 109 S.Ct. 2136, 104 L.Ed.2d 766 (1989) (rejecting free exercise challenge to payment of income taxes alleged to make religious activities more difficult).

The only decisions in which we have held that the First Amendment bars application of a neutral, generally applicable law to religiously motivated action have involved not the Free Exercise Clause alone, but the Free Exercise Clause in conjunction with other constitutional protections, such as freedom of speech and of the press, see *Cantwell v. Connecticut,* 310 U.S., at 304–307, 60 S.Ct., at 903–905 (invalidating a licensing system for religious and charitable solicitations under which the administrator had discretion to deny a license to any cause he deemed nonreligious); *Murdock v. Pennsylvania,* 319 U.S. 105, 63 S.Ct. 870, 87 L.Ed. 1292 (1943) (invalidating a flat tax on solicitation as applied to the dissemination of religious ideas); *Follett v. McCormick,* 321 U.S. 573, 64 S.Ct. 717, 88 L.Ed. 938 (1944) (same), or the right of parents, acknowledged in *Pierce v. Society of Sisters,* 268 U.S. 510, 45 S.Ct. 571, 69 L.Ed. 1070 (1925), to direct the education of their children, see *Wisconsin v. Yoder,* 406 U.S. 205, 92 S.Ct. 1526, 32 L.Ed.2d 15 (1972) (invalidating compulsory school-attendance laws as applied to Amish parents who refused on religious grounds to send their children to school). Some of our cases prohibiting compelled expression, decided exclusively upon free speech grounds, have also involved freedom of religion, cf. *Wooley v. Maynard,* 430 U.S. 705, 97 S.Ct. 1428, 51 L.Ed.2d 752 (1977) (invalidating compelled display of a license plate slogan that offended individual religious beliefs); *West Virginia Bd. of Education v. Barnette,* 319 U.S. 624, 63 S.Ct. 1178, 87 L.Ed. 1628 (1943) (invalidating compulsory flag salute statute challenged by religious objectors). And it is easy to envision a case in which a challenge on freedom of association grounds would likewise be reinforced by Free Exercise Clause concerns. *Cf. Roberts v. United States Jaycees,* 468 U.S. 609, 622, 104 S.Ct. 3244, 3251–52, 82 L.Ed.2d 462 (1984) ("An individual's freedom to speak, to worship, and to petition the government for the redress of grievances could not be vigorously protected from interference by the State [if] a correlative freedom to engage in group effort toward those ends were not also guaranteed").

The present case does not present such a hybrid situation, but a free exercise claim unconnected with any communicative activity or parental right. Respondents urge us to hold, quite simply, that when otherwise prohibitable conduct is accompanied by religious convictions, not only the convictions but the conduct itself must be free from governmental regulation. We have never held that, and decline to do so now. There being no contention that Oregon's drug law represents an attempt to regulate religious beliefs, the communication of religious beliefs, or the raising of one's children in those beliefs, the rule to which we have adhered ever since *Reynolds* plainly controls. "Our cases do not at their farthest reach support the proposition that a stance of conscientious opposition relieves an objector from any colliding duty fixed by a democratic government." *Gillette v. United States, supra,* 401 U.S., at 461, 91 S.Ct., at 842.

B

Respondents argue that even though exemption from generally applicable criminal laws need not automatically be extended to religiously motivated actors, at least the claim for a religious exemption must be evaluated under the balancing test set forth in *Sherbert v. Verner,* 374 U.S. 398, 83 S.Ct. 1790, 10

L.Ed.2d 965 (1963). Under the *Sherbert* test, governmental actions that substantially burden a religious practice must be justified by a compelling governmental interest. See *id.*, at 402–403, 83 S.Ct., at 1792–1794; see also *Hernandez v. Commissioner,* 490 U.S., at 699, 109 S.Ct., at 2148. Applying that test we have, on three occasions, invalidated state unemployment compensation rules that conditioned the availability of benefits upon an applicant's willingness to work under conditions forbidden by his religion. See *Sherbert v. Verner, supra; Thomas v. Review Bd. of Indiana Employment Security Div.,* 450 U.S. 707, 101 S.Ct. 1425, 67 L.Ed.2d 624 (1981); *Hobbie v. Unemployment Appeals Comm'n of Florida,* 480 U.S. 136, 107 S.Ct. 1046, 94 L.Ed.2d 190 (1987). We have never invalidated any governmental action on the basis of the *Sherbert* test except the denial of unemployment compensation. Although we have sometimes purported to apply the *Sherbert* test in contexts other than that, we have always found the test satisfied, see *United States v. Lee,* 455 U.S. 252, 102 S.Ct. 1051, 71 L.Ed.2d 127 (1982); *Gillette v. United States,* 401 U.S. 437, 91 S.Ct. 828, 28 L.Ed.2d 168 (1971). In recent years we have abstained from applying the *Sherbert* test (outside the unemployment compensation field) at all. In *Bowen v. Roy,* 476 U.S. 693, 106 S.Ct. 2147, 90 L.Ed.2d 735 (1986), we declined to apply *Sherbert* analysis to a federal statutory scheme that required benefit applicants and recipients to provide their Social Security numbers. The plaintiffs in that case asserted that it would violate their religious beliefs to obtain and provide a Social Security number for their daughter. We held the statute's application to the plaintiffs valid regardless of whether it was necessary to effectuate a compelling interest. See 476 U.S., at 699–701, 106 S.Ct., at 2151–53. In *Lyng v. Northwest Indian Cemetery Protective Assn.,* 485 U.S. 439, 108 S.Ct. 1319, 99 L.Ed.2d 534

(1988), we declined to apply *Sherbert* analysis to the Government's logging and road construction activities on lands used for religious purposes by several Native American Tribes, even though it was undisputed that the activities "could have devastating effects on traditional Indian religious practices," 485 U.S., at 451, 108 S.Ct., at 1326. In *Goldman v. Weinberger,* 475 U.S. 503, 106 S.Ct. 1310, 89 L.Ed.2d 478 (1986), we rejected application of the *Sherbert* test to military dress regulations that forbade the wearing of yarmulkes. In *O'Lone v. Estate of Shabazz,* 482 U.S. 342, 107 S.Ct. 2400, 96 L.Ed.2d 282 (1987), we sustained, without mentioning the *Sherbert* test, a prison's refusal to excuse inmates from work requirements to attend worship services.

Even if we were inclined to breathe into *Sherbert* some life beyond the unemployment compensation field, we would not apply it to require exemptions from a generally applicable criminal law. The *Sherbert* test, it must be recalled, was developed in a context that lent itself to individualized governmental assessment of the reasons for the relevant conduct. As a plurality of the Court noted in *Roy,* a distinctive feature of unemployment compensation programs is that their eligibility criteria invite consideration of the particular circumstances behind an applicant's unemployment: "The statutory conditions [in *Sherbert* and *Thomas*] provided that a person was not eligible for unemployment compensation benefits if, 'without good cause,' he had quit work or refused available work. The 'good cause' standard created a mechanism for individualized exemptions." *Bowen v. Roy, supra,* 476 U.S., at 708, 106 S.Ct., at 2156 (opinion of Burger, C.J., joined by Powell and Rehnquist, JJ.). See also *Sherbert, supra,* 374 U.S., at 401, n. 4, 83 S.Ct., at 1792, n. 4 (reading state unemployment compensation law as allowing benefits for unemployment caused by at least some "personal reasons"). As the plurality pointed out in *Roy,* our decisions in the unemployment cases stand for the proposition that where the State has in place a system of individual exemptions, it may not refuse to extend that system to cases of "religious hardship" without compelling reason. *Bowen v. Roy, supra,* 476 U.S., at 708, 106 S.Ct., at 2156–57.

Whether or not the decisions are that limited, they at least have nothing to do with an across-the-board criminal prohibition on a particular form of conduct. Although, as noted earlier, we have sometimes used the *Sherbert* test to analyze free exercise challenges to such laws, see *United States v. Lee, supra,* 455 U.S., at 257–260, 102 S.Ct., at 1055–1057; *Gillette v. United States, supra,* 401 U.S., at 462, 91 S.Ct., at 842–43, we have never applied the test to invalidate one. We conclude today that the sounder approach, and the approach in accord with the vast majority of our precedents, is to hold the test inapplicable to such challenges. The government's ability to enforce generally applicable prohibitions of socially harmful conduct, like its ability to carry out other aspects of public policy, "cannot depend on measuring the effects of a governmental action on a religious objector's spiritual development." *Lyng, supra,* 485 U.S., at 451, 108 S.Ct., at 1326. To make an individual's obligation to obey such a law contingent upon the law's coincidence with his religious beliefs, except where the State's interest is "compelling," permitting him, by virtue of his beliefs, "to become a law unto himself," *Reynolds v. United States,* 98 U.S., at 167—contradicts both constitutional tradition and common sense.

The "compelling government interest" requirement seems benign, because it is familiar from other fields. But using it as the standard that must be met before the government may accord different treatment on the basis of race, see, *e.g., Palmore v. Sidoti,* 466 U.S. 429, 432, 104 S.Ct. 1879, 1881–82,

80 L.Ed.2d 421 (1984), or before the government may regulate the content of speech, see, *e.g.*, *Sable Communications of California v. FCC,* 492 U.S. 115, 126, 109 S.Ct. 2829, 2836, 106 L.Ed.2d 93 (1989), is not remotely comparable to using it for the purpose asserted here. What it produces in those other fields—equality of treatment and an unrestricted flow of contending speech—are constitutional norms; what it would produce here—a private right to ignore generally applicable laws—is a constitutional anomaly.

Nor is it possible to limit the impact of respondents' proposal by requiring a "compelling state interest" only when the conduct prohibited is "central" to the individual's religion. Cf. *Lyng v. Northwest Indian Cemetery Protective Assn.,* 485 U.S., at 474–476, 108 S.Ct., at 1338–1339 (BRENNAN, J., dissenting). It is no more appropriate for judges to determine the "centrality" of religious beliefs before applying a "compelling interest" test in the free exercise field, than it would be for them to determine the "importance" of ideas before applying the "compelling interest" test in the free speech field. What principle of law or logic can be brought to bear to contradict a believer's assertion that a particular act is "central" to his personal faith? Judging the centrality of different religious practices is akin to the unacceptable "business of evaluating the relative merits of differing religious claims." *United States v. Lee,* 455 U.S., at 263 n. 2, 102 S.Ct., at 1058 n. 2 (Stevens, J., concurring). As we reaffirmed only last Term, "[i]t is not within the judicial ken to question the centrality of particular beliefs or practices to a faith, or the validity of particular litigants' interpretations of those creeds." *Hernandez v. Commissioner,* 490 U.S., at 699, 109 S.Ct., at 2148. Repeatedly and in many different contexts, we have warned that courts must not presume to determine the place of a particular belief in a religion or the plausibility of a religious claim. See, *e.g., Thomas v. Review Bd. of Indiana Employment Security Div.,* 450 U.S., at 716, 101 S.Ct., at 1431; *Presbyterian Church in U.S. v. Mary Elizabeth Blue Hull Memorial Presbyterian Church,* 393 U.S., at 450, 89 S.Ct., at 606–07; *Jones v. Wolf,* 443 U.S. 595, 602–606, 99 S.Ct. 3020, 3024–3027, 61 L.Ed.2d 775 (1979); *United States v. Ballard,* 322 U.S. 78, 85–87, 64 S.Ct. 882, 885–87, 88 L.Ed. 1148 (1944).

If the "compelling interest" test is to be applied at all, then, it must be applied across the board, to all actions thought to be religiously commanded. Moreover, if "compelling interest" really means what it says (and watering it down here would subvert its rigor in the other fields where it is applied), many laws will not meet the test. Any society adopting such a system would be courting anarchy, but that danger increases in direct proportion to the society's diversity of religious beliefs, and its determination to coerce or suppress none of them. Precisely because "we are a cosmopolitan nation made up of people of almost every conceivable religious preference," *Braunfeld v. Brown,* 366 U.S., at 606, 81 S.Ct., at 1147, and precisely because we value and protect that religious divergence, we cannot afford the luxury of deeming *presumptively invalid,* as applied to the religious objector, every regulation of conduct that does not protect an interest of the highest order. The rule respondents favor would open the prospect of constitutionally required religious exemptions from civic obligations of almost every conceivable kind—ranging from compulsory military service, see, *e.g., Gillette v. United States,* 401 U.S. 437, 91 S.Ct. 828, 28 L.Ed.2d 168 (1971), to the payment of taxes, see, *e.g., United States v. Lee, supra;* to health and safety regulation such as manslaughter and child neglect laws, see, *e.g., Funkhouser v. State,* 763 P.2d 695 (Okla.Crim.App.1 988), compulsory vaccination laws, see, *e.g., Cude v. State,* 237 Ark. 927, 377 S.W.2d 816 (1964), drug laws, see, *e.g., Olsen v. Drug*

Enforcement Administration, 279 U.S.App.D.C. 1, 878 F.2d 1458 (1989), and traffic laws, see *Cox v. New Hampshire,* 312 U.S. 569, 61 S.Ct. 762, 85 L.Ed. 1049 (1941); to social welfare legislation such as minimum wage laws, see *Tony and Susan Alamo Foundation v. Secretary of Labor,* 471 U.S. 290, 105 S.Ct. 1953, 85 L.Ed.2d 278 (1985), child labor laws, see *Prince v. Massachusetts,* 321 U.S. 158, 64 S.Ct. 438, 88 L.Ed. 645 (1944), animal cruelty laws, see, *e.g., Church of the Lukumi Babalu Aye Inc. v. City of Hialeah,* 723 F.Supp. 1467 (SD Fla.1989), cf. *State v. Massey,* 229 N.C. 734, 51 S.E.2d 179, appeal dism'd, 336 U.S. 942, 69 S.Ct. 813, 93 L.Ed. 1099 (1949), environmental protection laws, see *United States v. Little,* 638 F.Supp. 337 (Mont.1986), and laws providing for equality of opportunity for the races, see, *e.g., Bob Jones University v. United States,* 461 U.S. 574, 603–604, 103 S.Ct. 2017, 2034–2035, 76 L.Ed.2d 157 (1983). The First Amendment's protection of religious liberty does not require this.

Values that are protected against government interference through enshrinement in the Bill of Rights are not thereby banished from the political process. Just as a society that believes in the negative protection accorded to the press by the First Amendment is likely to enact laws that affirmatively foster the dissemination of the printed word, so also a society that believes in the negative protection accorded to religious belief can be expected to be solicitous of that value in its legislation as well. It is therefore not surprising that a number of States have made an exception to their drug laws for sacramental peyote use. See, *e.g.,* Ariz.Rev.Stat.Ann. §§ 13-3402(B)(1)-(3) (1989); Colo.Rev.Stat. § 12-22-317(3) (1985); N.M. Stat. Ann. § 30-31-6(D) (Supp.1989). But to say that a nondiscriminatory religious-practice exemption is permitted, or even that it is desirable, is not to say that it is constitutionally required, and that the appropriate occasions for its creation can be discerned by the courts. It may fairly be said that leaving accommodation to the political process will place at a relative disadvantage those religious practices that are not widely engaged in; but that unavoidable consequence of democratic government must be preferred to a system in which each conscience is a law unto itself or in which judges weigh the social importance of all laws against the centrality of all religious beliefs.

* * *

Because respondents' ingestion of peyote was prohibited under Oregon law, and because that prohibition is constitutional, Oregon may, consistent with the Free Exercise Clause, deny respondents unemployment compensation when their dismissal results from use of the drug. The decision of the Oregon Supreme Court is accordingly reversed.

It is so ordered.

Justice O'Connor, with whom Justice Brennan, Justice Marshall, and Justice Blackmun join as to Parts I and II, concurring in the judgment.[*]

Justice Blackmun, with whom Justice Brennan and Justice Marshall join, dissenting.

"Takings" and the Destruction of Property Value
Lucas v. South Carolina Coastal Council,
505 U.S. 1003 (1992)

Justice Scalia delivered the opinion of the Court.

In 1986, petitioner David H. Lucas paid $975,000 for two residential lots on the Isle of Palms in Charleston County, South Carolina, on which he intended to build single-family homes. In 1988, however, the South Carolina Legislature enacted the Beachfront Management Act, S.C.Code Ann. § 48-39-250 *et seq.* (Supp.1990), which had the direct effect of barring petitioner from erecting any permanent habitable structures on his two parcels. See § 48-39-290(A). A state trial court found that this prohibition rendered Lucas's parcels "valueless." App. to Pet. for Cert. 37. This case requires us to decide whether the Act's dramatic effect on the economic value of Lucas's lots accomplished a taking of private property under the Fifth and Fourteenth Amendments requiring the payment of "just compensation." U.S. Const., Amdt. 5.

I

A

South Carolina's expressed interest in intensively managing development activities in the so-called "coastal zone" dates from 1977 when, in the aftermath of Congress's passage of the federal Coastal Zone Management Act of 1972, 86 Stat. 1280, as amended, 16 U.S.C. § 1451 *et seq.*, the legislature enacted a Coastal Zone Management Act of its own. See S.C.Code Ann. § 48-39-10 *et seq.* (1987). In its original form, the South Carolina Act required owners of coastal zone land that qualified as a "critical area" (defined in the legislation to include beaches and immediately adjacent sand dunes, § 48-39-10(J)) to obtain a permit from the newly created South Carolina Coastal Council (Council) (respondent here) prior to committing the land to a "use other than the use the critical area was devoted to on [September 28, 1977]." § 48-39-130(A).

In the late 1970's, Lucas and others began extensive residential development of the Isle of Palms, a barrier island situated eastward of the city of Charleston. Toward the close of the development cycle for one residential subdivision known as "Beachwood East," Lucas in 1986 purchased the two lots at issue in this litigation for his own account. No portion of the lots, which were located approximately 300 feet from the beach, qualified as a "critical area" under the 1977 Act; accordingly, at the time Lucas acquired these parcels, he was not legally obliged to obtain a permit from the Council in advance of any development activity. His intention with respect to the lots was to do what the owners of the immediately adjacent parcels had already done: erect single-family residences. He commissioned architectural drawings for this purpose.

The Beachfront Management Act brought Lucas's plans to an abrupt end. Under that 1988 legislation, the Council was directed to establish a "baseline" connecting the landward-most "point[s] of erosion ... during the past forty years" in the region of the Isle of Palms that includes Lucas's lots. S.C.Code Ann. § 48-39-280(A)(2) (Supp.1988). In action not challenged here, the Council fixed this baseline landward of Lucas's parcels. That was significant, for under the Act construction of occupiable improvements was flatly prohibited seaward of a line drawn 20 feet landward of, and parallel to, the baseline. § 48-39-290(A). The Act provided no exceptions.

B

Lucas promptly filed suit in the South Carolina Court of Common Pleas, contending that the Beachfront Management Act's construction bar effected a taking of his property without just compensation. Lucas did not take issue with the validity of the Act as a lawful exercise of South Carolina's police power, but contended that the Act's complete extinguishment of his property's value entitled him to compensation regardless of whether the legislature had acted in furtherance of legitimate police power objectives. Following a bench trial, the court agreed. Among its factual determinations was the finding that "at the time Lucas purchased the two lots, both were zoned for single-family residential construction and ... there were no restrictions imposed upon such use of the property by either the State of South Carolina, the County of Charleston, or the Town of the Isle of Palms." App. to Pet. for Cert. 36. The trial court further found that the Beachfront Management Act decreed a permanent ban on construction insofar as Lucas's lots were concerned, and that this prohibition "deprive[d] Lucas of any reasonable economic use of the lots, ... eliminated the unrestricted right of use, and render[ed] them valueless." *Id.*, at 37. The court thus concluded that Lucas's properties had been "taken" by operation of the Act, and it ordered respondent to pay "just compensation" in the amount of $1,232,387.50. *Id.*, at 40.

The Supreme Court of South Carolina reversed. It found dispositive what it described as Lucas's concession "that the Beachfront Management Act [was] properly and validly designed to preserve ... South Carolina's beaches." 304 S.C. 376, 379, 404 S.E.2d 895, 896 (1991). Failing an attack on the validity of the statute as such, the court believed itself bound to accept the "uncontested ... findings" of the South Carolina Legislature that new construction in the coastal zone—such as petitioner intended—threatened this public resource. *Id.,* at 383, 404 S.E.2d, at 898. The court ruled that when a regulation respecting the use of property is designed "to prevent serious public harm," *id.,* at 383, 404 S.E.2d, at 899 (citing, *inter alia, Mugler v. Kansas,* 123 U.S. 623, 8 S.Ct. 273, 31 L.Ed. 205 (1887)), no compensation is owing under the Takings Clause regardless of the regulation's effect on the property's value.

Two justices dissented. They acknowledged that our *Mugler* line of cases recognizes governmental power to prohibit "noxious" uses of property—*i.e.,* uses of property akin to "public nuisances"—without having to pay compensation. But they would not have characterized the Beachfront Management Act's "*primary* purpose [as] the prevention of a nuisance." 304 S.C., at 395, 404 S.E.2d, at 906 (Harwell, J., dissenting). To the dissenters, the chief purposes of the legislation, among them the promotion of tourism and the creation of a "habitat for indigenous flora and fauna," could not fairly be compared to nuisance abatement. *Id.,* at 396, 404 S.E.2d, at 906. As a consequence, they would have affirmed the trial court's conclusion that the Act's obliteration of the value of petitioner's lots accomplished a taking.

We granted certiorari. 502 U.S. 966, 112 S.Ct. 436, 116 L.Ed.2d 455 (1991).

II

As a threshold matter, we must briefly address the Council's suggestion that this case is inappropriate for plenary review. After briefing and argument before the South Carolina Supreme Court, but prior to issuance of that court's opinion, the Beachfront Management Act was amended to authorize the Council, in certain circumstances, to issue "special permits" for the construction or reconstruction of habitable structures seaward of the baseline. See S.C.Code Ann. § 48-39-290(D)(1) (Supp.1991). According to the Council, this amendment renders Lucas's claim of a permanent deprivation unripe, as Lucas may yet be able to secure permission to build on his property. "[The Court's] cases," we are reminded, "uniformly reflect an insistence on knowing the nature and extent of permitted development before adjudicating the constitutionality of the regulations that purport to limit it." *MacDonald, Sommer & Frates v. Yolo County,* 477 U.S. 340, 351, 106 S.Ct. 2561, 2567, 91 L.Ed.2d 285 (1986). See also *Agins v. City of Tiburon,* 447 U.S. 255, 260, 100 S.Ct. 2138, 2141, 65 L.Ed.2d 106 (1980). Because petitioner "has not yet obtained a final decision regarding how [he] will be allowed to develop [his] property," *Williamson County Regional Planning Comm'n v. Hamilton Bank of Johnson City,* 473 U.S. 172, 190, 105 S.Ct. 3108, 3118, 87 L.Ed.2d 126 (1985), the Council argues that he is not yet entitled to definitive adjudication of his takings claim in this Court.

We think these considerations would preclude review had the South Carolina Supreme Court rested its judgment on ripeness grounds, as it was (essentially) invited to do by the Council. See Brief for Respondent 9, n. 3. The South Carolina Supreme Court shrugged off the possibility of further administrative and trial proceedings, however, preferring to dispose of Lucas's takings claim on the merits. Cf., *e.g., San Diego Gas & Electric Co. v. San Diego,* 450 U.S. 621, 631–632, 101 S.Ct. 1287, 1293–1294, 67 L.Ed.2d 551 (1981). This unusual disposition does not preclude Lucas from applying for a permit under the 1990 amendment for *future* construction, and challenging, on takings grounds, any denial. But it does preclude, both practically and legally, any takings claim with respect to Lucas's *past* deprivation, *i.e.,* for his having been denied construction rights during the period before the 1990 amendment. See generally *First English Evangelical Lutheran Church of Glendale v. County of Los Angeles,* 482 U.S. 304, 107 S.Ct. 2378, 96 L.Ed.2d 250 (1987) (holding that temporary deprivations of use are compensable under the Takings Clause). Without even so much as commenting upon the consequences of the South Carolina Supreme Court's judgment in this respect, the Council insists that permitting Lucas to press his claim of a past deprivation on this appeal would be improper, since "the issues of whether and to what extent [Lucas] has incurred a temporary taking ... have simply never been addressed." Brief for Respondent 11. Yet Lucas had no reason to proceed on a "temporary taking" theory at trial, or even to seek remand for that purpose prior to submission of the case to the South Carolina Supreme Court, since as the Act then read, the taking was unconditional and permanent. Moreover, given the breadth of the South Carolina Supreme Court's holding and judgment, Lucas would plainly be unable (absent our intervention now) to obtain further state-court adjudication with respect to the 1988–1990 period.

In these circumstances, we think it would not accord with sound process to insist that Lucas pursue the late-created "special permit" procedure before his takings claim can be considered ripe. Lucas has properly alleged Article III injury in fact in this case, with respect to both the pre-1990 and post-1990 constraints placed on the use of his parcels by the Beachfront Management Act. That there is a discretionary "special permit" procedure by which he may regain—for the future, at least—beneficial use of his land goes only to the prudential "ripeness" of Lucas's challenge, and for the reasons discussed we do not think it prudent to apply that prudential requirement here. See *Esposito v. South Carolina Coastal Council,* 939 F.2d 165, 168 (CA4 1991), cert. denied, 505 U.S. 1219, 112 S.Ct. 3027, 120 L.Ed.2d 898 (1992). We leave for decision on remand, of course, the questions left unaddressed by the South Carolina Supreme Court as a consequence of its categorical disposition.

III

A

Prior to Justice Holmes's exposition in *Pennsylvania Coal Co. v. Mahon,* 260 U.S. 393, 43 S.Ct. 158, 67 L.Ed. 322 (1922), it was generally thought that the Takings Clause reached only a "direct appropriation" of property, *Legal Tender Cases,* 12 Wall. 457, 551, 20 L.Ed. 287 (1871), or the functional equivalent of a "practical ouster of [the owner's] possession," *Transportation Co. v. Chicago,* 99 U.S. 635, 642, 25 L.Ed. 336 (1879). See also *Gibson v. United States,* 166 U.S. 269, 275–276, 17 S.Ct. 578, 580, 41 L.Ed. 996 (1897). Justice Holmes recognized in *Mahon,* however, that if the protection against physical appropriations of private property was to be meaningfully enforced, the government's power to redefine the range of interests included in the ownership of property was necessarily constrained by constitutional limits. 260 U.S., at 414–415, 43 S.Ct., at 160. If, instead, the uses of private property were subject to unbridled, uncompensated qualification under the police power, "the natural tendency of human nature [would be] to extend the qualification more and more until at last private property disappear[ed]." *Id.,* at 415, 43 S.Ct., at 160. These considerations gave birth in that case to the oft-cited maxim that, "while property may be regulated to a certain extent, if regulation goes too far it will be recognized as a taking." *Ibid.*

Nevertheless, our decision in *Mahon* offered little insight into when, and under what circumstances, a given regulation would be seen as going "too far" for purposes of the Fifth Amendment. In 70-odd years of succeeding "regulatory takings" jurisprudence, we have generally eschewed any "'set formula'" for determining how far is too far, preferring to "engag [e] in ... essentially ad hoc, factual inquiries." *Penn Central Transportation Co. v. New York City,* 438 U.S. 104, 124, 98 S.Ct. 2646, 2659, 57 L.Ed.2d 631 (1978) (quoting *Goldblatt v. Hempstead,* 369 U.S. 590, 594, 82 S.Ct. 987, 990, 8 L.Ed.2d 130 (1962)). See Epstein, "Takings: Descent and Resurrection," 1987 *S.Ct. Rev.* 1, 4. We have, however, described at least two discrete categories of regulatory action as compensable without case-specific inquiry into the public interest advanced in support of the restraint. The first encompasses regulations that compel the property owner to suffer a physical "invasion" of his property. In general (at least with regard to permanent invasions), no matter how minute the intrusion, and no matter how weighty the public purpose behind it, we have required compensation. For example, in *Loretto v. Teleprompter Manhattan CATV Corp.,* 458 U.S. 419, 102 S.Ct. 3164, 73 L.Ed.2d 868 (1982), we determined that New York's law requiring landlords to allow television cable companies to emplace cable facilities in their apartment buildings constituted a taking, *id.,* at 435–440, 102 S.Ct., at 3175–3178, even though the facilities occupied at most only 1 ½ cubic feet of the landlords' property, see *id.,* at 438, n. 16, 102 S.Ct., at 3177. See also *United States v. Causby,* 328 U.S. 256, 265, and n. 10, 66 S.Ct. 1062, 1067, and n. 10, 90 L.Ed. 1206 (1946) (physical invasions of airspace); cf. *Kaiser Aetna v. United States,* 444 U.S. 164, 100 S.Ct. 383, 62 L.Ed.2d 332 (1979) (imposition of navigational servitude upon private marina).

The second situation in which we have found categorical treatment appropriate is where regulation denies all economically beneficial or productive use of land. See *Agins,* 447 U.S., at 260, 100 S.Ct., at 2141; see also *Nollan v. California Coastal Comm'n,* 483 U.S. 825, 834, 107 S.Ct. 3141, 3147, 97 L.Ed.2d 677 (1987); *Keystone Bituminous Coal Assn. v.*

DeBenedictis, 480 U.S. 470, 495, 107 S.Ct. 1232, 1247, 94 L.Ed.2d 472 (1987); *Hodel v. Virginia Surface Mining & Reclamation Assn., Inc.,* 452 U.S. 264, 295–296, 101 S.Ct. 2352, 2370, 69 L.Ed.2d 1 (1981). As we have said on numerous occasions, the Fifth Amendment is violated when land-use regulation "does not substantially advance legitimate state interests *or denies an owner economically viable use of his land.*" *Agins, supra,* 447 U.S., at 260, 100 S.Ct., at 2141 (citations omitted) (emphasis added).

We have never set forth the justification for this rule. Perhaps it is simply, as Justice Brennan suggested, that total deprivation of beneficial use is, from the landowner's point of view, the equivalent of a physical appropriation. See *San Diego Gas & Electric Co. v. San Diego,* 450 U.S., at 652, 101 S.Ct., at 1304 (dissenting opinion). "[F]or what is the land but the profits thereof[?]" 1 E. Coke, *Institutes,* ch. 1, § 1 (1st Am. ed. 1812). Surely, at least, in the extraordinary circumstance when *no* productive or economically beneficial use of land is permitted, it is less realistic to indulge our usual assumption that the legislature is simply "adjusting the benefits and burdens of economic life," *Penn Central Transportation Co.,* 438 U.S., at 124, 98 S.Ct., at 2659, in a manner that secures an "average reciprocity of advantage" to everyone concerned, *Pennsylvania Coal Co. v. Mahon,* 260 U.S., at 415, 43 S.Ct., at 160. And the *functional* basis for permitting the government, by regulation, to affect property values without compensation —that "Government hardly could go on if to some extent values incident to property could not be diminished without paying for every such change in the general law," *id.,* at 413, 43 S.Ct., at 159—does not apply to the relatively rare situations where the government has deprived a landowner of all economically beneficial uses.

On the other side of the balance, affirmatively supporting a compensation requirement, is the fact that regulations that leave the owner of land without economically beneficial or productive options for its use—typically, as here, by requiring land to be left substantially in its natural state—carry with them a heightened risk that private property is being pressed into some form of public service under the guise of mitigating serious public harm. See, *e.g.*, *Annicelli v. South Kingstown*, 463 A.2d 133, 140–141 (R.I.1983) (prohibition on construction adjacent to beach justified on twin grounds of safety and "conservation of open space"); *Morris County Land Improvement Co. v. Parsippany-Troy Hills Township*, 40 N.J. 539, 552–553, 193 A.2d 232, 240 (1963) (prohibition on filling marshlands imposed in order to preserve region as water detention basin and create wildlife refuge). As Justice Brennan explained: "From the government's point of view, the benefits flowing to the public from preservation of open space through regulation may be equally great as from creating a wildlife refuge through formal condemnation or increasing electricity production through a dam project that floods private property." *San Diego Gas & Elec. Co., supra*, 450 U.S., at 652, 101 S.Ct., at 1304 (dissenting opinion). The many statutes on the books, both state and federal, that provide for the use of eminent domain to impose servitudes on private scenic lands preventing developmental uses, or to acquire such lands altogether, suggest the practical equivalence in this setting of negative regulation and appropriation. See, *e.g.*, 16 U.S.C. § 410ff-1(a) (authorizing acquisition of "lands, waters, or interests [within Channel Islands National Park] (including but not limited to scenic easements)"); § 460aa-2(a) (authorizing acquisition of "any lands, or lesser interests therein, including mineral interests and scenic easements" within Sawtooth National Recreation Area); §§ 3921–3923 (authorizing acquisition of wetlands); N.C. Gen.Stat. § 113A-38 (1990) (authorizing acquisition of, *inter alia,* "'scenic easements'" within the North Carolina natural and scenic rivers system); Tenn.Code Ann. §§ 11-15-101 to 11-15-108 (1987) (authorizing acquisition of "protective easements" and other rights in real property adjacent to State's historic, architectural, archaeological, or cultural resources).

We think, in short, that there are good reasons for our frequently expressed belief that when the owner of real property has been called upon to sacrifice *all* economically beneficial uses in the name of the common good, that is, to leave his property economically idle, he has suffered a taking.

B

The trial court found Lucas's two beachfront lots to have been rendered valueless by respondent's enforcement of the coastal-zone construction ban. Under Lucas's theory of the case, which rested upon our "no economically viable use" statements, that finding entitled him to compensation. Lucas believed it unnecessary to take issue with either the purposes behind the Beachfront Management Act, or the means chosen by the South Carolina Legislature to effectuate those purposes. The South Carolina Supreme Court, however, thought otherwise. In its view, the Beachfront Management Act was no ordinary enactment, but involved an exercise of South Carolina's "police powers" to mitigate the harm to the public interest that petitioner's use of his land might occasion. 304 S.C., at 384, 404 S.E.2d, at 899. By neglecting to dispute the findings enumerated in the Act or otherwise to challenge the legislature's purposes, petitioner "concede [d] that the beach/dune area of South Carolina's shores is an extremely valuable public resource; that the erection of new construction, *inter alia,* contributes to the erosion and destruction of this public resource; and that discouraging new construction in close proximity to the beach/dune area is necessary to prevent a great public harm." *Id.*, at 382–383, 404 S.E.2d, at 898. In the court's view, these concessions brought petitioner's challenge within a long line of this Court's cases sustaining against Due Process and Takings Clause challenges the State's use of its "police powers" to enjoin a property owner from activities akin to public nuisances. See *Mugler v. Kansas,* 123 U.S. 623, 8 S.Ct. 273, 31 L.Ed. 205 (1887) (law prohibiting manufacture of alcoholic beverages); *Hadacheck v. Sebastian,* 239 U.S. 394, 36 S.Ct. 143, 60 L.Ed. 348 (1915) (law barring operation of brick mill in residential area); *Miller v. Schoene,* 276 U.S. 272, 48 S.Ct. 246, 72 L.Ed. 568 (1928) (order to destroy diseased cedar trees to prevent infection of nearby orchards); *Goldblatt v. Hempstead,* 369 U.S. 590, 82 S.Ct. 987, 8 L.Ed.2d 130 (1962) (law effectively preventing continued operation of quarry in residential area).

It is correct that many of our prior opinions have suggested that "harmful or noxious uses" of property may be proscribed by government regulation without the requirement of compensation. For a number of reasons, however, we think the South Carolina Supreme Court was too quick to conclude that that principle decides the present case. The "harmful or noxious uses" principle was the Court's early attempt to describe in theoretical terms why government may, consistent with the Takings Clause, affect property values by regulation without incurring an obligation to compensate—a reality we nowadays acknowledge explicitly with respect to the full scope of the State's police power. See, *e.g., Penn Central Transportation Co.,* 438 U.S., at 125, 98 S.Ct., at 2659 (where State "reasonably conclude[s] that 'the health, safety, morals, or general welfare' would be promoted by prohibiting particular contemplated uses of land," compensation need not accompany prohibition); see also *Nollan v. California Coastal*

Comm'n, 483 U.S., at 834–835, 107 S.Ct., at 3147 ("Our cases have not elaborated on the standards for determining what constitutes a 'legitimate state interest[,]' [but] [t]hey have made clear ... that a broad range of governmental purposes and regulations satisfy these requirements"). We made this very point in *Penn Central Transportation Co.,* where, in the course of sustaining New York City's landmarks preservation program against a takings challenge, we rejected the petitioner's suggestion that *Mugler* and the cases following it were premised on, and thus limited by, some objective conception of "noxiousness":

> "[T]he uses in issue in *Hadacheck, Miller,* and *Goldblatt* were perfectly lawful in themselves. They involved no 'blameworthiness, ... moral wrongdoing or conscious act of dangerous risk-taking which induce[d society] to shift the cost to a pa[rt]icular individual.' Sax, "Takings and the Police Power," 74 *Yale L.J.* 36, 50 (1964). These cases are better understood as resting not on any supposed 'noxious' quality of the prohibited uses but rather on the ground that the restrictions were reasonably related to the implementation of a policy—not unlike historic preservation—expected to produce a widespread public benefit and applicable to all similarly situated property." 438 U.S., at 133–134, n. 30, 98 S.Ct., at 2664, n. 30.

"Harmful or noxious use" analysis was, in other words, simply the progenitor of our more contemporary statements that "land-use regulation does not effect a taking if it 'substantially advance[s] legitimate state interests'...." *Nollan, supra,* 483 U.S., at 834, 107 S.Ct., at 3147 (quoting *Agins v. Tiburon,* 447 U.S., at 260, 100 S.Ct., at 2141); see also *Penn Central Transportation Co., supra,* 438 U.S., at 127, 98 S.Ct., at 2660; *Euclid v. Ambler Realty Co.,* 272 U.S. 365, 387–388, 47 S.Ct. 114, 118, 71 L.Ed. 303 (1926).

The transition from our early focus on control of "noxious" uses to our contemporary understanding of the broad realm within which government may regulate without compensation was an easy one, since the distinction between "harm-preventing" and "benefit-conferring" regulation is often in the eye of the beholder. It is quite possible, for example, to describe in *either* fashion the ecological, economic, and esthetic concerns that inspired the South Carolina Legislature in the present case. One could say that imposing a servitude on Lucas's land is necessary in order to prevent his use of it from "harming" South Carolina's ecological resources; or, instead, in order to achieve the "benefits" of an ecological preserve. Compare, *e.g.*, *Claridge v. New Hampshire Wetlands Board,* 125 N.H. 745, 752, 485 A.2d 287, 292 (1984) (owner may, without compensation, be barred from filling wetlands because landfilling would deprive adjacent coastal habitats and marine fisheries of ecological support), with, *e.g.*, *Bartlett v. Zoning Comm'n of Old Lyme,* 161 Conn. 24, 30, 282 A.2d 907, 910 (1971) (owner barred from filling tidal marshland must be compensated, despite municipality's "laudable" goal of "preserv[ing] marshlands from encroachment or destruction"). Whether one or the other of the competing characterizations will come to one's lips in a particular case depends primarily upon one's evaluation of the worth of competing uses of real estate. See *Restatement* (*Second*) *of Torts* § 822, Comment g, p. 112 (1979) ("Practically all human activities unless carried on in a wilderness interfere to some extent with others or involve some risk of interference"). A given restraint will be seen as mitigating "harm" to the adjacent parcels or securing a "benefit" for them, depending upon the observer's evaluation of the relative importance of the use that the restraint favors. See Sax, "Takings and the Police Power," 74 *Yale L.J.* 36, 49 (1964) ("[T]he problem [in this area] is not one of noxiousness or harm-creating activity at all; rather it is a problem of inconsistency between perfectly innocent and independently desirable uses"). Whether Lucas's construction of single-family residences on his parcels should be described as bringing "harm" to South Carolina's adjacent ecological resources thus depends principally upon whether the describer believes that the State's use interest in nurturing those resources is so important that *any* competing adjacent use must yield.

When it is understood that "prevention of harmful use" was merely our early formulation of the police power justification necessary to sustain (without compensation) *any* regulatory diminution in value; and that the distinction between regulation that "prevents harmful use" and that which "confers benefits" is difficult, if not impossible, to discern on an objective, value-free basis; it becomes self-evident that noxious-use logic cannot serve as a touchstone to distinguish regulatory "takings"—which require compensation—from regulatory deprivations that do not require compensation. *A fortiori* the legislature's recitation of a noxious-use justification cannot be the basis for departing from our categorical rule that total regulatory takings must be compensated. If it were, departure would virtually always be allowed. The South Carolina Supreme Court's approach would essentially nullify *Mahon*'s affirmation of limits to the noncompensable exercise of the police power. Our cases provide no support for this: None of them that employed the logic of "harmful use" prevention to sustain a regulation involved an allegation that the regulation wholly eliminated the value of the claimant's land. See *Keystone Bituminous Coal Assn.,* 480 U.S., at 513–514, 107 S.Ct., at 1257 (Rehnquist, C.J., dissenting).

Where the State seeks to sustain regulation that deprives land of all economically beneficial use, we think it may resist compensation only if the logically antecedent inquiry into the nature of the owner's estate shows that the proscribed use interests were not part of his title to begin with. This accords, we think, with our "takings" jurisprudence, which has traditionally been guided by the understandings of our citizens regarding the content of, and the State's power over, the "bundle of rights" that they acquire when they obtain title to property. It seems to us that the property owner necessarily expects the uses of his property to be restricted, from time to time, by various measures newly enacted by the State in legitimate exercise of its police powers; "[a]s long recognized, some values are enjoyed under an implied limitation and must yield to the police power." *Pennsylvania Coal Co. v. Mahon,* 260 U.S., at 413, 43 S.Ct., at 159. And in the case of personal property, by reason of the State's traditionally high degree of control over commercial dealings, he ought to be aware of the possibility that new regulation might even render his property economically worthless (at least if the property's only economically productive use is sale or manufacture for sale). See *Andrus v. Allard,* 444 U.S. 51, 66–67, 100 S.Ct. 318, 327, 62 L.Ed.2d 210 (1979) (prohibition on sale of eagle feathers). In the case of land, however, we think the notion pressed by the Council that title is somehow held subject to the "implied limitation" that the State may subsequently eliminate all economically valuable use is inconsistent with the historical compact recorded in the Takings Clause that has become part of our constitutional culture.

Where "permanent physical occupation" of land is concerned, we have refused to allow the government to decree it anew (without compensation), no matter how weighty the asserted "public interests" involved, *Loretto v. Teleprompter Manhattan CATV Corp.,* 458 U.S., at 426, 102 S.Ct., at 3171—though we assuredly *would* permit the government to assert a permanent easement that was a pre-existing limitation upon the land owner's title. Compare *Scranton v. Wheeler,* 179 U.S. 141, 163, 21 S.Ct. 48, 57, 45 L.Ed. 126 (1900) (interests of "riparian owner in the submerged lands ... bordering on a public navigable water" held subject to Government's navigational servitude), with *Kaiser Aetna v. United States,* 444 U.S., at 178–180, 100 S.Ct., at 392–393 (imposition of navigational servitude on marina created and rendered navigable at private expense held to constitute a taking). We believe similar treatment must be accorded confiscatory regulations, *i.e.,* regulations that prohibit all economically beneficial use of land: Any limitation so severe cannot be newly legislated or decreed (without compensation), but must inhere in the title itself, in the restrictions that background principles of the State's law of property and nuisance already place upon land ownership. A law or decree with such an effect must, in other words, do no more than duplicate the result that could have been achieved in the courts—by adjacent landowners (or other uniquely affected persons) under the State's law of private nuisance, or by the State under its complementary power to abate nuisances that affect the public generally, or otherwise.

On this analysis, the owner of a lake-bed, for example, would not be entitled to compensation when he is denied the requisite permit to engage in a landfilling operation that would have the effect of flooding others' land. Nor the corporate owner of a nuclear generating plant, when it is directed to remove all improvements from its land upon discovery that the plant sits astride an earthquake fault. Such regulatory action may well have the effect of eliminating the land's only economically productive use, but it does not proscribe a productive use that was previously permissible under relevant property and nuisance principles. The use of these properties for what are now expressly prohibited purposes was *always* unlawful, and (subject to other constitutional limitations) it was open to the State at any point to make the implication of those background principles of nuisance and property law explicit. See Michelman, "Property, Utility, and Fairness, Comments on the Ethical Foundations of 'Just Compensation' Law," 80 *Harv.L.Rev.* 1165, 1239–1241 (1967). In light of our traditional resort to "existing rules or understandings that stem from an independent source such as state law" to define the range of interests that qualify for protection as "property" under the Fifth and Fourteenth Amendments, *Board of Regents of State Colleges v. Roth,* 408 U.S. 564, 577, 92 S.Ct. 2701, 2709, 33 L.Ed.2d 548 (1972); see, *e.g., Ruckelshaus v. Monsanto Co.,* 467 U.S. 986, 1011–1012, 104 S.Ct. 2862, 2877, 81 L.Ed.2d 815 (1984); *Hughes v. Washington,* 389 U.S. 290, 295, 88 S.Ct. 438, 441, 19 L.Ed.2d 530 (1967) (Stewart, J., concurring), this recognition that the Takings Clause does not require compensation when an owner is barred from putting land to a use that is proscribed by those "existing rules or understandings" is surely unexceptional. When, however, a regulation that declares "off-limits" all economically productive or beneficial uses of land goes beyond what the relevant background principles would dictate, compensation must be paid to sustain it.

The "total taking" inquiry we require today will ordinarily entail (as the application of state nuisance law ordinarily entails) analysis of, among other things, the degree of harm to public lands and resources, or adjacent private property, posed by the claimant's proposed activities, see, *e.g., Restatement (Second) of Torts* §§ 826, 827, the social value of the claimant's activities and their suitability to the locality in question, see, *e.g., id.,* §§ 828(a) and (b), 831, and the relative ease with which the alleged harm can be avoided through measures taken by the claimant and the government (or adjacent private landowners) alike, see, *e.g., id.,* §§ 827(e), 828(c), 830. The fact that a particular use has long been engaged in by similarly situated owners ordinarily imports a lack of any common-law prohibition (though changed circumstances or new knowledge may make what was previously permissible no longer so, see *id.*, § 827, Comment *g*. So also does the fact that other landowners, similarly situated, are permitted to continue the use denied to the claimant.

It seems unlikely that common-law principles would have prevented the erection of any habitable or productive improvements on petitioner's land; they rarely support prohibition of the "essential use" of land, *Curtin v. Benson,* 222 U.S. 78, 86, 32 S.Ct. 31, 33, 56 L.Ed. 102 (1911). The question, however, is one of state law to be dealt with on remand. We emphasize that to win its case South Carolina must do more than proffer the legislature's declaration that the uses Lucas desires are inconsistent with the public interest, or the conclusory assertion that they violate a common-law maxim such as *sic utere tuo ut alienum non laedas.* As we have said, a "State, by *ipse dixit,* may not transform private property into public property without compensation...." *Webb's Fabulous Pharmacies, Inc. v. Beckwith,* 449 U.S. 155, 164, 101 S.Ct. 446, 452, 66 L.Ed.2d 358 (1980). Instead, as it would be required to do if it sought to restrain Lucas in a common-law action for public nuisance, South Carolina must identify background principles of nuisance and property law that prohibit the uses he now intends in the circumstances in which the property is presently found. Only on this showing can the State fairly claim that, in proscribing all such beneficial uses, the Beachfront Management Act is taking nothing.

The judgment is reversed, and the case is remanded for proceedings not inconsistent with this opinion.

So ordered.

Background Checks, Gun Control, and State Rights

Printz v. United States,

521 U.S. 898 (1997)

Justice Scalia delivered the opinion of the Court.

The question presented in these cases is whether certain interim provisions of the Brady Handgun Violence Prevention Act, Pub.L. 103–159, 107 Stat. 1536, commanding state and local law enforcement officers to conduct background checks on prospective handgun purchasers and to perform certain related tasks, violate the Constitution.

I

The Gun Control Act of 1968(GCA), 18 U.S.C. § 921 *et seq.*, establishes a detailed federal scheme governing the distribution of firearms. It prohibits firearms dealers from transferring handguns to any person under 21, not resident in the dealer's State, or prohibited by state or local law from purchasing or possessing firearms, § 922(b). It also forbids possession of a firearm by, and transfer of a firearm to, convicted felons, fugitives from justice, unlawful users of controlled substances, persons adjudicated as mentally defective or committed to mental institutions, aliens unlawfully present in the United States, persons dishonorably discharged from the Armed Forces, persons who have renounced their citizenship, and persons who have been subjected to certain restraining orders or been convicted of a misdemeanor offense involving domestic violence. §§ 922(d) and (g).

In 1993, Congress amended the GCA by enacting the Brady Act. The Act requires the Attorney General to establish a national instant background-check system by November 30, 1998, Pub.L. 103–159, as amended, Pub.L. 103–322, 103 Stat. 2074, note following 18 U.S.C. § 922, and immediately puts in place certain interim provisions until that system becomes operative. Under the interim provisions, a firearms dealer who proposes to transfer a handgun must first: (1) receive from the transferee a statement (the Brady Form), § 922(s)(1)(A)(i)(I), containing the name, address, and date of birth of the proposed transferee along with a sworn statement that the transferee is not among any of the classes of prohibited purchasers, § 922(s)(3); (2) verify the identity of the transferee by examining an identification document, § 922(s)(1)(A)(i)(II); and (3) provide the "chief law enforcement officer" (CLEO) of the transferee's residence with notice of the contents (and a copy) of the Brady Form, §§ 922(s)(1)(A)(i)(III) and (IV). With some exceptions, the dealer must then wait five business days before consummating the sale, unless the CLEO earlier notifies the dealer that he has no reason to believe the transfer would be illegal. § 922(s)(1)(A)(ii).

The Brady Act creates two significant alternatives to the foregoing scheme. A dealer may sell a handgun immediately if the purchaser possesses a state handgun permit issued after a background check, § 922(s)(1)(C), or if state law provides for an instant background check, § 922(s)(1)(D). In States that have not rendered one of these alternatives applicable to all gun purchasers, CLEOs are required to perform certain duties. When a CLEO receives the required notice of a proposed transfer from the firearms dealer, the CLEO must "make a reasonable effort to ascertain within 5 business days whether receipt or possession would be in violation of the law, including research in whatever State and local recordkeeping systems are available and in a national system designated by the Attorney General." § 922(s)(2). The Act does not require the CLEO to take any particular action if he determines that a pending transaction would be unlawful; he may notify the firearms dealer to that effect, but is not required to do so. If, however, the CLEO notifies a gun dealer that a prospective purchaser is ineligible to receive a handgun, he must, upon request, provide the would-be purchaser with a written statement of the reasons for that determination. § 922(s)(6)(C). Moreover, if the CLEO does not discover any basis for objecting to the sale, he must destroy any records in his possession relating to the transfer, including his copy of the Brady Form. § 922(s)(6)(B)(i). Under a separate provision of the GCA, any person who "knowingly violates [the section of the GCA amended by the Brady Act] shall be fined under this title, imprisoned for not more than 1 year, or both." § 924(a)(5).

Petitioners Jay Printz and Richard Mack, the CLEOs for Ravalli County, Montana, and Graham County, Arizona, respectively, filed separate actions challenging the constitutionality of the Brady Act's interim provisions. In each case, the District Court held that the provision requiring CLEOs to perform background checks was unconstitutional, but concluded that that provision was severable from the remainder of the Act, effectively leaving a voluntary background-check system in place. 856 F.Supp. 1372 (D.Ariz.1994); 854 F.Supp. 1503 (D.Mont.1994). A divided panel of the Court of Appeals for the Ninth Circuit reversed, finding none of the Brady Act's interim provisions to be unconstitutional. 66 F.3d 1025 (1995). We granted certiorari. 518 U.S. 1003, 116 S.Ct. 2521, 135 L.Ed.2d 1046 (1996).

II

From the description set forth above, it is apparent that the Brady Act purports to direct state law enforcement officers to participate, albeit only temporarily, in the administration of a federally enacted regulatory scheme. Regulated firearms dealers are required to forward Brady Forms not to a federal officer or employee, but to the CLEOs, whose obligation to accept those forms is implicit in the duty imposed upon them to make "reasonable efforts" within five days to determine whether the sales reflected in the forms are lawful. While the CLEOs are subjected to no federal requirement that they prevent the sales determined to be unlawful (it is perhaps assumed that their state-law duties will require prevention or apprehension), they are empowered to grant, in effect, waivers of the federally prescribed 5-day waiting period for handgun purchases by notifying the gun dealers that they have no reason to believe the transactions would be illegal.

Petitioners here object to being pressed into federal service, and contend that congressional action compelling state officers to execute federal laws is unconstitutional. Because there is no constitutional text speaking to this precise question, the answer to the CLEOs' challenge must be sought in historical understanding and practice, in the structure of the Constitution, and in the jurisprudence of this Court. We treat those three sources, in that order, in this and the next two sections of this opinion.

Petitioners contend that compelled enlistment of state executive officers for the administration of federal programs is, until very recent years at least, unprecedented. The Government contends, to the contrary, that "the earliest Congresses enacted statutes that required the participation of state officials in the implementation of federal laws," Brief for United States 28. The Government's contention demands our careful consideration, since early congressional enactments "provid[e] 'contemporaneous and weighty evidence' of the Constitution's meaning," *Bowsher v. Synar,* 478 U.S. 714, 723–

724, 106 S.Ct. 3181, 3186, 92 L.Ed.2d 583 (1986) (quoting *Marsh v. Chambers,* 463 U.S. 783, 790, 103 S.Ct. 3330, 3335, 77 L.Ed.2d 1019 (1983)). Indeed, such "contemporaneous legislative exposition of the Constitution ..., acquiesced in for a long term of years, fixes the construction to be given its provisions." *Myers v. United States,* 272 U.S. 52, 175, 47 S.Ct. 21, 45, 71 L.Ed. 160 (1926) (citing numerous cases). Conversely if, as petitioners contend, earlier Congresses avoided use of this highly attractive power, we would have reason to believe that the power was thought not to exist.

The Government observes that statutes enacted by the first Congresses required state courts to record applications for citizenship, Act of Mar. 26, 1790, ch. 3, § 1, 1 Stat. 103, to transmit abstracts of citizenship applications and other naturalization records to the Secretary of State, Act of June 18, 1798, ch. 54, § 2, 1 Stat. 567, and to register aliens seeking naturalization and issue certificates of registry, Act of Apr. 14, 1802, ch. 28, § 2, 2 Stat. 154–155. It may well be, however, that these requirements applied only in States that authorized their courts to conduct naturalization proceedings. See Act of Mar. 26, 1790, ch. 3, § 1, 1 Stat. 103; *Holmgren v. United States,* 217 U.S. 509, 516–517, 30 S.Ct. 588, 589, 54 L.Ed. 861 (1910) (explaining that the Act of March 26, 1790, "conferred authority upon state courts to admit aliens to citizenship" and refraining from addressing the question "whether the States can be required to enforce such naturalization laws against their consent"); *United States v. Jones,* 109 U.S. 513, 519–520, 3 S.Ct. 346, 351, 27 L.Ed. 1015 (1883) (stating that these obligations were imposed "with the consent of the States" and "could not be enforced against the consent of the States"). Other statutes of that era apparently or at least arguably required state courts to perform functions unrelated to naturalization, such as resolving controversies between a captain and the crew of his ship concerning the seaworthiness of the vessel, Act of July 20, 1790, ch. 29, § 3, 1 Stat. 132, hearing the claims of slave owners who had apprehended fugitive slaves and issuing certificates authorizing the slave's forced removal to the State from which he had fled, Act of Feb. 12, 1793, ch. 7, § 3, 1 Stat. 302–305, taking proof of the claims of Canadian refugees who had assisted the United States during the Revolutionary War, Act of Apr. 7, 1798, ch. 26, § 3, 1 Stat. 548, and ordering the deportation of alien enemies in times of war, Act of July 6, 1798, ch. 66, § 2, 1 Stat. 577–578.

These early laws establish, at most, that the Constitution was originally understood to permit imposition of an obligation on state *judges* to enforce federal prescriptions, insofar as those prescriptions related to matters appropriate for the judicial power. That assumption was perhaps implicit in one of the provisions of the Constitution, and was explicit in another. In accord with the so-called Madisonian Compromise, Article III, § 1, established only a Supreme Court, and made the creation of lower federal courts optional with the Congress—even though it was obvious that the Supreme Court alone could not hear all federal cases throughout the United States. See C. Warren, *The Making of the Constitution* 325–327 (1928). And the Supremacy Clause, Art. VI, cl. 2, announced that "the Laws of the United States ... shall be the supreme Law of the Land; and the Judges in every State shall be bound thereby." It is understandable why courts should have been viewed distinctively in this regard; unlike legislatures and executives, they applied the law of other sovereigns all the time. The principle underlying so-called "transitory" causes of action was that laws which operated elsewhere created obligations in justice that courts of the forum State would enforce. See, *e.g.*, *McKenna v. Fisk*, 1 How. 241, 247–249, 11 L.Ed. 117 (1843). The Constitution itself, in the Full Faith and Credit Clause, Art. IV, § 1, generally required such enforcement with respect to obligations arising in other States. See *Hughes v. Fetter*, 341 U.S. 609, 71 S.Ct. 980, 95 L.Ed. 1212 (1951).

For these reasons, we do not think the early statutes imposing obligations on state courts imply a power of Congress to impress the state executive into its service. Indeed, it can be argued that the numerousness of these statutes, contrasted with the utter lack of statutes imposing obligations on the States' executive (notwithstanding the attractiveness of that course to Congress), suggests an assumed *absence* of such power. The only early federal law the Government has brought to our attention that imposed duties on state executive officers is the Extradition Act of 1793, which required the "executive authority" of a State to cause the arrest and delivery of a fugitive from justice upon the request of the executive authority of the State from which the fugitive had fled. See Act of Feb. 12, 1793, ch. 7, § 1, 1 Stat. 302. That was in direct implementation, however, of the Extradition Clause of the Constitution itself, see Art. IV, § 2.

Not only do the enactments of the early Congresses, as far as we are aware, contain no evidence of an assumption that the Federal Government may command the States' executive power in the absence of a particularized constitutional authorization, they contain some indication of precisely the opposite assumption. On September 23, 1789—the day before its proposal of the Bill of Rights, see 1 Annals of Congress 912–913—the First Congress enacted a law aimed at obtaining state assistance of the most rudimentary and necessary sort for the enforcement of the new Government's laws: the holding of federal prisoners in state jails at federal expense. Significantly, the law issued not a command to the States' executive, but a recommendation to their legislatures. Congress "recommended to the legislatures of the several States to pass laws, making it expressly the duty of the keepers of their gaols, to receive and safe keep therein all prisoners committed under the authority of the United States," and offered to pay 50 cents per month for each prisoner. Act of Sept. 23, 1789, 1 Stat. 96. Moreover, when Georgia refused to comply with the request, see L. White, *The Federalists* 402 (1948), Congress's only reaction was a law authorizing the marshal in any State that failed to comply with the Recommendation of September 23, 1789, to rent a temporary jail until provision for a permanent one could be made, see Resolution of Mar. 3, 1791, 1 Stat. 225.

In addition to early legislation, the Government also appeals to other sources we have usually regarded as indicative of the original understanding of the Constitution. It points to portions of *The Federalist* which reply to criticisms that Congress's power to tax will produce two sets of revenue officers—for example, "Brutus's" assertion in his letter to the New York Journal of December 13, 1787, that the Constitution "opens a door to the appointment of a swarm of revenue and excise officers to prey upon the honest and industrious part of the community, eat up their substance, and riot on the spoils of the country," reprinted in 1 *Debate on the Constitution* 502 (B. Bailyn ed. 1993). "Publius' responded that Congress will probably "make use of the State officers and State regulations, for collecting" federal taxes, *The Federalist* No. 36, p. 221 (C. Rossiter ed. 1961) (A. Hamilton) (hereinafter *The Federalist*), and predicted that "the eventual collection [of internal revenue] under the immediate authority of the Union, will generally be made by the officers, and according to the rules, appointed by the several States," *id.*, No. 45, at 292 (J. Madison). The Government also invokes *The Federalist*'s more general observations that the Constitution would "enable the [national] government to employ the ordinary magistracy of each [State] in the execution of its laws," *id.*, No. 27, at 176 (A. Hamilton), and that it was "extremely probable that in other instances, particularly in the organization of the judicial power, the officers of the States will be clothed with the correspondent authority of the Union," *id.*, No. 45, at 292 (J. Madison). But none of these statements necessarily implies—what is the critical point here—that Congress could impose these responsibilities *without the consent of the States.* They appear to rest on the natural assumption that the States would consent to allowing their officials to assist the Federal Government, see *FERC v. Mississippi,* 456 U.S. 742, 796, n. 35, 102 S.Ct. 2126, 2157, n. 35, 72 L.Ed.2d 532 (1982) (O'Connor, J., concurring in judgment in part and dissenting in part), an assumption proved correct by the extensive mutual assistance the States and Federal Government voluntarily provided one another in the early days of the Republic, see generally White, *supra,* at 401–404, including voluntary *federal implementation of state law,* see, *e.g.*, Act of Apr. 2, 1790, ch. 5, § 1, 1 Stat. 106 (directing federal tax collectors and customs officers to assist in enforcing state inspection laws).

Another passage of *The Federalist* reads as follows:

> "It merits particular attention ... that the laws of the Confederacy as to the *enumerated* and *legitimate* objects of its jurisdiction will become the supreme law of the land; to the observance of which all officers, legislative, executive, and judicial in each State will be bound by the sanctity of an oath. Thus, the legislatures, courts, and magistrates, of the respective members will be incorporated into the operations of the national government *as far as its just and constitutional authority extends;* and will be rendered auxiliary to the enforcement of its laws." *The Federalist* No. 27, at 177 (A. Hamilton) (emphasis in original).

The Government does not rely upon this passage, but Justice Souter (with whose conclusions on this point the dissent is in agreement, see *post,* at 2390 makes it the very foundation of his position; so we pause to examine it in some detail. Justice Souter finds "[t]he natural reading" of the phrases "'will be incorporated into the operations of the national government'" and "'will be rendered auxiliary to the enforcement of its laws'" to be that the National Government will have "authority ..., when exercising an otherwise legitimate power (the commerce power, say), to require state 'auxiliaries' to take appropriate action." *Post,* at 2402. There are several obstacles to such an interpretation. First, the consequences in question ("incorporated into the operations of the national government" and "rendered auxiliary to the enforcement of its laws") are said in the quoted passage to flow *automatically* from the officers' oath to observe "the laws of the Confederacy as to the *enumerated* and *legitimate* objects of its jurisdiction." Thus, if the passage means that state officers must take an active role in the implementation of federal law, it means that they must do so without the necessity for a congressional directive that they implement it. But no one has ever thought, and no one asserts in the present litigation, that that is the law. The second problem with Justice Souter's reading is that it makes state *legislatures* subject to federal direction. (The passage in question, after all, does not include legislatures merely incidentally, as by referring to "all state officers"; it refers to legislatures *specifically* and *first of all.*) We have held, however, that state legislatures are *not* subject to federal direction. *New York v. United States,* 505 U.S. 144, 112 S.Ct. 2408, 120 L.Ed.2d 120 (1992).

These problems are avoided, of course, if the calculatedly vague consequences the passage recites—"incorporated into the operations of the national government" and "rendered auxiliary to the enforcement of its laws"—are taken to refer to nothing more (or less) than the duty owed to the National Government, on the part of *all* state officials, to enact, enforce, and interpret state law in such fashion as not to obstruct the operation of federal law, and the attendant reality that all state actions constituting such obstruction, even legislative Acts, are *ipso facto* invalid. See *Silkwood v. Kerr-McGee Corp.*, 464 U.S. 238, 248, 104 S.Ct. 615, 621, 78 L.Ed.2d 443 (1984) (federal pre-emption of conflicting state law). This meaning accords well with the context of the passage, which seeks to explain why the new system of federal law directed to individual citizens, unlike the old one of federal law directed to the States, will "bid much fairer to avoid the necessity of using force" against the States, *The Federalist* No. 27, at 176. It also reconciles the passage with Hamilton's statement in *The Federalist* No. 36, at 222, that the Federal Government would in some circumstances do well "to employ the State officers as much as possible, and to attach them to the Union by an accumulation of their emoluments"—which surely suggests inducing state officers to come aboard by paying them, rather than merely commandeering their official services.

Justice Souter contends that his interpretation of *The Federalist* No. 27 is "supported by No. 44," written by Madison, wherefore he claims that "Madison and Hamilton" together stand opposed to our view. *Post,* at 2402, 2404. In fact, *The Federalist* No. 44 quite clearly contradicts Justice Souter's reading. In that Number, Madison justifies the requirement that state officials take an oath to support the Federal Constitution on the ground that they "will have an essential agency in giving effect to the federal Constitution." If the dissent's reading of *The Federalist* No. 27 were correct (and if Madison agreed with it), one would surely have expected that "essential agency" of state executive officers (if described further) to be described as their responsibility to execute the laws enacted under the Constitution. Instead, however, *The Federalist* No. 44 continues with the following description:

> "The election of the President and Senate will depend, in all cases, on the legislatures of the several States. And the election of the House of Representatives will equally depend on the same authority in the first instance; and will, probably, forever *be conducted by the officers* and according to the laws *of the States.*" *Id.*, at 287 (emphasis added).

It is most implausible that the person who labored for that example of state executive officers' assisting the Federal Government believed, but neglected to mention, that they had a responsibility to execute federal laws. If it was indeed Hamilton's view that the Federal Government could direct the officers of the States, that view has no clear support in Madison's writings, or as far as we are aware, in text, history, or early commentary elsewhere.

To complete the historical record, we must note that there is not only an absence of executive-commandeering statutes in the early Congresses, but there is an absence of them in our later history as well, at least until very recent years. The Government points to the Act of August 3, 1882, ch. 376, §§ 2, 4, 22 Stat. 214, which enlisted state officials "to take charge of the local affairs of immigration in the ports within such State, and to provide for the support and relief of such immigrants therein landing as may fall into distress or need of public aid"; to inspect arriving immigrants and exclude any person found to be a "convict, lunatic, idiot," or indigent; and to send convicts back to their country of origin "without compensation." The statute did not, however, *mandate* those duties, but merely empowered the Secretary of the Treasury "to *enter into contracts* with such State ... officers as *may be designated* for that purpose *by the governor* of any State." (Emphasis added.)

The Government cites the World War I selective draft law that authorized the President "to utilize the service of any or all departments and any or all officers or agents of the United States *and of the several States,* Territories, and the District of Columbia, and subdivisions thereof, in the execution of this Act," and made any person who refused to comply with the President's directions guilty of a misdemeanor. Act of May 18, 1917, ch. 15, § 6, 40 Stat. 80–81 (emphasis added). However, it is far from clear that the authorization "to utilize the service" of state officers was an authorization to *compel* the service of state officers; and the misdemeanor provision surely applied only to refusal to comply with the President's *authorized* directions, which might not have included directions to officers of States whose Governors had not volunteered their services. It is interesting that in implementing the Act President Wilson did not commandeer the services of state officers, but instead requested the assistance of the States' Governors, see Proclamation of May 18, 1917, 40 Stat. 1665 ("call[ing] upon the Governor of each of the several States ... and all officers and agents of the several States ... to perform certain duties"); Registration Regulations Prescribed by the President Under the Act of Congress Approved May 18, 1917, pt. 1, § 7 ("[T]he governor [of each State] is *requested* to act under the regulations and rules prescribed by the President or under his direction" (emphasis added)), obtained the consent of each of the Governors, see Note, The President, the Senate, the Constitution, and the Executive Order of May 8, 1926, 21 Ill. L.Rev. 142, 144 (1926), and left it to the Governors to issue orders to their subordinate state officers, see Selective Service Regulations Prescribed by the President Under the Act of May 18, 1917, § 27 (1918); J. Clark, The Rise of a New Federalism 91 (1965). See generally Note, 21 Ill. L.Rev., at 144. It is impressive that even with respect to a wartime measure the President should have been so solicitous of state independence.

The Government points to a number of federal statutes enacted within the past few decades that require the participation of state or local officials in implementing federal regulatory schemes. Some of these are connected to federal funding measures, and can perhaps be more accurately described as conditions upon the grant of federal funding than as mandates to the States; others, which require only the provision of information to the Federal Government, do not involve the precise issue before us here, which is the forced participation of the States' executive in the actual administration of a federal program. We of course do not address these or other currently operative enactments that are not before us; it will be time enough to do so if and when their validity is challenged in a proper case. For deciding the issue before us here, they are of little relevance. Even assuming they represent assertion of the very same congressional power challenged here, they are of such recent vintage that they are no more probative than the statute before us of a constitutional tradition that lends meaning to the text. Their persuasive force is far outweighed by almost two centuries of apparent congressional avoidance of the practice. Compare *INS v. Chadha,* 462 U.S. 919, 103 S.Ct. 2764, 77 L.Ed.2d 317 (1983), in which the legislative veto, though enshrined in perhaps hundreds of federal statutes, most of which were enacted in the 1970's and the earliest of which was enacted in 1932, see *id.,* at 967–975, 103 S.Ct., at 2792–2796 (White, J., dissenting), was nonetheless held unconstitutional.

III

The constitutional practice we have examined above tends to negate the existence of the congressional power asserted here, but is not conclusive. We turn next to consideration of the structure of the Constitution, to see if we can discern among its "essential postulate[s]," *Principality of Monaco v. Mississippi,* 292 U.S. 313, 322, 54 S.Ct. 745, 748, 78 L.Ed. 1282 (1934), a principle that controls the present cases.

A

It is incontestible that the Constitution established a system of "dual sovereignty." *Gregory v. Ashcroft,* 501 U.S. 452, 457, 111 S.Ct. 2395, 2399, 115 L.Ed.2d 410 (1991); *Tafflin v. Levitt,* 493 U.S. 455, 458, 110 S.Ct. 792, 795, 107 L.Ed.2d 887 (1990). Although the States surrendered many of their powers to the new Federal Government, they retained "a residuary and inviolable sovereignty," *The Federalist* No. 39, at 245 (J. Madison). This is reflected throughout the Constitution's text, *Lane County v. Oregon,* 7 Wall. 71, 76, 19 L.Ed. 101 (1869); *Texas v. White,* 7 Wall. 700, 725, 19 L.Ed. 227 (1869), including (to mention only a few examples) the prohibition on any involuntary reduction or combination of a State's territory, Art. IV, § 3; the Judicial Power Clause, Art. III, § 2, and the Privileges and Immunities Clause, Art. IV, § 2, which speak of the "Citizens" of the States; the amendment provision, Article V, which requires the votes of three-fourths of the States to amend the Constitution; and the Guarantee Clause, Art. IV, § 4, which "presupposes the continued existence of the states and ... those means and instrumentalities which are the creation of their sovereign and reserved rights," *Helvering v. Gerhardt,* 304 U.S. 405, 414–415, 58 S.Ct. 969, 973, 82 L.Ed. 1427 (1938). Residual state sovereignty was also implicit, of course, in the Constitution's conferral upon Congress of not all governmental powers, but only discrete, enumerated ones, Art. I, § 8, which implication was rendered express by the Tenth Amendment's assertion that "[t]he powers not delegated to the

United States by the Constitution, nor prohibited by it to the States, are reserved to the States respectively, or to the people."

The Framers' experience under the Articles of Confederation had persuaded them that using the States as the instruments of federal governance was both ineffectual and provocative of federal-state conflict. See *The Federalist* No. 15. Preservation of the States as independent political entities being the price of union, and "[t]he practicality of making laws, with coercive sanctions, for the States as political bodies" having been, in Madison's words, "exploded on all hands," 2 *Records of the Federal Convention of 1787*, p. 9 (M. Farrand ed.1911), the Framers rejected the concept of a central government that would act upon and through the States, and instead designed a system in which the State and Federal Governments would exercise concurrent authority over the people—who were, in Hamilton's words, " the only proper objects of government," *The Federalist* No. 15, at 109. We have set forth the historical record in more detail elsewhere, see *New York v. United States,* 505 U.S., at 161–166, 112 S.Ct., at 2420–2423, and need not repeat it here. It suffices to repeat the conclusion: "the Framers explicitly chose a Constitution that confers upon Congress the power to regulate individuals, not States." *Id.,* at 166, 112 S.Ct., at 2423. The great innovation of this design was that "our citizens would have two political capacities, one state and one federal, each protected from incursion by the other"—"a legal system unprecedented in form and design, establishing two orders of government, each with its own direct relationship, its own privity, its own set of mutual rights and obligations to the people who sustain it and are governed by it." *U.S. Term Limits, Inc. v. Thornton,* 514 U.S. 779, 838, 115 S.Ct. 1842, 1872, 131 L.Ed.2d 881 (1995) (Kennedy, J., concurring). The Constitution thus contemplates that a State's government will represent and remain accountable to its own citizens. *See New York, supra,* at 168–169, 112 S.Ct., at 2424; *United States v. Lopez,* 514 U.S. 549, 576–577, 115 S.Ct. 1624, 1638–1639, 131 L.Ed.2d 626 (1995) (Kennedy, J., concurring). Cf. *Edgar v. MITE Corp.,* 457 U.S. 624, 644, 102 S.Ct. 2629, 2641, 73 L.Ed.2d 269 (1982) ("the State has no legitimate interest in protecting nonresident [s]"). As Madison expressed it: "[T]he local or municipal authorities form distinct and independent portions of the supremacy, no more subject, within their respective spheres, to the general authority than the general authority is subject to them, within its own sphere." *The Federalist* No. 39, at 245.

This separation of the two spheres is one of the Constitution's structural protections of liberty. "Just as the separation and independence of the coordinate branches of the Federal Government serve to prevent the accumulation of excessive power in any one branch, a healthy balance of power between the States and the Federal Government will reduce the risk of tyranny and abuse from either front." 501 U.S., *supra,* at 458, 111 S.Ct., at 2400. To quote Madison once again:

> "In the compound republic of America, the power surrendered by the people is first divided between two distinct governments, and then the portion allotted to each subdivided among distinct and separate departments. Hence a double security arises to the rights of the people. The different governments will control each other, at the same time that each will be controlled by itself." *The Federalist* No. 51, at 323.

See also *The Federalist* No. 28, at 180–181 (A.Hamilton). The power of the Federal Government would be augmented immeasurably if it were able to impress into its service—and at no cost to itself—the police officers of the 50 States.

B

We have thus far discussed the effect that federal control of state officers would have upon the first element of the "double security" alluded to by Madison: the division of power between State and Federal Governments. It would also have an effect upon the second element: the separation and equilibration of powers between the three branches of the Federal Government itself. The Constitution does not leave to speculation who is to administer the laws enacted by Congress; the President, it says, "shall take Care that the Laws be faithfully executed," Art. II, § 3, personally and through officers whom he appoints (save for such inferior officers as Congress may authorize to be appointed by the "Courts of Law" or by "the Heads of Departments" who are themselves Presidential appointees), Art. II, § 2. The Brady Act effectively transfers this responsibility to thousands of CLEOs in the 50 States, who are left to implement the program without meaningful Presidential control (if indeed meaningful Presidential control is possible without the power to appoint and remove). The insistence of the Framers upon unity in the Federal Executive—to ensure both vigor and accountability—is well known. See *The Federalist* No. 70 (A.Hamilton); 2 *Documentary History of the Ratification of the Constitution* 495 (M. Jensen ed.1976) (statement of James Wilson); see also Calabresi & Prakash, "The President's Power to Execute the Laws," 104 *Yale L.J.* 541 (1994). That unity would be shattered, and the power of the President would be subject to reduction, if Congress could act as effectively without the President as with him, by simply requiring state officers to execute its laws.

The dissent of course resorts to the last, best hope of those who defend ultra vires congressional action, the Necessary and Proper Clause. It reasons, *post,* at 2387, that the power to regulate the sale of handguns under the Commerce Clause, coupled with the power to "make all Laws which shall be necessary and proper for carrying into Execution the foregoing Powers," Art. I, § 8, conclusively establishes the Brady Act's constitutional validity, because the Tenth Amendment imposes no limitations on the exercise of *delegated* powers but merely prohibits the exercise of powers "*not* delegated to the United States." What destroys the dissent's Necessary and Proper Clause argument, however, is not the Tenth Amendment but the Necessary and Proper Clause itself. When a "La [w] ... for carrying into Execution" the Commerce Clause violates the principle of state sovereignty reflected in the various constitutional provisions we mentioned earlier, *supra,* at 2376–2377, it is not a "La[w] ... *proper* for carrying into Execution the Commerce Clause," and is thus, in the words of *The Federalist,* "merely [an] ac[t] of usurpation" which "deserve[s] to be treated as such." *The Federalist* No. 33, at 204 (A. Hamilton). See Lawson & Granger, "The 'Proper' Scope of Federal Power: A Jurisdictional Interpretation of the Sweeping Clause," 43 *Duke L.J.* 267, 297–326, 330–333 (1993). We in fact answered the dissent's Necessary and Proper Clause argument in *New York:*

> "[E]ven where Congress has the authority under the Constitution to pass laws requiring or prohibiting certain acts, it lacks the power directly to compel the States to require or prohibit those acts.... [T]he Commerce Clause, for example, authorizes Congress to regulate interstate commerce directly; it does not authorize Congress to regulate state governments' regulation of interstate commerce." 505 U.S., at 166, 112 S.Ct., at 2423.

The dissent perceives a simple answer in that portion of Article VI which requires that "all executive and judicial Officers, both of the United States and of the several States, shall be bound by Oath or Affirmation, to support this

Constitution," arguing that by virtue of the Supremacy Clause this makes "not only the Constitution, but every law enacted by Congress as well," binding on state officers, including laws requiring state-officer enforcement. *Post,* at 2389. The Supremacy Clause, however, makes "Law of the Land" only "Laws of the United States which shall be made in Pursuance [of the Constitution]," Art. VI, cl. 2, so the Supremacy Clause merely brings us back to the question discussed earlier, whether laws conscripting state officers violate state sovereignty and are thus not in accord with the Constitution.

IV

Finally, and most conclusively in the present litigation, we turn to the prior jurisprudence of this Court. Federal commandeering of state governments is such a novel phenomenon that this Court's first experience with it did not occur until the 1970's, when the Environmental Protection Agency promulgated regulations requiring States to prescribe auto emissions testing, monitoring and retrofit programs, and to designate preferential bus and carpool lanes. The Courts of Appeals for the Fourth and Ninth Circuits invalidated the regulations on statutory grounds in order to avoid what they perceived to be grave constitutional issues, see *Maryland v. EPA,* 530 F.2d 215, 226 (C.A.4 1975); *Brown v. EPA,* 521 F.2d 827, 838–842 (C.A.9 1975); and the District of Columbia Circuit invalidated the regulations on both constitutional and statutory grounds, see *District of Columbia v. Train,* 521 F.2d 971, 994 (1975). After we granted certiorari to review the statutory and constitutional validity of the regulations, the Government declined even to defend them, and instead rescinded some and conceded the invalidity of those that remained, leading us to vacate the opinions below and remand for consideration of mootness. *EPA v. Brown,* 431 U.S. 99, 97 S.Ct. 1635, 52 L.Ed.2d 166 (1977) (*per curiam*).

Although we had no occasion to pass upon the subject in *Brown,* later opinions of ours have made clear that the Federal Government may not compel the States to implement, by legislation or executive action, federal regulatory programs. In *Hodel v. Virginia Surface Mining & Reclamation Assn., Inc.,* 452 U.S. 264, 101 S.Ct. 2352, 69 L.Ed.2d 1 (1981), and *FERC v. Mississippi,* 456 U.S. 742, 102 S.Ct. 2126, 72 L.Ed.2d 532 (1982), we sustained statutes against constitutional challenge only after assuring ourselves that they did not require the States to enforce federal law. In *Hodel* we cited the lower court cases in *EPA v. Brown, supra,* but concluded that the Surface Mining Control and Reclamation Act of 1977 did not present the problem they raised because it merely made compliance with federal standards a precondition to continued state regulation in an otherwise pre-empted field, *Hodel, supra,* at 288, 101 S.Ct., at 2366. In *FERC,* we construed the most troubling provisions of the Public Utility Regulatory Policies Act of 1978 to contain only the "command" that state agencies "consider" federal standards, and again only as a precondition to continued state regulation of an otherwise pre-empted field. 456 U.S., at 764–765, 102 S.Ct., at 2140–2141. We warned that "this Court never has sanctioned explicitly a federal command to the States to promulgate and enforce laws and regulations," *id.,* at 761–762, 102 S.Ct., at 2138–2139.

When we were at last confronted squarely with a federal statute that unambiguously required the States to enact or administer a federal regulatory program, our decision should have come as no surprise. At issue in *New York v. United States,* 505 U.S. 144, 112 S.Ct. 2408, 120 L.Ed.2d 120 (1992), were the so-called "take title" provisions of the Low-Level Radioactive Waste Policy Amendments Act of 1985, which required States either to enact legislation providing for the disposal of radioactive waste generated within their borders, or to take title to, and possession of, the waste—effectively requiring the States either to legislate pursuant to Congress's directions, or to implement an administrative solution. *Id.*, at 175–176, 112 S.Ct., at 2428. We concluded that Congress could constitutionally require the States to do neither. *Id.*, at 176, 112 S.Ct., at 2428. "The Federal Government," we held, "may not compel the States to enact or administer a federal regulatory program." *Id.*, at 188, 112 S.Ct., at 2435.

The Government contends that *New York* is distinguishable on the following ground: Unlike the "take title" provisions invalidated there, the background-check provision of the Brady Act does not require state legislative or executive officials to make policy, but instead issues a final directive to state CLEOs. It is permissible, the Government asserts, for Congress to command state or local officials to assist in the implementation of federal law so long as "Congress itself devises a clear legislative solution that regulates private conduct" and requires state or local officers to provide only "limited, non-policymaking help in enforcing that law." "[T]he constitutional line is crossed only when Congress compels the States to make law in their sovereign capacities." Brief for United States 16.

The Government's distinction between "making" law and merely "enforcing" it, between "policymaking" and mere "implementation," is an interesting one. It is perhaps not meant to be the same as, but it is surely reminiscent of, the line that separates proper congressional conferral of Executive power from unconstitutional delegation of legislative authority for federal separation-of-powers purposes. See *A.L.A. Schechter Poultry Corp. v. United States*, 295 U.S. 495, 530, 55 S.Ct. 837, 843, 79 L.Ed. 1570 (1935); *Panama Refining Co. v.*

Ryan, 293 U.S. 388, 428–429, 55 S.Ct. 241, 251–252, 79 L.Ed. 446 (1935). This Court has not been notably successful in describing the latter line; indeed, some think we have abandoned the effort to do so. See *FPC v. New England Power Co.*, 415 U.S. 345, 352–353, 94 S.Ct. 1151, 1156, 39 L.Ed.2d 383 (1974) (Marshall, J., concurring in result); Schoenbrod, "The Delegation Doctrine: Could the Court Give it Substance?," 83 *Mich. L.Rev.* 1223, 1233 (1985). We are doubtful that the new line the Government proposes would be any more distinct. Executive action that has utterly no policymaking component is rare, particularly at an executive level as high as a jurisdiction's chief law enforcement officer. Is it really true that there is no policymaking involved in deciding, for example, what "reasonable efforts" shall be expended to conduct a background check? It may well satisfy the Act for a CLEO to direct that (a) no background checks will be conducted that divert personnel time from pending felony investigations, and (b) no background check will be permitted to consume more than one-half hour of an officer's time. But nothing in the Act *requires* a CLEO to be so parsimonious; diverting at least *some* felony-investigation time, and permitting at least *some* background checks beyond one-half hour would certainly not be *un* reasonable. Is this decision whether to devote maximum "reasonable efforts" or minimum "reasonable efforts" not preeminently a matter of policy? It is quite impossible, in short, to draw the Government's proposed line at "no policymaking," and we would have to fall back upon a line of "not too much policymaking." How much is too much is not likely to be answered precisely; and an imprecise barrier against federal intrusion upon state authority is not likely to be an effective one.

Even assuming, moreover, that the Brady Act leaves no "policymaking" discretion with the States, we fail to see how that improves rather than worsens the intrusion upon state sovereignty. Preservation of the States as independent and autonomous political entities is arguably less undermined by requiring them to make policy in certain fields than (as Judge Sneed aptly described it over two decades ago) by "reduc[ing] [them] to puppets of a ventriloquist Congress," *Brown v. EPA*, 521 F.2d, at 839. It is an essential attribute of the States' retained sovereignty that they remain independent and autonomous within their proper sphere of authority. See *Texas v. White,* 7 Wall., at 725. It is no more compatible with this independence and autonomy that their officers be "dragooned" (as Judge Fernandez put it in his dissent below, 66 F.3d, at 1035) into administering federal law, than it would be compatible with the independence and autonomy of the United States that its officers be impressed into service for the execution of state laws.

The Government purports to find support for its proffered distinction of *New York* in our decisions in *Testa v. Katt,* 330 U.S. 386, 67 S.Ct. 810, 91 L.Ed. 967 (1947), and *FERC v. Mississippi,* 456 U.S. 742, 102 S.Ct. 2126, 72 L.Ed.2d 532 (1982). We find neither case relevant. *Testa* stands for the proposition that state courts cannot refuse to apply federal law—a conclusion mandated by the terms of the Supremacy Clause ("the Judges in every State shall be bound [by federal law]"). As we have suggested earlier, *supra,* at 2370, that says nothing about whether state executive officers must administer federal law. Accord, *New York,* 505 U.S., at 178–179, 112 S.Ct., at 2429–2430. As for *FERC,* it stated (as we have described earlier) that "this Court never has sanctioned explicitly a federal command to the States to promulgate and enforce laws and regulations," 456 U.S., at 761–762, 102 S.Ct., at 2138–2139, and upheld the statutory provisions at issue precisely because they did *not* commandeer state government, but merely imposed preconditions to continued state regulation of an otherwise pre-empted field, in accord with *Hodel,* 452 U.S., at 288, 101 S.Ct., at 2366, and required state administrative agencies to apply federal law while acting in a judicial capacity, in accord with *Testa,* see *FERC, supra,* at 759–771, and n. 24, 102 S.Ct., at 2137–2144, and n. 24.

The Government also maintains that requiring state officers to perform discrete, ministerial tasks specified by Congress does not violate the principle of *New York* because it does not diminish the accountability of state or federal officials. This argument fails even on its own terms. By forcing state governments to absorb the financial burden of implementing a federal regulatory program, Members of Congress can take credit for "solving" problems without having to ask their constituents to pay for the solutions with higher federal taxes. And even when the States are not forced to absorb the costs of implementing a federal program, they are still put in the position of taking the blame for its burdensomeness and for its defects. See Merritt, "Three Faces of Federalism: Finding a Formula for the Future," 47 *Vand. L.Rev.* 1563, 1580, n. 65 (1994). Under the present law, for example, it will be the CLEO and not some federal official who stands between the gun purchaser and immediate possession of his gun. And it will likely be the CLEO, not some federal official, who will be blamed for any error (even one in the designated federal database) that causes a purchaser to be mistakenly rejected.

The dissent makes no attempt to defend the Government's basis for distinguishing *New York,* but instead advances what seems to us an even more implausible theory. The Brady Act, the dissent asserts, is different from the "take title" provisions invalidated in *New York* because the former is addressed to individuals—namely, CLEOs—while the latter were directed to the State itself. That is certainly a difference, but it cannot be a constitutionally significant one. While the Brady Act is directed to "individuals," it is directed to them in their official capacities as state officers; it controls their actions, not as private citizens, but as the agents of the State. The distinction between judicial writs and other government action directed against individuals in their personal capacity, on the one hand, and in their official capacity, on the other hand, is an ancient one, principally because it is dictated by common sense. We have observed that "a suit against a state official in his or her official capacity is not a suit against the official but rather is a suit against the official's office.... As such, it is no different from a suit against the State itself." *Will v. Michigan Dept. of State Police,* 491 U.S. 58, 71, 109 S.Ct. 2304, 2312, 105 L.Ed.2d 45 (1989). And the same must be said of a directive to an official in his or her official capacity. To say that the Federal Government cannot control the State, but can control all of its officers, is to say nothing of significance. Indeed, it merits the description "empty formalistic reasoning of the highest order," *post,* at 2392. By resorting to this, the dissent not so much distinguishes *New York* as disembowels it.

Finally, the Government puts forward a cluster of arguments that can be grouped under the heading: "The Brady Act serves very important purposes, is most efficiently administered by CLEOs during the interim period, and places a minimal and only temporary burden upon state officers." There is considerable disagreement over the extent of the burden, but we need not pause over that detail. Assuming *all* the mentioned factors were true, they might be relevant if we were evaluating whether the incidental application to the States of a federal law of general applicability excessively interfered with the functioning of state governments. See, *e.g., Fry v. United States,* 421 U.S. 542, 548, 95 S.Ct. 1792, 1796, 44

L.Ed.2d 363 (1975); *National League of Cities v. Usery*, 426 U.S. 833, 853, 96 S.Ct. 2465, 2475, 49 L.Ed.2d 245 (1976) (overruled by *Garcia v. San Antonio Metropolitan Transit Authority*, 469 U.S. 528, 105 S.Ct. 1005, 83 L.Ed.2d 1016 (1985)); *South Carolina v. Baker*, 485 U.S. 505, 529, 108 S.Ct. 1355, 1370, 99 L.Ed.2d 592 (1988) (Rehnquist, C.J., concurring in judgment). But where, as here, it is the whole *object* of the law to direct the functioning of the state executive, and hence to compromise the structural framework of dual sovereignty, such a "balancing" analysis is inappropriate. It is the very *principle* of separate state sovereignty that such a law offends, and no comparative assessment of the various interests can overcome that fundamental defect. Cf. *Bowsher*, 478 U.S., at 736, 106 S.Ct., at 3192–3193 (declining to subject principle of separation of powers to a balancing test); *Chadha*, 462 U.S., at 944–946, 103 S.Ct., at 2780–2782 (same); *Plaut v. Spendthrift Farm, Inc.*, 514 U.S. 933211, 239–240, 115 S.Ct. 1447, 1462–1463, 131 L.Ed.2d 328 (1995) (holding legislated invalidation of final judgments to be categorically unconstitutional). We expressly rejected such an approach in *New York*, and what we said bears repeating:

> "Much of the Constitution is concerned with setting forth the form of our government, and the courts have traditionally invalidated measures deviating from that form. The result may appear 'formalistic' in a given case to partisans of the measure at issue, because such measures are typically the product of the era's perceived necessity. But the Constitution protects us from our own best intentions: It divides power among sovereigns and among branches of government precisely so that we may resist the temptation to concentrate power in one location as an expedient solution to the crisis of the day." 505 U.S., at 187, 112 S.Ct., at 2434.

We adhere to that principle today, and conclude categorically, as we concluded categorically in *New York:* "The Federal Government may not compel the States to enact or administer a federal regulatory program." *Id.*, at 188, 112 S.Ct., at 2435. The mandatory obligation imposed on CLEOs to perform background checks on prospective handgun purchasers plainly runs afoul of that rule.

V

What we have said makes it clear enough that the central obligation imposed upon CLEOs by the interim provisions of the Brady Act—the obligation to "make a reasonable effort to ascertain within 5 business days whether receipt or possession [of a handgun] would be in violation of the law, including research in whatever State and local recordkeeping systems are available and in a national system designated by the Attorney General," 18 U.S.C. § 922(s)(2)—is unconstitutional. Extinguished with it, of course, is the duty implicit in the background-check requirement that the CLEO accept notice of the contents of, and a copy of, the completed Brady Form, which the firearms dealer is required to provide to him, §§ 922(s)(1)(A)(i) (III) and (IV).

Petitioners also challenge, however, two other provisions of the Act: (1) the requirement that any CLEO "to whom a [Brady Form] is transmitted" destroy the form and any record containing information derived from it, § 922(s)(6)(B)(i), and (2) the requirement that any CLEO who "determines that an individual is ineligible to receive a handgun" provide the would-be purchaser, upon request, a written statement of the reasons for that determination, § 922(s)(6)(C). With the background-check and implicit receipt-of-forms requirements invalidated, however, these provisions require no action whatsoever on the part of the CLEO. Quite obviously, the obligation to destroy all Brady Forms that he has received when he has received none, and the obligation to give reasons for a determination of ineligibility when he never makes a determination of ineligibility, are no obligations at all. These two provisions have conceivable application to a CLEO, in other words, only if he has chosen, voluntarily, to participate in administration of the federal scheme. The present petitioners are not in that position. As to them, these last two challenged provisions are not unconstitutional, but simply inoperative.

There is involved in this Brady Act conundrum a severability question, which the parties have briefed and argued: whether firearms dealers in the jurisdictions at issue here, and in other jurisdictions, remain obliged to forward to the CLEO (even if he will not accept it) the requisite notice of the contents (and a copy) of the Brady Form, §§ 922(s)(1)(A)(i)(III) and (IV); and to wait five business days before consummating the sale, § 922(s)(1)(A)(ii). These are important questions, but we have no business answering them in these cases. These provisions burden only firearms dealers and purchasers, and no plaintiff in either of those categories is before us here. We decline to speculate regarding the rights and obligations of parties not before the Court. Cf., *e.g., New York, supra,* at 186–187, 112 S.Ct., at 2434 (addressing severability where remaining provisions at issue affected the plaintiffs).

* * *

We held in *New York* that Congress cannot compel the States to enact or enforce a federal regulatory program. Today we hold that Congress cannot circumvent that prohibition by conscripting the State's officers directly. The Federal Government may neither issue directives requiring the States to address particular problems, nor command the States' officers, or those of their political subdivisions, to administer or enforce a federal regulatory program. It matters not whether policymaking is involved, and no case-by-case weighing of the burdens or benefits is necessary; such commands are fundamentally incompatible with our constitutional system of dual sovereignty. Accordingly, the judgment of the Court of Appeals for the Ninth Circuit is reversed.

It is so ordered.

Justice O'Connor, concurring.

Justice Thomas, concurring.

Justice Stevens, with whom Justice Souter, Justice Ginsburg, and Justice Breyer join, dissenting.

Justice Souter, dissenting.

Justice Breyer, with whom Justice Stevens joins, dissenting.

Limits on Gun Ownership and the Fourth Amendment

District of Columbia v. Heller, 554 U.S. 570 (2008)

Justice Scalia delivered the opinion of the Court.

We consider whether a District of Columbia prohibition on the possession of usable handguns in the home violates the Second Amendment to the Constitution.

I

The District of Columbia generally prohibits the possession of handguns. It is a crime to carry an unregistered firearm, and the registration of handguns is prohibited. See D.C.Code §§ 7-2501.01(12), 7-2502.01(a), 7-2502.02(a)(4)

(2001). Wholly apart from that prohibition, no person may carry a handgun without a license, but the chief of police may issue licenses for 1-year periods. See §§ 22-4504(a), 22-4506. District of Columbia law also requires residents to keep their lawfully owned firearms, such as registered long guns, "unloaded and dissembled or bound by a trigger lock or similar device" unless they are located in a place of business or are being used for lawful recreational activities. See § 7-2507.02.

Respondent Dick Heller is a D.C. special police officer authorized to carry a handgun while on duty at the Thurgood Marshall Judiciary Building. He applied for a registration certificate for a handgun that he wished to keep at home, but the District refused. He thereafter filed a lawsuit in the Federal District Court for the District of Columbia seeking, on Second Amendment grounds, to enjoin the city from enforcing the bar on the registration of handguns, the licensing requirement insofar as it prohibits the carrying of a firearm in the home without a license, and the trigger-lock requirement insofar as it prohibits the use of "functional firearms within the home." App. 59a. The District Court dismissed respondent's complaint, see *Parker v. District of Columbia,* 311 F.Supp.2d 103, 109 (2004). The Court of Appeals for the District of Columbia Circuit, construing his complaint as seeking the right to render a firearm operable and carry it about his home in that condition only when necessary for self-defense, reversed, see *Parker v. District of Columbia,* 478 F.3d 370, 401 (2007). It held that the Second Amendment protects an individual right to possess firearms and that the city's total ban on handguns, as well as its requirement that firearms in the home be kept nonfunctional even when necessary for self-defense, violated that right. See *id.,* at 395, 399–401. The Court of Appeals directed the District Court to enter summary judgment for respondent.

We granted certiorari. 552 U.S. 1035, 128 S.Ct. 645, 169 L.Ed.2d 417 (2007).

II

We turn first to the meaning of the Second Amendment.

A

The Second Amendment provides: "A well regulated Militia, being necessary to the security of a free State, the right of the people to keep and bear Arms, shall not be infringed." In interpreting this text, we are guided by the principle that "[t]he Constitution was written to be understood by the voters; its words and phrases were used in their normal and ordinary as distinguished from technical meaning." *United States v.*

Sprague, 282 U.S. 716, 731, 51 S.Ct. 220, 75 L.Ed. 640 (1931); see also *Gibbons v. Ogden,* 9 Wheat. 1, 188, 6 L.Ed. 23 (1824). Normal meaning may of course include an idiomatic meaning, but it excludes secret or technical meanings that would not have been known to ordinary citizens in the founding generation.

The two sides in this case have set out very different interpretations of the Amendment. Petitioners and today's dissenting Justices believe that it protects only the right to possess and carry a firearm in connection with militia service. See Brief for Petitioners 11–12; *post,* at 2822 (Stevens, J., dissenting). Respondent argues that it protects an individual right to possess a firearm unconnected with service in a militia, and to use that arm for traditionally lawful purposes, such as self-defense within the home. See Brief for Respondent 2–4.

The Second Amendment is naturally divided into two parts: its prefatory clause and its operative clause. The former does not limit the latter grammatically, but rather announces a purpose. The Amendment could be rephrased, "Because a well regulated Militia is necessary to the security of a free State, the right of the people to keep and bear Arms shall not be infringed." See J. Tiffany, *A Treatise on Government and Constitutional Law* § 585, p. 394 (1867); Brief for Professors of Linguistics and English as *Amici Curiae* 3 (hereinafter Linguists' Brief). Although this structure of the Second Amendment is unique in our Constitution, other legal documents of the founding era, particularly individual-rights provisions of state constitutions, commonly included a prefatory statement of purpose. See generally Volokh, "The Commonplace Second Amendment," 73 *N.Y.U. L.Rev.* 793, 814–821 (1998).

Logic demands that there be a link between the stated purpose and the command. The Second Amendment would be nonsensical if it read, "A well regulated Militia, being necessary to the security of a free State, the right of the people to petition for redress of grievances shall not be infringed." That requirement of logical connection may cause a prefatory clause to resolve an ambiguity in the operative clause. ("The separation of church and state being an important objective, the teachings of canons shall have no place in our jurisprudence." The preface makes clear that the operative clause refers not to canons of interpretation but to clergymen.) But apart from that clarifying function, a prefatory clause does not limit or expand the scope of the operative clause. See F. Dwarris, *A General Treatise on Statutes* 268–269 (P. Potter ed. 1871); T. Sedgwick, *The Interpretation and Construction of Statutory and Constitutional Law* 42–45 (2d ed. 1874). "'It is nothing unusual in acts ... for the enacting part to go beyond the preamble; the remedy often extends beyond the particular act or mischief which first suggested the necessity of the law.'" J. Bishop, *Commentaries on Written Laws and Their Interpretation* § 51, p. 49 (1882) (quoting *Rex v. Marks,* 3 East 157, 165, 102 Eng.Rep. 557, 560 (K.B.1802)). Therefore, while we will begin our textual analysis with the operative clause, we will return to the prefatory clause to ensure that our reading of the operative clause is consistent with the announced purpose.

1. Operative Clause.

a. "Right of the People." The first salient feature of the operative clause is that it codifies a "right of the people." The unamended Constitution and the Bill of Rights use the phrase "right of the people" two other times, in the First Amendment's Assembly-and-Petition Clause and in the Fourth Amendment's Search-and-Seizure Clause. The Ninth Amendment uses very similar terminology ("The enumeration in the Constitution, of certain rights, shall not be construed to deny or disparage others retained by the people"). All three of these instances unambiguously refer to individual rights, not "collective" rights, or rights that may be exercised only through participation in some corporate body.

Three provisions of the Constitution refer to "the people" in a context other than "rights"—the famous preamble ("We the people"), § 2 of Article I (providing that "the people" will choose members of the House), and the Tenth Amendment (providing that those powers not given the Federal Government remain with "the States" or "the people"). Those provisions arguably refer to "the people" acting collectively—but they deal with the exercise or reservation of powers, not rights. Nowhere else in the Constitution does a "right" attributed to "the people" refer to anything other than an individual right.

What is more, in all six other provisions of the Constitution that mention "the people," the term unambiguously refers to all members of the political community, not an unspecified subset. As we said in *United States v. Verdugo-Urquidez,* 494 U.S. 259, 265, 110 S.Ct. 1056, 108 L.Ed.2d 222 (1990):

> "'[T]he people' seems to have been a term of art employed in select parts of the Constitution .... [Its uses] sugges[t] that 'the people' protected by the Fourth Amendment, and by the First and Second Amendments, and to whom rights and powers are reserved in the Ninth and Tenth Amendments, refers to a class of persons who are part of a national community or who have otherwise developed sufficient connection with this country to be considered part of that community."

This contrasts markedly with the phrase "the militia" in the prefatory clause. As we will describe below, the "militia" in colonial America consisted of a subset of "the people"—those who were male, able bodied, and within a certain age range. Reading the Second Amendment as protecting only the right to "keep and bear Arms" in an organized militia therefore fits poorly with the operative clause's description of the holder of that right as "the people."

We start therefore with a strong presumption that the Second Amendment right is exercised individually and belongs to all Americans.

b. "Keep and Bear Arms." We move now from the holder of the right—"the people"—to the substance of the right: "to keep and bear Arms."

Before addressing the verbs "keep" and "bear," we interpret their object: "Arms." The 18th-century meaning is no different from the meaning today. The 1773 edition of Samuel Johnson's dictionary defined "arms" as "[w]eapons of offence, or armour of defence." 1 *Dictionary of the English Language* 106 (4th ed.) (reprinted 1978) (hereinafter *Johnson*). Timothy Cunningham's important 1771 legal dictionary defined "arms" as "any thing that a man wears for his defence, or takes into his hands, or useth in wrath to cast at or strike another." 1 *A New and Complete Law Dictionary*; see also N. Webster, *American Dictionary of the English Language* (1828) (reprinted 1989) (hereinafter *Webster*) (similar).

The term was applied, then as now, to weapons that were not specifically designed for military use and were not employed in a military capacity. For instance, Cunningham's legal dictionary gave as an example of usage: "Servants and labourers shall use bows and arrows on *Sundays*, & c. and not bear other arms." See also, *e.g.*, An Act for the trial of Negroes,

1797 Del. Laws ch. XLIII, § 6, in 1 *First Laws of the State of Delaware* 102, 104 (J. Cushing ed.1981 (pt. 1)); see generally *State v. Duke,* 42 Tex. 455, 458 (1874) (citing decisions of state courts construing "arms"). Although one founding-era thesaurus limited "arms" (as opposed to "weapons") to "instruments of offence *generally* made use of in war," even that source stated that all firearms constituted "arms." 1 J. Trusler, *The Distinction Between Words Esteemed Synonymous in the English Language* 37 (3d ed. 1794) (emphasis added).

Some have made the argument, bordering on the frivolous, that only those arms in existence in the 18th century are protected by the Second Amendment. We do not interpret constitutional rights that way. Just as the First Amendment protects modern forms of communications, *e.g., Reno v. American Civil Liberties Union,* 521 U.S. 844, 849, 117 S.Ct. 2329, 138 L.Ed.2d 874 (1997), and the Fourth Amendment applies to modern forms of search, *e.g., Kyllo v. United States,* 533 U.S. 27, 35–36, 121 S.Ct. 2038, 150 L.Ed.2d 94 (2001), the Second Amendment extends, prima facie, to all instruments that constitute bearable arms, even those that were not in existence at the time of the founding.

We turn to the phrases "keep arms" and "bear arms." Johnson defined "keep" as, most relevantly, "[t]o retain; not to lose," and "[t]o have in custody." *Johnson* 1095. Webster defined it as "[t]o hold; to retain in one's power or possession." No party has apprised us of an idiomatic meaning of "keep Arms." Thus, the most natural reading of "keep Arms" in the Second Amendment is to "have weapons."

The phrase "keep arms" was not prevalent in the written documents of the founding period that we have found, but there are a few examples, all of which favor viewing the right to "keep Arms" as an individual right unconnected with militia service. William Blackstone, for example, wrote that Catholics convicted of not attending service in the Church of England suffered certain penalties, one of which was that they were not permitted to "keep arms in their houses." 4 *Commentaries on the Laws of England* 55 (1769) (hereinafter *Blackstone*); see also 1 W. & M., ch. 15, § 4, in 3 Eng. Stat. at Large 422 (1689) ("[N]o Papist ... shall or may have or keep in his House ... any Arms ..."); 1 W. Hawkins, *Treatise on the Pleas of the Crown* 26 (1771) (similar). Petitioners point to militia laws of the founding period that required militia members to "keep" arms in connection with militia service, and they conclude from this that the phrase "keep Arms" has a militia-related connotation. See Brief for Petitioners 16–17 (citing laws of Delaware, New Jersey, and Virginia). This is rather like saying that, since there are many statutes that authorize aggrieved employees to "file complaints" with federal agencies, the phrase "file complaints" has an employment-related connotation. "Keep arms" was simply a common way of referring to possessing arms, for militiamen *and everyone else.*

At the time of the founding, as now, to "bear" meant to "carry." See *Johnson* 161; *Webster*; T. Sheridan, *A Complete Dictionary of the English Language* (1796); 2 *Oxford English Dictionary* 20 (2d ed.1989) (hereinafter *Oxford*). When used with "arms," however, the term has a meaning that refers to carrying for a particular purpose—confrontation. In *Muscarello v. United States,* 524 U.S. 125, 118 S.Ct. 1911, 141 L.Ed.2d 111 (1998), in the course of analyzing the meaning of "carries a firearm" in a federal criminal statute, Justice Ginsburg wrote that "[s]urely a most familiar meaning is, as the Constitution's Second Amendment ... indicate[s]: 'wear, bear, or carry ... upon the person or in the clothing or in a pocket, for the purpose ... of being armed and ready for offensive or defensive action in a case of conflict with another person.'" *Id.,* at 143, 118 S.Ct. 1911 (dissenting opinion) (quoting *Black's Law Dictionary* 214 (6th ed.1990)). We think that Justice GINSBURG accurately captured the natural meaning of "bear arms." Although the phrase implies that the carrying of the weapon is for the purpose of "offensive or defensive action," it in no way connotes participation in a structured military organization.

From our review of founding-era sources, we conclude that this natural meaning was also the meaning that "bear arms" had in the 18th century. In numerous instances, "bear arms" was unambiguously used to refer to the carrying of weapons outside of an organized militia. The most prominent examples are those most relevant to the Second Amendment: nine state constitutional provisions written in the 18th century or the first two decades of the 19th, which enshrined a right of citizens to "bear arms in defense of themselves and the state" or "bear arms in defense of himself and the state." It is clear from those formulations that "bear arms" did not refer only to carrying a weapon in an organized military unit. Justice James Wilson interpreted the Pennsylvania Constitution's arms-bearing right, for example, as a recognition of the natural right of defense "of one's person or house"—what he called the law of "self preservation." 2 *Collected Works of James Wilson* 1142, and n. x (K. Hall & M. Hall eds.2007) (citing Pa. Const., Art. IX, § 21 (1790)); see also T. Walker, *Introduction to American Law* 198 (1837) ("Thus the right of self-defence [is] guaranteed by the [Ohio] constitution"); see also *id.*, at 157 (equating Second Amendment with that provision of the Ohio Constitution). That was also the interpretation of those state constitutional provisions adopted by pre-Civil War state courts. These provisions demonstrate—again, in the most analogous linguistic context—that "bear arms" was not limited to the carrying of arms in a militia.

The phrase "bear Arms" also had at the time of the founding an idiomatic meaning that was significantly different from its natural meaning: "to serve as a soldier, do military service, fight" or "to wage war." See Linguists' Brief 18; *post,* at 2827–2828 (Stevens, J., dissenting). But it *unequivocally* bore that idiomatic meaning only when followed by the preposition "against," which was in turn followed by the target of the hostilities. See 2 *Oxford* 21. (That is how, for example, our Declaration of Independence ¶ 28 used the phrase: "He has constrained our fellow Citizens taken Captive on the high Seas to bear Arms against their Country ....") Every example given by petitioners' *amici* for the idiomatic meaning of "bear arms" from the founding period either includes the preposition "against" or is not clearly idiomatic. See Linguists' Brief 18–23. Without the preposition, "bear arms" normally meant (as it continues to mean today) what Justice Ginsburg's opinion in *Muscarello* said.

In any event, the meaning of "bear arms" that petitioners and Justice Stevens propose is *not even* the (sometimes) idiomatic meaning. Rather, they manufacture a hybrid definition, whereby "bear arms" connotes the actual carrying of arms (and therefore is not really an idiom) but only in the service of an organized militia. No dictionary has ever adopted that definition, and we have been apprised of no source that indicates that it carried that meaning at the time of the founding. But it is easy to see why petitioners and the dissent are driven to the hybrid definition. Giving "bear Arms" its idiomatic meaning would cause the protected right to consist of the right to be a soldier or to wage war—an absurdity that no commentator has ever endorsed. See L. Levy, *Origins of the Bill of Rights* 135 (1999). Worse still, the phrase "keep and bear Arms" would be incoherent. The word "Arms" would have two different meanings at once: "weapons" (as the object of "keep") and (as the object of "bear") one-half of an idiom. It would be rather like saying "He filled and kicked the bucket" to mean "He filled the bucket and died." Grotesque.

Petitioners justify their limitation of "bear arms" to the military context by pointing out the unremarkable fact that it was often used in that context—the same mistake they made with respect to "keep arms." It is especially unremarkable that the phrase was often used in a military context in the federal legal sources (such as records of congressional debate) that have been the focus of petitioners' inquiry. Those sources would have had little occasion to use it *except* in discussions about the standing army and the militia. And the phrases used primarily in those military discussions include not only "bear arms" but also "carry arms," "possess arms," and "have arms"—though no one thinks that those *other* phrases also had special military meanings. See Barnett, "Was the Right to Keep and Bear Arms Conditioned on Service in an Organized Militia?" 83 *Texas L.Rev.* 237, 261 (2004). The common references to those "fit to bear arms" in congressional discussions about the militia are matched by use of the same phrase in the few nonmilitary federal contexts where the concept would be relevant. See, *e.g.*, 30 *Journals of Continental Congress* 349–351 (J. Fitzpatrick ed.1934). Other legal sources frequently used "bear arms" in nonmilitary contexts. Cunningham's legal dictionary, cited above, gave as an example of its usage a sentence unrelated to military affairs ("Servants and labourers shall use bows and arrows on *Sundays,* & c. and not bear other arms"). And if one looks beyond legal sources, "bear arms" was frequently used in nonmilitary contexts. See Cramer & Olson, "What Did 'Bear Arms' Mean in the Second Amendment?" 6 *Georgetown J.L. & Pub. Pol'y* 511 (2008) (identifying numerous nonmilitary uses of "bear arms" from the founding period).

Justice Stevens points to a study by *amici* supposedly showing that the phrase "bear arms" was most frequently used in the military context. See *post,* at 2828–2829, n. 9; Linguists' Brief 24. Of course, as we have said, the fact that the phrase was commonly used in a particular context does not show that it is limited to that context, and, in any event, we have given many sources where the phrase was used in nonmilitary contexts. Moreover, the study's collection appears to include (who knows how many times) the idiomatic phrase "bear arms against," which is irrelevant. The *amici* also dismiss examples such as "bear arms ... for the purpose of killing game" because those uses are "expressly qualified." Linguists' Brief 24. (Justice Stevens uses the same excuse for dismissing the state constitutional provisions analogous to the Second Amendment that identify private-use purposes for which the individual right can be asserted. See *post,* at 2828.) That analysis is faulty. A purposive qualifying phrase that contradicts the word or phrase it modifies is unknown this side of the looking glass (except, apparently, in some courses on linguistics). If "bear arms" means, as we think, simply the carrying of arms, a modifier can limit the purpose of the carriage ("for the purpose of self-defense" or "to make war against the King"). But if "bear arms" means, as the petitioners and the dissent think, the carrying of arms only for military purposes, one simply cannot add "for the purpose of killing game." The right "to carry arms in the militia for the purpose of killing game" is worthy of the Mad Hatter. Thus, these purposive qualifying phrases positively establish that "to bear arms" is not limited to military use.

Justice Stevens places great weight on James Madison's inclusion of a conscientious-objector clause in his original draft of the Second Amendment: "but no person religiously scrupulous of bearing arms, shall be compelled to render military service in person." *Creating the Bill of Rights* 12 (H. Veit, K. Bowling, & C. Bickford eds.1991) (hereinafter *Veit*). He argues that this clause establishes that the drafters of the Second Amendment intended "bear Arms" to refer only to military service. See *post,* at 2836. It is always perilous to derive the meaning of an adopted provision from another provision deleted in the drafting process. In any case, what Justice Stevens would conclude from the deleted provision does not follow. It was not meant to exempt from military service those who objected to going to war but had no scruples about personal gunfights. Quakers opposed the use of arms not just for militia service, but for any violent purpose whatsoever—so much so that Quaker frontiersmen were forbidden to use arms to defend their families, even though "[i]n such circumstances the temptation to seize a hunting rifle or knife in self-defense ... must sometimes have been almost overwhelming." P. Brock, *Pacifism in the United States* 359 (1968); see M. Hirst, *The Quakers in Peace and War* 336–339 (1923); 3 T. Clarkson, *Portraiture of Quakerism* 103–104 (3d ed. 1807). The Pennsylvania Militia Act of 1757 exempted from service those "*scrupling the use of arms*"—a phrase that no one contends had an idiomatic meaning. See 5 Stat. at Large of Pa. 613 (J. Mitchell & H. Flanders comm'rs 1898) (emphasis in original). Thus, the most natural interpretation of Madison's deleted text is that those opposed to carrying weapons for potential violent confrontation would not be "compelled to render military service," in which such carrying would be required.

Finally, Justice Stevens suggests that "keep and bear Arms" was some sort of term of art, presumably akin to "hue and cry" or "cease and desist." (This suggestion usefully evades the problem that there is no evidence whatsoever to support a military reading of "keep arms.") Justice Stevens believes that the unitary meaning of "keep and bear Arms" is established by the Second Amendment's calling it a "right" (singular) rather than "rights" (plural). See *post,* at 2830–2831. There is nothing to this. State constitutions of the founding period routinely grouped multiple (related) guarantees under a singular "right," and the First Amendment protects the "right [singular] of the people peaceably to assemble, and to petition the Government for a redress of grievances." See, *e.g.,* Pa. Declaration of Rights §§ IX, XII, XVI, in 5 Thorpe 3083–3084; Ohio Const., Art. VIII, §§ 11, 19 (1802), in *id.,* at 2910–2911. And even if "keep and bear Arms" were a unitary phrase, we find no evidence that it bore a military meaning. Although the phrase was not at all common (which would be unusual for a term of art), we have found instances of its use with a clearly nonmilitary connotation. In a 1780 debate in the House of Lords, for example, Lord Richmond described an order to disarm private citizens (not militia members) as "a violation of the constitutional right of Protestant subjects to keep and bear arms for their own defence." 49 *The London Magazine or Gentleman's Monthly Intelligencer* 467 (1780). In response, another member of Parliament referred to "the right of bearing arms for personal defence," making clear that no special military meaning for "keep and bear arms" was intended in the discussion. *Id.,* at 467–468.

c. **Meaning of the Operative Clause.** Putting all of these textual elements together, we find that they guarantee the individual right to possess and carry weapons in case of confrontation. This meaning is strongly confirmed by the historical background of the Second Amendment. We look to this because it has always been widely understood that the Second Amendment, like the First and Fourth Amendments, codified a *pre-existing* right. The very text of the Second Amendment implicitly recognizes the pre-existence of the right and declares only that it "shall not be infringed." As we said in *United States v. Cruikshank,* 92 U.S. 542, 553, 23 L.Ed. 588 (1876), "[t]his is not a right granted by the Constitution. Neither is it in any manner dependent upon that instrument for its existence. The second amendment declares that it shall not be infringed ...."

Between the Restoration and the Glorious Revolution, the Stuart Kings Charles II and James II succeeded in using select militias loyal to them to suppress political dissidents, in part by disarming their opponents. See J. Malcolm, *To Keep and Bear Arms* 31–53 (1994) (hereinafter *Malcolm*); L. Schwoerer, *The Declaration of Rights,* 1689, p. 76 (1981). Under the auspices of the 1671 Game Act, for example, the Catholic Charles II had ordered general disarmaments of regions home to his Protestant enemies. See *Malcolm* 103–106. These experiences caused Englishmen to be extremely wary of concentrated military forces run by the state and to be jealous of their arms. They accordingly obtained an assurance from William and Mary, in the Declaration of Rights (which was codified as the English Bill of Rights), that Protestants would never be disarmed: "That the Subjects which are Protestants, may have Arms for their Defence suitable to their Conditions, and as allowed by Law." 1 W. & M., ch. 2, § 7, in 3 *Eng. Stat. at Large* 441. This right has long been understood to be the predecessor to our Second Amendment. See E. Dumbauld, *The Bill of Rights and What It Means Today* 51 (1957); W. Rawle, *A View of the Constitution of the United States of America* 122 (1825) (hereinafter *Rawle*). It was clearly an individual right, having nothing whatever to do with service in a militia. To be sure, it was an individual right not available to the whole population, given that it was restricted to Protestants, and like all written English rights it was held only against the Crown, not Parliament. See Schwoerer, "To Hold and Bear Arms: The

English Perspective," in *Bogus* 207, 218; but see 3 J. Story, *Commentaries on the Constitution of the United States* § 1858 (1833) (hereinafter *Story*) (contending that the "right to bear arms" is a "limitatio[n] upon the power of parliament" as well). But it was secured to them as individuals, according to "libertarian political principles," not as members of a fighting force. Schwoerer, *Declaration of Rights*, at 283; see also *id.*, at 78; G. Jellinek, *The Declaration of the Rights of Man and of Citizens* 49, and n. 7 (1901) (reprinted 1979).

By the time of the founding, the right to have arms had become fundamental for English subjects. See *Malcolm* 122–134. Blackstone, whose works, we have said, "constituted the preeminent authority on English law for the founding generation," *Alden v. Maine,* 527 U.S. 706, 715, 119 S.Ct. 2240, 144 L.Ed.2d 636 (1999), cited the arms provision of the Bill of Rights as one of the fundamental rights of Englishmen. See 1 *Blackstone* 136, 139–140 (1765). His description of it cannot possibly be thought to tie it to militia or military service. It was, he said, "the natural right of resistance and self-preservation," *id.*, at 139, and "the right of having and using arms for self-preservation and defence," *id.*, at 140; see also 3 *id.*, at 2–4 (1768). Other contemporary authorities concurred. See G. Sharp, *Tracts, Concerning the Ancient and Only True Legal Means of National Defence, by a Free Militia* 17–18, 27 (3d ed. 1782); 2 J. de Lolme, *The Rise and Progress of the English Constitution* 886–887 (1784) (A. Stephens ed. 1838); W. Blizard, *Desultory Reflections on Police* 59–60 (1785). Thus, the right secured in 1689 as a result of the Stuarts' abuses was by the time of the founding understood to be an individual right protecting against both public and private violence.

And, of course, what the Stuarts had tried to do to their political enemies, George III had tried to do to the colonists. In the tumultuous decades of the 1760's and 1770's, the Crown began to disarm the inhabitants of the most rebellious areas. That provoked polemical reactions by Americans invoking their rights as Englishmen to keep arms. A New York article of April 1769 said that "[i]t is a natural right which the people have reserved to themselves, confirmed by the Bill of Rights, to keep arms for their own defence." *A Journal of the Times: Mar. 17, New York Journal*, Supp. 1, Apr. 13, 1769, in *Boston Under Military Rule* 79 (O. Dickerson ed.1936) (reprinted 1970); see also, *e.g.*, Shippen, *Boston Gazette*, Jan. 30, 1769, in 1 *The Writings of Samuel Adams* 299 (H. Cushing ed. 1904) (reprinted 1968). They understood the right to enable individuals to defend themselves. As the most important early American edition of *Blackstone's Commentaries* (by the law professor and former Antifederalist St. George Tucker) made clear in the notes to the description of the arms right, Americans understood the "right of self-preservation" as permitting a citizen to "repe[l] force by force" when "the intervention of society in his behalf, may be too late to prevent an injury." 1 *Blackstone's Commentaries* 145–146, n. 42 (1803) (hereinafter *Tucker's Blackstone*). See also W. Duer, *Outlines of the Constitutional Jurisprudence of the United States* 31–32 (1833).

There seems to us no doubt, on the basis of both text and history, that the Second Amendment conferred an individual right to keep and bear arms. Of course the right was not unlimited, just as the First Amendment's right of free speech was not, see, *e.g., United States v. Williams,* 553 U.S. 285, 128 S.Ct. 1830, 170 L.Ed.2d 650 (2008). Thus, we do not read the Second Amendment to protect the right of citizens to carry arms for *any sort* of confrontation, just as we do not read the First Amendment to protect the right of citizens to speak for *any purpose.* Before turning to limitations upon the individual right, however, we must determine whether the prefatory clause of the Second Amendment comports with our interpretation of the operative clause.

2. Prefatory Clause.

The prefatory clause reads: "A well regulated Militia, being necessary to the security of a free State ...."

a. "Well-Regulated Militia." In *United States v. Miller,* 307 U.S. 174, 179, 59 S.Ct. 816, 83 L.Ed. 1206 (1939), we explained that "the Militia comprised all males physically capable of acting in concert for the common defense." That definition comports with founding-era sources. See, *e.g., Webster* ("The militia of a country are the able bodied men organized into companies, regiments and brigades ... and required by law to attend military exercises on certain days only, but at other times left to pursue their usual occupations"); *The Federalist* No. 46, pp. 329, 334 (B. Wright ed.1961) (J. Madison) ("near half a million of citizens with arms in their hands"); Letter to Destutt de Tracy (Jan. 26, 1811), in *The Portable Thomas Jefferson* 520, 524 (M. Peterson ed. 1975) ("the militia of the State, that is to say, of every man in it able to bear arms").

Petitioners take a seemingly narrower view of the militia, stating that "[m]ilitias are the state- and congressionally-regulated military forces described in the Militia Clauses (art. I, § 8, cls. 15–16)." Brief for Petitioners 12. Although we agree with petitioners' interpretive assumption that "militia" means the same thing in Article I and the Second Amendment, we believe that petitioners identify the wrong thing, namely, the organized militia. Unlike armies and navies, which Congress is given the power to create ("to raise ... Armies"; "to provide ... a Navy," Art. I, § 8, cls. 12–13), the militia is assumed by Article I already to be *in existence.* Congress is given the power to "provide for calling forth the Militia," § 8, cl. 15; and the power not to create, but to "organiz[e]" it—and not to organize "a" militia, which is what one would expect if the militia were to be a federal creation, but to organize "the" militia, connoting a body already in existence, *ibid.*, cl. 16. This is fully consistent with the ordinary definition of the militia as all able-bodied men. From that pool, Congress has plenary power to organize the units that will make up an effective fighting force. That is what Congress did in the first Militia Act, which specified that "each and every free able-bodied white male citizen of the respective states, resident therein, who is or shall be of the age of eighteen years, and under the age of forty-five years (except as is herein after excepted) shall severally and respectively be enrolled in the militia." Act of May 8, 1792, 1 Stat. 271. To be sure, Congress need not conscript every able-bodied man into the militia, because nothing in Article I suggests that in exercising its power to organize, discipline, and arm the militia, Congress must focus upon the entire body. Although the militia consists of all able-bodied men, the federally organized militia may consist of a subset of them.

Finally, the adjective "well-regulated" implies nothing more than the imposition of proper discipline and training. See *Johnson* 1619 ("Regulate": "To adjust by rule or method"); *Rawle* 121–122; cf. Va. Declaration of Rights § 13 (1776), in 7 Thorpe 3812, 3814 (referring to "a well-regulated militia, composed of the body of the people, trained to arms").

b. "Security of a Free State." The phrase "security of a free State" meant "security of a free polity," not security of each of the several States as the dissent below argued, see 478 F.3d, at 405, and n. 10. Joseph Story wrote in his treatise on the Constitution that "the word 'state' is used in various senses [and in] its most enlarged sense it means the people composing a particular nation or community." 1 *Story* § 208; see also 3 *id.*, § 1890 (in reference to the Second Amendment's prefatory clause: "The militia is the natural defence of a free country"). It is true that the term "State" elsewhere in the Constitution refers to individual States, but the phrase "security of a free State" and close variations seem to have been terms of art in 18th-century political discourse, meaning a "free country" or free polity. See Volokh, "Necessary to the Security of a Free State," 83 *Notre Dame L.Rev.* 1, 5 (2007); see, *e.g.*, 4 *Blackstone* 151 (1769); Brutus Essay III (Nov. 15, 1787), in *The Essential Antifederalist* 251, 253 (W. Allen & G. Lloyd eds., 2d ed.2002). Moreover, the other instances of "state" in the Constitution are typically accompanied by modifiers making clear that the reference is to the several States—"each state," "several states," "any state," "that state," "particular states," "one state," "no state." And the presence of the term "foreign state" in Article I and Article III shows that the word "state" did not have a single meaning in the Constitution.

There are many reasons why the militia was thought to be "necessary to the security of a free State." See 3 *Story* § 1890. First, of course, it is useful in repelling invasions and suppressing insurrections. Second, it renders large standing armies unnecessary—an argument that Alexander Hamilton made in favor of federal control over the militia. *The Federalist* No. 29, pp. 226, 227 (B. Wright ed.1961). Third, when the able-bodied men of a nation are trained in arms and organized, they are better able to resist tyranny.

3. Relationship Between Prefatory Clause and Operative Clause.

We reach the question, then: Does the preface fit with an operative clause that creates an individual right to keep and bear arms? It fits perfectly, once one knows the history that the founding generation knew and that we have described above. That history showed that the way tyrants had eliminated a militia consisting of all the able-bodied men was not by banning the militia but simply by taking away the people's arms, enabling a select militia or standing army to suppress political opponents. This is what had occurred in England that prompted codification of the right to have arms in the English Bill of Rights.

The debate with respect to the right to keep and bear arms, as with other guarantees in the Bill of Rights, was not over whether it was desirable (all agreed that it was) but over whether it needed to be codified in the Constitution. During the 1788 ratification debates, the fear that the Federal Government would disarm the people in order to impose rule through a standing army or select militia was pervasive in Antifederalist rhetoric. See, *e.g.*, "Letters from The Federal Farmer" III (Oct. 10, 1787), in 2 *The Complete Anti-Federalist* 234, 242 (H. Storing ed.1981). John Smilie, for example, worried not only that Congress's "command of the militia" could be used to create a "select militia," or to have "no militia at all," but also, as a separate concern, that "[w]hen a select militia is formed; the people in general may be disarmed." 2 *Documentary History of the Ratification of the Constitution* 508–509 (M. Jensen ed.1976) (hereinafter *Documentary Hist.*). Federalists responded that because Congress was given no power to abridge the ancient right of individuals to keep and bear arms, such a force could never oppress the people. See, *e.g.*, A Pennsylvanian III (Feb. 20, 1788), in *The Origin of the Second Amendment* 275, 276 (D. Young ed., 2d ed.2001) (hereinafter *Young*); White, To the Citizens of Virginia (Feb. 22, 1788), in *id.*, at 280, 281; A Citizen of America (Oct. 10, 1787), in *id.*, at 38, 40; Foreign Spectator, Remarks on the

Amendments to the Federal Constitution, Nov. 7, 1788, in *id.*, at 556. It was understood across the political spectrum that the right helped to secure the ideal of a citizen militia, which might be necessary to oppose an oppressive military force if the constitutional order broke down.

It is therefore entirely sensible that the Second Amendment's prefatory clause announces the purpose for which the right was codified: to prevent elimination of the militia. The prefatory clause does not suggest that preserving the militia was the only reason Americans valued the ancient right; most undoubtedly thought it even more important for self-defense and hunting. But the threat that the new Federal Government would destroy the citizens' militia by taking away their arms was the reason that right—unlike some other English rights—was codified in a written Constitution. Justice Breyer's assertion that individual self-defense is merely a "subsidiary interest" of the right to keep and bear arms, see *post,* at 2841 (dissenting opinion), is profoundly mistaken. He bases that assertion solely upon the prologue—but that can only show that self-defense had little to do with the right's *codification;* it was the *central component* of the right itself.

Besides ignoring the historical reality that the Second Amendment was not intended to lay down a "novel principl[e]" but rather codified a right "inherited from our English ancestors," *Robertson v. Baldwin,* 165 U.S. 275, 281, 17 S.Ct. 326, 41 L.Ed. 715 (1897), petitioners' interpretation does not even achieve the narrower purpose that prompted codification of the right. If, as they believe, the Second Amendment right is no more than the right to keep and use weapons as a member of an organized militia, see Brief for Petitioners 8—if, that is, the *organized* militia is the sole institutional beneficiary of the Second Amendment's guarantee—it does not assure the existence of a "citizens' militia" as a safeguard against tyranny. For Congress retains plenary authority to organize the militia, which must include the authority to say who will belong to the organized force. That is why the first Militia Act's requirement that only whites enroll caused States to amend their militia laws to exclude free blacks. See Siegel, "The Federal Government's Power to Enact Color-Conscious Laws," 92 *Nw. U.L.Rev.* 477, 521–525 (1998). Thus, if petitioners are correct, the Second Amendment protects citizens' right to use a gun in an organization from which Congress has plenary authority to exclude them. It guarantees a select militia of the sort the Stuart kings found useful, but not the people's militia that was the concern of the founding generation.

B

Our interpretation is confirmed by analogous arms-bearing rights in state constitutions that preceded and immediately followed adoption of the Second Amendment. Four States adopted analogues to the Federal Second Amendment in the period between independence and the ratification of the Bill of Rights. Two of them—Pennsylvania and Vermont—clearly adopted individual rights unconnected to militia service. Pennsylvania's Declaration of Rights of 1776 said: "That the people have a right to bear arms *for the defence of themselves* and the state ...." § XIII, in 5 Thorpe 3082, 3083 (emphasis added). In 1777, Vermont adopted the identical provision, except for inconsequential differences in punctuation and capitalization. See Vt. Const., ch. 1, § XV, in 6 *id.*, at 3741.

North Carolina also codified a right to bear arms in 1776: "That the people have a right to bear arms, for the defence of the State ...." Declaration of Rights § XVII, in 5 *id.*, at 2787, 2788. This could plausibly be read to support only a right to bear arms in a militia—but that is a peculiar way to make the point in a constitution that elsewhere repeatedly mentions the militia explicitly. See N. C. Const., §§ XIV, XVIII, XXXV, in *id.,* at 2789, 2791, 2793. Many colonial statutes required individual arms bearing for public-safety reasons—such as the 1770 Georgia law that "for the security and *defence of this province* from internal dangers and insurrections" required those men who qualified for militia duty individually "to carry fire arms" "to places of public worship." 19 *Colonial Records of the State of Georgia* 137–139 (A. Candler ed.1911 (pt. 1)) (emphasis added). That broad public-safety understanding was the connotation given to the North Carolina right by that State's Supreme Court in 1843. See *State v. Huntly,* 25 N.C. 418, 25 N. C. 418, 422–423.

The 1780 Massachusetts Constitution presented another variation on the theme: "The people have a right to keep and to bear arms for the common defence ...." Pt. First, Art. XVII, in 3 Thorpe 1888, 1892. Once again, if one gives narrow meaning to the phrase "common defence" this can be thought to limit the right to the bearing of arms in a state-organized military force. But once again the State's highest court thought otherwise. Writing for the court in an 1825 libel case, Chief Justice Parker wrote: "The liberty of the press was to be unrestrained, but he who used it was to be responsible in cases of its abuse; like the right to keep fire arms, which does not protect him who uses them for annoyance or destruction."*Commonwealth v. Blanding,* 20 Mass. 304, 313–314. The analogy makes no sense if firearms could not be used for any individual purpose at all. See also Kates, Handgun Prohibition and the Original Meaning of the Second Amendment, 82 Mich. L.Rev. 204, 244 (1983) (19th-century courts never read "common defence" to limit the use of weapons to militia service).

We therefore believe that the most likely reading of all four of these pre-Second Amendment state constitutional provisions is that they secured an individual right to bear arms for defensive purposes. Other States did not include rights to bear arms in their pre-1789 constitutions—although in Virginia a Second Amendment analogue was proposed (unsuccessfully) by Thomas Jefferson. (It read: "No freeman shall ever be debarred the use of arms [within his own lands or tenements]." 1 *The Papers of Thomas Jefferson* 344 (J. Boyd ed.1950).)

Between 1789 and 1820, nine States adopted Second Amendment analogues. Four of them—Kentucky, Ohio, Indiana, and Missouri—referred to the right of the people to "bear arms in defence of themselves and the State." See n. 8, *supra.* Another three States—Mississippi, Connecticut, and Alabama—used the even more individualistic phrasing that each citizen has the "right to bear arms in defence of himself and the State." See *ibid.* Finally, two States—Tennessee and Maine—used the "common defence" language of Massachusetts. See Tenn. Const., Art. XI, § 26 (1796), in 6 Thorpe 3414, 3424; Me. Const., Art. I, § 16 (1819), in 3 *id.*, at 1646, 1648. That of the nine state constitutional protections for the right to bear arms enacted immediately after 1789 at least seven unequivocally protected an individual citizen's right to self-defense is strong evidence that that is how the founding generation conceived of the right. And with one possible exception that we discuss in Part II-D-2, 19th-century courts and commentators interpreted these state constitutional provisions to protect an individual right to use arms for self-defense. See n. 9, *supra; Simpson v. State,* 13 Tenn. 356, 5 Yer. 356, 360 (1833).

The historical narrative that petitioners must endorse would thus treat the Federal Second Amendment as an odd outlier, protecting a right unknown in state constitutions or at

English common law, based on little more than an overreading of the prefatory clause.

C

Justice Stevens relies on the drafting history of the Second Amendment—the various proposals in the state conventions and the debates in Congress. It is dubious to rely on such history to interpret a text that was widely understood to codify a pre-existing right, rather than to fashion a new one. But even assuming that this legislative history is relevant, Justice Stevens flatly misreads the historical record.

It is true, as Justice Stevens says, that there was concern that the Federal Government would abolish the institution of the state militia. See *post,* at 2832–2833. That concern found expression, however, *not* in the various Second Amendment precursors proposed in the state conventions, but in separate structural provisions that would have given the States concurrent and seemingly non-pre-emptible authority to organize, discipline, and arm the militia when the Federal Government failed to do so. See *Veit* 17, 20 (Virginia proposal); 4 J. Eliot, *The Debates in the Several State Conventions on the Adoption of the Federal Constitution* 244, 245 (2d ed. 1836) (reprinted 1941) (North Carolina proposal); see also 2 *Documentary Hist.* 624 (Pennsylvania minority's proposal). The Second Amendment precursors, by contrast, referred to the individual English right already codified in two (and probably four) state constitutions. The Federalist-dominated first Congress chose to reject virtually all major structural revisions favored by the Antifederalists, including the proposed militia amendments. Rather, it adopted primarily the popular and uncontroversial (though, in the Federalists' view, unnecessary) individual-rights amendments. The Second

Amendment right, protecting only individuals' liberty to keep and carry arms, did nothing to assuage Antifederalists' concerns about federal control of the militia. See, *e.g.*, "Centinel, Revived, No. XXIX," *Philadelphia Independent Gazetteer*, Sept. 9, 1789, in *Young* 711, 712.

Justice Stevens thinks it significant that the Virginia, New York, and North Carolina Second Amendment proposals were "embedded ... within a group of principles that are distinctly military in meaning," such as statements about the danger of standing armies. *Post*, at 2833–2834. But so was the highly influential minority proposal in Pennsylvania, yet that proposal, with its reference to hunting, plainly referred to an individual right. See 2 *Documentary Hist.* 624. Other than that erroneous point, Justice Stevens has brought forward absolutely no evidence that those proposals conferred only a right to carry arms in a militia. By contrast, New Hampshire's proposal, the Pennsylvania minority's proposal, and Samuel Adams' proposal in Massachusetts unequivocally referred to individual rights, as did two state constitutional provisions at the time. See *Veit* 16, 17 (New Hampshire proposal); 6 *Documentary Hist.* 1452, 1453 (J. Kaminski & G. Saladino eds. 2000) (Samuel Adams' proposal). Justice Stevens' view thus relies on the proposition, unsupported by any evidence, that different people of the founding period had vastly different conceptions of the right to keep and bear arms. That simply does not comport with our longstanding view that the Bill of Rights codified venerable, widely understood liberties.

D

We now address how the Second Amendment was interpreted from immediately after its ratification through the end of the 19th century. Before proceeding, however, we take issue with Justice Stevens' equating of these sources with postenactment legislative history, a comparison that betrays a fundamental misunderstanding of a court's interpretive task. See *post,* at 2837, n. 28. "[L]egislative history," of course, refers to the pre-enactment statements of those who drafted or voted for a law; it is considered persuasive by some, not because they reflect the general understanding of the disputed terms, but because the legislators who heard or read those statements presumably voted with that understanding. *Ibid.* "[P]osten-actment legislative history," *ibid.*, a deprecatory contradiction in terms, refers to statements of those who drafted or voted for the law that are made after its enactment and hence could have had no effect on the congressional vote. It most certainly does not refer to the examination of a variety of legal and other sources to determine *the public understanding* of a legal text in the period after its enactment or ratification. That sort of inquiry is a critical tool of constitutional interpretation. As we will show, virtually all interpreters of the Second Amendment in the century after its enactment interpreted the Amendment as we do.

1. Postratification Commentary.

Three important founding-era legal scholars interpreted the Second Amendment in published writings. All three understood it to protect an individual right unconnected with militia service.

St. George Tucker's version of *Blackstone's Commentaries*, as we explained above, conceived of the Blackstonian arms right as necessary for self-defense. He equated that right, absent the religious and class-based restrictions, with the Second Amendment. See 2 *Tucker's Blackstone* 143. In Note D, entitled, "View of the Constitution of the United States," Tucker elaborated on the Second Amendment: "This may be considered as the true palladium of liberty .... The right to self defence is the first law of nature: in most governments it has been the study of rulers to confine the right within the narrowest limits possible. Wherever standing armies are kept up, and the right of the people to keep and bear arms is, under any colour or pretext whatsoever, prohibited, liberty, if not already annihilated, is on the brink of destruction." 1 *id.*, at App. 300 (ellipsis in original). He believed that the English game laws had abridged the right by prohibiting "keeping a gun or other engine for the destruction of game." *Ibid.*; see also 2 *id.*, at 143, and nn. 40 and 41. He later grouped the right with some of the individual rights included in the First Amendment and said that if "a law be passed by congress, prohibiting" any of those rights, it would "be the province of the judiciary to pronounce whether any such act were constitutional, or not; and if not, to acquit the accused ...." 1 *id.*, at App. 357. It is unlikely that Tucker was referring to a person's being "accused" of violating a law making it a crime to bear arms in a state militia.

In 1825, William Rawle, a prominent lawyer who had been a member of the Pennsylvania Assembly that ratified the Bill of Rights, published an influential treatise, which analyzed the Second Amendment as follows:

> "The first [principle] is a declaration that a well regulated militia is necessary to the security of a free state; a proposition from which few will dissent ....
>
> "The corollary, from the first position is, that the right of the people to keep and bear arms shall not be infringed.
>
> "The prohibition is general. No clause in the constitution could by any rule of construction be conceived to give to congress a power to disarm the people. Such a flagitious attempt could only be made under some general pretence by a state legislature. But if in any blind pursuit of inordinate

> power, either should attempt it, this amendment may be appealed to as a restraint on both." *Rawle* 121–122.

Like Tucker, Rawle regarded the English game laws as violating the right codified in the Second Amendment. See *id.*, at 122–123. Rawle clearly differentiated between the people's right to bear arms and their service in a militia: "In a people permitted and accustomed to bear arms, we have the rudiments of a militia, which properly consists of armed citizens, divided into military bands, and instructed at least in part, in the use of arms for the purposes of war." *Id.*, at 140. Rawle further said that the Second Amendment right ought not "be abused to the disturbance of the public peace," such as by assembling with other armed individuals "for an unlawful purpose"—statements that make no sense if the right does not extend to *any* individual purpose. *Id.*, at 123.

Joseph Story published his famous *Commentaries on the Constitution of the United States* in 1833. Justice Stevens suggests that "[t]here is not so much as a whisper" in Story's explanation of the Second Amendment that favors the individual-rights view. *Post,* at 2840. That is wrong. Story explained that the English Bill of Rights had also included a "right to bear arms," a right that, as we have discussed, had nothing to do with militia service. 3 *Story* § 1858. He then equated the English right with the Second Amendment:

> "§ 1891. A similar provision [to the Second Amendment] in favour of protestants (for to them it is confined) is to be found in the bill of rights of 1688, it being declared, 'that the subjects, which are protestants, may have arms for their defence suitable to their condition, and as allowed by law.' But under various pretences the effect of this provision has been greatly narrowed; and it is at present in

England more nominal than real, as a defensive privilege." (Footnotes omitted.)

This comparison to the Declaration of Right would not make sense if the Second Amendment right was the right to use a gun in a militia, which was plainly not what the English right protected. As the Tennessee Supreme Court recognized 38 years after Story wrote his *Commentaries*, "[t]he passage from Story, shows clearly that this right was intended ... and was guaranteed to, and to be exercised and enjoyed by the citizen as such, and not by him as a soldier, or in defense solely of his political rights." *Andrews v. State*, 50 Tenn. 165, 183–184 (1871). Story's *Commentaries* also cite as support Tucker and Rawle, both of whom clearly viewed the right as unconnected to militia service. See 3 *Story* § 1890, n. 2, § 1891, n. 3. In addition, in a shorter 1840 work Story wrote: "One of the ordinary modes, by which tyrants accomplish their purposes without resistance, is, by disarming the people, and making it an offence to keep arms, and by substituting a regular army in the stead of a resort to the militia." *A Familiar Exposition of the Constitution of the United States* § 450 (reprinted 1986).

Antislavery advocates routinely invoked the right to bear arms for self-defense. Joel Tiffany, for example, citing Blackstone's description of the right, wrote that "the right to keep and bear arms, also implies the right to use them if necessary in self defence; without this right to use the guaranty would have hardly been worth the paper it consumed." *A Treatise on the Unconstitutionality of American Slavery* 117–118 (1849); see also L. Spooner, *The Unconstitutionality of Slavery* 116 (1845) (right enables "personal defence"). In his famous Senate speech about the 1856 "Bleeding Kansas" conflict, Charles Sumner proclaimed:

> "The rifle has ever been the companion of the pioneer and, under God, his tutelary protector against the red man and the beast of the forest. Never was this efficient weapon more needed in just self-defense, than now in Kansas, and at least one article in our National Constitution must be blotted out, before the complete right to it can in any way be impeached. And yet such is the madness of the hour, that, in defiance of the solemn guarantee, embodied in the Amendments to the Constitution, that 'the right of the people to keep and bear arms shall not be infringed,' the people of Kansas have been arraigned for keeping and bearing them, and the Senator from South Carolina has had the face to say openly, on this floor, that they should be disarmed—of course, that the fanatics of Slavery, his allies and constituents, may meet no impediment." The Crime Against Kansas, May 19–20, 1856, in *American Speeches: Political Oratory From the Revolution to the Civil War* 553, 606–607 (T. Widmer ed. 2006).

We have found only one early-19th century-commentator who clearly conditioned the right to keep and bear arms upon service in the militia—and he recognized that the prevailing view was to the contrary. "The provision of the constitution, declaring the right of the people to keep and bear arms, & c. was probably intended to apply to the right of the people to bear arms for such [militia-related] purposes only, and not to prevent congress or the legislatures of the different states from enacting laws to prevent the citizens from always going armed. A different construction however has been given to it." B. Oliver, *The Rights of an American Citizen* 177 (1832).

2. Pre-Civil War Case Law.

The 19th-century cases that interpreted the Second Amendment universally support an individual right unconnected to militia service. In *Houston v. Moore,* 5 Wheat. 1, 24, 5 L.Ed. 19 (1820), this Court held that States have concurrent power over the militia, at least where not pre-empted by Congress. Agreeing in dissent that States could "organize, arm, and discipline" the militia in the absence of conflicting federal regulation, Justice Story said that the Second Amendment "may not, perhaps, be thought to have any important bearing on this point. If it have, it confirms and illustrates, rather than impugns the reasoning already suggested." *Id.,* at 51–53. Of course, if the Amendment simply "protect[ed] the right of the people of each of the several States to maintain a well-regulated militia," *post,* at 2822 (Stevens, J., dissenting), it would have enormous and obvious bearing on the point. But the Court and Story derived the States' power over the militia from the nonexclusive nature of federal power, not from the Second Amendment, whose preamble merely "confirms and illustrates" the importance of the militia. Even clearer was Justice Baldwin. In the famous fugitive-slave case of *Johnson v. Tompkins,* 13 F. Cas. 840, 850, 852 (CC Pa. 1833), Baldwin, sitting as a Circuit Judge, cited both the Second Amendment and the Pennsylvania analogue for his conclusion that a citizen has "a right to carry arms in defence of his property or person, and to use them, if either were assailed with such force, numbers or violence as made it necessary for the protection or safety of either."

Many early-19th century state cases indicated that the Second Amendment right to bear arms was an individual right unconnected to militia service, though subject to certain restrictions. A Virginia case in 1824 holding that the Constitution did not extend to free blacks explained: "[N]umerous restrictions imposed on [blacks] in our Statute Book, many of which are inconsistent with the letter and spirit of the Constitution, both of this State and of the United States as respects the free whites, demonstrate, that, here, those instruments have not been considered to extend equally to both classes of our population. We will only instance the restriction upon the migration of free blacks into this State, and upon their right to bear arms." *Aldridge v. Commonwealth,* 4 Va. 447, 2 Va. Cas. 447, 449 (Gen.Ct.). The claim was obviously not that blacks were prevented from carrying guns in the militia. See also *Waters v. State,* 1 Gill 302, 309 (Md.1843) (because free blacks were treated as a "dangerous population," "laws have been passed to prevent their migration into this State; to make it unlawful for them to bear arms; to guard even their religious assemblages with peculiar watchfulness"). An 1829 decision by the Supreme Court of Michigan said: "The constitution of the United States also grants to the citizen the right to keep and bear arms. But the grant of this privilege cannot be construed into the right in him who keeps a gun to destroy his neighbor. No rights are intended to be granted by the constitution for an unlawful or unjustifiable purpose." *United States v. Sheldon,* in 5 *Transactions of the Supreme Court of the Territory of Michigan* 337, 346 (W. Blume ed.1940) (hereinafter *Blume*). It is not possible to read this as discussing anything other than an individual right unconnected to militia service. If it did have to do with militia service, the limitation upon it would not be any "unlawful or unjustifiable purpose," but any nonmilitary purpose whatsoever.

In *Nunn v. State,* 1 Ga. 243, 251 (1846), the Georgia Supreme Court construed the Second Amendment as protecting the "*natural* right of self-defence" and therefore struck down a ban on carrying pistols openly. Its opinion perfectly captured the way in which the operative clause of the Second Amendment furthers the purpose announced in the prefatory clause, in continuity with the English right:

> "The right of the whole people, old and young, men, women and boys, and not militia only, to keep and bear *arms* of every description, and not *such* merely as are used by the *militia,* shall not be *infringed,* curtailed, or broken in upon, in the smallest degree; and all this for the important end to be attained: the rearing up and qualifying a well-regulated militia, so vitally necessary to the security of a free State. Our opinion is, that any law, State or Federal, is repugnant to the Constitution, and void, which contravenes this *right,* originally belonging to our forefathers, trampled under foot by Charles I. and his two wicked sons and successors, re-established by the revolution of 1688, conveyed to this land of liberty by the colonists, and finally incorporated conspicuously in our own *Magna Charta!*" *Ibid.*

Likewise, in *State v. Chandler,* 5 La. Ann. 489, 490 (1850), the Louisiana Supreme Court held that citizens had a right to carry arms openly: "This is the right guaranteed by the Constitution of the United States, and which is calculated to incite men to a manly and noble defence of themselves, if necessary, and of their country, without any tendency to secret advantages and unmanly assassinations."

Those who believe that the Second Amendment preserves only a militia-centered right place great reliance on the Tennessee Supreme Court's 1840 decision in *Aymette v. State,* 21 Tenn. 154. The case does not stand for that broad proposition; in fact, the case does not mention the word "militia" at all, except in its quoting of the Second Amendment. *Aymette* held that the state constitutional guarantee of the right to "bear" arms did not prohibit the banning of concealed weapons. The opinion first recognized that both the state right and the federal right were descendents of the 1689 English right, but (erroneously, and contrary to virtually all other authorities) read that right to refer only to "protect[ion of] the public liberty" and "keep[ing] in awe those who are in power," *id.*, at 158. The court then adopted a sort of middle position, whereby citizens were permitted to carry arms openly, unconnected with any service in a formal militia, but were given the right to use them only for the military purpose of banding together to oppose tyranny. This odd reading of the right is, to be sure, not the one we adopt—but it is not petitioners' reading either. More importantly, seven years earlier the Tennessee Supreme Court had treated the state constitutional provision as conferring a right "to all the free citizens of the State to keep and bear arms for their defence," *Simpson,* 13 Tenn. 356, 5 Yer., at 360; and 21 years later the court held that the "keep" portion of the state constitutional right included the right to personal self-defense: "[T]he right to keep arms involves, necessarily, the right to use such arms for all the ordinary purposes, and in all the ordinary modes usual in the country, and to which arms are adapted, limited by the duties of a good citizen in times of peace." *Andrews,* 50 Tenn., at 178–179; see also *ibid.* (equating state provision with Second Amendment).

3. Post-Civil War Legislation.

In the aftermath of the Civil War, there was an outpouring of discussion of the Second Amendment in Congress and in public discourse, as people debated whether and how to secure constitutional rights for newly free slaves. See generally S. Halbrook, *Freedmen, the Fourteenth Amendment, and the Right to Bear Arms, 1866–1876* (1998) (hereinafter *Halbrook*); Brief for Institute for Justice as *Amicus Curiae.* Since those discussions took place 75 years after the ratification of the Second Amendment, they do not provide as much insight into its original meaning as earlier sources. Yet those born and educated in the early 19th century faced a widespread effort to limit arms ownership by a large number of citizens; their understanding of the origins and continuing significance of the Amendment is instructive.

Blacks were routinely disarmed by Southern States after the Civil War. Those who opposed these injustices frequently stated that they infringed blacks' constitutional right to keep and bear arms. Needless to say, the claim was not that blacks were being prohibited from carrying arms in an organized state militia. A Report of the Commission of the Freedmen's Bureau in 1866 stated plainly: "[T]he civil law [of Kentucky] prohibits the colored man from bearing arms .... Their arms are taken from them by the civil authorities .... Thus, the right of the people to keep and bear arms as provided in the Constitution is *infringed*." H.R. Exec. Doc. No. 70, 39th Cong., 1st Sess., 233, 236. A joint congressional Report decried:

> "[I]n some parts of [South Carolina,] armed parties are, without proper authority, engaged in seizing all fire-arms found in the hands of the freedmen. Such conduct is in plain and direct violation of their personal rights as guaranteed by the Constitution of the United States, which declares that 'the right of the people to keep and bear arms shall not be infringed.' The freedmen of South Carolina have shown by their peaceful and orderly conduct that they can safely be trusted with fire-arms, and they need them to kill game for subsistence, and to protect their crops from destruction by birds and animals." Joint Comm. on Reconstruction, H.R.Rep. No. 30, 39th Cong., 1st Sess., pt. 2, p. 229 (1866) (Proposed Circular of Brigadier General R. Saxton).

The view expressed in these statements was widely reported and was apparently widely held. For example, an editorial in The Loyal Georgian (Augusta) on February 3, 1866, assured blacks that "[a]ll men, without distinction of color, have the right to keep and bear arms to defend their homes, families or themselves." *Halbrook* 19.

Congress enacted the Freedmen's Bureau Act on July 16, 1866. Section 14 stated:

> "[T]he right ... to have full and equal benefit of all laws and proceedings concerning personal liberty, personal security, and the acquisition, enjoyment, and disposition of estate, real and personal, including the constitutional right to bear arms, shall be secured to and enjoyed by all the citizens... without respect to race or color, or previous condition of slavery ...." 14 Stat. 176–177.

The understanding that the Second Amendment gave freed blacks the right to keep and bear arms was reflected in congressional discussion of the bill, with even an opponent of it saying that the founding generation "were for every man bearing his arms about him and keeping them in his house, his castle, for his own defense." Cong. Globe, 39th Cong., 1st Sess., 362, 371 (1866) (Sen. Davis).

Similar discussion attended the passage of the Civil Rights Act of 1871 and the Fourteenth Amendment. For example, Representative Butler said of the Act: "Section eight is intended to enforce the well-known constitutional provision guaranteeing the right of the citizen to 'keep and bear arms,' and provides that whoever shall take away, by force or violence, or by threats and intimidation, the arms and weapons which any person may have for his defense, shall be deemed guilty of larceny of the same." H.R.Rep. No. 37, 41st Cong., 3d Sess., 7–8 (1871). With respect to the proposed Amendment, Senator Pomeroy described as one of the three "indispensable" "safeguards of liberty ... under the Constitution" a man's "right to bear arms for the defense of himself and family and his homestead." Cong. Globe, 39th Cong., 1st Sess., 1182 (1866). Representative Nye thought the Fourteenth Amendment unnecessary because "[a]s citizens of the United States [blacks] have equal right to protection, and to keep and bear arms for self-defense." *Id.*, at 1073.

It was plainly the understanding in the post-Civil War Congress that the Second Amendment protected an individual right to use arms for self-defense.

4. Post-Civil War Commentators.

Every late-19th-century legal scholar that we have read interpreted the Second Amendment to secure an individual right unconnected with militia service. The most famous was the judge and professor Thomas Cooley, who wrote a massively popular 1868 *Treatise on Constitutional Limitations.* Concerning the Second Amendment it said:

> "Among the other defences to personal liberty should be mentioned the right of the people to keep and bear arms .... The alternative to a standing army is 'a well-regulated militia,' but this cannot exist unless the people are trained to bearing arms. How far it is in the power of the legislature to regulate this right, we shall not undertake to say, as happily there has been very little occasion to discuss that subject by the courts." *Id.*, at 350.

That Cooley understood the right not as connected to militia service, but as securing the militia by ensuring a populace familiar with arms, is made even clearer in his 1880 work, *General Principles of Constitutional Law.* The Second Amendment, he said, "was adopted with some modification and enlargement from the English Bill of Rights of 1688, where it stood as a protest against arbitrary action of the overturned dynasty in disarming the people." *Id.*, at 270. In a section entitled "The Right in General," he continued:

> "It might be supposed from the phraseology of this provision that the right to keep and bear arms was only guaranteed to the militia; but this would be an interpretation not warranted by the intent. The militia, as has been elsewhere explained, consists of those persons who, under the law, are liable to the performance of military duty, and are officered and enrolled for service when called upon. But the law may make provision for the enrolment of all who are fit to perform military duty, or of a small number only, or it may wholly omit to make any provision at all; and if the right were limited to those enrolled, the purpose of this guaranty might be defeated altogether by the action or neglect to act of the government it was meant to hold in check. The meaning of the provision undoubtedly is, that the people, from whom the militia must be taken, shall have the right to keep and bear arms; and they need no permission or regulation of law for the purpose. But this enables government to have a well-regulated militia; for to bear arms implies something more than the mere keeping; it implies the learning to handle and use them in a way that makes those who keep them ready for their efficient use; in other words, it implies the right to meet for voluntary discipline in arms, observing in doing so the laws of public order." *Id.,* at 271.

All other post-Civil War 19th-century sources we have found concurred with Cooley. One example from each decade will convey the general flavor:

> "[The purpose of the Second Amendment is] to secure a well-armed militia .... But a militia would be useless unless the citizens were enabled to exercise themselves in the use of warlike weapons. To preserve this privilege, and to secure to the people the ability to oppose themselves in military force against the usurpations of government, as well as against enemies from without, that government is forbidden by any

law or proceeding to invade or destroy the right to keep and bear arms .... The clause is analogous to the one securing the freedom of speech and of the press. Freedom, not license, is secured; the fair use, not the libellous abuse, is protected." J. Pomeroy, *An Introduction to the Constitutional Law of the United States* § 239, pp. 152–153 (1868) (hereinafter *Pomeroy*).

"As the Constitution of the United States, and the constitutions of several of the states, in terms more or less comprehensive, declare the right of the people to keep and bear arms, it has been a subject of grave discussion, in some of the state courts, whether a statute prohibiting persons, when not on a journey, or as travellers, from *wearing or carrying concealed weapons,* be constitutional. There has been a great difference of opinion on the question." 2 J. Kent, *Commentaries on American Law* *340, n. 2 (O. Holmes ed., 12th ed. 1873) (hereinafter *Kent*).

"Some general knowledge of firearms is important to the public welfare; because it would be impossible, in case of war, to organize promptly an efficient force of volunteers unless the people had some familiarity with weapons of war. The Constitution secures the right of the people to keep and bear arms. No doubt, a citizen who keeps a gun or pistol under judicious precautions, practises in safe places the use of it, and in due time teaches his sons to do the same, exercises his individual right. No doubt, a person whose residence or duties involve peculiar peril may keep a pistol for prudent self-defence." B. Abbott, *Judge and Jury: A Popular Explanation of the Leading Topics in the Law of the Land* 333 (1880) (hereinafter *Abbott*).

"The right to bear arms has always been the distinctive privilege of freemen. Aside from any necessity of self-protection to the person, it represents among all nations power coupled with the exercise of a certain jurisdiction. ...

> [I]t was not necessary that the right to bear arms should be granted in the Constitution, for it had always existed." J. Ordronaux, *Constitutional Legislation in the United States* 241–242 (1891).

E

We now ask whether any of our precedents forecloses the conclusions we have reached about the meaning of the Second Amendment.

United States v. Cruikshank, 92 U.S. 542, 23 L.Ed. 588, in the course of vacating the convictions of members of a white mob for depriving blacks of their right to keep and bear arms, held that the Second Amendment does not by its own force apply to anyone other than the Federal Government. The opinion explained that the right "is not a right granted by the Constitution [or] in any manner dependent upon that instrument for its existence. The second amendment ... means no more than that it shall not be infringed by Congress." *Id.*, at 553. States, we said, were free to restrict or protect the right under their police powers. The limited discussion of the Second Amendment in *Cruikshank* supports, if anything, the individual-rights interpretation. There was no claim in *Cruikshank* that the victims had been deprived of their right to carry arms in a militia; indeed, the Governor had disbanded the local militia unit the year before the mob's attack, see C. Lane, *The Day Freedom Died* 62 (2008). We described the right protected by the Second Amendment as "'bearing arms for a lawful purpose'" and said that "the people [must] look for their protection against any violation by their fellow-citizens of the rights it recognizes" to the States' police power. 92 U.S., at 553. That discussion makes little sense if it is only a right to bear arms in a state militia.

Presser v. Illinois, 116 U.S. 252, 6 S.Ct. 580, 29 L.Ed. 615 (1886), held that the right to keep and bear arms was not violated by a law that forbade "bodies of men to associate together as military organizations, or to drill or parade with arms in cities and towns unless authorized by law." *Id.,* at 264–265, 6 S.Ct. 580. This does not refute the individual-rights interpretation of the Amendment; no one supporting that interpretation has contended that States may not ban such groups. Justice Stevens presses *Presser* into service to support his view that the right to bear arms is limited to service in the militia by joining *Presser's* brief discussion of the Second Amendment with a later portion of the opinion making the seemingly relevant (to the Second Amendment) point that the plaintiff was not a member of the state militia. Unfortunately for Justice Stevens' argument, that later portion deals with the *Fourteenth Amendment;* it was the *Fourteenth Amendment* to which the plaintiff's nonmembership in the militia was relevant. Thus, Justice Stevens' statement that *Presser* "suggested that ... nothing in the Constitution protected the use of arms outside the context of a militia," *post,* at 2843, is simply wrong. *Presser* said nothing about the Second Amendment's meaning or scope, beyond the fact that it does not prevent the prohibition of private paramilitary organizations.

Justice Stevens places overwhelming reliance upon this Court's decision in *Miller,* 307 U.S. 174, 59 S.Ct. 816, 83 L.Ed. 1206. "[H]undreds of judges," we are told, "have relied on the view of the Amendment we endorsed there," *post,* at 2823, and "[e]ven if the textual and historical arguments on both sides of the issue were evenly balanced, respect for the well-settled views of all of our predecessors on this Court, and for the rule of law itself ... would prevent most jurists from endorsing such a dramatic upheaval in the law," *post,* at 2824. And what is, according to Justice Stevens, the holding of

Miller that demands such obeisance? That the Second Amendment "protects the right to keep and bear arms for certain military purposes, but that it does not curtail the Legislature's power to regulate the nonmilitary use and ownership of weapons." *Post,* at 2823.

Nothing so clearly demonstrates the weakness of Justice Stevens' case. *Miller* did not hold that and cannot possibly be read to have held that. The judgment in the case upheld against a Second Amendment challenge two men's federal indictment for transporting an unregistered short-barreled shotgun in interstate commerce, in violation of the National Firearms Act, 48 Stat. 1236. It is entirely clear that the Court's basis for saying that the Second Amendment did not apply was *not* that the defendants were "bear [ing] arms" not "for ... military purposes" but for "nonmilitary use," *post,* at 2823. Rather, it was that the *type of weapon at issue* was not eligible for Second Amendment protection: "In the absence of any evidence tending to show that the possession or use of a [short-barreled shotgun] at this time has some reasonable relationship to the preservation or efficiency of a well regulated militia, we cannot say that the Second Amendment guarantees the right to keep and bear *such an instrument.*" 307 U.S., at 178, 59 S.Ct. 816 (emphasis added). "Certainly," the Court continued, "it is not within judicial notice that this weapon is any part of the ordinary military equipment or that its use could contribute to the common defense." *Ibid.* Beyond that, the opinion provided no explanation of the content of the right.

This holding is not only consistent with, but positively suggests, that the Second Amendment confers an individual right to keep and bear arms (though only arms that "have some reasonable relationship to the preservation or efficiency of a well regulated militia"). Had the Court believed that the Second Amendment protects only those serving in the militia, it would have been odd to examine the character of the weapon rather than simply note that the two crooks were not militiamen. Justice Stevens can say again and again that *Miller* did not "turn on the difference between muskets and sawed-off shotguns; it turned, rather, on the basic difference between the military and nonmilitary use and possession of guns," *post,* at 2845, but the words of the opinion prove otherwise. The most Justice Stevens can plausibly claim for *Miller* is that it declined to decide the nature of the Second Amendment right, despite the Solicitor General's argument (made in the alternative) that the right was collective, see Brief for United States, O.T.1938, No. 696, pp. 4–5. *Miller* stands only for the proposition that the Second Amendment right, whatever its nature, extends only to certain types of weapons.

It is particularly wrongheaded to read *Miller* for more than what it said, because the case did not even purport to be a thorough examination of the Second Amendment. Justice Stevens claims, *post,* at 2845, that the opinion reached its conclusion "[a]fter reviewing many of the same sources that are discussed at greater length by the Court today." Not many, which was not entirely the Court's fault. The defendants made no appearance in the case, neither filing a brief nor appearing at oral argument; the Court heard from no one but the Government (reason enough, one would think, not to make that case the beginning and the end of this Court's consideration of the Second Amendment). See Frye, "The Peculiar Story of *United States v. Miller,*" 3 *N.Y.U.J.L. & Liberty* 48, 65–68 (2008). The Government's brief spent two pages discussing English legal sources, concluding "that at least the carrying of weapons without lawful occasion or excuse was always a crime" and that (because of the class-based restrictions and the prohibition on terrorizing people with dangerous or unusual weapons) "the early English law did not guarantee an unrestricted right to bear arms." Brief for United States, O.T.1938, No. 696, at 9–11. It then went on to rely primarily on the discussion of the English right to bear arms in *Aymette v. State*, 21 Tenn. 154, for the proposition that the only uses of arms protected by the Second Amendment are those that relate to the militia, not self-defense. See Brief for United States, O.T.1938, No. 696, at 12–18. The final section of the brief recognized that "some courts have said that the right to bear arms includes the right of the individual to have them for the protection of his person and property," and launched an alternative argument that "weapons which are commonly used by criminals," such as sawed-off shotguns, are not protected. See *id.*, at 18–21. The Government's *Miller* brief thus provided scant discussion of the history of the Second Amendment—and the Court was presented with no counterdiscussion. As for the text of the Court's opinion itself, that discusses *none* of the history of the Second Amendment. It assumes from the prologue that the Amendment was designed to preserve the militia, 307 U.S., at 178, 59 S.Ct. 816 (which we do not dispute), and then reviews some historical materials dealing with the nature of the militia, and in particular with the nature of the arms their members were expected to possess, *id.*, at 178–182, 59 S.Ct. 816. Not a word *(not a word)* about the history of the Second Amendment. This is the mighty rock upon which the dissent rests its case.

We may as well consider at this point (for we will have to consider eventually) *what* types of weapons *Miller* permits. Read in isolation, *Miller*'s phrase "part of ordinary military equipment" could mean that only those weapons useful in warfare are protected. That would be a startling reading of the opinion, since it would mean that the National Firearms Act's restrictions on machineguns (not challenged in *Miller*) might be unconstitutional, machineguns being useful in warfare in

1939. We think that *Miller*'s "ordinary military equipment" language must be read in tandem with what comes after: "[O]rdinarily when called for [militia] service [able-bodied] men were expected to appear bearing arms supplied by themselves and of the kind in common use at the time." 307 U.S., at 179, 59 S.Ct. 816. The traditional militia was formed from a pool of men bringing arms "in common use at the time" for lawful purposes like self-defense. "In the colonial and revolutionary war era, [small-arms] weapons used by militiamen and weapons used in defense of person and home were one and the same." *State v. Kessler,* 289 Ore. 359, 368, 614 P.2d 94, 98 (1980) (citing G. Neumann, *Swords and Blades of the American Revolution* 6–15, 252–254 (1973)). Indeed, that is precisely the way in which the Second Amendment's operative clause furthers the purpose announced in its preface. We therefore read *Miller* to say only that the Second Amendment does not protect those weapons not typically possessed by law-abiding citizens for lawful purposes, such as short-barreled shotguns. That accords with the historical understanding of the scope of the right, see Part III, *infra.*

We conclude that nothing in our precedents forecloses our adoption of the original understanding of the Second Amendment. It should be unsurprising that such a significant matter has been for so long judicially unresolved. For most of our history, the Bill of Rights was not thought applicable to the States, and the Federal Government did not significantly regulate the possession of firearms by law-abiding citizens. Other provisions of the Bill of Rights have similarly remained unilluminated for lengthy periods. This Court first held a law to violate the First Amendment's guarantee of freedom of speech in 1931, almost 150 years after the Amendment was ratified, see *Near v. Minnesota ex rel. Olson,* 283 U.S. 697, 51 S.Ct. 625, 75 L.Ed. 1357 (1931), and it was not until after

World War II that we held a law invalid under the Establishment Clause, see *Illinois ex rel. McCollum v. Board of Ed. of School Dist. No. 71, Champaign Cty.*, 333 U.S. 203, 68 S.Ct. 461, 92 L.Ed. 649 (1948). Even a question as basic as the scope of proscribable libel was not addressed by this Court until 1964, nearly two centuries after the founding. See *New York Times Co. v. Sullivan*, 376 U.S. 254, 84 S.Ct. 710, 11 L.Ed.2d 686 (1964). It is demonstrably not true that, as Justice Stevens claims, *post*, at 2844–2845, "for most of our history, the invalidity of Second-Amendment-based objections to firearms regulations has been well settled and uncontroversial." For most of our history the question did not present itself.

III

Like most rights, the right secured by the Second Amendment is not unlimited. From Blackstone through the 19th-century cases, commentators and courts routinely explained that the right was not a right to keep and carry any weapon whatsoever in any manner whatsoever and for whatever purpose. See, *e.g.*, *Sheldon*, in 5 *Blume* 346; *Rawle* 123; *Pomeroy* 152–153; *Abbott* 333. For example, the majority of the 19th-century courts to consider the question held that prohibitions on carrying concealed weapons were lawful under the Second Amendment or state analogues. See, *e.g.*, *State v. Chandler*, 5 La. Ann., at 489–490; *Nunn v. State*, 1 Ga., at 251; see generally 2 *Kent* *340, n. 2; *The American Students' Blackstone* 84, n. 11 (G. Chase ed. 1884). Although we do not undertake an exhaustive historical analysis today of the full scope of the Second Amendment, nothing in our opinion should be taken to cast doubt on longstanding prohibitions on the possession of firearms by felons and the mentally ill, or laws forbidding the carrying of firearms in sensitive places such as schools and government buildings, or laws imposing conditions and qualifications on the commercial sale of arms.

We also recognize another important limitation on the right to keep and carry arms. *Miller* said, as we have explained, that the sorts of weapons protected were those "in common use at the time." 307 U.S., at 179, 59 S.Ct. 816. We think that limitation is fairly supported by the historical tradition of prohibiting the carrying of "dangerous and unusual weapons." See 4 *Blackstone* 148–149 (1769); 3 B. Wilson, *Works of the Honourable James Wilson* 79 (1804); J. Dunlap, *The New-York Justice* 8 (1815); C. Humphreys, *A Compendium of the Common Law in Force in Kentucky* 482 (1822); 1 W. Russell, *A Treatise on Crimes and Indictable Misdemeanors* 271–272 (1831); H. Stephen, *Summary of the Criminal Law* 48 (1840); E. Lewis, *An Abridgment of the Criminal Law of the United States* 64 (1847); F. Wharton, *A Treatise on the Criminal Law of the United States* 726 (1852). See also *State v. Langford,* 10 N.C. 381, 383–384 (1824); *O'Neill v. State,* 16 Ala. 65, 67 (1849); *English v. State,* 35 Tex. 473, 476 (1871); *State v. Lanier,* 71 N.C. 288, 289 (1874).

It may be objected that if weapons that are most useful in military service—M-16 rifles and the like—may be banned, then the Second Amendment right is completely detached from the prefatory clause. But as we have said, the conception of the militia at the time of the Second Amendment's ratification was the body of all citizens capable of military service, who would bring the sorts of lawful weapons that they possessed at home to militia duty.It may well be true today that a militia, to be as effective as militias in the 18th century, would require sophisticated arms that are highly unusual in society at large. Indeed, it may be true that no amount of small arms could be useful against modern-day bombers and tanks.

But the fact that modern developments have limited the degree of fit between the prefatory clause and the protected right cannot change our interpretation of the right.

IV

We turn finally to the law at issue here. As we have said, the law totally bans handgun possession in the home. It also requires that any lawful firearm in the home be disassembled or bound by a trigger lock at all times, rendering it inoperable.

As the quotations earlier in this opinion demonstrate, the inherent right of self-defense has been central to the Second Amendment right. The handgun ban amounts to a prohibition of an entire class of "arms" that is overwhelmingly chosen by American society for that lawful purpose. The prohibition extends, moreover, to the home, where the need for defense of self, family, and property is most acute. Under any of the standards of scrutiny that we have applied to enumerated constitutional rights, banning from the home "the most preferred firearm in the nation to 'keep' and use for protection of one's home and family," 478 F.3d, at 400, would fail constitutional muster.

Few laws in the history of our Nation have come close to the severe restriction of the District's handgun ban. And some of those few have been struck down. In *Nunn v. State,* the Georgia Supreme Court struck down a prohibition on carrying pistols openly (even though it upheld a prohibition on carrying concealed weapons). See 1 Ga., at 251. In *Andrews v. State,* the Tennessee Supreme Court likewise held that a statute that forbade openly carrying a pistol "publicly or privately, without regard to time or place, or circumstances," 50 Tenn., at 187, violated the state constitutional provision (which the court equated with the Second Amendment). That was so even though the statute did not restrict the carrying of long guns.

Ibid. See also *State v. Reid,* 1 Ala. 612, 616–617 (1840) ("A statute which, under the pretence of regulating, amounts to a destruction of the right, or which requires arms to be so borne as to render them wholly useless for the purpose of defence, would be clearly unconstitutional").

It is no answer to say, as petitioners do, that it is permissible to ban the possession of handguns so long as the possession of other firearms (*i.e.,* long guns) is allowed. It is enough to note, as we have observed, that the American people have considered the handgun to be the quintessential self-defense weapon. There are many reasons that a citizen may prefer a handgun for home defense: It is easier to store in a location that is readily accessible in an emergency; it cannot easily be redirected or wrestled away by an attacker; it is easier to use for those without the upper-body strength to lift and aim a long gun; it can be pointed at a burglar with one hand while the other hand dials the police. Whatever the reason, handguns are the most popular weapon chosen by Americans for self-defense in the home, and a complete prohibition of their use is invalid.

We must also address the District's requirement (as applied to respondent's handgun) that firearms in the home be rendered and kept inoperable at all times. This makes it impossible for citizens to use them for the core lawful purpose of self-defense and is hence unconstitutional. The District argues that we should interpret this element of the statute to contain an exception for self-defense. See Brief for Petitioners 56–57. But we think that is precluded by the unequivocal text, and by the presence of certain other enumerated exceptions: "Except for law enforcement personnel ..., each registrant shall keep any firearm in his possession unloaded and disassembled or bound by a trigger lock or similar device unless such firearm is kept at his place of business, or while being used for lawful recreational purposes within the District of Columbia." D.C.Code § 7-2507.02. The nonexistence of a self-defense exception is also suggested by the D.C. Court of Appeals' statement that the statute forbids residents to use firearms to stop intruders, see *McIntosh v. Washington,* 395 A.2d 744, 755–756 (1978).

Apart from his challenge to the handgun ban and the trigger-lock requirement respondent asked the District Court to enjoin petitioners from enforcing the separate licensing requirement "in such a manner as to forbid the carrying of a firearm within one's home or possessed land without a license." App. 59a. The Court of Appeals did not invalidate the licensing requirement, but held only that the District "may not prevent [a handgun] from being moved throughout one's house." 478 F.3d, at 400. It then ordered the District Court to enter summary judgment "consistent with [respondent's] prayer for relief." *Id.*, at 401. Before this Court petitioners have stated that "if the handgun ban is struck down and respondent registers a handgun, he could obtain a license, assuming he is not otherwise disqualified," by which they apparently mean if he is not a felon and is not insane. Brief for Petitioners 58. Respondent conceded at oral argument that he does not "have a problem with ... licensing" and that the District's law is permissible so long as it is "not enforced in an arbitrary and capricious manner." Tr. of Oral Arg. 74–75. We therefore assume that petitioners' issuance of a license will satisfy respondent's prayer for relief and do not address the licensing requirement.

Justice Breyer has devoted most of his separate dissent to the handgun ban. He says that, even assuming the Second Amendment is a personal guarantee of the right to bear arms, the District's prohibition is valid. He first tries to establish this by founding-era historical precedent, pointing to various restrictive laws in the colonial period. These demonstrate, in his view, that the District's law "imposes a burden upon gun owners that seems proportionately no greater than restrictions in existence at the time the Second Amendment was adopted." *Post,* at 2848. Of the laws he cites, only one offers even marginal support for his assertion. A 1783 Massachusetts law forbade the residents of Boston to "take into" or "receive into" "any Dwelling-House, Stable, Barn, Out-house, Ware-house, Store, Shop or other Building" loaded firearms, and permitted the seizure of any loaded firearms that "shall be found" there. Act of Mar. 1, 1783, ch. XIII, 1783 Mass. Acts p. 218. That statute's text and its prologue, which makes clear that the purpose of the prohibition was to eliminate the danger to firefighters posed by the "depositing of loaded Arms" in buildings, give reason to doubt that colonial Boston authorities would have enforced that general prohibition against someone who temporarily loaded a firearm to confront an intruder (despite the law's application in that case). In any case, we would not stake our interpretation of the Second Amendment upon a single law, in effect in a single city, that contradicts the overwhelming weight of other evidence regarding the right to keep and bear arms for defense of the home. The other laws Justice Breyer cites are gunpowder-storage laws that he concedes did not clearly prohibit loaded weapons, but required only that excess gunpowder be kept in a special container or on the top floor of the home. *Post,* at 2849–2850. Nothing about those fire-safety laws undermines our analysis; they do not remotely burden the right of self-defense as much as an absolute ban on handguns. Nor, correspondingly, does our analysis suggest the invalidity of laws regulating the storage of firearms to prevent accidents.

Justice Breyer points to other founding-era laws that he says "restricted the firing of guns within the city limits to at least some degree" in Boston, Philadelphia, and New York. *Post,* at 2848 (citing Churchill, "Gun Regulation, the Police Power, and the Right to Keep Arms in Early America," 25 *Law & Hist. Rev.* 139, 162 (2007)). Those laws provide no support for the severe restriction in the present case. The New York law levied a fine of 20 shillings on anyone who fired a gun in certain places (including houses) on New Year's Eve and the first two days of January, and was aimed at preventing the "great Damages ... frequently done on [those days] by persons going House to House, with Guns and other Fire Arms and being often intoxicated with Liquor." Ch. 1501, 5 *Colonial Laws of New York* 244–246 (1894). It is inconceivable that this law would have been enforced against a person exercising his right to self-defense on New Year's Day against such drunken hooligans. The Pennsylvania law to which Justice Breyer refers levied a fine of five shillings on one who fired a gun or set off fireworks in Philadelphia without first obtaining a license from the Governor. See Act of Aug. 26, 1721, ch. CCXLV, § IV, in 3 Stat. at Large of Pa. 253–254 (1896). Given Justice Wilson's explanation that the right to self-defense with arms was protected by the Pennsylvania Constitution, it is unlikely that this law (which in any event amounted to at most a licensing regime) would have been enforced against a person who used firearms for self-defense. Justice Breyer cites a Rhode Island law that simply levied a 5-shilling fine on those who fired guns in *streets* and *taverns,* a law obviously inapplicable to this case. See An Act for preventing Mischief being done in the town of *Newport,* or in any other Town in this Government, 1731 Rhode Island Session Laws, pp. 240–241. Finally, Justice Breyer points to a Massachusetts law similar to the Pennsylvania law, prohibiting "discharg[ing] any Gun or Pistol charged with Shot or Ball in the Town of *Boston.*" Act of May 28, 1746, ch. X, Acts and Laws of Mass. Bay p. 208. It is again implausible that this would have been enforced against a citizen acting in self-defense, particularly given its preambulatory reference to "the *indiscreet* firing of Guns." *Ibid.* (preamble) (emphasis added).

A broader point about the laws that Justice Breyer cites: All of them punished the discharge (or loading) of guns with a small fine and forfeiture of the weapon (or in a few cases a very brief stay in the local jail), not with significant criminal penalties. They are akin to modern penalties for minor public-safety infractions like speeding or jaywalking. And although such public-safety laws may not contain exceptions for self-defense, it is inconceivable that the threat of a jaywalking ticket would deter someone from disregarding a "Do Not Walk" sign in order to flee an attacker, or that the government would enforce those laws under such circumstances. Likewise, we do not think that a law imposing a 5-shilling fine and forfeiture of the gun would have prevented a person in the founding era from using a gun to protect himself or his family from violence, or that if he did so the law would be enforced against him. The District law, by contrast, far from imposing a minor fine, threatens citizens with a year in prison (five years for a second violation) for even obtaining a gun in the first place. See D.C.Code § 7-2507.06.

Justice Breyer moves on to make a broad jurisprudential point: He criticizes us for declining to establish a level of scrutiny for evaluating Second Amendment restrictions. He proposes, explicitly at least, none of the traditionally expressed levels (strict scrutiny, intermediate scrutiny, rational basis), but rather a judge-empowering "interest-balancing inquiry" that "asks whether the statute burdens a protected interest in a way or to an extent that is out of proportion to the statute's salutary effects upon other important governmental interests." *Post,* at 2852. After an exhaustive discussion of the arguments for and against gun control, Justice Breyer arrives at his interest-balanced answer: Because handgun violence is a problem, because the law is limited to an urban area, and because there were somewhat similar restrictions in the founding period (a false proposition that we have already discussed), the interest-balancing inquiry results in the constitutionality of the handgun ban. *QED.*

We know of no other enumerated constitutional right whose core protection has been subjected to a freestanding "interest-balancing" approach. The very enumeration of the right takes out of the hands of government—even the Third Branch of Government—the power to decide on a case-by-case basis whether the right is *really worth* insisting upon. A constitutional guarantee subject to future judges' assessments of its usefulness is no constitutional guarantee at all. Constitutional rights are enshrined with the scope they were understood to have when the people adopted them, whether or not future legislatures or (yes) even future judges think that scope too broad. We would not apply an "interest-balancing" approach to the prohibition of a peaceful neo-Nazi march through Skokie. See *National Socialist Party of America v. Skokie,* 432 U.S. 43, 97 S.Ct. 2205, 53 L.Ed.2d 96 (1977) (*per curiam*). The First Amendment contains the freedom-of-speech guarantee that the people ratified, which included exceptions for obscenity, libel, and disclosure of state secrets, but not for the expression of extremely unpopular and wrong headed views. The Second Amendment is no different. Like the First, it is the very *product* of an interest balancing by the people—which Justice Breyer would now conduct for them anew. And whatever else it leaves to future evaluation, it surely elevates above all other interests the right of law-abiding, responsible citizens to use arms in defense of hearth and home.

Justice Breyer chides us for leaving so many applications of the right to keep and bear arms in doubt, and for not providing extensive historical justification for those regulations of the right that we describe as permissible. See *post,* at 2869–2870. But since this case represents this Court's first in-depth examination of the Second Amendment, one should not expect it to clarify the entire field, any more than *Reynolds v. United States,* 98 U.S. 145, 25 L.Ed. 244 (1879), our first in-depth Free Exercise Clause case, left that area in a state of utter certainty. And there will be time enough to expound upon the historical justifications for the exceptions we have mentioned if and when those exceptions come before us.

In sum, we hold that the District's ban on handgun possession in the home violates the Second Amendment, as does its prohibition against rendering any lawful firearm in the home operable for the purpose of immediate self-defense. Assuming that Heller is not disqualified from the exercise of Second Amendment rights, the District must permit him to register his handgun and must issue him a license to carry it in the home.

* * *

We are aware of the problem of handgun violence in this country, and we take seriously the concerns raised by the many *amici* who believe that prohibition of handgun ownership is a solution. The Constitution leaves the District of Columbia a variety of tools for combating that problem, including some measures regulating handguns, see *supra,* at 2816–2817, and n. 26. But the enshrinement of constitutional rights necessarily takes certain policy choices off the table. These include the absolute prohibition of handguns held and used for self-defense in the home. Undoubtedly some think that the Second Amendment is outmoded in a society where our standing army is the pride of our Nation, where well-trained police forces provide personal security, and where gun violence is a serious problem. That is perhaps debatable, but what is not debatable is that it is not the role of this Court to pronounce the Second Amendment extinct.

We affirm the judgment of the Court of Appeals.

It is so ordered.

Justice Stevens, with whom Justice Souter, Justice Ginsburg, and Justice Breyer join, dissenting.

Justice Breyer, with whom Justice Stevens, Justice Souter, and Justice Ginsburg join, dissenting.

Of Religious Freedom, Headscarves and Employment Rights

EEOC v. Abercrombie & Fitch Stores, Inc.,

135 S. Ct. 2028 (2015)

Justice Scalia delivered the opinion of the Court.

Title VII of the Civil Rights Act of 1964 prohibits a prospective employer from refusing to hire an applicant in order to avoid accommodating a religious practice that it could accommodate without undue hardship. The question presented is whether this prohibition applies only where an applicant has informed the employer of his need for an accommodation.

I

We summarize the facts in the light most favorable to the Equal Employment Opportunity Commission (EEOC), against whom the Tenth Circuit granted summary judgment. Respondent Abercrombie & Fitch Stores, Inc., operates several lines of clothing stores, each with its own "style." Consistent with the image Abercrombie seeks to project for each store, the company imposes a Look Policy that governs its employees' dress. The Look Policy prohibits "caps"—a term the Policy does not define—as too informal for Abercrombie's desired image.

Samantha Elauf is a practicing Muslim who, consistent with her understanding of her religion's requirements, wears a headscarf. She applied for a position in an Abercrombie store, and was interviewed by Heather Cooke, the store's assistant manager. Using Abercrombie's ordinary system for evaluating applicants, Cooke gave Elauf a rating that qualified her to be hired; Cooke was concerned, however, that Elauf's headscarf would conflict with the store's Look Policy.

Cooke sought the store manager's guidance to clarify whether the headscarf was a forbidden "cap." When this yielded no answer, Cooke turned to Randall Johnson, the district manager. Cooke informed Johnson that she believed Elauf wore her headscarf because of her faith. Johnson told Cooke that Elauf's headscarf would violate the Look Policy, as would all other headwear, religious or otherwise, and directed Cooke not to hire Elauf.

The EEOC sued Abercrombie on Elauf's behalf, claiming that its refusal to hire Elauf violated Title VII. The District Court granted the EEOC summary judgment on the issue of liability, 798 F. Supp.2d 1272 (N.D.Okla.2011), held a trial on damages, and awarded $20,000. The Tenth Circuit reversed and awarded Abercrombie summary judgment. 731 F.3d 1106 (2013). It concluded that ordinarily an employer cannot be liable under Title VII for failing to accommodate a religious practice until the applicant (or employee) provides the employer with actual knowledge of his need for an accommodation. *Id.*, at 1131. We granted certiorari. 573 U.S. ----, 135 S.Ct. 44, 189 L.Ed.2d 897 (2014).

II

Title VII of the Civil Rights Act of 1964 78 Stat. 253, as amended, prohibits two categories of employment practices. It is unlawful for an employer:

> "(1) to fail or refuse to hire or to discharge any individual, or otherwise to discriminate against any individual with respect to his compensation, terms, conditions, or privileges of employment, because of such individual's race, color, religion, sex, or national origin; or

> (2) to limit, segregate, or classify his employees or applicants for employment in any way which would deprive or tend to deprive any individual of employment opportunities or otherwise adversely affect his status as an employee, because of such individual's race, color, religion, sex, or national origin." 42 U.S.C. § 2000e-2(a).

These two proscriptions, often referred to as the "disparate treatment" (or "intentional discrimination") provision and the "disparate impact" provision, are the only causes of action under Title VII. The word "religion" is defined to "includ[e] all aspects of religious observance and practice, as well as belief, unless an employer demonstrates that he is unable to reasonably accommodate to" a "religious observance or practice without undue hardship on the conduct of the employer's business." § 2000e(j).

Abercrombie's primary argument is that an applicant cannot show disparate treatment without first showing that an employer has "actual knowledge" of the applicant's need for an accommodation. We disagree. Instead, an applicant need only show that his need for an accommodation was a motivating factor in the employer's decision.

The disparate-treatment provision forbids employers to: (1) "fail ... to hire" an applicant (2) "because of" (3) "such individual's ... religion" (which includes his religious practice). Here, of course, Abercrombie (1) failed to hire Elauf. The parties concede that (if Elauf sincerely believes that her religion so requires) Elauf's wearing of a headscarf is (3) a "religious practice." All that remains is whether she was not hired (2) "because of" her religious practice.

The term "because of" appears frequently in antidiscrimination laws. It typically imports, at a minimum, the traditional standard of but-for causation. *University of Tex. Southwestern Medical Center* v. *Nassar,* 570 U.S. ----, 133 S.Ct.

2517, 186 L.Ed.2d 503 (2013). Title VII relaxes this standard, however, to prohibit even making a protected characteristic a "motivating factor" in an employment decision. 42 U.S.C. § 2000e-2(m). "Because of" in § 2000e-2(a)(1) links the forbidden consideration to each of the verbs preceding it; an individual's actual religious practice may not be a motivating factor in failing to hire, in refusing to hire, and so on.

It is significant that § 2000e-2(a)(1) does not impose a knowledge requirement. As Abercrombie acknowledges, some antidiscrimination statutes do. For example, the Americans with Disabilities Act of 1990 defines discrimination to include an employer's failure to make "reasonable accommodations to the *known* physical or mental limitations" of an applicant. § 12112(b)(5)(A) (emphasis added). Title VII contains no such limitation.

Instead, the intentional discrimination provision prohibits certain *motives,* regardless of the state of the actor's knowledge. Motive and knowledge are separate concepts. An employer who has actual knowledge of the need for an accommodation does not violate Title VII by refusing to hire an applicant if avoiding that accommodation is not his *motive.* Conversely, an employer who acts with the motive of avoiding accommodation may violate Title VII even if he has no more than an unsubstantiated suspicion that accommodation would be needed.

Thus, the rule for disparate-treatment claims based on a failure to accommodate a religious practice is straightforward: An employer may not make an applicant's religious practice, confirmed or otherwise, a factor in employment decisions. For example, suppose that an employer thinks (though he does not know for certain) that a job applicant may be an orthodox Jew who will observe the Sabbath, and thus be unable to work on Saturdays. If the applicant actually requires an accommodation of that religious practice, and the employer's desire to avoid the prospective accommodation is a motivating factor in his decision, the employer violates Title VII.

Abercrombie urges this Court to adopt the Tenth Circuit's rule "allocat[ing] the burden of raising a religious conflict." Brief for Respondent 46. This would require the employer to have actual knowledge of a conflict between an applicant's religious practice and a work rule. The problem with this approach is the one that inheres in most incorrect interpretations of statutes: It asks us to add words to the law to produce what is thought to be a desirable result. That is Congress's province. We construe Title VII's silence as exactly that: silence. Its disparate-treatment provision prohibits actions taken with the *motive* of avoiding the need for accommodating a religious practice. A request for accommodation, or the employer's certainty that the practice exists, may make it easier to infer motive, but is not a necessary condition of liability.

Abercrombie argues in the alternative that a claim based on a failure to accommodate an applicant's religious practice must be raised as a disparate-impact claim, not a disparate-treatment claim. We think not. That might have been true if Congress had limited the meaning of "religion" in Title VII to religious *belief*—so that discriminating against a particular religious *practice* would not be disparate treatment though it might have disparate impact. In fact, however, Congress defined "religion," for Title VII's purposes, as "includ[ing] all aspects of religious observance and practice, as well as belief." 42 U.S.C. § 2000e(j). Thus, religious practice is one of the protected characteristics that cannot be accorded disparate treatment and must be accommodated.

Nor does the statute limit disparate-treatment claims to only those employer policies that treat religious practices less favorably than similar secular practices. Abercrombie's argument that a neutral policy cannot constitute "intentional discrimination" may make sense in other contexts. But Title VII does not demand mere neutrality with regard to religious practices—that they be treated no worse than other practices. Rather, it gives them favored treatment, affirmatively obligating employers not "to fail or refuse to hire or discharge any individual ... because of such individual's" "religious observance and practice." An employer is surely entitled to have, for example, a no-headwear policy as an ordinary matter. But when an applicant requires an accommodation as an "aspec[t] of religious ... practice," it is no response that the subsequent "fail[ure] ... to hire" was due to an otherwise-neutral policy. Title VII requires otherwise-neutral policies to give way to the need for an accommodation.

* * *

The Tenth Circuit misinterpreted Title VII's requirements in granting summary judgment. We reverse its judgment and remand the case for further consideration consistent with this opinion.

It is so ordered.

Justice Alito, concurring in the judgment.
Justice Thomas, concurring in part and dissenting in part.

Visa Rights and the Fifth Amendment
Kerry v. Din,
135 S. Ct. 2128 (2015)

Justice Scalia announced the judgment of the Court and delivered an opinion, in which the Chief Justice and Justice Thomas join.

Fauzia Din is a citizen and resident of the United States. Her husband, Kanishka Berashk, is an Afghan citizen and former civil servant in the Taliban regime who resides in that country. When the Government declined to issue an immigrant visa to Berashk, Din sued.

The state action of which Din complains is the denial of *Berashk's* visa application. Naturally, one would expect him—not Din—to bring this suit. But because Berashk is an unadmitted and nonresident alien, he has no right of entry into the United States, and no cause of action to press in furtherance of his claim for admission. See *Kleindienst v. Mandel,* 408 U.S. 753, 762, 92 S.Ct. 2576, 33 L.Ed.2d 683 (1972). So, Din attempts to bring suit on his behalf, alleging that the Government's denial of her *husband's* visa application violated *her* constitutional rights. See App. 36–37, Complaint ¶ 56. In particular, she claims that the Government denied her due process of law when, without adequate explanation of the reason for the visa denial, it deprived her of her constitutional right to live in the United States with her spouse. There is no such constitutional right. What Justice Breyer's dissent strangely describes as a "deprivation of her freedom to live together with her spouse in America," *post,* at 2142, is, in any world other than the artificial world of ever-expanding constitutional rights, nothing more than a deprivation of her spouse's freedom to immigrate into America.

For the reasons given in this opinion and in the opinion concurring in the judgment, we vacate and remand.

I

A

Under the Immigration and Nationality Act (INA), 66 Stat. 163, as amended, 8 U.S.C. § 1101 *et seq.*, an alien may not enter and permanently reside in the United States without a visa. § 1181(a). The INA creates a special visa-application process for aliens sponsored by "immediate relatives" in the United States. §§ 1151(b), 1153(a). Under this process, the citizen-relative first files a petition on behalf of the alien living abroad, asking to have the alien classified as an immediate relative. See §§ 1153(f), 1154(a)(1). If and when a petition is approved, the alien may apply for a visa by submitting the required documents and appearing at a United States Embassy or consulate for an interview with a consular officer. See §§ 1201(a)(1), 1202. Before issuing a visa, the consular officer must ensure the alien is not inadmissible under any provision of the INA. § 1361.

One ground for inadmissibility, § 1182(a)(3)(B), covers "[t]errorist activities." In addition to the violent and destructive acts the term immediately brings to mind, the INA defines "terrorist activity" to include providing material support to a terrorist organization and serving as a terrorist organization's representative. § 1182(a)(3)(B)(i), (iii)-(vi).

B

Fauzia Din came to the United States as a refugee in 2000, and became a naturalized citizen in 2007. She filed a petition to have Kanishka Berashk, whom she married in 2006, classified as her immediate relative. The petition was granted, and Berashk filed a visa application. The U.S. Embassy in Islamabad, Pakistan, interviewed Berashk and denied his application. A consular officer informed Berashk that he was inadmissible under § 1182(a)(3)(B) but provided no further explanation.

Din then brought suit in Federal District Court seeking a writ of mandamus directing the United States to properly adjudicate Berashk's visa application; a declaratory judgment that 8 U.S.C. § 1182(b)(2)-(3), which exempts the Government from providing notice to an alien found inadmissible under the terrorism bar, is unconstitutional as applied; and a declaratory judgment that the denial violated the Administrative Procedure Act. App. 36-39, Complaint ¶¶ 55–68. The District Court granted the Government's motion to dismiss, but the Ninth Circuit reversed. The Ninth Circuit concluded that Din "has a protected liberty interest in marriage that entitled [her] to review of the denial of [her] spouse's visa," 718 F.3d 856, 860 (2013), and that the Government's citation of § 1182(a)(3)(B) did not provide Din with the "limited judicial review" to which she was entitled under the Due Process Clause, *id.*, at 868. This Court granted certiorari. 573 U.S. ----, 135 S.Ct. 44, 189 L.Ed.2d 896 (2014).

II

The Fifth Amendment provides that "[n]o person shall be ... deprived of life, liberty, or property, without due process of law." Although the amount and quality of process that our precedents have recognized as "due" under the Clause has changed considerably since the founding, see *Pacific Mut. Life Ins. Co. v. Haslip,* 499 U.S. 1, 28–36, 111 S.Ct. 1032, 113 L.Ed.2d 1 (1991) (SCALIA, J., concurring in judgment), it remains the case that *no* process is due if one is not deprived of "life, liberty, or property," *Swarthout v. Cooke,* 562 U.S. 216,

219, 131 S.Ct. 859, 178 L.Ed.2d 732 (2011) (*per curiam*). The first question that we must ask, then, is whether the denial of Berashk's visa application deprived Din of any of these interests. Only if we answer in the affirmative must we proceed to consider whether the Government's explanation afforded sufficient process.

A

The Due Process Clause has its origin in Magna Carta. As originally drafted, the Great Charter provided that "[n]o freeman shall be taken, or imprisoned, or be disseised of his freehold, or liberties, or free customs, or be outlawed, or exiled, or any otherwise destroyed; nor will we not pass upon him, nor condemn him, but by lawful judgment of his peers, or *by the law of the land*." Magna Carta, ch. 29, in 1 E. Coke, *The Second Part of the Institutes of the Laws of England* 45 (1797) (emphasis added). The Court has recognized that at the time of the Fifth Amendment's ratification, the words "due process of law" were understood "to convey the same meaning as the words 'by the law of the land'" in Magna Carta. *Murray's Lessee v. Hoboken Land & Improvement Co.*, 18 How. 272, 276, 15 L.Ed. 372 (1856). Although the terminology associated with the guarantee of due process changed dramatically between 1215 and 1791, the general scope of the underlying rights protected stayed roughly constant.

Edward Coke, whose *Institutes* "were read in the American Colonies by virtually every student of law," *Klopfer v. North Carolina,* 386 U.S. 213, 225, 87 S.Ct. 988, 18 L.Ed.2d 1 (1967), thoroughly described the scope of the interests that could be deprived only pursuant to "the law of the land." Magna Carta, he wrote, ensured that, without due process, "no man [may] be taken or imprisoned"; "disseised of his lands, or tenements, or dispossessed of his goods, or chattels"; "put from his livelihood without answer"; "barred to have the benefit of the law"; denied "the franchises, and priviledges, which the subjects have of the gift of the king"; "exiled"; or "forejudged of life, or limbe, disherited, or put to torture, or death." 1 Coke, *supra,* at 46–48. Blackstone's description of the rights protected by Magna Carta is similar, although he discusses them in terms much closer to the "life, liberty, or property" terminology used in the Fifth Amendment. He described first an interest in "personal security," "consist[ing] in a person's legal and uninterrupted enjoyment of his life, his limbs, his body, his health, and his reputation." 1 W. Blackstone, *Commentaries on the Laws of England* 125 (1769). Second, the "personal liberty of individuals" "consist[ed] in the power of locomotion, of changing situation, or removing one's person to whatsoever place one's own inclination may direct; without imprisonment or restraint." *Id.,* at 130. And finally, a person's right to property included "the free use, enjoyment, and disposal of all his acquisitions." *Id.,* at 134.

Din, of course, could not conceivably claim that the denial of Berashk's visa application deprived her—or for that matter even Berashk—of life or property; and under the above described historical understanding, a claim that it deprived her of liberty is equally absurd. The Government has not "taken or imprisoned" Din, nor has it "confine[d]" her, either by "keeping [her] against h[er] will in a private house, putting h[er] in the stocks, arresting or forcibly detaining h[er] in the street." *Id.,* at 132. Indeed, not even Berashk has suffered a deprivation of liberty so understood.

B

Despite this historical evidence, this Court has seen fit on several occasions to expand the meaning of "liberty" under the Due Process Clause to include certain implied "fundamental rights." (The reasoning presumably goes like this: If you have a right to do something, you are free to do it, and deprivation of freedom is a deprivation of "liberty"—never mind the original meaning of that word in the Due Process Clause.) These implied rights have been given *more* protection than "life, liberty, or property" properly understood. While one may be dispossessed of property, thrown in jail, or even executed so long as proper procedures are followed, the enjoyment of implied constitutional rights cannot be limited at all, except by provisions that are "narrowly tailored to serve a compelling state interest." *Reno v. Flores,* 507 U.S. 292, 301–302, 113 S.Ct. 1439, 123 L.Ed.2d 1 (1993). Din does not explicitly argue that the Government has violated this absolute prohibition of the *substantive* component of the Due Process Clause, likely because it is obvious that a law barring aliens engaged in terrorist activities from entering this country *is* narrowly tailored to serve a compelling state interest. She nevertheless insists that, because enforcement of the law affects her enjoyment of an implied fundamental liberty, the Government must first provide her a full battery of procedural-due-process protections.

I think it worth explaining why, *even if* one accepts the textually unsupportable doctrine of implied fundamental rights, Din's arguments would fail. Because "extending constitutional protection to an asserted right or liberty interest ... place[s] the matter outside the arena of public debate and legislative action," *Washington v. Glucksberg,* 521 U.S. 702, 720, 117 S.Ct. 2258, 138 L.Ed.2d 772 (1997), and because the "guideposts for responsible decisionmaking in this unchartered area are scarce and open-ended," *Collins v. Harker Heights,* 503 U.S. 115, 125, 112 S.Ct. 1061, 117 L.Ed.2d 261 (1992), "[t]he doctrine of judicial self-restraint requires us to exercise the utmost care whenever we are asked to break new ground in this field," *ibid.* Accordingly, before conferring constitutional status upon a previously unrecognized "liberty," we have required "a careful description of the asserted fundamental liberty interest," as well as a demonstration that the interest is "objectively, deeply rooted in this Nation's history and tradition, and implicit in the concept of ordered liberty, such that neither liberty nor justice would exist if [it was] sacrificed." *Glucksberg, supra,* at 720–721, 117 S.Ct. 2258 (citations and internal quotation marks omitted).

Din describes the denial of Berashk's visa application as implicating, alternately, a "liberty interest in her marriage," Brief for Respondent 28, a "right of association with one's spouse," *id.,* at 18, "a liberty interest in being reunited with certain blood relatives," *id.,* at 22, and "the liberty interest of a U.S. citizen under the Due Process Clause to be free from arbitrary restrictions on his right to live with his spouse," *ibid.* To be sure, this Court has at times indulged a propensity for grandiloquence when reviewing the sweep of implied rights, describing them so broadly that they would include not only the interests Din asserts but many others as well. For example: "Without doubt, [the liberty guaranteed by the Due Process Clause] denotes not merely freedom from bodily restraint but also the right of the individual to contract, to engage in any of the common occupations of life, to acquire useful knowledge, to marry, establish a home and bring up children, [and] to worship God according to the dictates of his own conscience" *Meyer v. Nebraska,* 262 U.S. 390, 399, 43 S.Ct. 625, 67 L.Ed. 1042 (1923). But this Court is not bound by dicta, especially dicta that have been repudiated by the holdings of our subsequent cases. And the actual holdings of the cases Din relies upon hardly establish the capacious right she now asserts.

Unlike the States in *Loving v. Virginia,* 388 U.S. 1, 87 S.Ct. 1817, 18 L.Ed.2d 1010 (1967), *Zablocki v. Redhail,* 434 U.S. 374, 98 S.Ct. 673, 54 L.Ed.2d 618 (1978), and *Turner v. Safley,* 482 U.S. 78, 107 S.Ct. 2254, 96 L.Ed.2d 64 (1987), the Federal Government here has not attempted to forbid a marriage. Although Din and the dissent borrow language from those cases invoking a fundamental right to marriage, they both implicitly concede that no such right has been infringed in this case. Din relies on the "associational interests in marriage that necessarily are protected by the right to marry," and that are "presuppose[d]" by later cases establishing a right to marital privacy. Brief for Respondent 16, 18. The dissent supplements the fundamental right to marriage with a fundamental right to live in the United States in order to find an affected liberty interest. *Post,* at 2142–2143 (Breyer, J., dissenting).

Attempting to abstract from these cases some liberty interest that might be implicated by Berashk's visa denial, Din draws on even more inapposite cases. *Meyer,* for example, invalidated a state statute proscribing the teaching of foreign language to children who had not yet passed the eighth grade, reasoning that it violated the teacher's "right thus to teach and the right of parents to engage him so to instruct their children." 262 U.S., at 400, 43 S.Ct. 625. *Pierce v. Society of Sisters,* 268 U.S. 510, 534–535, 45 S.Ct. 571, 69 L.Ed. 1070 (1925), extended *Meyer,* finding that a law requiring children to attend public schools "interferes with the liberty of parents and guardians to direct the upbringing and education of children under their control." *Moore v. East Cleveland,* 431 U.S. 494, 505–506, 97 S.Ct. 1932, 52 L.Ed.2d 531 (1977), extended this interest in raising children to caretakers in a child's extended family, striking down an ordinance that limited occupancy of a single-family house to members of a nuclear family on the ground that "[d]ecisions concerning child rearing ... long have been shared with grandparents or other relatives." And *Griswold v. Connecticut,* 381 U.S. 479, 485, 85 S.Ct. 1678, 14 L.Ed.2d 510 (1965), concluded that a law criminalizing the use of contraceptives by married couples violated "penumbral rights of 'privacy and repose'" protecting "the sacred precincts of the marital bedroom"—rights which do not plausibly extend into the offices of our consulates abroad.

Nothing in the cases Din cites establishes a free-floating and categorical liberty interest in marriage (or any other formulation Din offers) sufficient to trigger constitutional protection whenever a regulation in any way touches upon an aspect of the marital relationship. Even if our cases could be construed so broadly, the relevant question is not whether the asserted interest "is consistent with this Court's substantive-due-process line of cases," but whether it is supported by "this Nation's history and practice." *Glucksberg,* 521 U.S., at 723–724, 117 S.Ct. 2258 (emphasis deleted). Even if we might "imply" a liberty interest in marriage generally speaking, that must give way when there is a tradition denying the specific application of that general interest. Thus, *Glucksberg* rejected a claimed liberty interest in "self-sovereignty" and "personal autonomy" that extended to assisted suicide when there was a longstanding tradition of outlawing the practice of suicide. *Id.,* at 724, 727–728, 117 S.Ct. 2258 (internal quotation marks omitted).

Here, a long practice of regulating spousal immigration precludes Din's claim that the denial of Berashk's visa application has deprived her of a fundamental liberty interest. Although immigration was effectively unregulated prior to 1875, as soon as Congress began legislating in this area it enacted a complicated web of regulations that erected serious impediments to a person's ability to bring a spouse into the

United States. See Abrams, "What Makes the Family Special?" 80 *U. Chi. L. Rev.* 7, 10–16 (2013).

Most strikingly, perhaps, the Expatriation Act of 1907 provided that "any American woman who marries a foreigner shall take the nationality of her husband." Ch. 2534, 34 Stat. 1228. Thus, a woman in Din's position not only lacked a liberty interest that might be affected by the Government's disposition of her husband's visa application, she lost her *own* rights as a citizen upon marriage. When Congress began to impose quotas on immigration by country of origin less than 15 years later, with the Immigration Act of 1921, it omitted fiances and husbands from the family relations eligible for preferred status in the allocation of quota spots. § 2(d), 42 Stat. 6. Such relations were similarly excluded from the relations eligible for nonquota status, when that status was expanded three years later. Immigration Act of 1924, § 4(a), 43 Stat. 155.

To be sure, these early regulations were premised on the derivative citizenship of women, a legacy of the law of coverture that was already in decline at the time. C. Bredbenner, *A Nationality of Her Own* 5 (1998). Modern equal-protection doctrine casts substantial doubt on the permissibility of such asymmetric treatment of women citizens in the immigration context, and modern moral judgment rejects the premises of such a legal order. Nevertheless, this all-too-recent practice repudiates any contention that Din's asserted liberty interest is "deeply rooted in this Nation's history and tradition, and implicit in the concept of ordered liberty." *Glucksberg, supra,* at 720, 117 S.Ct. 2258 (citations and internal quotations marks omitted).

Indeed, the law showed little more solicitude for the marital relationship when it was a male resident or citizen seeking admission for his fiancee or wife. The Immigration Act of 1921 granted nonquota status only to unmarried, minor children of citizens, § 2(a), while granting fiancees and wives preferred status *within* the allocation of quota spots, § 2(d). In other words, a citizen could move his spouse forward in the line, but once all the quota spots were filled for the year, the spouse was barred without exception. This was not just a theoretical possibility: As one commentator has observed, "[f]or many immigrants, the family categories did little to help, because the quotas were so small that the number of family members seeking slots far outstripped the number available." Abrams, *supra,* at 13.

Although Congress has tended to show "a continuing and kindly concern ... for the unity and the happiness of the immigrant family," E. Hutchinson, *Legislative History of American Immigration Policy 1798–1965*, p. 518 (1981), this has been a matter of legislative grace rather than fundamental right. Even where Congress has provided special privileges to promote family immigration, it has also "written in careful checks and qualifications." *Ibid.* This Court has consistently recognized that these various distinctions are "policy questions entrusted exclusively to the political branches of our Government, and we have no judicial authority to substitute our political judgment for that of the Congress." *Fiallo v. Bell,* 430 U.S. 787, 798, 97 S.Ct. 1473, 52 L.Ed.2d 50 (1977). Only by diluting the meaning of a fundamental liberty interest and jettisoning our established jurisprudence could we conclude that the denial of Berashk's visa application implicates any of Din's fundamental liberty interests.

C

Justice Breyer suggests that procedural due process rights attach to liberty interests that either are (1) created by nonconstitutional law, such as a statute, or (2) "sufficiently important" so as to "flow 'implicit[ly]' from the design, object, and nature of the Due Process Clause." *Post,* at 2142.

The first point is unobjectionable, at least given this Court's case law. See, *e.g., Goldberg v. Kelly,* 397 U.S. 254, 262, and n. 8, 90 S.Ct. 1011, 25 L.Ed.2d 287 (1970); *Collins,* 503 U.S., at 129, 112 S.Ct. 1061. But it is unhelpful to Din, who does not argue that a statute confers on her a liberty interest protected by the Due Process Clause. Justice Breyer attempts to make this argument for Din, latching onto language in *Wilkinson v. Austin,* 545 U.S. 209, 221, 125 S.Ct. 2384, 162 L.Ed.2d 174 (2005), saying that a liberty interest "may arise from an expectation or interest created by state laws or policies." Such an "expectation" has been created here, he asserts, because "the law ... surrounds marriage with a host of legal protections to the point that it creates a strong expectation that government will not deprive married individuals of their freedom to live together without strong reasons and (in individual cases) without fair procedure," *post,* at 2143. But what *Wilkinson* meant by an "expectation or interest" was not that sort of judicially unenforceable substantial hope, but a present and legally recognized substantive entitlement. As sole support for its conclusion that nonconstitutional law can create constitutionally protected liberty interests, *Wilkinson* cited *Wolff v. McDonnell,* 418 U.S. 539, 556–558, 94 S.Ct. 2963, 41 L.Ed.2d 935 (1974), which held that a prisoner could not be deprived of statutory good-time credit without procedural due process. That was not because a prisoner might have "'a strong expectation'" that the government would not deprive him of good-time credit "'without strong reasons'" or "'fair procedure,'" but because "the State itself has not only provided a statutory *right* to good time [credit] but also specifies that it is to be forfeited *only* for serious misbehavior," *id.,* at 557, 94 S.Ct. 2963 (emphasis added). The legal benefits afforded to marriages and the preferential treatment accorded to visa applicants with citizen relatives are insufficient to confer on Din a right that can be deprived only pursuant to procedural due process.

Justice Breyer's second point—that procedural due process rights attach even to some nonfundamental liberty interests that have *not* been created by statute—is much more troubling. He relies on the implied-fundamental-rights cases discussed above to divine a "right of spouses to live together and to raise a family," along with "a citizen's right to live within this country." *Post,* at 2142. But perhaps recognizing that our established methodology for identifying fundamental rights cuts against his conclusion, see Part II-B, *supra,* he argues that the term "liberty" in the Due Process Clause includes implied rights that, although not so fundamental as to deserve substantive-due-process protection, are important enough to deserve procedural-due-process protection. *Post,* at 2142. In other words, there are two categories of implied rights protected by the Due Process Clause: really fundamental rights, which cannot be taken away at all absent a compelling state interest; and not-so-fundamental rights, which can be taken away so long as procedural due process is observed.

The dissent fails to cite a single case supporting its novel theory of implied nonfundamental rights. It is certainly true that *Vitek v. Jones,* 445 U.S. 480, 100 S.Ct. 1254, 63 L.Ed.2d 552 (1980), and *Washington v. Harper,* 494 U.S. 210, 110 S.Ct. 1028, 108 L.Ed.2d 178 (1990), do not entail implied *fundamental* rights, but this is because they do not entail *implied* rights at all. *Vitek* concerned the involuntary commitment of a prisoner, deprivation of the expressly protected right of liberty under the original understanding of the term, see Part II-A, *supra.* "'Among the historic liberties' protected by the Due Process Clause is the 'right to be free from, and to obtain judicial relief for, unjustified intrusions on personal security.'" *Vitek, supra,* at 492, 100 S.Ct. 1254. The same is true of *Harper,* which concerned forced administration of psychotropic drugs to an inmate. 494 U.S., at 214, 110 S.Ct. 1028. Arguably, *Paul v. Davis,* 424 U.S. 693, 96 S.Ct. 1155, 47 L.Ed.2d 405 (1976), also addressed an interest expressly contemplated within the meaning of "liberty." See 1 W. Blackstone, *Commentaries on the Laws of England* 125 ("The right of personal security consists in a person's ... reputation"). But that case is of no help to the dissent anyway, since it found no liberty interest entitled to the Due Process Clause's protection. *Paul, supra,* at 713–714, 96 S.Ct. 1155. Finally, the dissent points to *Goss v. Lopez,* 419 U.S. 565, 574, 95 S.Ct. 729, 42 L.Ed.2d 725 (1975), a case that "recognize[d] ... as a property interest" a student's right to a public education conferred by Ohio's express statutory creation of a public school system; and further concluded that the student's 10-day suspension implicated the constitutionally grounded liberty interest in "'a person's good name, reputation, honor, or integrity.'"

Ultimately, the dissent identifies no case holding that there is an implied nonfundamental right protected by procedural due process, and only one case even *suggesting* that there is. That suggestion, in *Smith v. Organization of Foster Families For Equality and Reform,* 431 U.S. 816, 97 S.Ct. 2094, 53 L.Ed.2d 14 (1977), is contained in dictum in a footnote, *id.,* at 842, n. 48, 97 S.Ct. 2094. The holding of the case was that "the procedures provided by New York State ... and by New York Cit[y] ... are adequate to protect *whatever* liberty interests appellees *may* have." *Id.,* at 856, 97 S.Ct. 2094 (emphasis added).

The footnoted dictum that Justice Breyer proposes to elevate to constitutional law is a dangerous doctrine. It vastly expands the scope of our implied-rights jurisprudence by setting it free from the requirement that the liberty interest be "objectively, deeply rooted in this Nation's history and tradition, and implicit in the concept of ordered liberty," *Glucksberg,* 521 U.S., at 720–721, 117 S.Ct. 2258 (internal quotation marks omitted). Even shallow-rooted liberties would, thanks to this new procedural-rights-only notion of quasi-fundamental rights, qualify for judicially imposed procedural requirements. Moreover, Justice Breyer gives no basis for distinguishing the fundamental rights recognized in the cases he depends on from the *nonfundamental* right he believes they give rise to in the present case.

Neither Din's right to live with her spouse nor her right to live within this country is implicated here. There is a "simple distinction between government action that directly affects a citizen's legal rights, or imposes a direct restraint on his liberty, and action that is directed against a third party and affects the citizen only indirectly or incidentally." *O'Bannon v. Town Court Nursing Center,* 447 U.S. 773, 788, 100 S.Ct. 2467, 65 L.Ed.2d 506 (1980). The Government has not refused to recognize Din's marriage to Berashk, and Din remains free to live with her husband anywhere in the world that both individuals are permitted to reside. And the Government has not expelled Din from the country. It has simply determined that Kanishka Berashk engaged in terrorist activities within the meaning of the Immigration and Nationality Act, and has therefore denied him admission into the country. This might, indeed, deprive Din of something "important," *post,* at 2142, but if that is the criterion for Justice Breyer's new pairing of substantive and procedural due process, we are in for quite a ride.

* * *

Because Fauzia Din was not deprived of "life, liberty, or property" when the Government denied Kanishka Berashk admission to the United States, there is no process due to her under the Constitution. To the extent that she received any explanation for the Government's decision, this was more than the Due Process Clause required. The judgment of the Ninth Circuit is vacated, and the case is remanded for further proceedings.

It is so ordered.

Justice Kennedy, with whom Justice Alito joins, concurring in the judgment.

Justice Breyer, with whom Justice Ginsburg, Justice Sotomayor, and Justice Kagan join, dissenting.

4

Rights of the Accused

The "Confrontation Clause" and Minors
Coy v. Iowa, 487 U.S. 1012 (1988)

Due Process, Employment Rights and Illegal Drugs
Gilbert v. Homar, 520 U.S. 924 (1997)

On the "Confrontation Clause" in Court
Crawford v. Washington, 541 U.S. 36 (2004)

In the three cases presented in this chapter, The Court was asked to interpret the rights of individuals accused of criminal acts under the "Due Process" clause of the Fourteenth Amendment and the "Confrontation" clause of the Sixth Amendment. These two constitutional provisions provide the most basic rights accorded to Americans, the right not to be deprived of "life, liberty or property" without "due process" of law and the right to be able to confront a witness against oneself and, most critically, to question such a hostile witness. Interestingly, in two of these cases, the Court was unanimous in its decision and in the third, Justice Scalia wrote for a 6-2 majority.

The "Confrontation Clause" and Minors

Coy v. Iowa,

487 U.S. 1012 (1988)

Justice Scalia delivered the opinion of the Court.

Appellant was convicted of two counts of lascivious acts with a child after a jury trial in which a screen placed between him and the two complaining witnesses blocked him from their sight. Appellant contends that this procedure, authorized by state statute, violated his Sixth Amendment right to confront the witnesses against him.

I

In August 1985, appellant was arrested and charged with sexually assaulting two 13-year-old girls earlier that month while they were camping out in the backyard of the house next door to him. According to the girls, the assailant entered their tent after they were asleep wearing a stocking over his head, shined a flashlight in their eyes, and warned them not to look at him; neither was able to describe his face. In November 1985, at the beginning of appellant's trial, the State made a motion pursuant to a recently enacted statute, Act of May 23, 1985, § 6, 1985 Iowa Acts 338, now codified at Iowa Code § 910A.14 (1987), to allow the complaining witnesses to testify either via closed-circuit television or behind a screen. See App. 4–5. The trial court approved the use of a large screen to be placed between appellant and the witness stand during the girls' testimony. After certain lighting adjustments in the courtroom, the screen would enable appellant dimly to perceive the witnesses, but the witnesses to see him not at all.

Appellant objected strenuously to use of the screen, based first of all on his Sixth Amendment confrontation right. He argued that, although the device might succeed in its apparent aim of making the complaining witnesses feel less uneasy in giving their testimony, the Confrontation Clause directly addressed this issue by giving criminal defendants a right to face-to-face confrontation. He also argued that his right to due process was violated, since the procedure would make him appear guilty and thus erode the presumption of innocence. The trial court rejected both constitutional claims, though it instructed the jury to draw no inference of guilty from the screen.

The Iowa Supreme Court affirmed appellant's conviction, 397 N.W.2d 730 (1986). It rejected appellant's confrontation argument on the ground that, since the ability to cross-examine the witnesses was not impaired by the screen, there was no violation of the Confrontation Clause. It also rejected the due process argument, on the ground that the screening procedure was not inherently prejudicial. We noted probable jurisdiction, 483 U.S. 1019, 107 S.Ct. 3260, 97 L.Ed.2d 760 (1987).

II

The Sixth Amendment gives a criminal defendant the right "to be confronted with the witnesses against him." This language "comes to us on faded parchment," *California v. Green,* 399 U.S. 149, 174, 90 S.Ct. 1930, 1943, 26 L.Ed.2d 489 (1970) (Harlan, J., concurring), with a lineage that traces back to the beginnings of Western legal culture. There are indications that a right of confrontation existed under Roman law. The Roman Governor Festus, discussing the proper treatment of his prisoner, Paul, stated: "It is not the manner of the Romans to deliver any man up to die before the accused has met his accusers face to face, and has been given a chance to defend himself against the charges." Acts 25:16. It has been argued that a form of the right of confrontation was recognized in England well before the right to jury trial. Pollitt, "The Right of Confrontation: Its History and Modern Dress," 8 *J.Pub.L.* 381, 384–387 (1959).

Most of this Court's encounters with the Confrontation Clause have involved either the admissibility of out-of-court statements, see, *e.g., Ohio v. Roberts,* 448 U.S. 56, 100 S.Ct. 2531, 65 L.Ed.2d 597 (1980); *Dutton v. Evans,* 400 U.S. 74, 91 S.Ct. 210, 27 L.Ed.2d 213 (1970), or restrictions on the scope of cross-examination, *Delaware v. Van Arsdall,* 475 U.S. 673, 106 S.Ct. 1431, 89 L.Ed.2d 674 (1986); *Davis v. Alaska,* 415 U.S. 308, 94 S.Ct. 1105, 39 L.Ed.2d 347 (1974). Cf. *Delaware v. Fensterer,* 474 U.S. 15, 18–19, 106 S.Ct. 292, 294, 88 L.Ed.2d 15 (1985) (*per curiam*) (noting these two categories and finding neither applicable). The reason for that is not, as the State suggests, that these elements are the essence of the Clause's protection—but rather, quite to the contrary, that there is at least some room for doubt (and hence litigation) as to the extent to which the Clause includes those elements, whereas, as Justice Harlan put it, "[s]imply as a matter of English" it confers at least "a right to meet face to face all those who appear and give evidence at trial." *California v. Green, supra,* at 175, 90 S.Ct., at 1943–1944. Simply as a matter of Latin as well, since the word "confront" ultimately derives from the prefix "con-" (from "contra" meaning "against" or "opposed") and the noun "frons" (forehead). Shakespeare was thus describing the root meaning of confrontation when he had Richard the Second say: "Then call them to our presence—face to face, and frowning brow to brow, ourselves will hear the accuser and the accused freely speak...." *Richard II,* Act 1, sc. 1.

We have never doubted, therefore, that the Confrontation Clause guarantees the defendant a face-to-face meeting with witnesses appearing before the trier of fact. See *Kentucky v.*

Stincer, 482 U.S. 730, 748, 749–750, 107 S.Ct. 2658, 2668, 96 L.Ed.2d 631 (1987) (MARSHALL, J., dissenting). For example, in *Kirby v. United States,* 174 U.S. 47, 55, 19 S.Ct. 574, 577, 43 L.Ed. 890 (1899), which concerned the admissibility of prior convictions of codefendants to prove an element of the offense of receiving stolen Government property, we described the operation of the Clause as follows: "[A] fact which can be primarily established only by witnesses cannot be proved against an accused ... except by witnesses who confront him at the trial, upon whom he can look while being tried, whom he is entitled to cross-examine, and whose testimony he may impeach in every mode authorized by the established rules governing the trial or conduct of criminal cases." Similarly, in *Dowdell v. United States,* 221 U.S. 325, 330, 31 S.Ct. 590, 592, 55 L.Ed. 753 (1911), we described a provision of the Philippine Bill of Rights as substantially the same as the Sixth Amendment, and proceeded to interpret it as intended "to secure the accused the right to be tried, so far as facts provable by witnesses are concerned, by only such witnesses as meet him face to face at the trial, who give their testimony in his presence, and give to the accused an opportunity of cross-examination." More recently, we have described the "literal right to 'confront' the witness at the time of trial" as forming "the core of the values furthered by the Confrontation Clause." *California v. Green, supra,* at 157, 90 S.Ct., at 1934–1935. Last Term, the plurality opinion in *Pennsylvania v. Ritchie,* 480 U.S. 39, 51, 107 S.Ct. 989, 998, 94 L.Ed.2d 40 (1987), stated that "[t]he Confrontation Clause provides two types of protections for a criminal defendant: the right physically to face those who testify against him, and the right to conduct cross-examination."

The Sixth Amendment's guarantee of face-to-face encounter between witness and accused serves ends related both to appearances and to reality. This opinion is embellished with references to and quotations from antiquity in part to convey that there is something deep in human nature that regards face-to-face confrontation between accused and accuser as "essential to a fair trial in a criminal prosecution." *Pointer v. Texas,* 380 U.S. 400, 404, 85 S.Ct. 1065, 1068, 13 L.Ed.2d 923 (1965). What was true of old is no less true in modern times. President Eisenhower once described face-to-face confrontation as part of the code of his hometown of Abilene, Kansas. In Abilene, he said, it was necessary to "[m]eet anyone face to face with whom you disagree. You could not sneak up on him from behind, or do any damage to him, without suffering the penalty of an outraged citizenry.... In this country, if someone dislikes you, or accuses you, he must come up in front. He cannot hide behind the shadow." Press release of remarks given to the B'nai B'rith Anti–Defamation League, November 23, 1953, quoted in Pollitt, *supra,* at 381. The phrase still persists, "Look me in the eye and say that." Given these human feelings of what is necessary for fairness, the right of confrontation "contributes to the establishment of a system of criminal justice in which the perception as well as the reality of fairness prevails." *Lee v. Illinois,* 476 U.S. 530, 540, 106 S.Ct. 2056, 2062, 90 L.Ed.2d 514 (1986).

The perception that confrontation is essential to fairness has persisted over the centuries because there is much truth to it. A witness "may feel quite differently when he has to repeat his story looking at the man whom he will harm greatly by distorting or mistaking the facts. He can now understand what sort of human being that man is." Z. Chafee, *The Blessings of Liberty* 35 (1956), quoted in *Jay v. Boyd,* 351 U.S. 345, 375–376, 76 S.Ct. 919, 935–936, 100 L.Ed. 1242 (1956) (Douglas, J., dissenting). It is always more difficult to tell a lie about a person "to his face" than "behind his back." In the former context, even if the lie is told, it will often be told less convincingly. The Confrontation Clause does not, of course, compel the witness to fix his eyes upon the defendant; he may studiously look elsewhere, but the trier of fact will draw its own conclusions. Thus the right to face-to-face confrontation serves much the same purpose as a less explicit component of the Confrontation Clause that we have had more frequent occasion to discuss the right to cross-examine the accuser; both "ensur[e] the integrity of the fact-finding process." *Kentucky v. Stincer, supra,* 482 U.S., at 736, 107 S.Ct., at 2662. The State can hardly gainsay the profound effect upon a witness of standing in the presence of the person the witness accuses, since that is the very phenomenon it relies upon to establish the potential "trauma" that allegedly justified the extraordinary procedure in the present case. That face-to-face presence may, unfortunately, upset the truthful rape victim or abused child; but by the same token it may confound and undo the false accuser, or reveal the child coached by a malevolent adult. It is a truism that constitutional protections have costs.

III

The remaining question is whether the right to confrontation was in fact violated in this case. The screen at issue was specifically designed to enable the complaining witnesses to avoid viewing appellant as they gave their testimony, and the record indicates that it was successful in this objective. App. 10–11. It is difficult to imagine a more obvious or damaging violation of the defendant's right to a face-to-face encounter.

The State suggests that the confrontation interest at stake here was outweighed by the necessity of protecting victims of sexual abuse. It is true that we have in the past indicated that rights conferred by the Confrontation Clause are not absolute, and may give way to other important interests. The rights referred to in those cases, however, were not the right narrowly and explicitly set forth in the Clause, but rather rights that are, or were asserted to be, reasonably implicit—namely, the right to cross-examine, see *Chambers v. Mississippi,* 410 U.S. 284, 295, 93 S.Ct. 1038, 1045–1046, 35 L.Ed.2d 297 (1973); the right to exclude out-of-court statements, see *Ohio v. Roberts,* 448 U.S., at 63–65, 100 S.Ct., at 2537–2539; and the asserted right to face-to-face confrontation at some point in the proceedings other than the trial itself, *Kentucky v. Stincer, supra.* To hold that our determination of what implications are reasonable must take into account other important interests is not the same as holding that we can identify exceptions, in light of other important interests, to the irreducible literal meaning of the Clause: "a right to *meet face to face* all those who appear and give evidence *at trial.*" *California v. Green,* 399 U.S., at 175, 90 S.Ct., at 1943–1944 (Harlan, J., concurring) (emphasis added). We leave for another day, however, the question whether any exceptions exist. Whatever they may be, they would surely be allowed only when necessary to further an important public policy. Cf *Ohio v. Roberts, supra,* 448 U.S., at 64, 100 S.Ct., at 2538; *Chambers v. Mississippi, supra,* at 295, 93 S.Ct., at 1045–1046. The State maintains that such necessity is established here by the statute, which creates a legislatively imposed presumption of trauma. Our cases suggest, however, that even as to exceptions from the normal implications of the Confrontation Clause, as opposed to its most literal application, something more than the type of generalized finding underlying such a statute is needed when the exception is not "firmly ... rooted in our jurisprudence." *Bourjaily v. United States,* 483 U.S. 171, 183, 107 S.Ct. 2775, 2782, 97 L.Ed.2d 144 (1987) (citing *Dutton v. Evans,* 400 U.S. 74, 91 S.Ct. 210, 27 L.Ed.2d 213 (1970)). The exception created by the Iowa statute, which was passed in 1985, could hardly be viewed as firmly rooted. Since there have been no individualized findings that these particular witnesses needed special protection, the judgment here could not be sustained by any conceivable exception.

The State also briefly suggests that any Confrontation Clause error was harmless beyond a reasonable doubt under the standard of *Chapman v. California*, 386 U.S. 18, 24, 87 S.Ct. 824, 828, 17 L.Ed.2d 705 (1967). We have recognized that other types of violations of the Confrontation Clause are subject to that harmless-error analysis, see *e.g., Delaware v. Van Arsdall,* 475 U.S., at 679, 684, 106 S.Ct., at 1436, 1438, and see no reason why denial of face-to-face confrontation should not be treated the same. An assessment of harmlessness cannot include consideration of whether the witness' testimony would have been unchanged, or the jury's assessment unaltered, had there been confrontation; such an inquiry would obviously involve pure speculation, and harmlessness must therefore be determined on the basis of the remaining evidence. The Iowa Supreme Court had no occasion to address the harmlessness issue, since it found no constitutional violation. In the circumstances of this case, rather than decide whether the error was harmless beyond a reasonable doubt, we leave the issue for the court below.

We find it unnecessary to reach appellant's due process claim. Since his constitutional right to face-to-face confrontation was violated, we reverse the judgment of the Iowa Supreme Court and remand the case for further proceedings not inconsistent with this opinion.

It is so ordered.

Due Process, Employment Rights and Illegal Drugs

Gilbert v. Homar, 520 U.S. 924 (1997)

Justice Scalia, delivered the opinion of the Court.

This case presents the question whether a State violates the Due Process Clause of the Fourteenth Amendment by failing to provide notice and a hearing before suspending a tenured public employee without pay.

I

Respondent Richard J. Homar was employed as a police officer at East Stroudsburg University (ESU), a branch of Pennsylvania's State System of Higher Education. On August 26, 1992, when respondent was at the home of a family friend, he was arrested by the Pennsylvania State Police in a drug raid. Later that day, the state police filed a criminal complaint charging respondent with possession of marijuana, possession with intent to deliver, and criminal conspiracy to violate the controlled substance law, which is a felony. The state police notified respondent's supervisor, University Police Chief David Marazas, of the arrest and charges. Chief Marazas in turn informed Gerald Levanowitz, ESU's Director of Human Resources, to whom ESU President James Gilbert had delegated authority to discipline ESU employees. Levanowitz suspended respondent without pay effective immediately. Respondent failed to report to work on the day of his arrest, and learned of his suspension the next day, when he called Chief Marazas to inquire whether he had been suspended. That same day, respondent received a letter from Levanowitz confirming that he had been suspended effective August 26 pending an investigation into the criminal charges filed against him. The letter explained that any action taken by ESU would not necessarily coincide with the disposition of the criminal charges.

Although the criminal charges were dismissed on September 1, respondent's suspension remained in effect while ESU continued with its own investigation. On September 18, Levanowitz and Chief Marazas met with respondent in order to give him an opportunity to tell his side of the story. Respondent was informed at the meeting that the state police had given ESU information that was "very serious in nature," Record, Doc. No. 26, p. 48, but he was not informed that that included a report of an alleged confession he had made on the day of his arrest; he was consequently unable to respond to damaging statements attributed to him in the police report.

In a letter dated September 23, Levanowitz notified respondent that he was being demoted to the position of groundskeeper effective the next day, and that he would receive backpay from the date the suspension took effect at the rate of pay of a groundskeeper. (Respondent eventually received backpay for the period of his suspension at the rate of pay of a university police officer.) The letter maintained that the demotion was being imposed "as a result of admissions made by yourself to the Pennsylvania State Police on August 26, 1992 that you maintained associations with individuals whom you knew were dealing in large quantities of marijuana and that you obtained marijuana from one of those individuals for your own use. Your actions constitute a clear and flagrant violation of Sections 200 and 200.2 of the [ESU] Police Department Manual." App. 82a. Upon receipt of this letter, the president of respondent's union requested a meeting with President Gilbert. The requested meeting took place on September 24, at which point respondent had received and read the police report containing the alleged confession. After providing respondent with an opportunity to respond to the charges, Gilbert sustained the demotion.

Respondent filed this suit under Rev. Stat. § 1979, 42 U.S. C. § 1983, in the United States District Court for the Middle District of Pennsylvania against President Gilbert, Chief Marazas, Levanowitz, and a Vice President of ESU, Curtis English, all in both their individual and official capacities. He contended, *inter alia,* that petitioners' failure to provide him with notice and an opportunity to be heard before suspending him without pay violated due process. The District Court entered summary judgment for petitioners. A divided Court of Appeals reversed the District Court's determination that it was permissible for ESU to suspend respondent without pay without first providing a hearing. 89 F.3d 1009 (CA3 1996). We granted certiorari. 519 U.S. 1052 (1997).

II

The protections of the Due Process Clause apply to government deprivation of those perquisites of government employment in which the employee has a constitutionally protected "property" interest. Although we have previously held that public employees who can be discharged only for cause have a constitutionally protected property interest in their tenure and cannot be fired without due process, see *Board of Regents of State Colleges* v. *Roth,* 408 U.S. 564, 578 (1972); *Perry* v. *Sindermann,* 408 U.S. 593, 602–603 (1972), we have not had occasion to decide whether the protections of the Due Process Clause extend to discipline of tenured public employees short of termination. Petitioners, however, do not contest this preliminary point, and so without deciding it we will, like the District Court, "[a]ssum[e] that the suspension infringed a protected property interest," App. to Pet. for Cert.

59a, and turn at once to petitioners' contention that respondent received all the process he was due.

A

In *Cleveland Bd. of Ed.* v. *Loudermill*, 470 U.S. 532 (1985), we concluded that a public employee dismissable only for cause was entitled to a very limited hearing prior to his termination, to be followed by a more comprehensive posttermination hearing. Stressing that the pretermination hearing 'should be an initial check against mistaken decisions—essentially, a determination of whether there are reasonable grounds to believe that the charges against the employee are true and support the proposed action," *id.*, at 545–546, we held that pretermination process need only include oral or written notice of the charges, an explanation of the employer's evidence, and an opportunity for the employee to tell his side of the story, *id.*, at 546. In the course of our assessment of the governmental interest in immediate termination of a tenured employee, we observed that "in those situations where the employer perceives a significant hazard in keeping the employee on the job, it can avoid the problem by suspending *with pay*." *Id.*, at 544–545 (emphasis added; footnote omitted).

Relying on this dictum, which it read as "strongly suggest[ing] that suspension without pay must be preceded by notice and an opportunity to be heard *in all instances*," 89 F. 3d, at 1015 (emphasis added), and determining on its own that such a rule would be "eminently sensible," *id.*, at 1016, the Court of Appeals adopted a categorical prohibition: "[A] governmental employer may not suspend an employee without pay unless that suspension is preceded by some kind of presuspension hearing, providing the employee with notice and an opportunity to be heard." *Ibid.* Respondent (as well as most of his *amici*) makes no attempt to defend this absolute rule, which spans all types of government employment and all types of unpaid suspensions. Brief for Respondent 8, 12–13. This is eminently wise, since under our precedents such an absolute rule is indefensible.

It is by now well established that "'due process,' unlike some legal rules, is not a technical conception with a fixed content unrelated to time, place and circumstances." *Cafeteria & Restaurant Workers* v. *McElroy,* 367 U.S. 886, 895 (1961). "[D]ue process is flexible and calls for such procedural protections as the particular situation demands." *Morrissey* v. *Brewer,* 408 U.S. 471, 481 (1972). This Court has recognized, on many occasions, that where a State must act quickly, or where it would be impractical to provide predeprivation process, postdeprivation process satisfies the requirements of the Due Process Clause. See, *e. g., United States* v. *James Daniel Good Real Property,* 510 U.S. 43, 53 (1993); *Zinermon* v. *Burch,* 494 U.S. 113, 128 (1990) (collecting cases); *Barry* v. *Barchi,* 443 U.S. 55, 64–65 (1979); *Dixon* v. *Love,* 431 U.S. 105, 115 (1977); *North American Cold Storage Co.* v. *Chicago,* 211 U.S. 306, 314–320 (1908). Indeed, in *Parratt* v. *Taylor,* 451 U.S. 527 (1981), overruled in part on other grounds, *Daniels* v. *Williams,* 474 U.S. 327 (1986), we specifically noted that "we have rejected the proposition that [due process] *always* requires the State to provide a hearing prior to the initial deprivation of property." 451 U. S., at 540. And in *FDIC* v. *Mallen,* 486 U.S. 230 (1988), where we unanimously approved the Federal Deposit Insurance Corporation's (FDIC's) suspension, without prior hearing, of an indicted private bank employee, we said: "An important government interest, accompanied by a substantial assurance that the deprivation is not baseless or unwarranted, may in limited cases demanding prompt action justify postponing the opportunity to be heard until after the initial deprivation." *Id.*, at 240.

The dictum in *Loudermill* relied upon by the Court of Appeals is of course not inconsistent with these precedents. To say that when the government employer perceives a hazard in leaving the employee on the job it "can avoid the problem by suspending with pay" is not to say that that is the only way of avoiding the problem. Whatever implication the phrase "with pay" might have conveyed is far outweighed by the clarity of our precedents which emphasize the flexibility of due process as contrasted with the sweeping and categorical rule adopted by the Court of Appeals.

B

To determine what process is constitutionally due, we have generally balanced three distinct factors:

> "First, the private interest that will be affected by the official action; second, the risk of an erroneous deprivation of such interest through the procedures used, and the probable value, if any, of additional or substitute procedural safeguards; and finally, the Government's interest." *Mathews* v. *Eldridge,* 424 U.S. 319, 335 (1976). See also, *e. g.*, *Mallen, supra,* at 242; *Logan* v. *Zimmerman Brush Co.*, 455 U.S. 422, 434 (1982).

Respondent contends that he has a significant private interest in the uninterrupted receipt of his paycheck. But while our opinions have recognized the severity of depriving someone of the means of his livelihood, see, *e. g., Mallen, supra,* at 243; *Loudermill,* 470 U. S., at 543, they have also emphasized that in determining what process is due, account must be taken of "the *length* " and "*finality* of the deprivation," *Logan, supra,* at 434 (emphasis added). Unlike the employee in

Loudermill, who faced *termination,* respondent faced only a *temporary suspension* without pay. So long as the suspended employee receives a sufficiently prompt postsuspension hearing, the lost income is relatively insubstantial (compared with termination), and fringe benefits such as health and life insurance are often not affected at all, Brief for United States as *Amicus Curiae* 18; Record, Doc. No. 19, p. 7.

On the other side of the balance, the State has a significant interest in immediately suspending, when felony charges are filed against them, employees who occupy positions of great public trust and high public visibility, such as police officers. Respondent contends that this interest in maintaining public confidence could have been accommodated by suspending him *with* pay until he had a hearing. We think, however, that the government does not have to give an employee charged with a felony a paid leave at taxpayer expense. If his services to the government are no longer useful once the felony charge has been filed, the Constitution does not require the government to bear the added expense of hiring a replacement while still paying him. ESU's interest in preserving public confidence in its police force is at least as significant as the State's interest in preserving the integrity of the sport of horse racing, see *Barry* v. *Barchi, supra,* at 64, an interest we "deemed sufficiently important … to justify a brief period of suspension prior to affording the suspended trainer a hearing," *Mallen,* 486 U. S., at 241.

The last factor in the *Mathews* balancing, and the factor most important to resolution of this case, is the risk of erroneous deprivation and the likely value of any additional procedures. Petitioners argue that any presuspension hearing would have been worthless because pursuant to an Executive Order of the Governor of Pennsylvania a state employee is automatically to be suspended without pay "[a]s soon as practicable after [being] formally charged with … a felony." 4

Pa. Code § 7.173 (1997). According to petitioners, supervisors have no discretion under this rule, and the mandatory suspension without pay lasts until the criminal charges are finally resolved. See Tr. of Oral Arg. 20. If petitioners' interpretation of this order is correct, there is no need for any presuspension process since there would be nothing to consider at the hearing except the independently verifiable fact of whether an employee had indeed been formally charged with a felony. See *Codd* v. *Velger*, 429 U.S. 624, 627–628 (1977) (*per curiam*). Cf. *Loudermill, supra,* at 543. Respondent, however, challenges petitioners' reading of the Code, and contends that in any event an order of the Governor of Pennsylvania is a "mere directiv[e] which do[es] not confer a legally enforceable right." Brief for Respondent 20. We need not resolve this disputed issue of state law because even assuming the Code is only advisory (or has no application at all), the State had no constitutional obligation to provide respondent with a presuspension hearing. We noted in *Loudermill* that the purpose of a pre-*termination* hearing is to determine "whether there are reasonable grounds to believe that the charges against the employee are true and support the proposed action." 470 U. S., at 545–546. By parity of reasoning, the purpose of any pre*suspension* hearing would be to assure that there are reasonable grounds to support the suspension without pay. Cf. *Mallen,* 486 U. S., at 240. But here that has already been assured by the arrest and the filing of charges.

In *Mallen,* we concluded that an "*ex parte* finding of probable cause" such as a grand jury indictment provides adequate assurance that the suspension is not unjustified. *Id.,* at 240–241. The same is true when an employee is arrested and then formally charged with a felony. First, as with an indictment, the arrest and formal charges imposed upon respondent "by an independent body demonstrat[e] that the suspension is not arbitrary." *Id.,* at 244. Second, like an indictment, the imposition of felony charges "itself is an objective fact that will in most cases raise serious public concern." *Id.*, at 244–245. It is true, as respondent argues, that there is more reason to believe an employee has committed a felony when he is indicted rather than merely arrested and formally charged; but for present purposes arrest and charge give reason enough. They serve to assure that the state employer's decision to suspend the employee is not "baseless or unwarranted," *id.*, at 240, in that an independent third party has determined that there is probable cause to believe the employee committed a serious crime.

Respondent further contends that since (as we have agreed to assume) Levanowitz had discretion *not* to suspend despite the arrest and filing of charges, he had to be given an opportunity to persuade Levanowitz of his innocence before the decision was made. We disagree. In *Mallen,* despite the fact that the FDIC had *discretion* whether to suspend an indicted bank employee, see 64 Stat. 879, as amended, 12 U.S. C. § 1818(g)(1); *Mallen, supra,* at 234–235, and n. 5, we nevertheless did not believe that a presuspension hearing was necessary to protect the private interest. Unlike in the case of a termination, where we have recognized that "the only meaningful opportunity to invoke the discretion of the decisionmaker is likely to be before the termination takes effect," *Loudermill, supra,* at 543, in the case of a suspension there will be ample opportunity to invoke discretion later—and a short delay actually benefits the employee by allowing state officials to obtain more accurate information about the arrest and charges. Respondent "has an interest in seeing that a decision concerning his or her continued suspension is not made with excessive haste." *Mallen,* 486 U. S., at 243. If the State is forced to act too quickly, the decisionmaker "may give greater weight to the public interest and leave the suspension in place." *Ibid.*

C

Much of respondent's argument is dedicated to the proposition that he had a due process right to a presuspension hearing because the suspension was open-ended and he "theoretically may not have had the opportunity to be heard for weeks, months, or even years after his initial suspension without pay." Brief for Respondent 23. But, as respondent himself asserts in his attempt to downplay the governmental interest, "[b]ecause the employee is entitled, in any event, to a prompt post-suspension opportunity to be heard, the period of the suspension should be short and the amount of pay during the suspension minimal." *Id.,* at 24–25.

Whether respondent was provided an adequately prompt *post*-suspension hearing in the present case is a separate question. Although the charges against respondent were dropped on September 1 (petitioners apparently learned of this on September 2), he did not receive any sort of hearing until September 18. Once the charges were dropped, the risk of erroneous deprivation increased substantially, and, as petitioners conceded at oral argument, there was likely value in holding a prompt hearing, Tr. of Oral Arg. 19. Cf. *Mallen, supra,* at 243 (holding that 90 days before the agency hears and decides the propriety of a suspension does not exceed the permissible limits where coupled with factors that minimize the risk of an erroneous deprivation). Because neither the Court of Appeals nor the District Court addressed whether, under the particular facts of this case, petitioners violated due process by failing to provide a sufficiently prompt postsuspension hearing, we will not consider this issue in the first instance, but remand for consideration by the Court of Appeals.

* * *

The judgment of the Court of Appeals is reversed, and the case is remanded for further proceedings consistent with this opinion.

It is so ordered.

On the "Confrontation Clause" in Court
Crawford v. Washington,
541 U.S. 36 (2004)

Justice Scalia delivered the opinion of the Court.

Petitioner Michael Crawford stabbed a man who allegedly tried to rape his wife, Sylvia. At his trial, the State played for the jury Sylvia's tape-recorded statement to the police describing the stabbing, even though he had no opportunity for cross-examination. The Washington Supreme Court upheld petitioner's conviction after determining that Sylvia's statement was reliable. The question presented is whether this procedure complied with the Sixth Amendment's guarantee that, "[i]n all criminal prosecutions, the accused shall enjoy the right ... to be confronted with the witnesses against him."

I

On August 5, 1999, Kenneth Lee was stabbed at his apartment. Police arrested petitioner later that night. After giving petitioner and his wife *Miranda* warnings, detectives interrogated each of them twice. Petitioner eventually confessed that he and Sylvia had gone in search of Lee because he was upset over an earlier incident in which Lee had tried to rape her. The two had found Lee at his apartment, and a fight ensued in which Lee was stabbed in the torso and petitioner's hand was cut.

Petitioner gave the following account of the fight:

"Q. Okay. Did you ever see anything in [Lee's] hands?

"A. I think so, but I'm not positive.

> "Q. Okay, when you think so, what do you mean by that?
>
> "A. I could a swore I seen him goin' for somethin' before, right before everything happened. He was like reachin', fiddlin' around down here and stuff ... and I just ... I don't know, I think, this is just a possibility, but I think, I think that he pulled somethin' out and I grabbed for it and that's how I got cut ... but I'm not positive. I, I, my mind goes blank when things like this happen. I mean, I just, I remember things wrong, I remember things that just doesn't, don't make sense to me later." App. 155 (punctuation added).

Sylvia generally corroborated petitioner's story about the events leading up to the fight, but her account of the fight itself was arguably different—particularly with respect to whether Lee had drawn a weapon before petitioner assaulted him:

> "Q. Did Kenny do anything to fight back from this assault?
>
> "A. (pausing) I know he reached into his pocket ... or somethin' ... I don't know what.
>
> "Q. After he was stabbed?
>
> "A. He saw Michael coming up. He lifted his hand ... his chest open, he might [have] went to go strike his hand out or something and then (inaudible).
>
> "Q. Okay, you, you gotta speak up.
>
> "A. Okay, he lifted his hand over his head maybe to strike Michael's hand down or something and then he put his hands in his ... put his right hand in his right pocket ... took a step back ... Michael proceeded to stab him ... then his hands were like ... how do you explain this ... open arms ...

> with his hands open and he fell down ... and we ran (describing subject holding hands open, palms toward assailant).
>
> "Q. Okay, when he's standing there with his open hands, you're talking about Kenny, correct?
>
> "A. Yeah, after, after the fact, yes.
>
> "Q. Did you see anything in his hands at that point?
>
> "A. (pausing) um um (no)." *Id.*, at 137 (punctuation added).

The State charged petitioner with assault and attempted murder. At trial, he claimed self-defense. Sylvia did not testify because of the state marital privilege, which generally bars a spouse from testifying without the other spouse's consent. See Wash. Rev.Code § 5.60.060(1) (1994).

In Washington, this privilege does not extend to a spouse's out-of-court statements admissible under a hearsay exception, see *State v. Burden*, 120 Wash.2d 371, 377, 841 P.2d 758, 761 (1992), so the State sought to introduce Sylvia's tape-recorded statements to the police as evidence that the stabbing was not in self-defense. Noting that Sylvia had admitted she led petitioner to Lee's apartment and thus had facilitated the assault, the State invoked the hearsay exception for statements against penal interest, Wash. Rule Evid. 804(b)(3) (2003).

Petitioner countered that, state law notwithstanding, admitting the evidence would violate his federal constitutional right to be "confronted with the witnesses against him." Amdt. 6. According to our description of that right in *Ohio v. Roberts*, 448 U.S. 56, 100 S.Ct. 2531, 65 L.Ed.2d 597 (1980), it does not bar admission of an unavailable witness's statement against a criminal defendant if the statement bears "adequate 'indicia of reliability.'" *Id.,* at 66, 100 S.Ct. 2531. To meet that test, evidence must either fall within a "firmly rooted hearsay exception" or bear "particularized guarantees of trustworthiness." *Ibid.* The trial court here admitted the statement on the latter ground, offering several reasons why it was trustworthy: Sylvia was not shifting blame but rather corroborating her husband's story that he acted in self-defense or "justified reprisal"; she had direct knowledge as an eyewitness; she was describing recent events; and she was being questioned by a "neutral" law enforcement officer. App. 76–77. The prosecution played the tape for the jury and relied on it in closing, arguing that it was "damning evidence" that "completely refutes [petitioner's] claim of self-defense." Tr. 468 (Oct. 21, 1999). The jury convicted petitioner of assault.

The Washington Court of Appeals reversed. It applied a nine-factor test to determine whether Sylvia's statement bore particularized guarantees of trustworthiness, and noted several reasons why it did not: The statement contradicted one she had previously given; it was made in response to specific questions; and at one point she admitted she had shut her eyes during the stabbing. The court considered and rejected the State's argument that Sylvia's statement was reliable because it coincided with petitioner's to such a degree that the two "interlocked." The court determined that, although the two statements agreed about the events leading up to the stabbing, they differed on the issue crucial to petitioner's self-defense claim: "[Petitioner's] version asserts that Lee may have had something in his hand when he stabbed him; but Sylvia's version has Lee grabbing for something only after he has been stabbed." App. 32.

The Washington Supreme Court reinstated the conviction, unanimously concluding that, although Sylvia's statement did not fall under a firmly rooted hearsay exception, it bore guarantees of trustworthiness: "'[W]hen a codefendant's confession is virtually identical [to, *i.e.,* interlocks with,] that of a defendant, it may be deemed reliable.'" 147 Wash.2d 424, 437, 54 P.3d 656, 663 (2002) (quoting *State v. Rice,* 120 Wash.2d 549, 570, 844 P.2d 416, 427 (1993)). The court explained:

> "Although the Court of Appeals concluded that the statements were contradictory, upon closer inspection they appear to overlap....
>
> "[B]oth of the Crawfords' statements indicate that Lee was possibly grabbing for a weapon, but they are equally unsure when this event may have taken place. They are also equally unsure how Michael received the cut on his hand, leading the court to question when, if ever, Lee possessed a weapon. In this respect they overlap....
>
> "[N]either Michael nor Sylvia clearly stated that Lee had a weapon in hand from which Michael was simply defending himself. And it is this omission by both that interlocks the statements and makes Sylvia's statement reliable." 147 Wash.2d, at 438–439, 54 P.3d, at 664 (internal quotation marks omitted).

We granted certiorari to determine whether the State's use of Sylvia's statement violated the Confrontation Clause. 539 U.S. 914, 123 S.Ct. 2275, 156 L.Ed.2d 129 (2003).

II

The Sixth Amendment's Confrontation Clause provides that, "[i]n all criminal prosecutions, the accused shall enjoy the right ... to be confronted with the witnesses against him." We have held that this bedrock procedural guarantee applies to both federal and state prosecutions. *Pointer v. Texas,* 380 U.S. 400, 406, 85 S.Ct. 1065, 13 L.Ed.2d 923 (1965). As noted above,

Roberts says that an unavailable witness's out-of-court statement may be admitted so long as it has adequate indicia of reliability—*i.e.,* falls within a "firmly rooted hearsay exception" or bears "particularized guarantees of trustworthiness." 448 U.S., at 66, 100 S.Ct. 2531. Petitioner argues that this test strays from the original meaning of the Confrontation Clause and urges us to reconsider it.

A

The Constitution's text does not alone resolve this case. One could plausibly read "witnesses against" a defendant to mean those who actually testify at trial, cf. *Woodsides v. State,* 3 Miss. 655, 664–665 (1837), those whose statements are offered at trial, see 3 J. Wigmore, *Evidence* § 1397, p. 104 (2d ed.1923) (hereinafter *Wigmore*), or something in-between, see *infra,* at 1364. We must therefore turn to the historical background of the Clause to understand its meaning.

The right to confront one's accusers is a concept that dates back to Roman times. See *Coy v. Iowa,* 487 U.S. 1012, 1015, 108 S.Ct. 2798, 101 L.Ed.2d 857 (1988); Herrmann & Speer, "Facing the Accuser: Ancient and Medieval Precursors of the Confrontation Clause," 34 *Va. J. Int'l L.* 481 (1994). The founding generation's immediate source of the concept, however, was the common law. English common law has long differed from continental civil law in regard to the manner in which witnesses give testimony in criminal trials. The common-law tradition is one of live testimony in court subject to adversarial testing, while the civil law condones examination in private by judicial officers. See 3 W. Blackstone, *Commentaries on the Laws of England* 373–374 (1768).

Nonetheless, England at times adopted elements of the civil-law practice. Justices of the peace or other officials examined suspects and witnesses before trial. These examinations were sometimes read in court in lieu of live testimony, a practice that "occasioned frequent demands by the prisoner to have his 'accusers,' *i.e.* the witnesses against him, brought before him face to face." 1 J. Stephen, *History of the Criminal Law of England* 326 (1883). In some cases, these demands were refused. See 9 W. Holdsworth, *History of English Law* 216–217, 228 (3d ed.1944); *e.g., Raleigh's Case,* 2 How. St. Tr. 1, 15–16, 24 (1603); *Throckmorton's Case,* 1 How. St. Tr. 869, 875–876 (1554); cf. *Lilburn's Case,* 3 How. St. Tr. 1315, 1318–1322, 1329 (Star Chamber 1637).

Pretrial examinations became routine under two statutes passed during the reign of Queen Mary in the 16th century, 1 & 2 Phil. & M., c. 13 (1554), and 2 & 3 *id.,* c. 10 (1555). These Marian bail and committal statutes required justices of the peace to examine suspects and witnesses in felony cases and to certify the results to the court. It is doubtful that the original purpose of the examinations was to produce evidence admissible at trial. See J. Langbein, *Prosecuting Crime in the Renaissance* 21–34 (1974). Whatever the original purpose, however, they came to be used as evidence in some cases, see 2 M. Hale, *Pleas of the Crown* 284 (1736), resulting in an adoption of continental procedure. See 4 Holdsworth, *supra,* at 528–530.

The most notorious instances of civil-law examination occurred in the great political trials of the 16th and 17th centuries. One such was the 1603 trial of Sir Walter Raleigh for treason. Lord Cobham, Raleigh's alleged accomplice, had implicated him in an examination before the Privy Council and in a letter. At Raleigh's trial, these were read to the jury. Raleigh argued that Cobham had lied to save himself: "Cobham is absolutely in the King's mercy; to excuse me cannot avail him; by accusing me he may hope for favour." 1 D. Jardine, *Criminal Trials* 435 (1832). Suspecting that

Cobham would recant, Raleigh demanded that the judges call him to appear, arguing that "[t]he Proof of the Common Law is by witness and jury: let Cobham be here, let him speak it. Call my accuser before my face ...." 2 How. St. Tr., at 15–16. The judges refused, *id.*, at 24, and, despite Raleigh's protestations that he was being tried "by the Spanish Inquisition," *id.*, at 15, the jury convicted, and Raleigh was sentenced to death.

One of Raleigh's trial judges later lamented that "'the justice of England has never been so degraded and injured as by the condemnation of Sir Walter Raleigh.'" 1 Jardine, *supra,* at 520. Through a series of statutory and judicial reforms, English law developed a right of confrontation that limited these abuses. For example, treason statutes required witnesses to confront the accused "face to face" at his arraignment. *E.g.*, 13 Car. 2, c. 1, § 5 (1661); see 1 Hale, *supra,* at 306. Courts, meanwhile, developed relatively strict rules of unavailability, admitting examinations only if the witness was demonstrably unable to testify in person. See *Lord Morley's Case,* 6 How. St. Tr. 769, 770–771 (H.L.1666); 2 Hale, *supra,* at 284; 1 Stephen, *supra,* at 358. Several authorities also stated that a suspect's confession could be admitted only against himself, and not against others he implicated. See 2 W. Hawkins, *Pleas of the Crown,* ch. 46, § 3, pp. 603–604 (T. Leach 6th ed. 1787); 1 Hale, *supra,* at 585, n. *(k);* 1 G. Gilbert, *Evidence* 216 (C. Lofft ed. 1791); cf. *Tong's Case,* Kel. J. 17, 18, 84 Eng. Rep. 1061, 1062 (1662) (treason). But see *King v. Westbeer,* 1 Leach 12, 168 Eng. Rep. 108, 109 (1739).

One recurring question was whether the admissibility of an unavailable witness's pretrial examination depended on whether the defendant had had an opportunity to cross-examine him. In 1696, the Court of King's Bench answered this question in the affirmative, in the widely reported misdemeanor libel case of *King v. Paine,* 5 Mod. 163, 87 Eng. Rep. 584. The court ruled that, even though a witness was dead, his examination was not admissible where "the defendant not being present when [it was] taken before the mayor ... had lost the benefit of a cross-examination." *Id.,* at 165, 87 Eng. Rep., at 585. The question was also debated at length during the infamous proceedings against Sir John Fenwick on a bill of attainder. Fenwick's counsel objected to admitting the examination of a witness who had been spirited away, on the ground that Fenwick had had no opportunity to cross-examine. See *Fenwick's Case,* 13 How. St. Tr. 537, 591–592 (H.C. 1696) (Powys) ("[T]hat which they would offer is something that Mr. Goodman hath sworn when he was examined ...; sir J.F. not being present or privy, and no opportunity given to cross-examine the person; and I conceive that cannot be offered as evidence ..."); *id.,* at 592 (Shower) ("[N]o deposition of a person can be read, though beyond sea, unless in cases where the party it is to be read against was privy to the examination, and might have cross-examined him .... [O]ur constitution is, that the person shall see his accuser"). The examination was nonetheless admitted on a closely divided vote after several of those present opined that the common-law rules of procedure did not apply to parliamentary attainder proceedings—one speaker even admitting that the evidence would normally be inadmissible. See *id.,* at 603–604 (Williamson); *id.,* at 604–605 (Chancellor of the Exchequer); *id.,* at 607; 3 *Wigmore* § 1364, at 22–23, n. 54. Fenwick was condemned, but the proceedings "must have burned into the general consciousness the vital importance of the rule securing the right of cross-examination." *Id.,* § 1364, at 22; cf. *Carmell v. Texas,* 529 U.S. 513, 526–530, 120 S.Ct. 1620, 146 L.Ed.2d 577 (2000).

Paine had settled the rule requiring a prior opportunity for cross-examination as a matter of common law, but some doubts remained over whether the Marian statutes prescribed an exception to it in felony cases. The statutes did not identify the circumstances under which examinations were admissible, see 1 & 2 Phil. & M., c. 13 (1554); 2 & 3 *id.*, c. 10 (1555), and some inferred that no prior opportunity for cross-examination was required. See *Westbeer, supra,* at 12, 168 Eng. Rep., at 109; compare *Fenwick's Case,* 13 How. St. Tr., at 596 (Sloane), with *id.*, at 602 (Musgrave). Many who expressed this view acknowledged that it meant the statutes were in derogation of the common law. See *King v. Eriswell,* 3 T.R. 707, 710, 100 Eng. Rep. 815, 817 (K.B.1790) (Grose, J.) (dicta); *id.*, at 722–723, 100 Eng. Rep., at 823–824 (Kenyon, C.J.) (same); compare 1 Gilbert, *Evidence*, at 215 (admissible only "by Force 'of the Statute'"), with *id.*, at 65. Nevertheless, by 1791 (the year the Sixth Amendment was ratified), courts were applying the cross-examination rule even to examinations by justices of the peace in felony cases. See *King v. Dingler,* 2 Leach 561, 562–563, 168 Eng. Rep. 383, 383–384 (1791); *King v. Woodcock,* 1 Leach 500, 502–504, 168 Eng. Rep. 352, 353 (1789); cf. *King v. Radbourne,* 1 Leach 457, 459–461, 168 Eng. Rep. 330, 331–332 (1787); 3 *Wigmore* § 1364, at 23. Early 19th-century treatises confirm that requirement. See 1 T. Starkie, *Evidence* 95 (1826); 2 *id.*, at 484–492; T. Peake, *Evidence* 63–64 (3d ed. 1808). When Parliament amended the statutes in 1848 to make the requirement explicit, see 11 & 12 Vict., c. 42, § 17, the change merely "introduced in terms" what was already afforded the defendant "by the equitable construction of the law." *Queen v. Beeston,* 29 Eng. L. & Eq. R. 527, 529 (Ct.Crim.App.1854) (Jervis, C. J.).

B

Controversial examination practices were also used in the Colonies. Early in the 18th century, for example, the Virginia Council protested against the Governor for having "privately issued several commissions to examine witnesses against particular men *ex parte*," complaining that "the person accused is not admitted to be confronted with, or defend himself against his defamers." A Memorial Concerning the Maladministrations of His Excellency Francis Nicholson, reprinted in 9 *English Historical Documents* 253, 257 (D. Douglas ed.1955). A decade before the Revolution, England gave jurisdiction over Stamp Act offenses to the admiralty courts, which followed civil-law rather than common-law procedures and thus routinely took testimony by deposition or private judicial examination. See 5 Geo. 3, c. 12, § 57 (1765); Pollitt, "The Right of Confrontation: Its History and Modern Dress," 8 J. *Pub.L.* 381, 396–397 (1959). Colonial representatives protested that the Act subverted their rights "by extending the jurisdiction of the courts of admiralty beyond its ancient limits." Resolutions of the Stamp Act Congress § 8th (Oct. 19, 1765), reprinted in *Sources of Our Liberties* 270, 271 (R. Perry & J. Cooper eds.1959). John Adams, defending a merchant in a high-profile admiralty case, argued: "Examinations of witnesses upon Interrogatories, are only by the Civil Law. Interrogatories are unknown at common Law, and Englishmen and common Lawyers have an aversion to them if not an Abhorrence of them." Draft of Argument in *Sewall v. Hancock* (Oct. 1768–Mar. 1769), in 2 *Legal Papers of John Adams* 194, 207 (L. Wroth & H. Zobel eds.1965).

Many declarations of rights adopted around the time of the Revolution guaranteed a right of confrontation. See Virginia Declaration of Rights § 8 (1776); Pennsylvania Declaration of Rights § IX (1776); Delaware Declaration of Rights § 14 (1776);

Maryland Declaration of Rights § XIX (1776); North Carolina Declaration of Rights § VII (1776); Vermont Declaration of Rights Ch. I, § X (1777); Massachusetts Declaration of Rights § XII (1780); New Hampshire Bill of Rights § XV (1783), all reprinted in 1 B. Schwartz, *The Bill of Rights: A Documentary History* 235, 265, 278, 282, 287, 323, 342, 377 (1971). The proposed Federal Constitution, however, did not. At the Massachusetts ratifying convention, Abraham Holmes objected to this omission precisely on the ground that it would lead to civil-law practices: "The mode of trial is altogether indetermined; ... whether [the defendant] is to be allowed to confront the witnesses, and have the advantage of cross-examination, we are not yet told .... [W]e shall find Congress possessed of powers enabling them to institute judicatories little less inauspicious than a certain tribunal in Spain, ... the *Inquisition.*" 2 *Debates on the Federal Constitution* 110–111 (J. Elliot 2d ed. 1863). Similarly, a prominent Antifederalist writing under the pseudonym Federal Farmer criticized the use of "written evidence" while objecting to the omission of a vicinage right: "Nothing can be more essential than the cross examining [of] witnesses, and generally before the triers of the facts in question .... [W]ritten evidence ... [is] almost useless; it must be frequently taken ex parte, and but very seldom leads to the proper discovery of truth." R. Lee, *Letter IV by the Federal Farmer* (Oct. 15, 1787), reprinted in 1 Schwartz, *supra,* at 469, 473. The First Congress responded by including the Confrontation Clause in the proposal that became the Sixth Amendment.

Early state decisions shed light upon the original understanding of the common-law right. *State v. Webb,* 2 N.C. 103 (Super. L. & Eq. 1794) *(per curiam),* decided a mere three years after the adoption of the Sixth Amendment, held that depositions could be read against an accused only if they were taken in his presence. Rejecting a broader reading of the English authorities, the court held: "[I]t is a rule of the common law, founded on natural justice, that no man shall be prejudiced by evidence which he had not the liberty to cross examine." *Id.*, at 104.

Similarly, in *State v. Campbell,* 30 S.C.L. 124, 1844 WL 2558 (App.L.1844), South Carolina's highest law court excluded a deposition taken by a coroner in the absence of the accused. It held: "[I]f we are to decide the question by the established rules of the common law, there could not be a dissenting voice. For, notwithstanding the death of the witness, and whatever the respectability of the court taking the depositions, the solemnity of the occasion and the weight of the testimony, such depositions are *ex parte,* and, therefore, utterly incompetent." *Id.,* at 125. The court said that one of the "indispensable conditions" implicitly guaranteed by the State Constitution was that "prosecutions be carried on to the conviction of the accused, by witnesses confronted by him, and subjected to his personal examination." *Ibid.*

Many other decisions are to the same effect. Some early cases went so far as to hold that prior testimony was inadmissible in criminal cases *even if* the accused had a previous opportunity to cross-examine. See *Finn v. Commonwealth,* 26 Va. 701, 708 (1827); *State v. Atkins,* 1 Tenn. 229 (Super. L. & Eq. 1807) *(per curiam).* Most courts rejected that view, but only after reaffirming that admissibility depended on a prior opportunity for cross-examination. See *United States v. Macomb,* 26 F.Cas. 1132, 1133 (No. 15,702) (CC Ill. 1851); *State v. Houser,* 26 Mo. 431, 435–436 (1858); *Kendrick v. State,* 29 Tenn. 479, 485–488 (1850); *Bostick v. State,* 22 Tenn. 344, 345–346 (1842); *Commonwealth v. Richards,* 35 Mass. 434, 437 (1837); *State v. Hill,* 20 S.C.L. 607, 608–610 (App. 1835); *Johnston v. State,* 10 Tenn. 58, 59 (Err. &

App. 1821). Nineteenth-century treatises confirm the rule. See 1 J. Bishop, *Criminal Procedure* § 1093, p. 689 (2d ed. 1872); T. Cooley, *Constitutional Limitations* *318.

III

This history supports two inferences about the meaning of the Sixth Amendment.

A

First, the principal evil at which the Confrontation Clause was directed was the civil-law mode of criminal procedure, and particularly its use of *ex parte* examinations as evidence against the accused. It was these practices that the Crown deployed in notorious treason cases like Raleigh's; that the Marian statutes invited; that English law's assertion of a right to confrontation was meant to prohibit; and that the founding-era rhetoric decried. The Sixth Amendment must be interpreted with this focus in mind.

Accordingly, we once again reject the view that the Confrontation Clause applies of its own force only to in-court testimony, and that its application to out-of-court statements introduced at trial depends upon "the law of Evidence for the time being." 3 *Wigmore* § 1397, at 101; accord, *Dutton v. Evans,* 400 U.S. 74, 94, 91 S.Ct. 210, 27 L.Ed.2d 213 (1970) (Harlan, J., concurring in result). Leaving the regulation of out-of-court statements to the law of evidence would render the Confrontation Clause powerless to prevent even the most flagrant inquisitorial practices. Raleigh was, after all, perfectly free to confront those who read Cobham's confession in court.

This focus also suggests that not all hearsay implicates the Sixth Amendment's core concerns. An off-hand, overheard remark might be unreliable evidence and thus a good candidate for exclusion under hearsay rules, but it bears little resemblance to the civil-law abuses the Confrontation Clause targeted. On the other hand, *ex parte* examinations might sometimes be admissible under modern hearsay rules, but the Framers certainly would not have condoned them.

The text of the Confrontation Clause reflects this focus. It applies to "witnesses" against the accused—in other words, those who "bear testimony." 2 N. Webster, *An American Dictionary of the English Language* (1828). "Testimony," in turn, is typically "[a] solemn declaration or affirmation made for the purpose of establishing or proving some fact." *Ibid.* An accuser who makes a formal statement to government officers bears testimony in a sense that a person who makes a casual remark to an acquaintance does not. The constitutional text, like the history underlying the common-law right of confrontation, thus reflects an especially acute concern with a specific type of out-of-court statement.

Various formulations of this core class of "testimonial" statements exist: "*ex parte* in-court testimony or its functional equivalent—that is, material such as affidavits, custodial examinations, prior testimony that the defendant was unable to cross-examine, or similar pretrial statements that declarants would reasonably expect to be used prosecutorially," Brief for Petitioner 23; "extrajudicial statements ... contained in formalized testimonial materials, such as affidavits, depositions, prior testimony, or confessions," *White v. Illinois,* 502 U.S. 346, 365, 112 S.Ct. 736, 116 L.Ed.2d 848 (1992) (Thomas, J., joined by Scalia, J., concurring in part and concurring in judgment); "statements that were made under circumstances which would lead an objective witness reasonably to believe that the statement would be available for use at a later trial," Brief for National Association of Criminal Defense Lawyers et al. as *Amici Curiae* 3. These formulations all share a common nucleus and then define the Clause's coverage at various levels of abstraction around it. Regardless of the precise articulation, some statements qualify under any definition—for example, *ex parte* testimony at a preliminary hearing.

Statements taken by police officers in the course of interrogations are also testimonial under even a narrow standard. Police interrogations bear a striking resemblance to examinations by justices of the peace in England. The statements are not *sworn* testimony, but the absence of oath was not dispositive. Cobham's examination was unsworn, see 1 Jardine, *Criminal Trials*, at 430, yet Raleigh's trial has long been thought a paradigmatic confrontation violation, see, *e.g.*, *Campbell*, 30 S.C.L., at 130. Under the Marian statutes, witnesses were typically put on oath, but suspects were not. See 2 Hale, *Pleas of the Crown*, at 52. Yet Hawkins and others went out of their way to caution that such unsworn confessions were not admissible against anyone but the confessor. See *supra*, at 1360.

That interrogators are police officers rather than magistrates does not change the picture either. Justices of the peace conducting examinations under the Marian statutes were not magistrates as we understand that office today, but had an essentially investigative and prosecutorial function. See 1 Stephen, *Criminal Law of England*, at 221; Langbein, *Prosecuting Crime in the Renaissance*, at 34–45. England did not have a professional police force until the 19th century, see 1 Stephen, *supra*, at 194–200, so it is not surprising that other government officers performed the investigative functions now associated primarily with the police. The involvement of government officers in the production of testimonial evidence presents the same risk, whether the officers are police or justices of the peace.

In sum, even if the Sixth Amendment is not solely concerned with testimonial hearsay, that is its primary object, and interrogations by law enforcement officers fall squarely within that class.

B

The historical record also supports a second proposition: that the Framers would not have allowed admission of testimonial statements of a witness who did not appear at trial unless he was unavailable to testify, and the defendant had had a prior opportunity for cross-examination. The text of the Sixth Amendment does not suggest any open-ended exceptions from the confrontation requirement to be developed by the courts. Rather, the "right ... to be confronted with the witnesses against him," Amdt. 6, is most naturally read as a reference to the right of confrontation at common law, admitting only those exceptions established at the time of the founding. See *Mattox v. United States,* 156 U.S. 237, 243, 15 S.Ct. 337, 39 L.Ed. 409 (1895); cf. *Houser,* 26 Mo., at 433–435. As the English authorities above reveal, the common law in 1791 conditioned admissibility of an absent witness's examination on unavailability and a prior opportunity to cross-examine. The Sixth Amendment therefore incorporates those limitations. The numerous early state decisions applying the same test confirm that these principles were received as part of the common law in this country.

We do not read the historical sources to say that a prior opportunity to cross-examine was merely a sufficient, rather than a necessary, condition for admissibility of testimonial statements. They suggest that this requirement was dispositive, and not merely one of several ways to establish reliability. This is not to deny, as the Chief Justice notes, that "[t]here were always exceptions to the general rule of exclusion" of hearsay evidence. *Post,* at 1377. Several had become well established by 1791. See 3 *Wigmore* § 1397, at 101; Brief for United States as

Amicus Curiae 13, n. 5. But there is scant evidence that exceptions were invoked to admit *testimonial* statements against the accused in a *criminal* case. Most of the hearsay exceptions covered statements that by their nature were not testimonial—for example, business records or statements in furtherance of a conspiracy. We do not infer from these that the Framers thought exceptions would apply even to prior testimony. Cf. *Lilly v. Virginia,* 527 U.S. 116, 134, 119 S.Ct. 1887, 144 L.Ed.2d 117 (1999) (plurality opinion) ("[A]ccomplices' confessions that inculpate a criminal defendant are not within a firmly rooted exception to the hearsay rule").

IV

Our case law has been largely consistent with these two principles. Our leading early decision, for example, involved a deceased witness's prior trial testimony. *Mattox v. United States,* 156 U.S. 237, 15 S.Ct. 337, 39 L.Ed. 409 (1895). In allowing the statement to be admitted, we relied on the fact that the defendant had had, at the first trial, an adequate opportunity to confront the witness: "The substance of the constitutional protection is preserved to the prisoner in the advantage he has once had of seeing the witness face to face, and of subjecting him to the ordeal of a cross-examination. This, the law says, he shall under no circumstances be deprived of ...." *Id.,* at 244, 15 S.Ct. 337.

Our later cases conform to *Mattox's* holding that prior trial or preliminary hearing testimony is admissible only if the defendant had an adequate opportunity to cross-examine. See *Mancusi v. Stubbs,* 408 U.S. 204, 213–216, 92 S.Ct. 2308, 33 L.Ed.2d 293 (1972); *California v. Green,* 399 U.S. 149, 165–168, 90 S.Ct. 1930, 26 L.Ed.2d 489 (1970); *Pointer v. Texas,* 380 U.S., at 406–408, 85 S.Ct. 1065; cf. *Kirby v. United States,* 174 U.S. 47, 55–61, 19 S.Ct. 574, 43 L.Ed. 890 (1899). Even where the defendant had such an opportunity, we excluded the testimony where the government had not established unavailability of the witness. See *Barber v. Page,* 390 U.S. 719, 722–725, 88 S.Ct. 1318, 20 L.Ed.2d 255 (1968); cf. *Motes v. United States,* 178 U.S. 458, 470–471, 20 S.Ct. 993, 44 L.Ed. 1150 (1900). We similarly excluded accomplice confessions where the defendant had no opportunity to cross-examine. See *Roberts v. Russell,* 392 U.S. 293, 294–295, 88 S.Ct. 1921, 20 L.Ed.2d 1100 (1968) *(per curiam); Bruton v. United States,* 391 U.S. 123, 126–128, 88 S.Ct. 1620, 20 L.Ed.2d 476 (1968); *Douglas v. Alabama,* 380 U.S. 415, 418–420, 85 S.Ct. 1074, 13 L.Ed.2d 934 (1965). In contrast, we considered reliability factors beyond prior opportunity for cross-examination when the hearsay statement at issue was not testimonial. See *Dutton v. Evans,* 400 U.S., at 87–89, 91 S.Ct. 210 (plurality opinion).

Even our recent cases, in their outcomes, hew closely to the traditional line. *Ohio v. Roberts,* 448 U.S., at 67–70, 100 S.Ct. 2531, admitted testimony from a preliminary hearing at which the defendant had examined the witness. *Lilly v. Virginia, supra,* excluded testimonial statements that the defendant had had no opportunity to test by cross-examination. And *Bourjaily v. United States,* 483 U.S. 171, 181–184, 107 S.Ct. 2775, 97 L.Ed.2d 144 (1987), admitted statements made unwittingly to a Federal Bureau of Investigation informant after applying a more general test that did *not* make prior cross-examination an indispensable requirement.

Lee v. Illinois, 476 U.S. 530, 106 S.Ct. 2056, 90 L.Ed.2d 514 (1986), on which the State relies, is not to the contrary. There, we *rejected* the State's attempt to admit an accomplice confession. The State had argued that the confession was admissible because it "interlocked" with the defendant's. We dealt with the argument by rejecting its premise, holding that "when the discrepancies between the statements are not insignificant, the codefendant's confession may not be admitted." *Id.*, at 545, 106 S.Ct. 2056. Respondent argues that "[t]he logical inference of this statementis that when the discrepancies between the statements *are* insignificant, then the codefendant's statement *may* be admitted." Brief for Respondent 6. But this is merely a possible inference, not an inevitable one, and we do not draw it here. If *Lee* had meant authoritatively to announce an exception—previously unknown to this Court's jurisprudence—for interlocking confessions, it would not have done so in such an oblique manner. Our only precedent on interlocking confessions had addressed the entirely different question whether a limiting instruction cured prejudice to codefendants from admitting a defendant's *own* confession against him in a joint trial. See *Parker v. Randolph,* 442 U.S. 62, 69–76, 99 S.Ct. 2132, 60 L.Ed.2d 713 (1979) (plurality opinion), abrogated by *Cruz v. New York,* 481 U.S. 186, 107 S.Ct. 1714, 95 L.Ed.2d 162 (1987).

Our cases have thus remained faithful to the Framers' understanding: Testimonial statements of witnesses absent from trial have been admitted only where the declarant is unavailable, and only where the defendant has had a prior opportunity to cross-examine.

V

Although the results of our decisions have generally been faithful to the original meaning of the Confrontation Clause, the same cannot be said of our rationales. *Roberts* conditions the admissibility of all hearsay evidence on whether it falls under a "firmly rooted hearsay exception" or bears "particularized guarantees of trustworthiness." 448 U.S., at 66,

100 S.Ct. 2531. This test departs from the historical principles identified above in two respects. First, it is too broad: It applies the same mode of analysis whether or not the hearsay consists of *ex parte* testimony. This often results in close constitutional scrutiny in cases that are far removed from the core concerns of the Clause. At the same time, however, the test is too narrow: It admits statements that *do* consist of *ex parte* testimony upon a mere finding of reliability. This malleable standard often fails to protect against paradigmatic confrontation violations.

Members of this Court and academics have suggested that we revise our doctrine to reflect more accurately the original understanding of the Clause. See, *e.g., Lilly,* 527 U.S., at 140–143, 119 S.Ct. 1887 (Breyer, J., concurring); *White,* 502 U.S., at 366, 112 S.Ct. 736 Thomas, J., joined by Scalia, J., concurring in part and concurring in judgment); A. Amar, *The Constitution and Criminal Procedure* 125–131 (1997); Friedman, "Confrontation: The Search for Basic Principles," 86 *Geo. L.J.* 1011 (1998). They offer two proposals: First, that we apply the Confrontation Clause only to testimonial statements, leaving the remainder to regulation by hearsay law—thus eliminating the overbreadth referred to above. Second, that we impose an absolute bar to statements that are testimonial, absent a prior opportunity to cross-examine—thus eliminating the excessive narrowness referred to above.

In *White,* we considered the first proposal and rejected it. 502 U.S., at 352–353, 112 S.Ct. 736. Although our analysis in this case casts doubt on that holding, we need not definitively resolve whether it survives our decision today, because Sylvia Crawford's statement is testimonial under any definition. This case does, however, squarely implicate the second proposal.

A

Where testimonial statements are involved, we do not think the Framers meant to leave the Sixth Amendment's protection to the vagaries of the rules of evidence, much less to amorphous notions of "reliability." Certainly none of the authorities discussed above acknowledges any general reliability exception to the common-law rule. Admitting statements deemed reliable by a judge is fundamentally at odds with the right of confrontation. To be sure, the Clause's ultimate goal is to ensure reliability of evidence, but it is a procedural rather than a substantive guarantee. It commands, not that evidence be reliable, but that reliability be assessed in a particular manner: by testing in the crucible of cross-examination. The Clause thus reflects a judgment, not only about the desirability of reliable evidence (a point on which there could be little dissent), but about how reliability can best be determined. Cf. 3 Blackstone, *Commentaries*, at 373 ("This open examination of witnesses ... is much more conducive to the clearing up of truth"); M. Hale, *History and Analysis of the Common Law of England* 258 (1713) (adversarial testing "beats and bolts out the Truth much better").

The *Roberts* test allows a jury to hear evidence, untested by the adversary process, based on a mere judicial determination of reliability. It thus replaces the constitutionally prescribed method of assessing reliability with a wholly foreign one. In this respect, it is very different from exceptions to the Confrontation Clause that make no claim to be a surrogate means of assessing reliability. For example, the rule of forfeiture by wrongdoing (which we accept) extinguishes confrontation claims on essentially equitable grounds; it does not purport to be an alternative means of determining reliability. See *Reynolds v. United States,* 98 U.S. 145, 158–159, 25 L.Ed. 244 (1879).

The Raleigh trial itself involved the very sorts of reliability determinations that *Roberts* authorizes. In the face of Raleigh's repeated demands for confrontation, the prosecution responded with many of the arguments a court applying *Roberts* might invoke today: that Cobham's statements were self-inculpatory, 2 How. St. Tr., at 19, that they were not made in the heat of passion, *id.*, at 14, and that they were not "extracted from [him] upon any hopes or promise of Pardon," *id.*, at 29. It is not plausible that the Framers' only objection to the trial was that Raleigh's judges did not properly weigh these factors before sentencing him to death. Rather, the problem was that the judges refused to allow Raleigh to confront Cobham in court, where he could cross-examine him and try to expose his accusation as a lie.

Dispensing with confrontation because testimony is obviously reliable is akin to dispensing with jury trial because a defendant is obviously guilty. This is not what the Sixth Amendment prescribes.

B

The legacy of *Roberts* in other courts vindicates the Framers' wisdom in rejecting a general reliability exception. The framework is so unpredictable that it fails to provide meaningful protection from even core confrontation violations.

Reliability is an amorphous, if not entirely subjective, concept. There are countless factors bearing on whether a statement is reliable; the nine-factor balancing test applied by the Court of Appeals below is representative. See, *e.g.*, *People v. Farrell,* 34 P.3d 401, 406–407 (Colo.2001) (eight-factor test). Whether a statement is deemed reliable depends heavily on which factors the judge considers and how much weight he accords each of them. Some courts wind up attaching the same significance to opposite facts. For example, the Colorado Supreme Court held a statement more reliable because its inculpation of the defendant was "detailed," *id.*, at 407, while the Fourth Circuit found a statement more reliable because the portion implicating another was "fleeting," *United States v. Photogrammetric Data Servs., Inc.*, 259 F.3d 229, 245 (C.A.4 2001). The Virginia Court of Appeals found a statement more reliable because the witness was in custody and charged with a crime (thus making the statement more obviously against her penal interest), see *Nowlin v. Commonwealth*, 40 Va.App. 327, 335–338, 579 S.E.2d 367, 371–372 (2003), while the Wisconsin Court of Appeals found a statement more reliable because the witness was *not* in custody and *not* a suspect, see *State v. Bintz*, 2002 WI App. 204, ¶ 13, 257 Wis.2d 177, ¶ 13, 650 N.W.2d 913, ¶ 13. Finally, the Colorado Supreme Court in one case found a statement more reliable because it was given "immediately after" the events at issue, *Farrell, supra*, at 407, while that same court, in another case, found a statement more reliable because two years had elapsed, *Stevens v. People*, 29 P.3d 305, 316 (Colo.2001).

The unpardonable vice of the *Roberts* test, however, is not its unpredictability, but its demonstrated capacity to admit core testimonial statements that the Confrontation Clause plainly meant to exclude. Despite the plurality's speculation in *Lilly*, 527 U.S., at 137, 119 S.Ct. 1887, that it was "highly unlikely" that accomplice confessions implicating the accused could survive *Roberts*, courts continue routinely to admit them. See *Photogrammetric Data Servs., supra*, at 245–246; *Farrell, supra*, at 406–408; *Stevens, supra*, at 314–318; *Taylor v. Commonwealth*, 63 S.W.3d 151, 166–168 (Ky.2001); *State v. Hawkins*, No.2001–P–0060, 2002 WL 31895118, ¶¶ 34–37, *6 (Ohio App., Dec. 31, 2002); *Bintz, supra*, ¶¶ 7–14, 257 Wis.2d, at 183–188, 650 N.W.2d, at 916–918; *People v. Lawrence,* 55 P.3d 155, 160–161 (Colo.App.2001); *State v. Jones,* 171 Or.App. 375, 387–391, 15 P.3d 616, 623–625 (2000); *State v. Marshall,* 136 Ohio App.3d 742, 747–748, 737 N.E.2d 1005, 1009 (2000); *People v. Schutte,* 240 Mich.App. 713, 718–721, 613 N.W.2d 370, 376–377 (2000); *People v. Thomas,* 313 Ill.App.3d 998, 1005–1007, 246 Ill.Dec. 593, 730 N.E.2d 618, 625–626 (2000); cf. *Nowlin, supra,* at 335–338, 579 S.E.2d, at 371–372 (witness confessed to a related crime); *People v. Campbell,* 309 Ill.App.3d 423, 431–432, 242 Ill.Dec. 694, 699, 721 N.E.2d 1225, 1230 (1999) (same). One recent study found that, after *Lilly,* appellate courts admitted accomplice statements to the authorities in 25 out of 70 cases—more than one-third of the time. Kirst, Appellate Court Answers to the Confrontation Questions in *Lilly v. Virginia,* 53 Syracuse L.Rev. 87, 105 (2003). Courts have invoked *Roberts* to admit other sorts of plainly testimonial statements despite the absence of any opportunity to cross-examine. See *United States v. Aguilar,* 295 F.3d 1018, 1021–1023 (C.A.9 2002) (plea allocution showing existence of a conspiracy); *United States v. Centracchio,* 265 F.3d 518, 527–530 (C.A.7 2001) (same); *United States v. Dolah,* 245 F.3d 98, 104–105 (C.A.2 2001) (same); *United States v. Petrillo,* 237 F.3d 119, 122–123 (C.A.2 2000) (same); *United States v. Moskowitz,* 215 F.3d 265, 268–269 (C.A.2 2000) *(per curiam)* (same); *United States v. Gallego,* 191 F.3d 156, 166–168 (C.A.2 1999) (same); *United States v. Papajohn,* 212 F.3d 1112, 1118–1120 (C.A.8 2000) (grand jury testimony); *United States v. Thomas,* 30 Fed.Appx. 277, 279 (C.A.4 2002) *(per curiam)* (same); *Bintz, supra,* ¶¶ 15–22, 257 Wis.2d, at 188–191, 650 N.W.2d, at 918–920 (prior trial testimony); *State v. McNeill,* 140 N.C.App. 450, 457–460, 537 S.E.2d 518, 523–524 (2000) (same).

To add insult to injury, some of the courts that admit untested testimonial statements find reliability in the very factors that *make* the statements testimonial. As noted earlier, one court relied on the fact that the witness's statement was made to police while in custody on pending charges—the theory being that this made the statement more clearly against penal interest and thus more reliable. *Nowlin, supra,* at 335–338, 579 S.E.2d, at 371–372. Other courts routinely rely on the fact that a prior statement is given under oath in judicial proceedings. *E.g., Gallego, supra,* at 168 (plea allocution); *Papajohn, supra,* at 1120 (grand jury testimony). That inculpating statements are given in a testimonial setting is not an antidote to the confrontation problem, but rather the trigger that makes the Clause's demands most urgent. It is not enough to point out that most of the usual safeguards of the adversary process attend the statement, when the single safeguard missing is the one the Confrontation Clause demands.

C

Roberts' failings were on full display in the proceedings below. Sylvia Crawford made her statement while in police custody, herself a potential suspect in the case. Indeed, she had been told that whether she would be released "depend[ed] on how the investigation continues." App. 81. In response to often leading questions from police detectives, she implicated her husband in Lee's stabbing and at least arguably undermined his self-defense claim. Despite all this, the trial court admitted her statement, listing several reasons why it was reliable. In its opinion reversing, the Court of Appeals listed several *other* reasons why the statement was *not* reliable. Finally, the State Supreme Court relied exclusively on the interlocking character of the statement and disregarded every other factor the lower courts had considered. The case is thus a self-contained demonstration of *Roberts*' unpredictable and inconsistent application.

Each of the courts also made assumptions that cross-examination might well have undermined. The trial court, for example, stated that Sylvia Crawford's statement was reliable because she was an eyewitness with direct knowledge of the events. But Sylvia at one point told the police that she had "shut [her] eyes and ... didn't really watch" part of the fight, and that she was "in shock." App. 134. The trial court also buttressed its reliability finding by claiming that Sylvia was "being questioned by law enforcement, and, thus, the [questioner] is ... neutral to her and not someone who would be inclined to advance her interests and shade her version of the truth unfavorably toward the defendant." *Id.*, at 77. The Framers would be astounded to learn that *ex parte* testimony could be admitted against a criminal defendant because it was elicited by "neutral" government officers. But even if the court's assessment of the officer's motives was accurate, it says nothing about Sylvia's perception of her situation. Only cross-examination could reveal that.

The State Supreme Court gave dispositive weight to the interlocking nature of the two statements—that they were both ambiguous as to when and whether Lee had a weapon. The court's claim that the two statements were *equally* ambiguous is hard to accept. Petitioner's statement is ambiguous only in the sense that he had lingering doubts about his recollection: "A. I could a swore I seen him goin' for somethin' before, right before everything happened .... [B]ut I'm not positive." *Id.*, at 155. Sylvia's statement, on the other hand, is truly inscrutable, since the key timing detail was simply assumed in the leading question she was asked: "Q. Did Kenny do anything to fight back from this assault?" *Id.*, at 137 (punctuation added). Moreover, Sylvia specifically said Lee had nothing in his hands after he was stabbed, while petitioner was not asked about that.

The prosecutor obviously did not share the court's view that Sylvia's statement was ambiguous—he called it "damning evidence" that "completely refutes [petitioner's] claim of self-defense." Tr. 468 (Oct. 21, 1999). We have no way of knowing whether the jury agreed with the prosecutor or the court. Far from obviating the need for cross-examination, the "interlocking" ambiguity of the two statements made it all the more imperative that they be tested to tease out the truth.

We readily concede that we could resolve this case by simply reweighing the "reliability factors" under *Roberts* and finding that Sylvia Crawford's statement falls short. But we view this as one of those rare cases in which the result below is so improbable that it reveals a fundamental failure on our part to interpret the Constitution in a way that secures its intended constraint on judicial discretion. Moreover, to reverse the Washington Supreme Court's decision after conducting our own reliability analysis would perpetuate, not avoid, what the Sixth Amendment condemns. The Constitution prescribes a procedure for determining the reliability of testimony in criminal trials, and we, no less than the state courts, lack authority to replace it with one of our own devising.

We have no doubt that the courts below were acting in utmost good faith when they found reliability. The Framers, however, would not have been content to indulge this assumption. They knew that judges, like other government officers, could not always be trusted to safeguard the rights of the people; the likes of the dread Lord Jeffreys were not yet too distant a memory. They were loath to leave too much discretion in judicial hands. Cf. U.S. Const., Amdt. 6 (criminal jury trial); Amdt. 7 (civil jury trial); *Ring v. Arizona,* 536 U.S.

584, 611–612, 122 S.Ct. 2428, 153 L.Ed.2d 556 (2002) (SCALIA, J., concurring). By replacing categorical constitutional guarantees with open-ended balancing tests, we do violence to their design. Vague standards are manipulable, and, while that might be a small concern in run-of-the-mill assault prosecutions like this one, the Framers had an eye toward politically charged cases like Raleigh's great state trials where the impartiality of even those at the highest levels of the judiciary might not be so clear. It is difficult to imagine *Roberts*' providing any meaningful protection in those circumstances.

* * *

Where nontestimonial hearsay is at issue, it is wholly consistent with the Framers' design to afford the States flexibility in their development of hearsay law—as does *Roberts,* and as would an approach that exempted such statements from Confrontation Clause scrutiny altogether. Where testimonial evidence is at issue, however, the Sixth Amendment demands what the common law required: unavailability and a prior opportunity for cross-examination. We leave for another day any effort to spell out a comprehensive definition of "testimonial." Whatever else the term covers, it applies at a minimum to prior testimony at a preliminary hearing, before a grand jury, or at a former trial; and to police interrogations. These are the modern practices with closest kinship to the abuses at which the Confrontation Clause was directed.

In this case, the State admitted Sylvia's testimonial statement against petitioner, despite the fact that he had no opportunity to cross-examine her. That alone is sufficient to make out a violation of the Sixth Amendment. *Roberts* notwithstanding, we decline to mine the record in search of indicia of reliability.

Where testimonial statements are at issue, the only indicium of reliability sufficient to satisfy constitutional demands is the one the Constitution actually prescribes: confrontation.

The judgment of the Washington Supreme Court is reversed, and the case is remanded for further proceedings not inconsistent with this opinion.

It is so ordered.

5

Statutory and Treaty Interpretation

Interpreting the Panama Canal Treaty
O'Connor v. United States, 479 U.S. 27 (1986)

Interpreting the Warsaw Convention
Chan v. Korean Air Lines, Ltd., 490 U.S. 122 (1989)

Union Rights and the Federal Labor-Management Relations Statute
Fort Stewart Schools v. FLRA, 495 U.S. 641 (1990)

The Limits of Actions under ERISA
Mertens v. Hewitt Assocs., 508 U.S. 248 (1993)

Interpreting a Decision of the Social Security Administration
Barnhart v. Thomas, 540 U.S. 20 (2003)

On the National Childhood Vaccine Injury Act and the Right to Sue
Bruesewitz v. Wyeth LLC, 562 U.S. 223 (2011)

Much of the Court's work involves the interpretation of texts, especially the Constitution, federal statutes, and treaties to which the United States is a party. There was no subject more dear to Justice Scalia's heart than textual interpretation. His father was a textual scholar; Justice Scalia himself was educated in the classical tradition, and throughout his life he devoted much of his vast energy and critical intelligence to the study of legal texts. Thus, it is not at all surprising that in the decisions presented in this chapter, we see Justice Scalia as a master of textual interpretation. The cases in this chapter range over such topics as the Panama Canal Treaty, the *Federal Service Labor-Management Relations Statute*, and *ERISA*.

Interpreting the Panama Canal Treaty
O'Connor v. United States,
479 U.S. 27 (1986)

Justice Scalia delivered the opinion of the Court.

The petitioners, United States citizen employees of the Panama Canal Commission and their spouses, seek refunds of income taxes collected on salaries paid by the Commission between 1979 and 1981. We granted certiorari to resolve conflicting appellate interpretations of an international agreement. 474 U.S. 1050, 106 S.Ct. 784, 88 L.Ed.2d 763 (1986).

From 1904 to 1979, the United States exercised sovereignty over the Panama Canal and the surrounding 10-mile-wide Panama Canal Zone under the Isthmian Canal Convention, 33 Stat. 2234. On September 7, 1977, the United States and Panama signed the Panama Canal Treaty, T.I.A.S. No. 10030, which was ratified by the Senate on April 17, 1978, and took effect on October 1, 1979. The Treaty transferred to Panama sovereignty over the Canal and Zone, but gave the United States the right to operate the Canal until December 31, 1999. The vehicle for United States administration of the Canal is the Panama Canal Commission, a United States Government agency supervised by a Board of nine members, four of whom are Panamanian nationals proposed by the Government of Panama. See 22 U.S.C. §§ 3611, 3612; Panama Canal Treaty, Art. III, § 3, T.I.A.S. No. 10030 (hereinafter Treaty).

Article III of the Treaty, entitled "Canal Operation and Management," specifies that "the rights and legal status of United States Government agencies and employees operating in the Republic of Panama pursuant to this Article, shall be governed by the Agreement in Implementation of this Article...." Treaty, Art. III, § 9. The latter agreement, signed simultaneously with the Treaty, see Panama Canal Treaty: Implementation of Article III, Sept. 7, 1977, T.I.A.S. No. 10031 (hereinafter Agreement), contains the provision that gives rise to the present dispute. Article XV of the Agreement, entitled "Taxation," provides as follows:

> "1. By virtue of this Agreement, the Commission, its contractors and subcontractors are exempt from payment in the Republic of Panama of all taxes, fees or other charges on their activities or property.
>
> "2. United States citizen employees and dependents shall be exempt from any taxes, fees or other charges on income received as a result of their work for the Commission. Similarly, they shall be exempt from payment of taxes, fees or other charges on income derived from sources outside the Republic of Panama.
>
> "3. United States citizen employees and dependents shall be exempt from taxes, fees or other charges on gifts or inheritance or on personal property, the presence of which within the territory of the Republic of Panama is due solely to the stay therein of such persons on account of their or their sponsor's work with the Commission.
>
> "4. The Coordinating Committee may establish such regulations as may be appropriate for the implementation of this Article."

The petitioners contend that § 2 of this Article constitutes an express exemption of their Commission salaries from both Panamanian and United States taxation. See 26 U.S.C. § 894(a) ("Income of any kind, to the extent required by any treaty obligation of the United States, shall not be included in gross income and shall be exempt from taxation under this subtitle"). The Claims Court agreed, 6 Cl.Ct. 115 (1984), but was reversed by a five-judge panel of the Federal Circuit. 761 F.2d 688 (1985). In a substantively identical case, the Eleventh Circuit has ruled for the taxpayers. *Harris v. United States,* 768

F.2d 1240 (1985), cert. pending, No. 85-1011. The same issue is presented in numerous cases still pending in the lower courts.

We agree with the Federal Circuit. The first section of Article XV, which confers upon the Commission and its contractors an exemption "from payment *in the Republic of Panama* of all taxes" (emphasis added), establishes the context for the discussion of tax exemptions in the entire Article—so that when §§ 2 and 3 state that "United States citizen employees ... shall be exempt" from taxes they are understood to be dealing only with taxes payable in Panama. In that regard the structure of Article XV is similar to that of Article XVI, which in most of its sections speaks generally of import duties, but is understood to refer only to *Panamanian* import duties principally because § 1 sets the stage in that fashion by referring to "the customs laws and regulations *of the Republic of Panama.*" Agreement, Art. XVI, § 1 (emphasis added).

There is some purely textual evidence, albeit subtle, of the understanding that Article XV applies only to Panamanian taxes: In conferring an exemption from property taxes, § 3 displays an assumption that only personal property within the Republic of Panama is at issue; otherwise, that significant qualification to the operation of § 3 would more naturally have been set forth as an explicit limitation ("personal property *within the territory of the Republic of Panama,* whose presence there," etc.) rather than being referred to incidentally in the modifying clause ("personal property, whose presence within the territory of the Republic of Panama," etc.). And the assumption that only personal property within Panama is at issue in turn reflects the more fundamental assumption that only *Panamanian* personal property taxes are being addressed.

More persuasive than the textual evidence, and in our view overwhelmingly convincing, is the contextual case for limiting Article XV to Panamanian taxes. Unless one posits the ellipsis of failing to repeat, in each section, § 1's limitation to taxes "in the Republic of Panama," the Article takes on a meaning that is utterly implausible and has no foundation in the negotiations leading to the Agreement. For if the first sentence of § 2 refers to United States as well as Panamanian taxes, then the second sentence of § 2, and the totality of § 3, must do so as well—with the consequence that United States citizen employees and their dependents would be exempt not only from United States income tax on their earnings from the Commission, but also from United States income tax on all income from sources outside Panama (*e.g.*, United States bank accounts), and from all United States gift and inheritance taxes. While, as the petitioners assert, there might have been some reason why Panama would insist that its inability to tax United States citizen Commission employees upon their earnings in Panama be matched by a detraction from the United States' sovereign power to tax those same earnings, there is no conceivable reason why this hypothetical "your-sovereignty-for-mine" negotiating strategy would escalate into a demand that the United States yield more sovereign prerogatives than it was asking Panama to forgo-and no imaginable reason why the United States would accept such an escalation, producing tax immunity of unprecedented scope.

The petitioners' attempts to explain why these broader tax consequences need not follow from their interpretation are unpersuasive. With regard to the second sentence of § 2, they argue that the opening word "similarly" should be read to incorporate into that sentence the first sentence's restriction to "income received as a result of ... work for the Commission." On this understanding, the second sentence provides a "simila[r]" tax exemption for Commission-related income "derived from sources outside the Republic of Panama," but allows both countries to tax non-Commission income. In addition to being an unnatural reading of "similarly" in this context, this interpretation is flatly inconsistent with the language of § 2. Contrary to the petitioners' tacit assumption, the first sentence contains nothing limiting the scope of its exemption to income received as a result of work for the Commission *in Panama.* A person receiving a Commission salary for work performed in, for example, Bogotá would seem plainly to qualify for exemption under this provision-rendering the second sentence, on the petitioners' understanding, superfluous. With regard to § 3, the petitioners assert that its reference to taxation of property "within the territory of the Republic of Panama" is sufficient to demonstrate that only Panamanian taxation is intended to be covered. But as a reading of the provision will readily demonstrate, that reference applies only to personal property taxes; there is no comparable qualification on § 3's exemption from taxes "on gifts or inheritance." That is limited, if at all, only by the implication that Panamanian taxes alone are at issue. In sum, we find the verbal distortions necessary to give plausible content, under the petitioners' theory, to the second sentence of § 2 and § 3, far less tolerable than the acknowledgement of ellipsis which forms the basis of the Government's interpretation.

Not only is limitation of Article XV to Panamanian taxes in accord with the consistent application of the Agreement by the Executive Branch—a factor which alone is entitled to great weight, see *Sumitomo Shoji America, Inc. v. Avagliano,* 457 U.S. 176, 184–185, 102 S.Ct. 2374, 2379, 72 L.Ed.2d 765 (1982)—but that application has gone unchallenged by Panama. It is undisputed that, pursuant to clear Executive Branch policy, the Panama Canal Commission consistently withheld United States income taxes from petitioners and others similarly situated, see Letter from John L. Haines, Jr.,

Deputy General Counsel, Panama Canal Commission, to David Slacter, United States Department of Justice, Dec. 20, 1982, pp. 2–3, 1 App. in Nos. 85–504, 85–505, 85–506, and 85–507 (CA Fed.), pp. 61–62, and that Panama, which had four of its own nationals on the Board of the Commission, did not object. The course of conduct of parties to an international agreement, like the course of conduct of parties to any contract, is evidence of its meaning. See *Trans World Airlines, Inc. v. Franklin Mint Corp.*, 466 U.S. 243, 259–260, 104 S.Ct. 1776, 1786–1787, 80 L.Ed.2d 273 (1984); *Pigeon River Improvement, Slide & Boom Co. v. Charles W. Cox, Ltd.*, 291 U.S. 138, 158–161, 54 S.Ct. 361, 366–367, 78 L.Ed. 695 (1934). Cf. Uniform Commercial Code § 2-208(1) (1978).

The petitioners contrast § 2 with the following provision of the simultaneously executed Agreement in Implementation of Article IV, relating to taxation of United States Armed Forces and associated civilian personnel:

> "(2) Members of the Forces or the civilian component, and dependents, shall be exempt from any taxes, fees, or other charges on income received as a result of their work for the United States Forces or for any of the service facilities referred to in Article XI or XVIII of this Agreement. Similarly, *as is provided by Panamanian law,* they shall be exempt from payment of taxes, fees or other charges on income derived from sources outside the Republic of Panama." Panama Canal Treaty: Implementation of Article IV, Sept. 7, 1977, Art. XVI, § 2, T.I.A.S. No. 10032 (emphasis added).

The petitioners contend that the variation in the phraseology of the two provisions demonstrates that the taxation provisions of the Article III Agreement were meant to be bilateral. We think not. It would be another matter if the variation at issue were alteration of the phrase "Panamanian taxes" in one agreement to merely "taxes" in the other; there would have been no reason to object to the former formulation *except* the belief that more than Panamanian taxes were covered. Several plausible reasons, however, would justify objection to the phrase "as is provided by Panamanian law." The most obvious is the concern that the phrase would be interpreted to leave future scope of the tax exemption within Panama's unilateral control, through the amendment of its domestic law. (To be sure, that reason would seemingly call for deletion of the phrase from both agreements rather than merely the Agreement in Implementation of Article III—but perhaps it was only with respect to the latter agreement, in which Panama had steadfastly opposed the whole concept of tax exemption, that unilateral Panamanian action was feared.) The surmise that the reason for deletion of the phrase in the Article III Agreement was its implication that only Panamanian taxes were covered would perhaps be reasonable if it were clear that the deletion was prompted by Panama. In fact, however, the deletion was made in the course of the American side's own internal drafting, before any text had even been presented to the Panamanians. (The phrase "as is provided by Panamanian law" was included in the June 26, 1977, United States draft of § 2 of Art. XV, 1 App. in Nos. 85–504, 85–505, 85–506, and 85–507 (CA Fed.), p. 74, but was dropped from subsequent United States drafts, *id.*, at 77, 81.) The petitioners assert that this occurred as a consequence of the American side's knowledge that Panama would not accept a unilateral tax exemption provision and would accept a bilateral one—but they point to no Panamanian negotiating proposal supporting that speculation, which seems to us not inordinately credible on its face.

We find the petitioners' attempted reliance upon other elements of the negotiating history unavailing. While the

Claims Court may have been correct that the negotiating history does not favor the Government's position sufficiently to overcome what that court regarded as a plain textual meaning in favor of the taxpayers, it certainly does not favor the taxpayers' position sufficiently to affect our view of the text. It contains, we may note, only a single (unhelpful) reference to United States income taxation—a silence that can perhaps be reconciled with the petitioners' position, but can hardly be said affirmatively to support it.

Finally, we find no significance in the fact, urged so strongly by the petitioners, that Article XV is entitled "Taxation" rather than "Panamanian Taxation." Of the 21 Articles of the Agreement, only 2—Articles V and IX—are limited by title to Panamanian subject matter, though it is plain that most are so limited in their application. See, *e.g.*, Article VII ("Water Rights"); Article XII ("Entry and Departure"); Article XVI ("Import Duties").

The judgment of the Court of Appeals is

Affirmed.

Interpreting the Warsaw Convention
Chan v. Korean Air Lines, Ltd.,
490 U.S. 122 (1989)

Justice Scalia delivered the opinion of the Court.

This case presents the question whether international air carriers lose the benefit of the limitation on damages for passenger injury or death provided by the multilateral treaty known as the Warsaw Convention if they fail to provide notice of that limitation in the 10-point type size required by a private accord among carriers, the Montreal Agreement.

I

On September 1, 1983, over the Sea of Japan, a military aircraft of the Soviet Union destroyed a Korean Air Lines, Ltd. (KAL), Boeing 747 en route from Kennedy Airport in New York to Seoul, South Korea. All 269 persons on board the plane perished. Survivors of the victims filed wrongful-death actions against KAL in several Federal District Courts, all of which were transferred for pretrial proceedings to the District Court for the District of Columbia pursuant to 28 U.S.C. § 1407. All parties agree that their rights are governed by the Warsaw Convention, a multilateral treaty governing the international carriage of passengers, baggage, and cargo by air. Convention for the Unification of Certain Rules Relating to International Transportation by Air, Oct. 12, 1929, 49 Stat. 3000, T.S. No. 876 (1934), reprinted in note following 49 U.S.C.App. § 1502.

The present controversy centers on the per passenger damages limitation for personal injury or death. This was fixed at approximately $8,300 by the Convention, but was raised to $75,000 by the Montreal Agreement, an agreement among carriers executed (and approved by the Civil Aeronautics Board (CAB)) in 1966, and joined by KAL in 1969. Agreement Relating to Liability Limitations of the Warsaw Convention and the Hague Protocol, CAB Agreement 18900, note following 49 U.S.C.App. § 1502 (approved by CAB Order E-23680, May 13, 1966, 31 Fed.Reg. 7302). In addition to providing for a higher damages limitation, this agreement required carriers to give passengers written notice of the Convention's damage limitations in print size no smaller than 10-point type. The notice of the Convention's liability rules printed on KAL's passenger tickets for the flight in question here appeared in only 8-point type. By motion for partial summary judgment, plaintiffs sought a declaration that this discrepancy deprived KAL of the benefit of the damages limitation.

On July 25, 1985, the District Court for the District of Columbia denied the motion, finding that neither the Warsaw Convention nor the Montreal Agreement prescribes that the sanction for failure to provide the required form of notice is the elimination of the damages limitation. *In re Korean Air Lines Disaster of September 1, 1983,* 664 F.Supp. 1463. Its opinion specifically considered and rejected contrary Second Circuit precedent. See *In re Air Crash Disaster at Warsaw, Poland, on March 14, 1980,* 705 F.2d 85, cert. denied *sub nom. Polskie Linie Lotnicze v. Robles,* 464 U.S. 845, 104 S.Ct. 147, 78 L.Ed.2d 138 (1983). On September 24, 1985, the District Court certified for interlocutory appeal under 28 U.S.C. § 1292(b) (1982 ed., Supp. IV) the question whether KAL "is entitled to avail itself of the limitation of damages provided by the Warsaw Convention and Montreal Agreement despite its defective tickets." The District of Columbia Circuit allowed the appeal and (following a remand of the record for clarification of the scope of the District Court's order) affirmed, adopting the District Court's opinion in full. *In re Korean Air Lines*

Disaster of September 1, 1983, 265 U.S.App.D.C. 39, 829 F.2d 1171 (1987). We granted certiorari, 485 U.S. 986, 108 S.Ct. 1288, 99 L.Ed.2d 499 (1988), to resolve the conflict among the Courts of Appeals. (In addition to the Second Circuit, the Fifth is in disagreement with the District of Columbia Circuit's resolution here. See *In re Air Crash Disaster Near New Orleans, Louisiana, on July 9, 1982,* 789 F.2d 1092 (1986), reinstated, 821 F.2d 1147 (1987) (en banc).)

II

Petitioners concede that by itself the Montreal Agreement imposes no sanction for failure to comply with its 10-point type requirement. They argue, however, that such a requirement is created by reading the Montreal Agreement in conjunction with the Warsaw Convention. This argument proceeds in two steps. First, petitioners assert that Article 3 of the Warsaw Convention removes the protection of limited liability if a carrier fails to provide adequate notice of the Convention's liability limitation in its passenger tickets. Second, they contend that the Montreal Agreement's 10-point type requirement supplies the standard of adequate notice under Article 3. Because we reject the first point, we need not reach the second.

Article 3 of the Warsaw Convention provides:

> "(1) For the transportation of passengers the carriers must deliver a passenger ticket which shall contain the following particulars:
>
> "*(a)* The place and date of issue;
>
> "*(b)* The place of departure and of destination;
>
> "*(c)* The agreed stopping places, provided that the carrier may reserve the right to alter the stopping places in case of necessity, and that if he exercises that right, the

alteration shall not have the effect of depriving the transportation of its international character;

"(*d*) The name and address of the carrier or carriers;

"(*e*) A statement that the transportation is subject to the rules relating to liability established by this convention.

"(2) The absence, irregularity, or loss of the passenger ticket shall not affect the existence or the validity of the contract of transportation, which shall none the less be subject to the rules of this convention. Nevertheless, if the carrier accepts a passenger without a passenger ticket having been delivered he shall not be entitled to avail himself of those provisions of this convention which exclude or limit his liability."

Although Article 3(1)(*e*) specifies that a passenger ticket shall contain "[a] statement that the transportation is subject to the rules relating to liability established by this convention," nothing in Article 3 or elsewhere in the Convention imposes a sanction for failure to provide an "adequate" statement. The only sanction in Article 3 appears in the second clause of Article 3(2), which subjects a carrier to unlimited liability if it "accepts a passenger without a passenger ticket having been delivered." Several courts have equated nondelivery of a ticket, for purposes of this provision, with the delivery of a ticket in a form that fails to provide adequate notice of the Warsaw limitation. See *In re Air Crash Disaster Near New Orleans, Louisiana, on July 9, 1982, supra; In re Air Crash Disaster at Warsaw, Poland, on March 14, 1980,* 705 F.2d 85 (CA2), cert. denied *sub nom. Polskie Linie Lotnicze v. Robles,* 464 U.S. 845, 104 S.Ct. 147, 78 L.Ed.2d 138 (1983); *Deutsche Lufthansa Aktiengesellschaft v. CAB,* 156 U.S.App.D.C. 191, 196–197, 479 F.2d 912, 917–918 (1973); *Lisi v. Alitalia-Linee Aeree Italiane, S.p.A.,* 370 F.2d 508 (CA2 1966), aff'd by equally divided Court, 390 U.S. 455, 88 S.Ct. 1193, 20 L.Ed.2d 27 (1968); *Egan v. Kollsman Instrument Corp.,* 21 N.Y.2d 160, 287 N.Y.S.2d 14, 234 N.E.2d 199 (1967), cert. denied, 390 U.S. 1039, 88 S.Ct.

1636, 20 L.Ed.2d 301 (1968). See also *Warren v. Flying Tiger Line, Inc.*, 352 F.2d 494 (CA9 1965) (conditioning liability limitation upon delivery of tickets in such manner as to afford passengers a reasonable opportunity to take measures to protect against liability limitation); *Mertens v. Flying Tiger Line, Inc.*, 341 F.2d 851 (CA2) (same), cert. denied, 382 U.S. 816, 86 S.Ct. 38, 15 L.Ed.2d 64 (1965). But see *Ludecke v. Canadian Pacific Airlines, Ltd.*, 98 D.L.R.3d 52, 57 (Can.1979) (rejecting the view of the American cases).

3456 We cannot accept this interpretation. All that the second sentence of Article 3(2) requires in order to avoid its sanction is the "deliver[y]" of "a passenger ticket." Expanding this to mean "a passenger ticket in compliance with the requirements of this Convention" is rendered implausible by the first sentence of Article 3(2), which specifies that "[t]he ... irregularity ... of the passenger ticket shall not affect the existence or the validity of the contract of transportation, which shall none the less be subject to the rules of this convention." It is clear from this (1) that an "irregularity" does not prevent a document from being a "passenger ticket"; and (2) that an "irregularity" in a passenger ticket does not eliminate the contractual damages limitation provided for by the Convention. "Irregularity" means the "[q]uality or state of not conforming to rule or law," *Webster's Second International Dictionary* (1950), and in the present context the word must surely refer to the rules established by the Convention, including the notice requirement. Thus, a delivered document does not fail to qualify as a "passenger ticket," and does not cause forfeiture of the damages limitation, merely because it contains a defective notice. When Article 3(2), after making this much clear, continues (in the second sentence) "Nevertheless, if a carrier accepts a passenger without a passenger ticket having been delivered, etc.," it can only be referring to the carrier's failure to deliver any document whatever, or its delivery of a document whose shortcomings are so extensive that it cannot reasonably be described as a "ticket" (for example, a mistakenly delivered blank form, with no data filled in). Quite obviously, the use of 8-point type instead of 10-point type for the liability limitation notice is not a shortcoming of such magnitude; indeed, one might well select that as a polar example of what could not possibly prevent a document from being a ticket.

Besides being incompatible with the language of the Convention, the proposition that, for purposes of Article 3(2), delivering a defective ticket is equivalent to failure to deliver a ticket, produces absurd results. It may seem reasonable enough that a carrier "shall not be entitled to avail himself of those provisions of this convention which exclude or limit his liability" when the ticket defect consists precisely of a failure to give the passenger proper notice of those provisions. But there is no textual basis for limiting the "defective-ticket-is-no-ticket" principle to that particular defect. Thus, the liability limitation would also be eliminated if the carrier failed to comply, for example, with the requirement of Article 3(1)*(d)* that the ticket contain the address of the carrier.

The conclusion that defective compliance with the notice provision does not eliminate the liability limitation is confirmed by comparing Article 3(2) with other provisions of the Convention. Article 3 is a part of Chapter II of the Convention, entitled "Transportation Documents." Just as Section I of that Chapter (which includes Article 3) specifies what information must be included in passenger tickets, Sections II and III specify what information must be included in, respectively, baggage checks and air waybills for cargo. All three sections require, in identical terms, "[a] statement that the transportation is subject to the rules relating to liability established by this convention." Articles 3(1)(*e*), 4(3)(*h*), 8(*q*). All three sections also provide, again in identical terms, that if the relevant document (ticket, baggage check, or air waybill) has not been delivered (or, in the case of air waybill, "made out"), the carrier "shall not be entitled to avail himself of the provisions of this convention which exclude or limit his liability." Articles 3(2), 4(4), and 9. But, *unlike Section I*, Sections II and III also specifically impose the latter sanction for failure to include in the documents certain particulars, including (though not limited to) the notice of liability limitation. Sections II and III thus make doubly clear what the text of Article 3(2) already indicates: that delivery of a defective document is something quite different from failure to deliver a document. And given the parallel structures of these provisions it would be a flouting of the text to imply in Section I a sanction not only withheld there but explicitly granted elsewhere. When such an interpretation is allowed, the art of draftsmanship will have become obsolete.

Petitioners and the United States as *amicus curiae* seek to explain the variance between Section I and Sections II and III (as well as the clear text of Article 3) as a drafting error, and lead us through the labyrinth of the Convention's drafting history in an effort to establish this point. It would be absurd, they urge, for defective notice to eliminate liability limits on baggage and air freight but not on personal injury and death. Perhaps not. It might have been thought, by the representatives from diverse countries who drafted the Convention in 1925 and 1929 (an era when even many States of this country had relatively low limits on wrongful-death recovery) that the $8,300 maximum liability established for personal injury or death was a "fair" recovery in any event, so that even if the defective notice caused the passenger to forgo the purchase of additional insurance, he or his heirs would be treated with rough equity in any event. Cf. C. McCormick, Law of Damages § 104 (1935) ("In about one-third of the states, a fixed limit upon the recovery under the Death Act is imposed in the statute. The usual limit is $10,000, but in some instances the maximum is $7,500 or $5,000"). Quite obviously, however, the limitation of liability for baggage and freight (about $16.50 per kilogram, see Article 22(2)) was not set with an eye to fair value (the very notion of a "fair" average value of goods per kilogram is absurd), but perhaps with an eye to fair level of liability in relation to profit on the carriage-so that the shipper of lost goods misled by the inadequate notice would not be compensated equitably. Another possible explanation for the difference in treatment is that the limitations on liability prescribed for baggage and freight are much more substantial and thus notice of them is much more important. They include not just a virtually nominal monetary limit, but also total exclusion of liability for "an error in piloting, in the handling of the aircraft, or in navigation." Article 20. Or perhaps the difference in treatment can be traced to a belief that people were much more likely, if adequate notice was given, to purchase additional insurance on goods than on their own lives-not only because baggage and freight are lost a lot more frequently than passengers, but also because the Convention itself establishes, in effect, an insurance-purchasing counter at the airport for baggage and freight, providing that if the consignor makes "a special declaration of the value at delivery and has paid a supplementary sum if the case so requires," the carrier will be liable for actual value up to the declared sum. Article 22(2); see also Articles 4(*g*), 8(*m*).

These estimations of what the drafters might have had in mind are of course speculation, but they suffice to establish that the result the text produces is not necessarily absurd, and hence cannot be dismissed as an obvious drafting error. We must thus be governed by the text-solemnly adopted by the governments of many separate nations-whatever conclusions might be drawn from the intricate drafting history that petitioners and the United States have brought to our attention. The latter may of course be consulted to elucidate a text that is ambiguous, see, *e.g., Air France v. Saks,* 470 U.S. 392, 105 S.Ct. 1338, 84 L.Ed.2d 289 (1985). But where the text is clear, as it is here, we have no power to insert an amendment. As Justice Story wrote for the Court more than a century and a half ago:

> "[T]o alter, amend, or add to any treaty, by inserting any clause, whether small or great, important or trivial, would be on our part an usurpation of power, and not an exercise of judicial functions. It would be to make, and not to construe a treaty. Neither can this Court supply a *casus omissus* in a treaty, any more than in a law. We are to find out the intention of the parties by just rules of interpretation applied to the subject matter; and having found that, our duty is to follow it as far as it goes, and to stop where that stops-whatever may be the imperfections or difficulties which it leaves behind." *The Amiable Isabella,* 6 Wheat. 1, 71, 5 L.Ed. 191 (1821).

For the reasons given above, we agree with the opinion of the Supreme Court of Canada, see *Ludecke v. Canadian Pacific Airlines, Ltd.,* 98 D.L.R.3d 52 (1979), that the Warsaw Convention does not eliminate the limitation on damages for passenger injury or death as a sanction for failure to provide adequate notice of that limitation. Accordingly, we affirm the judgment of the District of Columbia Circuit.

So ordered.

Justice Brennan, with whom Justice Marshall, Justice Blackmun, and Justice Stevens join, concurring in the judgment.

Union Rights and the Federal Labor-Management Relations Statute

Fort Stewart Schools v. FLRA,

495 U.S. 641 (1990)

Justice Scalia delivered the opinion of the Court.

In this case we review the decision of the Federal Labor Relations Authority that petitioner Fort Stewart Schools, a Federal Government employer, is required to bargain with the labor union representing its employees over a proposal relating to wages and fringe benefits.

I

Respondent Fort Stewart Association of Educators (Union), is the collective-bargaining representative of the employees of two elementary schools at Fort Stewart, a United States military facility in Georgia. The schools, petitioner here, are owned and operated by the United States Army under authority of 64 Stat. 1107, 20 U.S.C. § 241(a), which directs the Secretary of Health and Human Services to "make such arrangements ... as may be necessary to provide free public education" for children living on federally owned property. The present controversy arose when, during the course of collective-bargaining negotiations, the Union submitted to the schools proposals relating to mileage reimbursement, various types of paid leave, and a salary increase. Petitioner declined to negotiate these matters, claiming that they were not subject to bargaining under Title VII of the Civil Service Reform Act of 1978, sometimes referred to as the Federal Service Labor-Management Relations Statute, 5 U.S.C. § 7101 *et seq.* (FSLMRS or Statute). The Union sought the aid of the Federal

Labor Relations Authority pursuant to §§ 7105(a)(2)(D) and (E) and the Authority held that the Union's proposals were negotiable. *Fort Stewart Assn. of Educators,* 28 F.L.R.A. 547 (1987). Upon a petition for review by petitioner and cross-petitions for enforcement by the Authority and the Union, the Court of Appeals for the Eleventh Circuit upheld the Authority's decision, 860 F.2d 396 (1988), and we granted certiorari, 493 U.S. 807, 110 S.Ct. 47, 107 L.Ed.2d 16 (1989).

II

The FSLMRS requires a federal agency to negotiate in good faith with the chosen representative of employees covered by the Statute, 5 U.S.C. § 7114(a)(4), and makes it an unfair labor practice to refuse to do so, § 7116(a)(5). The scope of the negotiating obligation is set forth in § 7102, which confers upon covered employees the right, through their chosen representative, "to engage in collective bargaining with respect to conditions of employment." § 7102(2). Section 7103(a)(14) defines "conditions of employment" as follows:

> "'conditions of employment' means personnel policies, practices, and matters, whether established by rule, regulation, or otherwise, affecting working conditions, except that such term does not include policies, practices, and matters-
>
> "(A) relating to political activities prohibited under subchapter III of chapter 73 of this title;
>
> "(B) relating to the classification of any position; or
>
> "(C) to the extent such matters are specifically provided for by Federal statute...."

In construing these provisions, and the other provisions of the FSLMRS at issue in this case, the Authority was interpreting the statute that it is charged with implementing, see § 7105. We must therefore review its conclusions under the standard set forth in *Chevron U.S.A. Inc. v. Natural Resources Defense Council, Inc.*, 467 U.S. 837, 104 S.Ct. 2778, 81 L.Ed.2d 694 (1984). If, upon examination of "the particular statutory language at issue, as well as the language and design of the statute as a whole," *K mart Corp. v. Cartier, Inc.*, 486 U.S. 281, 291, 108 S.Ct. 1811, 1818, 100 L.Ed.2d 313 (1988), it is clear that the Authority's interpretation is incorrect, then we need look no further, "for the court, as well as the agency, must give effect to the unambiguously expressed intent of Congress." *Chevron*, 467 U.S., at 842–843, 104 S.Ct., at 2781–2782. If, on the other hand, "the statute is silent or ambiguous" on the point at issue, we must decide "whether the agency's answer is based on a permissible construction of the statute." *Ibid.*

The Authority concluded that the Union's proposals related to "conditions of employment," following its decision in *American Federation of Government Employees, AFL-CIO, Local 1897*, 24 F.L.R.A. 377, 379 (1986) (AFGE). 28 F.L.R.A., at 550–551. Petitioner claims that this was error because § 7103(a)(14) defines "conditions of employment" as matters affecting "working conditions," and because the latter term most naturally connotes "the physical conditions under which an employee labors," Brief for Petitioner 17. The difficulty here, of course, is that the word "conditions" has two common meanings. It can mean matters "established or agreed upon as a requisite to the doing ... of something else"; and it can also mean "attendant circumstances," or an "existing state of affairs." *Webster's Third New International Dictionary* 473 (1961). Whereas the term "conditions of employment" in § 7102 seems to us equally susceptible of both meanings, petitioner is correct that the term "working conditions" in the defining provision of § 7103(a)(14) more naturally refers, in isolation, only to the "circumstances" or "state of affairs" attendant to one's performance of a job. See *Department of Defense Dependents Schools v. FLRA,* 274 U.S.App.D.C. 299, 301, 863 F.2d 988, 990 (1988) ("The term "working conditions" ordinarily calls to mind the day-to-day circumstances under which an employee performs his or her job"), rehearing en banc granted, No. 87-1733 (Feb. 6, 1989). Even if, however, it could not reasonably be interpreted to bear the other meaning in isolation, here it is not in isolation, but forms part of a paragraph whose structure, as a whole, lends support to the Authority's broader reading.

As set forth above, § 7103(a)(14) specifically excepts from the definition of "conditions of employment" (and thus suggests *are covered* by the term "working conditions") "policies, practices, and matters ... relating to political activities prohibited under subchapter III of chapter 73 of this title." The subchapter referred to contains restrictions on partisan political activities of federal employees and protects them from being required or coerced to engage in political activity. It is barely conceivable, but most unlikely, that this provision of § 7103(a)(14) was meant to exclude from collective-bargaining proposals that would somehow infect with politics the "physical conditions" of the workplace; it seems much more plausibly directed at "conditions of employment" in the sense of qualifications demanded of, or obligations imposed upon, employees. And the second exception set forth in § 7103(a)(14), as set forth above, *unquestionably* assumes that "conditions of employment" (and hence "working conditions") bears this broader meaning. The exception of "policies, practices, and matters ... relating to the classification of any position" would be utterly unnecessary if petitioner's interpretation of "working conditions" were correct.

It might reasonably be argued, of course, that these two exceptions are indeed technically unnecessary, and were inserted out of an abundance of caution-a drafting imprecision venerable enough to have left its mark on legal Latin (*ex abundanti cautela*). But petitioner does not make this argument. Indeed, in its reply brief petitioner claims that it is "a serious distortion of [its] position," Reply Brief for Petitioner 2, to characterize it, as respondent Union does, as asserting that "negotiations over "working conditions" are limited to the physical conditions under which an employee labors." Brief for Respondent Union 11. Petitioner asserts that, to the contrary, it "recognize[s] that the phrase "conditions of employment" is no doubt susceptible of diverse interpretations," including an interpretation whereby it would embrace "any subject which is insisted upon as a prerequisite for continued employment," Reply Brief for Petitioner 2 (internal quotations omitted); and petitioner even acknowledges, with apparent approval, that the phrase in the present statute "has been extended beyond the purely physical conditions of the workplace," *ibid.* The textual argument is thus abandoned. Petitioner seeks to persuade us, not (as respondent Union does) that the term "conditions of employment" (as defined to include only "working conditions") bears one, rather than the other, of its two possible meanings; but rather to persuade us that it bears some third meaning no one has ever conceived of, so that it includes *other* insisted-upon prerequisites for continued employment, but does not include the insisted-upon prerequisite *par excellence,* wages. And this new unheard-of meaning, petitioner contends, is so "unambiguously expressed," *Chevron, supra,* 467 U.S., at 843, 104 S.Ct., at 2781, that we must impose it upon the agency initially responsible for interpreting the statute, despite the deference otherwise accorded under *Chevron.* To describe this position is sufficient to reject it, but we nonetheless examine briefly the elements petitioner sets forth to establish that "conditions of employment" clearly has a meaning here that it bears nowhere else.

Petitioner points to the National Labor Relations Act, 49 Stat. 449, as amended, 29 U.S.C. § 151 *et seq.*, which authorizes bargaining over "wages, hours, and other terms and conditions of employment," § 158(d), and to the Postal Reorganization Act, 39 U.S.C. § 1201 *et seq.*, which grants postal workers the right to bargain over "wages, hours, and working conditions." Note following § 1201. Because each of these statutes specifically refers to wages, the argument runs, we must infer from the absence of such a reference in the FSLMRS that Congress did not mean to include them. But those other statutes deal with labor-management relations in entirely different fields of employment, and the FSLMRS contains no indication that it is to be read *in pari materia* with them. The first of those provisions does (perhaps) show that the term "conditions of employment" can be used to refer only to physical circumstances of employment; and the second of them does (perhaps) show that "working conditions" is more naturally used to mean that—but those are points we have already conceded.

Petitioner discusses at great length the legislative history of the Statute, from which it has culled a formidable number of statements suggesting that certain members and committees of Congress did not think the duty to bargain would extend to proposals relating to wages and fringe benefits. A Senate Report, for example, states unequivocally that "[t]he bill permits unions to bargain collectively on personnel policies and practices, and other matters affecting working conditions within the authority of agency managers.... It excludes bargaining on economic matters...." S.Rep. No. 95-969, pp. 12–

13 (1978), *U.S.Code Cong. & Admin. News* 1978, pp. 2734, 2735. A House Report recounts that the bill "does not permit ... bargaining on wages and fringe benefits...." H.R.Rep. No. 95-1403, p. 12 (1978). To like effect are numerous floor statements by both sponsors and opponents.

The trouble with these statements, to the extent they are relevant to our inquiry, is that they may have been wrong. The wages and fringe benefits of the overwhelming majority of Executive Branch employees are fixed by law, in accordance with the General Schedules of the Civil Service Act, see 5 U.S.C. § 5332, and are therefore eliminated from the definition of "conditions of employment" by the third exception in § 7103(a)(14) set forth above-which excludes "matters ... specifically provided for by Federal statute." 5 U.S.C. § 7103(a)(14)(C). Employees of schools established under § 241 are among a miniscule minority of federal employees whose wages are exempted from operation of the General Schedules. Title 20 U.S.C. § 241(a) provides that an agency establishing such a school may fix "the compensation, tenure, leave, hours of work, and other incidents of the employment relationship" of its employees "without regard to the Civil Service Act and rules." *Ibid.* See also *AFGE,* 24 F.L.R.A., at 378. The legislative materials to which petitioner refers display no awareness of this exception. To the contrary, numerous statements, many from the same sources to which petitioner points, display the erroneous belief that the wages and fringe benefits of *all* Executive Branch employees were set by statute. See H.R.Rep. No. 95-1403, p. 12 (1978) ("Federal pay will continue to be set in accordance with the pay provisions of title 5, and fringe benefits, including retirement, insurance, and leave, will continue to be set by Congress"); *id.,* at 44 ("Rates of overtime pay are not bargainable, because they are specifically provided for by statute"). Thus, all of the statements to which petitioner refers may have rested upon the following syllogism: The wages and fringe benefits of all federal employees are specifically provided for by federal statute; "conditions of employment" subject to the duty to bargain do not include "matters ... specifically provided for by Federal statute"; therefore "conditions of employment" subject to the duty to bargain do not include the wages and fringe benefits of all federal employees. Since the premise of that syllogism is wrong, so may be its expressed conclusion. There is no conceivable persuasive effect in legislative history that may reflect nothing more than the speakers' incomplete understanding of the world upon which the statute will operate. Cf. *Yellow Freight System, Inc. v. Donnelly,* 494 U.S. 820, 824, 110 S.Ct. 1566, 1569, 108 L.Ed.2d 834 (1990) (expectation by Members of Congress that all Title VII suits would be tried in federal court, "even if universally shared," does not establish that the statute requires such suits to be brought in federal court).

III

Petitioner next argues that, even if the Union's proposals relate to "conditions of employment" subject to bargaining under § 7102, they are exempted from the statutory duty to bargain by § 7106, which provides that "nothing in this chapter shall affect the authority of any management official of any agency ... to determine the ... budget ... of the agency...." 5 U.S.C. § 7106. The Authority rejected that claim by applying the test established in its decision in *American Federation of Government Employees, AFL-CIO,* 2 F.L.R.A. 604 (1980), enf'd on other grounds *sub nom. Department of Defense v. FLRA,* 212 U.S.App.D.C. 256, 659 F.2d 1140 (1981), cert. denied, 455 U.S. 945, 102 S.Ct. 1443, 71 L.Ed.2d 658 (1982):

> "To establish that a proposal directly interferes with an agency's right to determine its budget under section 7106(a)(1) of the Statute, an agency must make a substantial showing that the proposal requires the inclusion of a particular program or amount in its budget *or that the proposal will result in significant and unavoidable increases in cost not affected* [sic: *offset*] *by compensating benefits.*" 28 F.L.R.A., at 551 (emphasis added).

Because petitioner did not contend that the Union's proposal required "the inclusion of a particular program or amount in its budget," the only question for the Authority was whether petitioner had made out its case under the underscored standard. The Authority held that it had not, finding that petitioner had shown neither that its costs would be significantly and unavoidably increased were it to accept the proposals offered by the Union, nor that "any increased costs ... would not be offset by compensating benefits." *Id.,* at 552.

The parties initially dispute which entity is the relevant "agency" for purposes of determining whether the Union's proposals would "affect the authority of any management official of any agency ... to determine the ... budget ... of the agency...." 5 U.S.C. § 7106(a). The Authority concluded only that petitioner had not satisfied § 7106(a) with respect to its own budget, *i.e.,* that of the schools at the Fort Stewart Army base. The Court of Appeals upheld the Authority's decision, but did so by reference to the budget of the Army as a whole, which it noted "includes bases, troops, weapons, vehicles, other equipment, salaries for all other officers, and expenses for its eight other schools." 860 F.2d, at 405–406. We cannot, however, uphold the Authority's decision on that basis, for it is elementary that if an agency's decision is to be sustained in the courts on any rationale under which the agency's factual or legal determinations are entitled to deference, it must be upheld on the rationale set forth by the agency itself. *SEC v. Chenery Corp.*, 318 U.S. 80, 93–95, 63 S.Ct. 454, 461–463, 87 L.Ed. 626 (1943). Because petitioner does not challenge, as a ground for reversing the Authority's decision, its determination to look only to petitioner's budget, we assume without deciding that that determination was correct.

Petitioner does not take issue with the Authority's premise that § 7106 does not make a proposal nonnegotiable simply because it "imposes a cost upon the agency which requires the expenditure of appropriated agency funds." See 28 F.L.R.A., at 607. Rather, petitioner argues that "the application of the FLRA's rule here—particularly the conclusion that the proposal calling for a 13.5% pay raise would not significantly affect the agency's budget—is plainly flawed." Brief for Petitioner 28. Petitioner also claims that "the other aspect of the FLRA's rule-requiring management to show that a significant increase in costs would not be offset by compensating benefits is not reasonable or consistent with the statute, because it negates management's right to set the agency budget." *Ibid.*

The latter observation has some force if the Authority's definition of "compensating benefits" is as petitioner describes it. Petitioner claims that, in order to prove that the cost of a given proposal is not outweighed by "compensating benefits," an agency must disprove not only monetary benefits, but also nonmonetary "intangible" benefits such as the positive effects that a proposed change might have on employee morale. Although counsel for the Authority agreed with petitioner's statement of its test at oral argument before this Court, it is not entirely clear from the Authority's cases that the "benefits" side of the calculus is as all embracing as petitioner suggests. Cf. *International Association of Fire Fighters Local F-61,* 3 F.L.R.A. 438, 452 (1980) (rejecting agency's claim of no "compensating benefits" where "the agency has made no substantial demonstration that the increased costs ... will not be offset by increased employee performance, reduced turnover, fewer grievances and the like"). Indeed, it is difficult to see how the Authority could possibly derive a test measured by nonmonetary benefits from a provision that speaks only to the agency's "authority ... to determine ... [its] budget," a phrase that can only be understood to refer to the allocation of funds within the agency.

We need not dwell on this point, however, because the Authority's first ground for its decision is supported by substantial evidence. Petitioner has challenged neither the Authority's requirement that an agency show a significant and unavoidable increase in its costs, nor the Authority's finding that petitioner failed to submit any evidence on that point in this case. Rather, it asks us to hold that a proposal calling for a 13.5% salary increase would necessarily result in a "significant and unavoidable" increase in the agency's overall costs. We cannot do that without knowing even so rudimentary a fact as the percentage of the agency's budget attributable to teachers' salaries. Under the Authority's precedents, petitioner had the burden of proof on this point, but it placed nothing in the record to document its total costs or even its current total teachers' salaries. The Authority reasonably determined that it could not conclude from an increase in one budget item of indeterminate amount whether petitioner's costs as a whole would be "significant[ly] and unavoidabl[y]" increased.

IV

Petitioner's final argument rests upon 20 U.S.C. § 241, which directs the agency establishing a school thereunder to "ensure that the education provided pursuant to such arrangement is comparable to free public education provided for children in comparable communities in the State," § 241(a), and to limit expenditures "[t]o the maximum extent practicable" to "an amount per pupil which will not exceed the per pupil cost of free public education provided for children in comparable communities in the State," § 241(e). In implementing this provision, the Army has promulgated a regulation stating that education provided under § 241 "will be considered comparable to free public education offered by selected communities of the State" when 10 specified factors, including "[s]alary schedules" are, "to the maximum extent practicable, equal." Army Reg. 352-3, 1-7(h) (1980). Petitioner claims—and we assume for purposes of this discussion that in order to accept the Union's proposals, it would have to contravene this regulation because the proposed salaries would exceed those of employees of the local school systems.

It is a familiar rule of administrative law that an agency must abide by its own regulations. *Vitarelli v. Seaton,* 359 U.S. 535, 547, 79 S.Ct. 968, 976, 3 L.Ed.2d 1012 (1959); *Service v. Dulles,* 354 U.S. 363, 388, 77 S.Ct. 1152, 1165, 1 L.Ed.2d 1403 (1957). That says nothing, however, about whether an agency can be compelled to negotiate about a change in its regulations. The latter question is addressed by 5 U.S.C. § 7117(a)(2), which provides, insofar as applicable to the regulation here, that "[t]he duty to bargain in good faith shall, to the extent not inconsistent with Federal law or any Government-wide rule or regulation, extend to matters which are the subject of any agency rule or regulation ... *only if the Authority has determined under subsection (b) of this section that no compelling need (as determined under regulations prescribed by the Authority) exists for the rule or regulation.*" (Emphasis added.) Section 7117(b) sets out the procedures by which the Authority is to make its "compelling need" determination, see generally *FLRA v. Aberdeen Proving Ground, Department of*

Army, 485 U.S. 409, 108 S.Ct. 1261, 99 L.Ed.2d 470 (1988), and § 7105(a)(2)(D) instructs the Authority to "prescribe criteria" for that determination.

Pursuant to this last provision, the Authority has adopted the following regulation:

> "A compelling need exists for an agency rule or regulation concerning any condition of employment when the agency demonstrates that the rule or regulation meets any one or more of the following illustrative criteria:
>
> > "(a) The rule or regulation is essential, as distinguished from helpful or desirable, to the accomplishment of the mission or the execution of functions of the agency ... in a manner which is consistent with the requirements of an effective and efficient government.
> >
> > "(b) The rule or regulation is necessary to insure the maintenance of basic merit principles.
> >
> > "(c) The rule or regulation implements a mandate to the agency ... under law or other outside authority, which implementation is essentially nondiscretionary in nature." 5 CFR § 2424.11 (1989).

Before the Authority, petitioner rested its entire case upon the assertion that the last of these criteria was satisfied by the provision of Army Regulation 352-3 which requires salaries equal to those of local schools, since that provision "implements the mandate" of § 241(a). The Authority disagreed, following its decision in *Fort Knox Teachers Assn.,* 27 F.L.R.A. 203, 215, 216 (1987), which said that no "compelling need" for Army Regulation 352-3 exists because § 241 does not require the agency "to match exactly the conditions of employment of teachers in local school districts" or "to restrict the Agency's discretion as to the particular employment practices which could be adopted."

Petitioner argues that, although "[s]ection 241 does not specifically provide that teachers' salaries ... must be set by comparison with those at local public schools," Brief for Petitioner 32, it does state that "[f]or the purpose of providing such comparable education," teachers' salaries and benefits "may be fixed without regard to the [General Schedules set out in the] Civil Service Act," 20 U.S.C. § 241(a). According to petitioner, "it is a fair reading of [§ 241] to conclude that Congress excepted [wages and fringe benefits] from the civil service laws so that they would be set by comparison with those at public schools." Brief for Petitioner 33. That is not so. All that can reasonably be deduced from the exclusion of the General Schedules is that Congress expected teachers' wages and benefits to be one of the elements that the federal agency could adjust in order to render per pupil expenditure comparable to that in local public schools. But to be able to adjust is not to be required to make equal. The statute requires equivalence ("[t]o the maximum extent practicable") in total per pupil expenditure, not in each separate element of educational cost. An agency may well decide to pay teachers more or less than teachers in local schools, in order that it may expend less or more than local schools for other needs of the educational program. It is thus impossible to say that the requirement of Army Reg. 352-3 that teachers' salaries be "to the maximum extent practicable, equal" was "essentially nondiscretionary in nature" within the meaning of § 2424.11(c).

Petitioner insists, however, that reading § 2424.11 this strictly renders that regulation in violation of the Statute, which never requires bargaining over any matter covered by a regulation except "to the extent not inconsistent with Federal law." See § 7117(a)(2); see also § 7117(a)(1). Thus, to recognize a compelling need for a regulation "only if it implements a statutory mandate that leaves an agency absolutely no room for discretion," Brief for Petitioner 33, n. 23, is to render the "compelling need" exception of § 7117(a)(2) a nullity, for bargaining over such a regulation would be "inconsistent with Federal law" anyway. We may assume, without deciding, that petitioner is correct that any rule that meets the § 2424.11(c) "essentially nondiscretionary" standard as interpreted by the Authority would necessarily be a rule required by law. There is some support for that equivalency in the Authority's cases. See, *e.g., Fort Knox Teachers Assn.,* 25 F.L.R.A. 1119 (1987). But see *National Border Patrol Council, American Federation of Government Employees, AFL-CIO,* 23 F.L.R.A. 106 (1986); *National Federation of Federal Employees, Local 1153,* 26 F.L.R.A. 505 (1987). Even so, the Authority's regulation does not eliminate the "compelling need" exception. Petitioner's argument ignores the existence of subsections (a) and (b) of § 2424.11, which provide alternative methods of proving "compelling need." In this case, to be sure, petitioner chose not to assert a claim that Army Regulation 352-3 was either "essential ... to the accomplishment of the mission or the execution of functions of the agency," 5 CFR § 2424.11(a) (1989), or "necessary to insure the maintenance of basic merit principles," § 2424.11(b). But, those alternatives were available and suffice to give the regulation for which there is a "compelling need" an existence quite independent of the regulation whose elimination would be inconsistent with law.

For the foregoing reasons, the judgment of the Court of Appeals for the Eleventh Circuit is *Affirmed.*

Justice Marshall, concurring.

The Limits of Actions under ERISA

Mertens v. Hewitt Assocs.,

508 U.S. 248 (1993)

Justice Scalia delivered the opinion of the Court.

The question presented is whether a nonfiduciary who knowingly participates in the breach of a fiduciary duty imposed by the Employee Retirement Income Security Act of 1974 (ERISA), 88 Stat. 832, as amended, 29 U.S.C. 1001 et seq., is liable for losses that an employee benefit plan suffers as a result of the breach.

I

According to the complaint, the allegations of which we take as true, petitioners represent a class of former employees of the Kaiser Steel Corporation (Kaiser) who participated in the Kaiser Steel Retirement Plan, a qualified pension plan under ERISA. Respondent was the plan's actuary in 1980, when Kaiser began to phase out its steelmaking operations, prompting early retirement by a large number of plan participants. Respondent did not, however, change the plan's actuarial assumptions to reflect the additional costs imposed by the retirements. As a result, Kaiser did not adequately fund the plan, and eventually the plan's assets became insufficient to satisfy its benefit obligations, causing the Pension Benefit Guaranty Corporation (PBGC) to terminate the plan pursuant to 29 U.S.C. 1341. Petitioners now receive only the benefits guaranteed by ERISA, see 1322, which are in general substantially lower than the fully vested pensions due them under the plan.

Petitioners sued the fiduciaries of the failed plan, alleging breach of fiduciary duties. See *Mertens v. Black*, 948 F.2d 1105 (CA9 1991) (per curiam) (affirming denial of summary judgment). They also commenced this action against respondent, alleging that it had caused the losses by allowing Kaiser to select the plan's actuarial assumptions, by failing to disclose that Kaiser was one of its clients, and by failing to disclose the plan's funding shortfall. Petitioners claimed that these acts and omissions violated ERISA by effecting a breach of respondent's "professional duties" to the plan, for which they sought, inter alia, monetary relief. In opposing respondent's motion to dismiss, petitioners fleshed out this claim, asserting that respondent was liable (1) as an ERISA fiduciary that committed a breach of its own fiduciary duties, (2) as a nonfiduciary that knowingly participated in the plan fiduciaries' breach of their fiduciary duties, and (3) as a nonfiduciary that committed a breach of nonfiduciary duties imposed on actuaries by ERISA. The District Court for the Northern District of California dismissed the complaint, App. to Pet. for Cert. A17, and the Court of Appeals for the Ninth Circuit affirmed in relevant part, 948 F.2d 607 (1991).

Petitioners sought certiorari only on the question whether ERISA authorizes suits for money damages against nonfiduciaries who knowingly participate in a fiduciary's breach of fiduciary duty. We agreed to hear the case. 506 U.S. 812 (1992).

II

ERISA is, we have observed, a "comprehensive and reticulated statute," the product of a decade of congressional study of the Nation's private employee benefit system. *Nachman Corp. v. Pension Benefit Guaranty Corporation*, 446 U.S. 359, 361 (1980). The statute provides that not only the persons named as fiduciaries by a benefit plan, see 29 U.S.C. 1102(a), but also anyone else who exercises discretionary control or authority over the plan's management, administration, or assets, see 1002(21)(A), is an ERISA "fiduciary." Fiduciaries are assigned a number of detailed duties and responsibilities, which include "the proper management, administration, and investment of [plan] assets, the maintenance of proper records, the disclosure of specified information, and the avoidance of conflicts of interest." *Massachusetts Mut. Life Ins. Co. v. Russell*, 473 U.S. 134, 142–143 (1985); see 29 U.S.C. 1104(a). Section 409(a), 29 U.S.C. 1109(a), makes fiduciaries liable for breach of these duties, and specifies the remedies available against them: The fiduciary is personally liable for damages ("to make good to [the] plan any losses to the plan resulting from each such breach"), for restitution ("to restore to [the] plan any profits of such fiduciary which have been made through use of assets of the plan by the fiduciary"), and for "such other equitable or remedial relief as the court may deem appropriate," including removal of the fiduciary. Section 502(a)(2), 29 U.S.C. 1132(a)(2)—the second of ERISA's "six carefully integrated civil enforcement provisions," Russell, supra, at 146—allows the Secretary of Labor or any plan beneficiary, participant, or fiduciary to bring a civil action "for appropriate relief under section 409."

The above described provisions are, however, limited by their terms to fiduciaries. The Court of Appeals decided that respondent was not a fiduciary, see 948 F.2d, at 610, and petitioners do not contest that holding. Lacking equivalent provisions specifying nonfiduciaries as potential defendants, or damages as a remedy available against them, petitioners have turned to 502(a)(3), 29 U.S.C. 1132(a)(3), which authorizes a plan beneficiary, participant, or fiduciary to bring a civil action:

> "(A) to enjoin any act or practice which violates any provision of [ERISA] or the terms of the plan, or (B) to obtain other appropriate equitable relief (i) to redress such violations or (ii) to enforce any provisions of [ERISA] or the terms of the plan. ..."

See also 502(a)(5), 29 U.S.C. 1132(a)(5) (providing, in similar language, for civil suits by the Secretary based upon violation of ERISA provisions). Petitioners contend that requiring respondent to make the Kaiser plan whole for the losses resulting from its alleged knowing participation in the breach of fiduciary duty by the Kaiser plan's fiduciaries would constitute "other appropriate equitable relief" within the meaning of 502(a)(3).

We note at the outset that it is far from clear that, even if this provision does make money damages available, it makes them available for the actions at issue here. It does not, after all, authorize "appropriate equitable relief" at large, but only "appropriate equitable relief" for the purpose of "redress[ing any] violations or ... enforc[ing] any provisions of ERISA or an ERISA plan. No one suggests that any term of the Kaiser plan has been violated, nor would any be enforced by the requested judgment. And while ERISA contains various provisions that can be read as imposing obligations upon nonfiduciaries, including actuaries, no provision explicitly requires them to avoid participation (knowing or unknowing) in a fiduciary's breach of fiduciary duty. It is unlikely, moreover, that this was an oversight, since ERISA does explicitly impose "knowing participation" liability on cofiduciaries. See 405(a), 29 U.S.C. 1105(a). That limitation appears all the more deliberate in light of the fact that "knowing participation" liability on the part of both cotrustees and third persons was well established under the common law of trusts. See 3 A. Scott & W. Fratcher, *Law of Trusts* 224.1, p.

404 (4th ed. 1988) (hereinafter *Scott & Fratcher*) (cotrustees); 4 *Scott & Fratcher* 326, p. 291 (third persons). In Russell, we emphasized our unwillingness to infer causes of action in the ERISA context, since that statute's carefully crafted and detailed enforcement scheme provides "strong evidence that Congress did not intend to authorize other remedies that it simply forgot to incorporate expressly." 473 U.S., at 146–147. All of this notwithstanding, petitioners and their amicus the United States seem to assume that respondent's alleged action (or inaction) violated ERISA, and address their arguments almost exclusively to what forms of relief are available. And respondent, despite considerable prompting by its amici, expressly disclaims reliance on this preliminary point. See Brief for Respondent 18, n. 15; Tr. of Oral Arg. 46. Thus, although we acknowledge the oddity of resolving a dispute over remedies where it is unclear that a remediable wrong has been alleged, we decide this case on the narrow battlefield the parties have chosen, and reserve decision of that antecedent question.

Petitioners maintain that the object of their suit is "appropriate equitable relief" under 502(a)(3) (emphasis added). They do not, however, seek a remedy traditionally viewed as "equitable," such as injunction or restitution. (The Court of Appeals held that restitution was unavailable, see 948 F.2d, at 612, and petitioners have not challenged that.) Although they often dance around the word, what petitioners in fact seek is nothing other than compensatory damages—monetary relief for all losses their plan sustained as a result of the alleged breach of fiduciary duties. Money damages are, of course, the classic form of legal relief. *Curtis v. Loether*, 415 U.S. 189, 196 (1974); *Teamsters v. Terry*, 494 U.S. 558, 570–571 (1990); D. Dobbs, *Remedies* 1.1, p. 3 (1973). And though we have never interpreted the precise phrase "other appropriate equitable relief," we have construed the similar language of

Title VII of the Civil Rights Act of 1964 (before its 1991 amendments)—"any other equitable relief as the court deems appropriate," 42 U.S.C. 2000e-5(g)—to preclude "awards for compensatory or punitive damages." *United States v. Burke*, 504 U.S. 229, 238 (1992).

Petitioners assert, however, that this reading of "equitable relief" fails to acknowledge ERISA's roots in the common law of trusts, see *Firestone Tire & Rubber Co. v. Bruch*, 489 U.S. 101, 110–111 (1989). "[A]lthough a beneficiary's action to recover losses resulting from a breach of duty superficially resembles an action at law for damages," the Solicitor General suggests, "such relief traditionally has been obtained in courts of equity" and therefore "is, by definition, 'equitable relief.'" Brief for United States as Amicus Curiae 13–14. It is true that, at common law, the courts of equity had exclusive jurisdiction over virtually all actions by beneficiaries for breach of trust. See *Lessee of Smith v. McCann*, 24 How. 398, 407 (1861); 3 *Scott & Fratcher* 197, p. 188. It is also true that money damages were available in those courts against the trustee, *see United States v. Mitchell*, 463 U.S. 206, 226 (1983); G. Bogert & G. Bogert, *Law of Trusts and Trustees* 701, p. 198 (rev.2d ed. 1982) (hereinafter *Bogert & Bogert*), and against third persons who knowingly participated in the trustee's breach, see *Seminole Nation v. United States*, 316 U.S. 286, 296–297 (1942); Scott, "Participation in a Breach of Trust," 34 *Harv. L.Rev.* 454 (1921).

At common law, however, there were many situations—not limited to those involving enforcement of a trust—in which an equity court could "establish purely legal rights and grant legal remedies which would otherwise be beyond the scope of its authority." 1 J. Pomeroy, *Equity Jurisprudence* 181, p. 257 (5th ed. 1941). The term "equitable relief" can assuredly mean, as petitioners and the Solicitor General would have it, whatever relief a court of equity is empowered to provide in the particular case at issue. But as indicated by the foregoing quotation—which speaks of "legal remedies" granted by an equity court—"equitable relief" can also refer to those categories of relief that were typically available in equity (such as injunction, mandamus, and restitution, but not compensatory damages). As memories of the divided bench, and familiarity with its technical refinements, recede further into the past, the former meaning becomes, perhaps, increasingly unlikely; but it remains a question of interpretation in each case which meaning is intended.

In the context of the present statute, we think there can be no doubt. Since all relief available for breach of trust could be obtained from a court of equity, limiting the sort of relief obtainable under 502(a)(3) to "equitable relief" in the sense of "whatever relief a common-law court of equity could provide in such a case" would limit the relief not at all. We will not read the statute to render the modifier superfluous. See *United State v. Nordic Village, Inc.*, 503 U.S. 30, 36 (1992); *Moskal v. United States*, 498 U.S. 103, 109–110 (1990). Regarding "equitable" relief in 502(a)(3) to mean "all relief available for breach of trust at common law" would also require us either to give the term a different meaning there than it bears elsewhere in ERISA or to deprive of all meaning the distinction Congress drew between "equitable" and "remedial" relief in 409(a), and between "equitable" and "legal" relief in the very same section of ERISA, see 29 U.S.C. 1132(g)(2)(E); in the same subchapter of ERISA, see 1024(a)(5)(C); and in the ERISA subchapter dealing with the PBGC, see 1303(e)(1), 1451(a)(1). Neither option is acceptable. See *Estate of Cowart v. Nicklos Drilling Co.*, 505 U.S. 469, 479 (1992); cf. *Lorillard v. Pons*, 434 U.S. 575, 583 (1978). The authority of courts to develop a "federal common law" under ERISA, see Firestone, 489 U.S., at 110, is not the authority to revise the text of the statute.

Petitioners point to ERISA 502(l), which was added to the statute in 1989, see Omnibus Budget Reconciliation Act of 1989 (OBRA), Pub.L. 101–239, 2101, 103 Stat. 2123, and provides as follows:

> "(1) In the case of -
>
> "(A) any breach of fiduciary responsibility under (or other violation of) part 4 by a fiduciary, or
>
> "(B) any knowing participation in such a breach or violation by any other person,
>
> "the Secretary shall assess a civil penalty against such fiduciary or other person in an amount equal to 20 percent of the applicable recovery amount." 29 U.S.C. 1132(1)(1) (1988 ed., Supp. III).

The Secretary may waive or reduce this penalty if he believes that "the fiduciary or other person will [otherwise] not be able to restore all losses to the plan without severe financial hardship." 1132(1)(3)(B). "[A]pplicable recovery amount" is defined (in 502(l)(2)(B)) as "any amount ... ordered by a court to be paid by such fiduciary or other person to a plan or its participants or beneficiaries in a judicial proceeding instituted by the Secretary under [502](a)(2) or (a)(5)." It will be recalled that the latter subsection, 502(a)(5), authorizes relief in actions by the Secretary on the same terms ("appropriate equitable relief") as in the private-party actions authorized by 502(a)(3). Petitioners argue that 502(l) confirms that 502(a)(5)—and hence, since it uses the same language, 502(a)(3) —allows actions for damages, since otherwise there could be no "applicable recovery amount" against some "other person" than the fiduciary, and the Secretary would have no occasion to worry about whether any such "other person" would be able to "restore all losses to the plan" without financial hardship.

We certainly agree with petitioners that language used in one portion of a statute (§ 502(a)(3)) should be deemed to have the same meaning as the same language used elsewhere in the statute (§ 502(a)(5)). Indeed, we are even more zealous advocates of that principle than petitioners, who stop short of applying it directly to the term "equitable relief." We cannot agree, however, that § 502(l) establishes the existence of a damages remedy under 502(a)(5) —*i.e.*, that it is otherwise so inexplicable that we must give the term "equitable relief" the expansive meaning "all relief available for breach of trust." For even in its more limited sense, the "equitable relief" awardable under 502(a)(5) includes restitution of ill-gotten plan assets or profits, providing an "applicable recovery amount" to use to calculate the penalty, which the Secretary may waive or reduce if paying it would prevent the restoration of those gains to the plan; and even assuming nonfiduciaries are not liable at all for knowing participation in a [508 U.S. 248, 261] fiduciary's breach of duty, see supra, at 5–6, cofiduciaries expressly are, see 405(a), so there are some "other person[s]" than fiduciaries-in-breach liable under 502(l)(1)(B). These applications of 502(l) give it meaning and scope without resort to the strange interpretation of "equitable relief" in 502(a)(3) that petitioners propose. The Secretary's initial interpretation of 502(l) accords with our view. The prologue of the proposed regulation implementing 502(l), to be codified at 29 CFR 2560.502l-1, states that, when a court awards "equitable relief"—as opposed to "monetary damages"—a 502(l) penalty will be assessed only if the award involves the transfer to the plan of money or property. 55 Fed.Reg. 25288, 25289, and n. 9 (1990).

In the last analysis, petitioners and the United States ask us to give a strained interpretation to 502(a)(3) in order to achieve the "purpose of ERISA to protect plan participants and beneficiaries." Brief for Petitioners 31. They note, as we have, that, before ERISA, nonfiduciaries were generally liable under state trust law for damages resulting from knowing participation in a trustee's breach of duty, and they assert that such actions are now preempted by ERISA's broad preemption clause, 514(a), 29 U.S.C. 1144(a), see *Ingersoll-Rand Co. v. McClendon*, 498 U.S. 133, 139–140 (1990). Thus, they contend, our construction of 502(a)(3) leaves beneficiaries like petitioners with less protection than existed before ERISA, contradicting ERISA's basic goal of "promot[ing] the interests of employees and their beneficiaries in employee benefit plans," *Shaw v. Delta Air Lines, Inc.*, 463 U.S. 85, 90 (1983). See *Firestone Tire & Rubber Co., v. Bruch*, supra, at 114.

Even assuming (without deciding) that petitioners are correct about the preemption of previously available state court actions, vague notions of a statute's "basic purpose" are nonetheless inadequate to overcome the words of its text regarding the specific issue under consideration. See *Pension Benefit Guaranty Corporation v. LTV Corp.*, 496 U.S. 633, 646–647 (1990). This is especially true with legislation such as ERISA, an enormously complex and detailed statute that resolved innumerable disputes between powerful competing interests—not all in favor of potential plaintiffs. See, *e.g.*, *Pilot Life Ins. Co. v. Dedeaux*, 481 U.S. 41, 54–56 (1987). The text that we have described is certainly not nonsensical; it allocates liability for plan-related misdeeds in reasonable proportion to respective actors" power to control and prevent the misdeeds. Under traditional trust law, although a beneficiary could obtain damages from third persons for knowing participation in a trustee's breach of fiduciary duties, only the trustee had fiduciary duties. See 1 *Scott & Fratcher* 2.5, p. 43. ERISA, however, defines "fiduciary" not in terms of formal trusteeship, but in functional terms of control and authority over the plan, see 29 U.S.C. 1002(21)(A), thus expanding the universe of persons subject to fiduciary duties—and to damages—under 409(a). Professional service providers such as actuaries become liable for damages when they cross the line from advisor to fiduciary; must disgorge assets and profits obtained through participation as parties-in-interest in transactions prohibited by 406, and pay related civil penalties, see 502(i), 29 U.S.C. 1132(i), or excise taxes, see 26 U.S.C. 4975; and (assuming nonfiduciaries can be sued under 502(a)(3)) may be enjoined from participating in a fiduciary's breaches, compelled to make restitution, and subjected to other equitable decrees. All that ERISA has eliminated, on these assumptions, is the common law's joint and several liability, for all direct and consequential damages suffered by the plan, on the part of persons who had no real power to control what the plan did. Exposure to that sort of liability would impose high insurance costs upon persons who regularly deal with and offer advice to ERISA plans, and hence upon ERISA plans themselves. There is, in other words, a "tension between the primary [ERISA] goal of benefitting employees and the subsidiary goal of containing pension costs." *Alessi v. Raybestos-Manhattan, Inc.*, 451 U.S. 504, 515 (1981); see also Russell, 473 U.S., at 148, n. 17. We will not attempt to adjust the balance between those competing goals that the text adopted by Congress has struck.

* * *

The judgment of the Court of Appeals is

Affirmed.

Justice White, with whom the Chief Justice, Justice Stevens and Justice O'Connor join, dissenting.

Interpreting a Decision of the Social Security Administration

Barnhart v. Thomas,

540 U.S. 20 (2003)

Justice Scalia delivered the opinion of the Court.

Under the Social Security Act, the Social Security Administration (SSA) is authorized to pay disability insurance benefits and Supplemental Security Income to persons who have a "disability." A person qualifies as disabled, and thereby eligible for such benefits, "only if his physical or mental impairment or impairments are of such severity that he is not only unable to do his previous work but cannot, considering his age, education, and work experience, engage in any other kind of substantial gainful work which exists in the national economy." 42 U.S.C. §§ 423(d)(2)(A), 1382c(a)(3)(B). The issue we must decide is whether the SSA may determine that a claimant is not disabled because she remains physically and mentally able to do her previous work, without investigating whether that previous work exists in significant numbers in the national economy.

I

Pauline Thomas worked as an elevator operator for six years until her job was eliminated in August 1995. In June 1996, at age 53, Thomas applied for disability insurance benefits under Title II and Supplemental Security Income under Title XVI of the Social Security Act. See 49 Stat. 622, as amended, 42 U.S.C. § 401 *et seq.* (Title II); as added, 86 Stat. 1465, and as amended, § 1381 *et seq.* (Title XVI). She claimed that she suffered from, and was disabled by, heart disease and cervical and lumbar radiculopathy.

After the SSA denied Thomas's application initially and on reconsideration, she requested a hearing before an Administrative Law Judge (ALJ). The ALJ found that Thomas had "hypertension, cardiac arrythmia, [and] cervical and lumbar strain/sprain." Decision of ALJ 5, Record 15. He concluded, however, that Thomas was not under a "disability" because her "impairments do not prevent [her] from performing her past relevant work as an elevator operator." *Id.*, at 6, Record 16. He rejected Thomas's argument that she is unable to do her previous work because that work no longer exists in significant numbers in the national economy. The SSA's Appeals Council denied Thomas's request for review.

Thomas then challenged the ALJ's ruling in the United States District Court for the District of New Jersey, renewing her argument that she is unable to do her previous work due to its scarcity. The District Court affirmed the ALJ, concluding that whether Thomas's old job exists is irrelevant under the SSA's regulations. *Thomas v. Apfel,* Civ. No. 99-2234 (Aug. 17, 2000). The Court of Appeals for the Third Circuit, sitting en banc, reversed and remanded. Over the dissent of three of its members, it held that the statute unambiguously provides that the ability to perform prior work disqualifies from benefits only if it is "substantial gainful work which exists in the national economy." 294 F.3d 568, 572 (2002). That holding conflicts with the decisions of four other Courts of Appeals. See *Quang Van Han v. Bowen,* 882 F.2d 1453, 1457 (C.A.9 1989); *Garcia v. Secretary of Health and Human Services,* 46 F.3d 552, 558 (C.A.6 1995); *Pass v. Chater,* 65 F.3d 1200, 1206–1207 (C.A.4 1995); *Rater v. Chater,* 73 F.3d 796, 799 (C.A.8 1996). We granted the SSA's petition for certiorari. 537 U.S. 1187, 123 S.Ct. 1251, 154 L.Ed.2d 1017 (2003).

II

As relevant to the present case, Title II of the Act defines "disability" as the "inability to engage in any substantial gainful activity by reason of any medically determinable physical or mental impairment which can be expected to result in death or which has lasted or can be expected to last for a continuous period of not less than 12 months." 42 U.S.C. § 423(d)(1)(A). That definition is qualified, however, as follows:

> "An individual shall be determined to be under a disability only if his physical or mental impairment or impairments are of such severity that *he is not only unable to do his previous work but cannot,* considering his age, education, and work experience, *engage in any other kind of substantial gainful work which exists in the national economy....*" § 423(d)(2)(A) (emphases added).

"[W]ork which exists in the national economy" is defined to mean "work which exists in significant numbers either in the region where such individual lives or in several regions of the country." *Ibid.* Title XVI of the Act, which governs Supplemental Security Income for disabled indigent persons, employs the same definition of "disability" used in Title II, including a qualification that is verbatim the same as § 423(d)(2)(A). See 42 U.S.C. § 1382c(a)(3)(B). For simplicity's sake, we will refer only to the Title II provisions, but our analysis applies equally to Title XVI.

Section 423(d)(2)(A) establishes two requirements for disability. First, an individual's physical or mental impairment must render him "unable to do his previous work." Second, the impairment must also preclude him from "engag [ing] in any other kind of substantial gainful work." The parties agree that the *latter* requirement is qualified by the clause that immediately follows it—"which exists in the national economy." The issue in this case is whether that clause also qualifies "previous work."

The SSA has answered this question in the negative. Acting pursuant to its statutory rulemaking authority, 42 U.S.C. §§ 405(a) (Title II), 1383(d)(1) (Title XVI), the agency has promulgated regulations establishing a five-step sequential evaluation process to determine disability. See 20 CFR § 404.1520 (2003) (governing claims for disability insurance benefits); § 416.920 (parallel regulation governing claims for Supplemental Security Income). If at any step a finding of disability or nondisability can be made, the SSA will not review the claim further. At the first step, the agency will find nondisability unless the claimant shows that he is not working at a "substantial gainful activity." §§ 404.1520(b), 416.920(b). At step two, the SSA will find nondisability unless the claimant shows that he has a "severe impairment," defined as "any impairment or combination of impairments which significantly limits [the claimant's] physical or mental ability to do basic work activities." §§ 404.1520(c), 416.920(c). At step three, the agency determines whether the impairment which enabled the claimant to survive step two is on the list of impairments presumed severe enough to render one disabled; if so, the claimant qualifies. §§ 404.1520(d), 416.920(d). If the claimant's impairment is not on the list, the inquiry proceeds to step four, at which the SSA assesses whether the claimant can do his previous work; unless he shows that he cannot, he is determined not to be disabled. If the claimant survives the fourth stage, the fifth, and final, step requires the SSA to consider so-called "vocational factors" (the claimant's age, education, and past work experience), and to determine whether the claimant is capable of performing other jobs existing in significant numbers in the national economy. §§ 404.1520(f), 404.1560(c), 416.920(f), 416.960(c).

As the above description shows, step four can result in a determination of no disability without inquiry into whether the claimant's previous work exists in the national economy; the regulations explicitly reserve inquiry into the national economy for step five. Thus, the SSA has made it perfectly clear that it does not interpret the clause "which exists in the national economy" in § 423(d)(2)(A) as applying to "previous work." The issue presented is whether this agency interpretation must be accorded deference.

As we held in *Chevron U.S.A. Inc. v. Natural Resources Defense Council, Inc.*, 467 U.S. 837, 843, 104 S.Ct. 2778, 81 L.Ed.2d 694 (1984), when a statute speaks clearly to the issue at hand we "must give effect to the unambiguously expressed intent of Congress," but when the statute "is silent or ambiguous" we must defer to a reasonable construction by the agency charged with its implementation. The Third Circuit held that, by referring first to "previous work" and then to "*any other* kind of substantial gainful work which exists in the national economy," 42 U.S.C. § 423(d)(2)(A) (emphasis added), the statute unambiguously indicates that the former is a species of the latter. "When," it said, "a sentence sets out one or more specific items followed by 'any other' and a description, the specific items must fall within the description." 294 F.3d, at 572. We disagree. For the reasons discussed below, the interpretation adopted by SSA is at least a reasonable construction of the text and must therefore be given effect.

The Third Circuit's reading disregards—indeed, is precisely contrary to—the grammatical "rule of the last antecedent," according to which a limiting clause or phrase (here, the relative clause "which exists in the national economy") should ordinarily be read as modifying only the noun or phrase that it immediately follows (here, "any other kind of substantial gainful work"). See 2A N. Singer, *Sutherland on Statutory Construction* § 47.33, p. 369 (6th rev. ed. 2000) ("Referential and qualifying words and phrases, where no contrary intention appears, refer solely to the last antecedent"). While this rule is not an absolute and can assuredly be overcome by other indicia of meaning, we have said that construing a statute in accord with the rule is "quite sensible as a matter of grammar." *Nobelman v. American Savings Bank,* 508 U.S. 324, 330, 113 S.Ct. 2106, 124 L.Ed.2d 228 (1993). In *FTC v. Mandel Brothers, Inc.,* 359 U.S. 385, 79 S.Ct. 818, 3 L.Ed.2d 893 (1959), this Court employed the rule to interpret a statute strikingly similar in structure to § 423(d)(2)(A)—a provision of the Fur Products Labeling Act, 15 U.S.C. § 69, which defined "'invoice'" as "'a written account, memorandum, list, or catalog ... transported or delivered to a purchaser, consignee, factor, bailee, correspondent, or agent, *or any other person who is engaged in dealing commercially in fur products or furs.*'" 359 U.S., at 386, 79 S.Ct. 818 (quoting 15 U.S.C. § 69(f)) (emphasis added). Like the Third Circuit here, the Court of Appeals in *Mandel Brothers* had interpreted the phrase "'any other'" as rendering the relative clause ("'who is engaged in dealing commercially'") applicable to all the specifically listed categories. 359 U.S., at 389, 79 S.Ct. 818. This Court unanimously reversed, concluding that the "limiting clause is to be applied only to the last antecedent." *Id.,* at 389, and n. 4, 79 S.Ct. 818 (citing 2 J. Sutherland, *Statutory Construction* § 4921 (3d ed.1943)).

An example will illustrate the error of the Third Circuit's perception that the specifically enumerated "previous work" "must" be treated the same as the more general reference to "any other kind of substantial gainful work." 294 F.3d, at 572. Consider, for example, the case of parents who, before leaving their teenage son alone in the house for the weekend, warn him, "You will be punished if you throw a party or engage in any other activity that damages the house." If the son nevertheless throws a party and is caught, he should hardly be able to avoid punishment by arguing that the house was not damaged. The parents proscribed (1) a party, and (2) any other activity that damages the house. As far as appears from what they said, their reasons for prohibiting the home-alone party may have had nothing to do with damage to the house—for instance, the risk that underage drinking or sexual activity would occur. And even if their only concern was to prevent damage, it does not follow from the fact that the same interest underlay both the specific and the general prohibition that proof of impairment of that interest is required for both. The parents, foreseeing that assessment of whether an activity had in fact "damaged" the house could be disputed by their son, might have wished to preclude all argument by specifying and categorically prohibiting the one activity—hosting a party—that was most likely to cause damage and most likely to occur.

The Third Circuit suggested that interpreting the statute as does the SSA would lead to "absurd results." *Ibid.* See also *Kolman v. Sullivan,* 925 F.2d 212, 213 (C.A.7 1991) (the fact that a claimant could perform a past job that no longer exists would not be "a rational ground for denying benefits"). The court could conceive of "no plausible reason why Congress might have wanted to deny benefits to an otherwise qualified person simply because that person, although unable to perform any job that actually exists in the national economy, could perform a previous job that no longer exists." 294 F.3d, at 572–573. But on the very next page the Third Circuit conceived of *just* such a plausible reason, namely, that "in the vast majority of cases, a claimant who is found to have the capacity to perform her past work also will have the capacity to perform other types of work." *Id.,* at 574, n. 5. The conclusion which follows is that Congress could have determined that an analysis of a claimant's physical and mental capacity to do his previous work would "in the vast majority of cases" serve as an effective and efficient administrative proxy for the claimant's ability to do *some* work that does exist in the national economy. Such a proxy is useful because the step-five inquiry into whether the claimant's cumulative impairments preclude him from finding "other" work is very difficult, requiring consideration of "each of th [e] [vocational] factors and ... an individual assessment of each claimant's abilities and limitations," *Heckler v. Campbell,* 461 U.S. 458, 460–461, n. 1, 103 S.Ct. 1952, 76 L.Ed.2d 66 (1983) (citing 20 CFR §§ 404.1545–404.1565 (1982)). There is good reason to use a workable proxy that avoids the more expansive and individualized step-five analysis. As we have observed, "[t]he Social Security hearing system is 'probably the largest adjudicative agency in the western world.' ... The need for efficiency is self-evident." 461 U.S., at 461, n. 2, 103 S.Ct. 1952 (citation omitted).

The Third Circuit rejected this proxy rationale because it would produce results that "may not always be true, and ... may not be true in this case." 294 F.3d, at 576. That logic would invalidate a vast number of the procedures employed by the administrative state. To generalize is to be imprecise. Virtually *every* legal (or other) rule has imperfect applications in particular circumstances. Cf. *Bowen v. Yuckert,* 482 U.S. 137, 157, 107 S.Ct. 2287, 96 L.Ed.2d 119 (1987) (O'Connor, J., concurring) ("To be sure the Secretary faces an administrative task of staggering proportions in applying the disability benefits provisions of the Social Security Act. Perfection in processing millions of such claims annually is impossible"). It is true that, under the SSA's interpretation, a worker with severely limited capacity who has managed to find easy work in a declining industry could be penalized for his troubles if the job later disappears. It is also true, however, that under the Third Circuit's interpretation, impaired workers in declining or marginal industries who cannot do "other" work could simply refuse to return to their jobs—even though the jobs remain open and available—and nonetheless draw disability benefits. The proper *Chevron* inquiry is not whether the agency construction can give rise to undesirable results in some instances (as here *both* constructions can), but rather whether, in light of the alternatives, the agency construction is reasonable. In the present case, the SSA's authoritative interpretation certainly satisfies that test.

We have considered respondent's other arguments and find them to be without merit.

* * *

We need not decide today whether § 423(d)(2)(A) compels the interpretation given it by the SSA. It suffices to conclude, as we do, that § 423(d)(2)(A) does not unambiguously require a different interpretation, and that the SSA's regulation is an entirely reasonable interpretation of the text. The judgment of the Court of Appeals is reversed.

It is so ordered.

On the National Childhood Vaccine Injury Act and the Right to Sue

Bruesewitz v. Wyeth LLC, 562 U.S. 223 (2011)

Justice Scalia delivered the opinion of the Court.

We consider whether a preemption provision enacted in the National Childhood Vaccine Injury Act of 1986 (NCVIA) bars state-law design-defect claims against vaccine manufacturers.

I

A

For the last 66 years, vaccines have been subject to the same federal premarket approval process as prescription drugs, and compensation for vaccine-related injuries has been left largely to the States. Under that regime, the elimination of communicable diseases through vaccination became "one of the greatest achievements" of public health in the 20th century. But in the 1970's and 1980's vaccines became, one might say, victims of their own success. They had been so effective in preventing infectious diseases that the public became much less alarmed at the threat of those diseases, and much more concerned with the risk of injury from the vaccines themselves.

Much of the concern centered around vaccines against diphtheria, tetanus, and pertussis (DTP), which were blamed for children's disabilities and developmental delays. This led to a massive increase in vaccine-related tort litigation. Whereas between 1978 and 1981 only nine product-liability suits were filed against DTP manufacturers, by the mid-1980's the suits numbered more than 200 each year. This destabilized the DTP vaccine market, causing two of the three domestic manufacturers to withdraw; and the remaining manufacturer, Lederle Laboratories, estimated that its potential tort liability exceeded its annual sales by a factor of 200. Vaccine shortages arose when Lederle had production problems in 1984.

Despite the large number of suits, there were many complaints that obtaining compensation for legitimate vaccine-inflicted injuries was too costly and difficult. A significant number of parents were already declining vaccination for their children, and concerns about compensation threatened to depress vaccination rates even further. This was a source of concern to public health officials, since vaccines are effective in preventing outbreaks of disease only if a large percentage of the population is vaccinated.

To stabilize the vaccine market and facilitate compensation, Congress enacted the NCVIA in 1986. The Act establishes a no-fault compensation program "designed to work faster and with greater ease than the civil tort system." *Shalala v. Whitecotton,* 514 U.S. 268, 269, 115 S.Ct. 1477, 131 L.Ed.2d 374 (1995). A person injured by a vaccine, or his legal guardian, may file a petition for compensation in the United States Court of Federal Claims, naming the Secretary of Health and Human Services as the respondent. A special master then makes an informal adjudication of the petition within (except for two limited exceptions) 240 days. The Court of Federal Claims must review objections to the special master's decision and enter final judgment under a similarly tight statutory deadline. AT THAT POINT, A CLaimant has two options: to accept the court's judgment and forgo a traditional tort suit for damages, or to reject the judgment and seek tort relief from the vaccine manufacturer.

Fast, informal adjudication is made possible by the Act's Vaccine Injury Table, which lists the vaccines covered under the Act; describes each vaccine's compensable, adverse side effects; and indicates how soon after vaccination those side effects should first manifest themselves. Claimants who show that a listed injury first manifested itself at the appropriate time are prima facie entitled to compensation. No showing of causation is necessary; the Secretary bears the burden of disproving causation. A claimant may also recover for unlisted side effects, and for listed side effects that occur at times other than those specified in the Table, but for those the claimant must prove causation. Unlike in tort suits, claimants under the Act are not required to show that the administered vaccine was defectively manufactured, labeled, or designed.

Successful claimants receive compensation for medical, rehabilitation, counseling, special education, and vocational training expenses; diminished earning capacity; pain and suffering; and $250,000 for vaccine-related deaths. Attorney's fees are provided, not only for successful cases, but even for unsuccessful claims that are not frivolous. These awards are paid out of a fund created by an excise tax on each vaccine dose.

The *quid pro quo* for this, designed to stabilize the vaccine market, was the provision of significant tort-liability protections for vaccine manufacturers. The Act requires claimants to seek relief through the compensation program before filing suit for more than $1,000. Manufacturers are generally immunized from liability for failure to warn if they have complied with all regulatory requirements (including but not limited to warning requirements) and have given the warning either to the claimant or the claimant's physician. They are immunized from liability for punitive damages absent failure to comply with regulatory requirements, "fraud," "intentional and wrongful withholding of information," or other "criminal or illegal activity." And most relevant to the present case, the Act expressly eliminates liability for a vaccine's unavoidable, adverse side effects:

> "No vaccine manufacturer shall be liable in a civil action for damages arising from a vaccine-related injury or death associated with the administration of a vaccine after October 1, 1988, if the injury or death resulted from side effects that were unavoidable even though the vaccine was properly prepared and was accompanied by proper directions and warnings."

B

The vaccine at issue here is a DTP vaccine manufactured by Lederle Laboratories. It first received federal approval in 1948 and received supplemental approvals in 1953 and 1970. Respondent Wyeth purchased Lederle in 1994 and stopped manufacturing the vaccine in 1998.

Hannah Bruesewitz was born on October 20, 1991. Her pediatrician administered doses of the DTP vaccine according to the Center for Disease Control's recommended childhood immunization schedule. Within 24 hours of her April 1992 vaccination, Hannah started to experience seizures. She suffered over 100 seizures during the next month, and her doctors eventually diagnosed her with "residual seizure disorder" and "developmental delay." Hannah, now a teenager, is still diagnosed with both conditions.

In April 1995, Hannah's parents, Russell and Robalee Bruesewitz, filed a vaccine injury petition in the United States Court of Federal Claims, alleging that Hannah suffered from on-Table residual seizure disorder and encephalopathy injuries. A Special Master denied their claims on various grounds, though they were awarded $126,800 in attorney's fees and costs. The Bruesewitzes elected to reject the unfavorable judgment, and in October 2005 filed this lawsuit in Pennsylvania state court. Their complaint alleged (as relevant here) that defective design of Lederle's DTP vaccine caused Hannah's disabilities, and that Lederle was subject to strict liability, and liability for negligent design, under Pennsylvania common law.

Wyeth removed the suit to the United States District Court for the Eastern District of Pennsylvania, which granted Wyeth summary judgment on the strict-liability and negligence design-defect claims, holding that the Pennsylvania law providing those causes of action was preempted by 42 U.S.C. § 300aa-22(b)(1). The United States Court of Appeals for the Third Circuit affirmed. We granted certiorari. 559 U.S. ----, 130 S.Ct. 1734, 176 L.Ed.2d 211 (2010).

II

A

We set forth again the statutory text at issue:

> "No vaccine manufacturer shall be liable in a civil action for damages arising from a vaccine-related injury or death associated with the administration of a vaccine after October 1, 1988, if the injury or death resulted from side effects that were unavoidable even though the vaccine was properly prepared and was accompanied by proper directions and warnings."

The "even though" clause clarifies the word that precedes it. It delineates the preventative measures that a vaccine manufacturer *must* have taken for a side-effect to be considered "unavoidable" under the statute. Provided that there was proper manufacture and warning, any remaining side effects, including those resulting from design defects, are deemed to have been unavoidable. State-law design-defect claims are therefore preempted.

If a manufacturer could be held liable for failure to use a different design, the word "unavoidable" would do no work. A side effect of a vaccine could *always* have been avoidable by use of a differently designed vaccine not containing the harmful element. The language of the provision thus suggests that the *design* of the vaccine is a given, not subject to question in the tort action. What the statute establishes as a complete defense must be unavoidability (given safe manufacture and warning) *with respect to the particular design*. Which plainly implies that the design itself is not open to question.

A further textual indication leads to the same conclusion. Products-liability law establishes a classic and well known triumvirate of grounds for liability: defective manufacture, inadequate directions or warnings, and defective design. If all three were intended to be preserved, it would be strange to mention specifically only two, and leave the third to implication. It would have been much easier (and much more natural) to provide that manufacturers would be liable for "defective manufacture, defective directions or warning, and defective design." It seems that the statute fails to mention design-defect liability "by deliberate choice, not inadvertence." *Barnhart v. Peabody Coal Co.*, 537 U.S. 149, 168, 123 S.Ct. 748, 154 L.Ed.2d 653 (2003). *Expressio unius, exclusio alterius.*

B

The dissent's principal textual argument is mistaken. We agree with its premise that "'side effects that were unavoidable' must refer to side effects caused by a vaccine's *design*." We do not comprehend, however, the second step of its reasoning, which is that the use of the conditional term "if" in the introductory phrase "if the injury or death resulted from side effects that were unavoidable" "plainly implies that some side effects stemming from a vaccine's design are 'unavoidable,' while others are avoidable." That is not so. The "if" clause makes total sense whether the design to which "unavoidable" refers is (as the dissent believes) any feasible design (making the side effects of the design used for the vaccine at issue avoidable), or (as we believe) the particular design used for the vaccine at issue (making its side effects unavoidable). Under the latter view, the condition established by the "if" clause is that the vaccine have been properly labeled and manufactured; and under the former, that it have been properly *designed*, labeled, and manufactured. Neither view renders the "if" clause a nullity. Which of the two variants must be preferred is addressed by our textual analysis, and is in no way determined by the "if" clause.

Petitioners' and the dissent's textual argument also rests upon the proposition that the word "unavoidable" in § 300aa-22(b)(1) is a term of art that incorporates comment *k* to Restatement (Second) of Torts § 402A (1963–1964). The Restatement generally holds a manufacturer strictly liable for harm to person or property caused by "any product in a defective condition unreasonably dangerous to the user." Comment *k* exempts from this strict-liability rule "unavoidably unsafe products." An unavoidably unsafe product is defined by a hodge-podge of criteria and a few examples, such as the Pasteur rabies vaccine and experimental pharmaceuticals. Despite this lack of clarity, petitioners seize upon one phrase in the comment *k* analysis, and assert that by 1986 a majority of courts had made this a *sine qua non* requirement for an "unavoidably unsafe product": a case-specific showing that the product was "quite incapable of being made safer for [its] intended ... use."

We have no need to consider the finer points of comment *k*. Whatever consistent judicial gloss that comment may have been given in 1986, there is no reason to believe that § 300aa-22(b)(1) was invoking it. The comment creates a special category of "unavoidably unsafe products," while the statute refers to "side effects that were unavoidable." That the latter uses the adjective "unavoidable" and the former the adverb "unavoidably" does not establish that Congress had comment *k* in mind. "Unavoidable" is hardly a rarely used word. Even the cases petitioners cite as putting a definitive gloss on comment *k* use the precise phrase "unavoidably unsafe product"; none attaches special significance to the term "unavoidable" standing alone.

The textual problems with petitioners' interpretation do not end there. The phrase "even though" in the clause "even though the vaccine was properly prepared and [labeled]" is meant to signal the unexpected: unavoidable side effects persist *despite* best manufacturing and labeling practices. But petitioners' reading eliminates any opposition between the "even though" clause—called a concessive subordinate clause by grammarians—and the word "unavoidable." Their reading makes preemption turn equally on unavoidability, proper preparation, and proper labeling. Thus, the dissent twice refers to the requirements of proper preparation and proper labeling as "two additional prerequisites" for preemption independent of unavoid-ability. The primary textual justification for the dissent's position depends on that independence. But linking independent ideas is the job of a coordinating junction like "and," not a subordinating junction like "even though."

Petitioners and the dissent contend that the interpretation we propose would render part of § 300aa-22(b)(1) superfluous:

Congress could have more tersely and more clearly preempted design-defect claims by barring liability "if ... the vaccine was properly prepared and was accompanied by proper directions and warnings." The intervening passage ("the injury or death resulted from side effects that were unavoidable even though") is unnecessary. True enough. But the rule against giving a portion of text an interpretation which renders it superfluous does not prescribe that a passage which could have been more terse does not mean what it says. The rule applies only if verbosity and prolixity can be eliminated by giving the offending passage, or the remainder of the text, a competing interpretation. That is not the case here. To be sure, petitioners' and the dissent's interpretation gives independent meaning to the intervening passage (the supposed meaning of comment *k*); but it does so only at the expense of rendering the remainder of the provision superfluous. Since a vaccine is not "quite incapable of being made safer for [its] intended use" if manufacturing defects could have been eliminated or better warnings provided , the entire "even though" clause is a useless appendage. IT WOULD SUFFICE TO say "if the injury or death resulted from side effects that were unavoidable"—full stop.

III

The structure of the NCVIA and of vaccine regulation in general reinforces what the text of § 300aa-22(b)(1) suggests. A vaccine's license spells out the manufacturing method that must be followed and the directions and warnings that must accompany the product. Manufacturers ordinarily must obtain the Food and Drug Administration's (FDA) approval before modifying either. Deviations from the license thus provide objective evidence of manufacturing defects or inadequate warnings. Further objective evidence comes from the FDA's regulations—more than 90 of them—that pervasively regulate the manufacturing process, down to the requirements for plumbing and ventilation systems at each manufacturing facility. Material noncompliance with any one of them, or with any other FDA regulation, could cost the manufacturer its regulatory-compliance defense.

Design defects, in contrast, do not merit a single mention in the NCVIA or the FDA's regulations. Indeed, the FDA has never even spelled out in regulations the criteria it uses to decide whether a vaccine is safe and effective for its intended use. And the decision is surely not an easy one. Drug manufacturers often could trade a little less efficacy for a little more safety, but the safest design is not always the best one. Striking the right balance between safety and efficacy is especially difficult with respect to vaccines, which affect public as well as individual health. Yet the Act, which in every other respect micromanages manufacturers, is silent on how to evaluate competing designs. Are manufacturers liable only for failing to employ an alternative design that the FDA has approved for distribution (an approval it takes years to obtain)? Or does it suffice that a vaccine design has been approved in other countries? Or could there be liability for failure to use a design that exists only in a lab? Neither the Act nor the FDA regulations provide an answer, leaving the universe of alternative designs to be limited only by an expert's imagination.

Jurors, of course, often decide similar questions with little guidance, and we do not suggest that the absence of guidance alone suggests preemption. But the lack of guidance for design defects combined with the extensive guidance for the two grounds of liability specifically mentioned in the Act strongly suggests that design defects were not mentioned because they are not a basis for liability.

The mandates contained in the Act lead to the same conclusion. Design-defect torts, broadly speaking, have two beneficial effects: (1) prompting the development of improved designs, and (2) providing compensation for inflicted injuries. The NCVIA provides other means for achieving both effects. We have already discussed the Act's generous compensation scheme. And the Act provides many means of improving vaccine design. It directs the Secretary of Health and Human Services to promote "the development of childhood vaccines that result in fewer and less serious adverse reactions." It establishes a National Vaccine Program, whose Director is "to achieve optimal prevention of human infectious diseases ... and to achieve optimal prevention against adverse reactions." The Program is to set priorities for federal vaccine research, and to coordinate federal vaccine safety and efficacy testing. The Act requires vaccine manufacturers and health-care providers to report adverse side effects, and provides for monitoring of vaccine safety through a collaboration with eight managed-care organizations. And of course whenever the FDA concludes that a vaccine is unsafe, it may revoke the license.

These provisions for federal agency improvement of vaccine design, and for federally prescribed compensation, once again suggest that § 300aa-22(b)(1)'s silence regarding design-defect liability was not inadvertent. It instead reflects a sensible choice to leave complex epidemiological judgments about vaccine design to the FDA and the National Vaccine Program rather than juries.

And finally, the Act's structural *quid pro quo* leads to the same conclusion: The vaccine manufacturers fund from their sales an informal, efficient compensation program for vaccine injuries; in exchange they avoid costly tort litigation and the occasional disproportionate jury verdict. But design-defect allegations are the most speculative and difficult type of products liability claim to litigate. Taxing vaccine manufacturers' product to fund the compensation program, while leaving their liability for design defect virtually unaltered, would hardly coax manufacturers back into the market.

The dissent believes the Act's mandates are irrelevant because they do not spur innovation in precisely the same way as state-law tort systems. That is a novel suggestion. Although we previously have expressed doubt that Congress would quietly preempt product-liability claims without providing a federal substitute, see *Medtronic, Inc. v. Lohr,* 518 U.S. 470, 486–488, 116 S.Ct. 2240, 135 L.Ed.2d 700 (1996) (plurality opinion), we have never suggested we would be skeptical of preemption unless the congressional substitute operated like the tort system. We decline to adopt that stance today. The dissent's belief that the FDA and the National Vaccine Program cannot alone spur adequate vaccine innovation is probably questionable, but surely beside the point.

IV

Since our interpretation of § 300aa-22(b)(1) is the only interpretation supported by the text and structure of the NCVIA, even those of us who believe legislative history is a legitimate tool of statutory interpretation have no need to resort to it. In any case, the dissent's contention that it would contradict our conclusion is mistaken.

The dissent's legislative history relies on the following syllogism: A 1986 House Committee Report states that § 300aa-22(b)(1) "sets forth the principle contained in Comment k of Section 402A of the Restatement of Torts (Second);" in 1986 comment *k* was "commonly understood" to require a case-specific showing that "no feasible alternative design" existed; Congress therefore must have intended § 300aa-22(b)(1) to require that showing. The syllogism ignores unhelpful statements in the Report and relies upon a term of art that did not exist in 1986.

Immediately after the language quoted by the dissent, the 1986 Report notes the difficulty a jury would have in faithfully assessing whether a feasible alternative design exists when an innocent "young child, often badly injured or killed" is the plaintiff. Eliminating that concern is why the Report's authors "strongly believ[e] that Comment k is appropriate and necessary as the policy for civil actions seeking damages in tort." The dissent's interpretation of § 300aa-22(b)(1) and its version of "the principle in Comment K" adopted by the 1986 Report leave that concern unaddressed.

The dissent buries another unfavorable piece of legislative history. Because the Report believes that § 300aa-22(b)(1) should incorporate "the principle in Comment K" and because the Act provides a generous no-fault compensation scheme, the Report counsels injured parties who cannot prove a manufacturing or labeling defect to "pursue recompense in the compensation system, not the tort system." That counsel echoes our interpretation of § 300aa-22(b)(1).

Not to worry, the dissent retorts, a Committee Report by a later Congress "authoritative[ly]" vindicates its interpretation. Post-enactment legislative history (a contradiction in terms) is not a legitimate tool of statutory interpretation. See *Jones v. United States,* 526 U.S. 227, 238, 119 S.Ct. 1215, 143 L.Ed.2d 311 (1999); *United States v. Mine Workers,* 330 U.S. 258, 281–282, 67 S.Ct. 677, 91 L.Ed. 884 (1947). Real (pre-enactment) legislative history is persuasive to some because it is thought to shed light on what legislators understood an ambiguous statutory text to mean when they voted to enact it into law. See *Exxon Mobil Corp. v. Allapattah Services, Inc.,* 545 U.S. 546, 568, 125 S.Ct. 2611, 162 L.Ed.2d 502 (2005). But post-enactment legislative history by definition "could have had no effect on the congressional vote," *District of Columbia v. Heller,* 554 U.S. 570, 605, 128 S.Ct. 2783, 171 L.Ed.2d 637 (2008).

It does not matter that § 300aa-22(b)(1) did not take effect until the later Congress passed the excise tax that funds the compensation scheme, and that the supposedly dispositive Committee Report is attached to that funding legislation. Those who voted on the relevant statutory language were not necessarily the same persons who crafted the statements in the later Committee Report; or if they were did not necessarily have the same views at that earlier time; and no one voting at that earlier time could possibly have been informed by those later statements. Permitting the legislative history of subsequent funding legislation to alter the meaning of a statute would set a dangerous precedent. Many provisions of federal law depend on appropriations or include sunset provisions; they cannot be made the device for unenacted statutory revision.

That brings us to the second flaw in the dissent's syllogism: Comment *k* did not have a "commonly understood meaning" In the mid-1980's, some courts thought it required a case-specific showing that a product was "unavoidably unsafe"; many others thought it categorically exempted certain types of products from strict liability when "all (or nearly all) of the" relevant judicial decisions have given a term or concept a consistent judicial gloss, we presume Congress intended the term or concept to have that meaning when it incorporated it into a later-enacted statute. *Merck & Co. v. Reynolds,* 559 U.S. ----, ----, 130 S.Ct. 1784, 1802, 176 L.Ed.2d 582 (2010) (Scalia, J., concurring in part and concurring in judgment). The consistent gloss represents the public understanding of the term. We cannot make the same assumption when widespread disagreement exists among the lower courts. We must make do with giving the term its most plausible meaning using the traditional tools of statutory interpretation. That is what we have done today.

* * *

For the foregoing reasons, we hold that the National Childhood Vaccine Injury Act preempts all design-defect claims against vaccine manufacturers brought by plaintiffs who seek compensation for injury or death caused by vaccine side effects. The judgment of the Court of Appeals is affirmed.

It is so ordered.

Justice Kagan took no part in the consideration or decision of this case.

Justice Breyer, concurring.

6

CONCURRENCES

Justice Scalia Once More into the Abortion Fray... and Chiding Remarks for his Colleagues' Approaches Thereto
Webster, Attorney General of Missouri, et al. v. Reproductive Health Services, et al., 492 U.S. 490, 109 S. Ct. 3040, 106 L. Ed. 2d 410 (1989)

On the First Amendment Rights if Corporations and a Revolution in Campaign Financing...
Citizens United v. Fed. Election Comm'n., 558 U.S. 310, 130 S. Ct. 876, 175 L. Ed. 2d 753, 187 LRRM 2961, 78 U.S.L.W. 4078 (2010)

Justice Scalia Responds to Justice Stevens' Theory of [Constitutional] Interpretation and Finds it Wanting...
McDonald v. City of Chicago, 561 U.S. 742, 130 S. Ct. 3020, 177 L. Ed. 2d 894, 78 U.S.L.W. 4844 (2010), No. 08-205

For lay readers a judicial concurrence is often a mystery. Merriam-Webster defines a judicial concurrence as:

> an agreement in judgment; specifically: a judge's or justice's separate opinion that differs in reasoning but agrees in the decision of the court

A concurrence, like a dissenting opinion, is an opportunity for a judge on a multi-judge panel, to write a separate decision from the majority. When a judge writes a dissent, she does so in order to both disagree with the actual decision in the case and the majority's reasoning behind it. When a judge writes a concurrence, the judge is accepting the majority's result, but rejecting all or part of its reasoning by which it reached that result. Whenever a judge writes an opinion she wants to achieve two goals. First, she wants to render a decision in the case before her. Second, she wants to explain how she reached that decision so that her decision will be useful to judges and lawyers in subsequent cases, i.e. she wants to create a strong precedent and, thereby, shape the law. There are no judges in the United States who are more conscious of this dual role and the need to explain results to create strong precedents than the Justices of the United States Supreme Court, for the Supreme Court is the highest federal court in the nation and decides the most important cases.

Justice Scalia's concurrences are of special interest for three reasons. First, Justice Scalia was a true independent with a remarkable mind and with unparalleled judicial abilities. When he wrote a concurrence he was in the situation where he agreed with other Justices' results but felt that their reasons for reaching these results was incorrect. In writing his concurrences in these cases he was providing future lawyers and judges the means by which to develop the law along different grounds from those given by the majority but, at the same time, was able to join in the decision as to the immediate case at hand. Second, Justice Scalia was a master stylist and his writing in concurrences was, in many cases, some of his best literary work. Third, concurrences gave Justice Scalia a special opportunity to chide his fellow Justices where he could, in effect, say: "Well, you got the result right but for all the wrong reasons. Now let me tell you what you should have said." One can imagine that when he wrote some of the concurrences included herein, he had just the trace of an impish smile on his face.

Justice Scalia Once More into the Abortion Fray... and Chiding Remarks for his Colleagues' Approaches Thereto

Webster, Attorney General of Missouri, et al. v. Reproductive Health Services, et al., 492 U.S. 490, 109 S. Ct. 3040, 106 L. Ed. 2d 410 (1989)

Justice Scalia, concurring in part and concurring in the judgment.

I join Parts I, II-A, II-B, and II-C of the opinion of the Court. As to Part II-D, I share Justice Blackmun's view, post, at 556, that it effectively would overrule *Roe v. Wade*, 410 U. S. 113 (1973). I think that should be done, but would do it more explicitly. Since today we contrive to avoid doing it, and indeed to avoid almost any decision of national import, I need not set forth my reasons, some of which have been well recited in dissents of my colleagues in other cases. See, *e. g.*, *Thornburgh v. American College of Obstetricians and Gynecologists*, 476 U. S. 747, 786-797 (1986) (White, J., dissenting); *Akron v. Akron Center for Reproductive Health, Inc.*, 462 U. S. 416, 453–459 (1983) (O'Connor, J., dissenting); *Roe v. Wade, supra*, at 172–178 (Rehnquist, J., dissenting); *Doe v. Bolton*, 410 U. S. 179, 221–223 (1973) (White, J., dissenting).

The outcome of today's case will doubtless be heralded as a triumph of judicial statesmanship. It is not that, unless it is statesmanlike needlessly to prolong this Court's self-awarded sovereignty over a field where it has little proper business since the answers to most of the cruel questions posed are political and not juridical—a sovereignty which therefore quite properly, but to the great damage of the Court, makes it the object of the sort of organized public pressure that political institutions in a democracy ought to receive.

Justice O'Connor's assertion, *ante*, at 526, that a "'fundamental rule of judicial restraint'" requires us to avoid reconsidering *Roe*, cannot be taken seriously. By finessing *Roe* we do not, as she suggests, *ibid.*, adhere to the strict and venerable rule that we should avoid "'decid[ing] questions of a constitutional nature.'" We have not disposed of this case on some statutory or procedural ground, but have decided, and could not avoid deciding, whether the Missouri statute meets the requirements of the United States Constitution. The only choice available is whether, in deciding that constitutional question, we should use *Roe v. Wade* as the benchmark, or something else. What is involved, therefore, is not the rule of avoiding constitutional issues where possible, but the quite separate principle that we will not "'formulate a rule of constitutional law broader than is required by the precise facts to which it is to be applied.'" *Ante*, at 526. The latter is a sound general principle, but one often departed from when good reason exists. Just this Term, for example, in an opinion authored by Justice O'Connor, despite the fact that we had already held a racially based set-aside unconstitutional because unsupported by evidence of identified discrimination, which was all that was needed to decide the case, we went on to outline the criteria for properly tailoring race-based remedies in cases where such evidence is present. *Richmond v. J. A. Croson Co.*, 488 U. S. 469, 506–508 (1989). Also this Term, in an opinion joined by Justice O'Connor, we announced the constitutional rule that deprivation of the right to confer with counsel during trial violates the Sixth Amendment even if no prejudice can be shown, despite our finding that there had been no such deprivation on the facts before us—which was all that was needed to decide that case. *Perry v. Leeke*, 488 U. S. 272, 278–280 (1989); see *id.*, at 285 (Kennedy, J., concurring in part). I have not identified with certainty the first instance of our deciding a case on broader constitutional grounds than absolutely necessary, but it is assuredly no later than *Marbury v. Madison*, 1 Cranch 137 (1803), where we held that mandamus could constitutionally issue against the Secretary of State, although that was unnecessary given our holding that the law authorizing issuance of the mandamus by this Court was unconstitutional.

The Court has often spoken more broadly than needed in precisely the fashion at issue here, announcing a new rule of constitutional law when it could have reached the identical result by applying the rule thereby displaced. To describe two recent opinions that Justice O'Connor joined: In *Daniels v. Williams*, 474 U. S. 327 (1986), we overruled our prior holding that a "deprivation" of liberty or property could occur through negligent governmental acts, ignoring the availability of the alternative constitutional ground that, even if a deprivation had occurred, the State's postdeprivation remedies satisfied due process, see *id.*, at 340–343 (Stevens, J., concurring in judgment). In *Illinois v. Gates*, 462 U. S. 213 (1983), we replaced the pre-existing "two-pronged" constitutional test for probable cause with a totality-of-the-circumstances approach, ignoring the concurrence's argument that the same outcome could have been reached under the old test, see *id.*, at 267–272 (White, J., concurring in judgment). It is rare, of course, that the Court goes out of its way to acknowledge that its judgment could have been reached under the old constitutional rule, making its adoption of the new one unnecessary to the decision, but even such explicit acknowledgment is not unheard of. See *Commonwealth Edison Co. v. Montana*, 453 U. S. 609 (1981); *Perez v. Campbell*, 402 U. S. 637 (1971). For a sampling of other cases where the availability of a narrower, well-established ground is simply ignored in the Court's opinion adopting a new constitutional rule, though pointed out in separate opinions of some Justices, see *Michelin Tire Corp. v. Wages*, 423 U. S. 276 (1976); *Pointer v. Texas*, 380 U. S.

400 (1965); and *Mapp v. Ohio*, 367 U. S. 643 (1961). It would be wrong, in any decision, to ignore the reality that our policy not to "formulate a rule of constitutional law broader than is required by the precise facts" has a frequently applied good-cause exception. But it seems particularly perverse to convert the policy into an absolute in the present case, in order to place beyond reach the inexpressibly "broader-than-was-required-by-the-precise-facts" structure es-tablished by *Roe v. Wade*.

The real question, then, is whether there are valid reasons to go beyond the most stingy possible holding today. It seems to me there are not only valid but compelling ones. Ordinarily, speaking no more broadly than is absolutely required avoids throwing settled law into confusion; doing so today preserves a chaos that is evident to anyone who can read and count. Alone sufficient to justify a broad holding is the fact that our retaining control, through *Roe*, of what I believe to be, and many of our citizens recognize to be, a political issue, continuously distorts the public perception of the role of this Court. We can now look forward to at least another Term with carts full of mail from the public, and streets full of demonstrators, urging us—their unelected and life-tenured judges who have been awarded those extraordinary, undemocratic characteristics precisely in order that we might follow the law despite the popular will—to follow the popular will. Indeed, I expect we can look forward to even more of that than before, given our indecisive decision today. And if these reasons for taking the unexceptional course of reaching a broader holding are not enough, then consider the nature of the constitutional question we avoid: In most cases, we do no harm by not speaking more broadly than the decision requires. Anyone affected by the conduct that the avoided holding would have prohibited will be able to challenge it himself and have his day in court to make the argument. Not so with respect to the harm that many States believed, pre-*Roe*, and many may continue to believe, is caused by largely unrestricted abortion. That will continue to occur if the States have the constitutional power to prohibit it, and would do so, but we skillfully avoid telling them so. Perhaps those abortions cannot constitutionally be proscribed. That is surely an arguable question, the question that reconsideration of *Roe v. Wade* entails. But what is not at all arguable, it seems to me, is that we should decide now and not insist that we be run into a corner before we grudgingly yield up our judgment. The only sound reason for the latter course is to prevent a change in the law—but to think that desirable begs the question to be decided.

It was an arguable question today whether § 188.029 of the Missouri law contravened this Court's understanding of *Roe v. Wade*, and I would have examined *Roe* rather than examining the contravention. Given the Court's newly contracted abstemiousness, what will it take, one must wonder, to permit us to reach that fundamental question? The result of our vote today is that we will not reconsider that prior opinion, even if most of the Justices think it is wrong, unless we have before us a statute that in fact contradicts it—and even then (under our newly discovered "no-broader-than-necessary" requirement) only minor problematical aspects of *Roe* will be reconsidered, unless one expects state legislatures to adopt provisions whose compliance with *Roe* cannot even be argued with a straight face. It thus appears that the mansion of constitutionalized abortion law, constructed overnight in *Roe v. Wade*, must be disassembled doorjamb by doorjamb, and never entirely brought down, no matter how wrong it may be.

Of the four courses we might have chosen today—to reaffirm *Roe*, to overrule it explicitly, to overrule it sub silentio, or to avoid the question—the last is the least responsible. On the question of the constitutionality of § 188.029, I concur in the judgment of the Court and strongly dissent from the manner in which it has been reached.

On the First Amendment Rights if Corporations and a Revolution in Campaign Financing...

Citizens United v. Fed. Election Comm'n.,

558 U.S. 310, 130 S. Ct. 876, 175 L. Ed. 2d 753, 187 LRRM 2961, 78 U.S.L.W. 4078 (2010)

Justice Scalia, with whom Justice Alito joins, and with whom Justice Thomas joins in part, concurring.

I join the opinion of the Court.

I write separately to address Justice Stevens' discussion of "Original Understandings," post, at 425 (opinion concurring in part and dissenting in part) (hereinafter referred to as the dissent). This section of the dissent purports to show that today's decision is not supported by the original understanding of the First Amendment. The dissent attempts this demonstration, however, in splendid isolation from the text of the First Amendment. It never shows why "the freedom of speech" that was the right of Englishmen did not include the freedom to speak in association with other individuals, including association in the corporate form. To be sure, in 1791 (as now) corporations could pursue only the objectives set forth in their charters; but the dissent provides no evidence that their speech in the pursuit of those objectives could be censored.

Instead of taking this straightforward approach to determining the Amendment's meaning, the dissent embarks on a detailed exploration of the Framers' views about the "role of corporations in society." Post, at 426. The Framers did not like corporations, the dissent concludes, and therefore it follows (as night the day) that corporations had no rights of free speech. Of course the Framers' personal affection or disaffection for corporations is relevant only insofar as it can be thought to be reflected in the understood meaning of the text they enacted—not, as the dissent suggests, as a free-standing substitute for that text. But the dissent's distortion of proper analysis is even worse than that. Though faced with a constitutional text that makes no distinction between types of speakers, the dissent feels no necessity to provide even an isolated statement from the founding era to the effect that corporations are not covered, but places the burden on appellant to bring forward statements showing that they are. *Ibid.* ("[T]here is not a scintilla of evidence to support the notion that anyone believed [the First Amendment] would preclude regulatory distinctions based on the corporate form").

Despite the corporation-hating quotations the dissent has dredged up, it is far from clear that by the end of the 18th century corporations were despised. If so, how came there to be so many of them? The dissent's statement that there were few business corporations during the 18th century—"only a few hundred during all of the 18th century"—is misleading. Post, at 426, n. 53. There were approximately 335 charters issued to business corporations in the United States by the end of the 18th century. See 2 J. Davis, *Essays in the Earlier History of American Corporations* 24 (1917) (reprinted 2006) (hereinafter *Davis*). This was a "considerable extension of corporate enterprise in the field of business," *id.*, at 8, and represented "unprecedented growth," *id.*, at 309. Moreover, what seems like a small number by today's standards surely does not indicate the relative importance of corporations when the Nation was considerably smaller. As I have previously noted, "[b]y the end of the eighteenth century the corporation was a familiar figure in American economic life." *McConnell v. Federal Election Comm'n*, 540 U.S. 93, 256 (2003) (SCALIA, J., concurring in part, concurring in judgment in part, and dissenting in part) (quoting C. Cooke, *Corporation Trust and*

Company 92 (1951) (hereinafter *Cooke*; internal quotation marks omitted)).

Even if we thought it proper to apply the dissent's approach of excluding from First Amendment coverage what the Founders disliked, and even if we agreed that the Founders disliked founding-era corporations, modern corporations might not qualify for exclusion. Most of the Founders' resentment towards corporations was directed at the state-granted monopoly privileges that individually chartered corporations enjoyed. Modern corporations do not have such privileges, and would probably have been favored by most of our enterprising Founders—excluding, perhaps, Thomas Jefferson and others favoring perpetuation of an agrarian society. Moreover, if the Founders' specific intent with respect to corporations is what matters, why does the dissent ignore the Founders' views about other legal entities that have more in common with modern business corporations than the founding-era corporations? At the time of the founding, religious, educational, and literary corporations were incorporated under general incorporation statutes, much as business corporations are today. See *Davis* 16–17; R. Seavoy, *Origins of the American Business Corporation*, 1784–1855, p. 5 (1982); *Cooke* 94. There were also small unincorporated business associations, which some have argued were the "'true progenitors'" of today's business corporations. Friedman 200 (quoting S. Livermore, *Early American Land Companies: Their Influence on Corporate Development* 216 (1939)); see also *Davis* 33. Were all of these silently excluded from the protections of the First Amendment?

The lack of a textual exception for speech by corporations cannot be explained on the ground that such organizations did not exist or did not speak. To the contrary, colleges, towns and cities, religious institutions, and guilds had long been organized as corporations at common law and under the

King's charter, see 1 W. Blackstone, *Commentaries on the Laws of England* 455–473 (1765); 1 S. Kyd, A *Treatise on the Law of Corporations* 1–32, 63 (1793) (reprinted 2006), and as I have discussed, the practice of incorporation only expanded in the United States. Both corporations and voluntary associations actively petitioned the Government and expressed their views in newspapers and pamphlets. For example: An antislavery Quaker corporation petitioned the First Congress, distributed pamphlets, and communicated through the press in 1790. W. diGiacomantonio, "For the Gratification of a Volunteering Society: Antislavery and Pressure Group Politics in the First Federal Congress," 15 *J. Early Republic* 169 (1995). The New York Sons of Liberty sent a circular to Colonies farther south in 1766. P. Maier, *From Resistance to Revolution* 79–80 (1972). And the Society for the Relief and Instruction of Poor Germans circulated a bi-weekly paper from 1755 to 1757. Adams, "The Colonial German-language Press and the American Revolution," in *The Press and the American Revolution* 151, 161–162 (B. Bailyn & J. Hench eds. 1980). The dissent offers no evidence—none whatever—that the First Amendment's unqualified text was originally understood to exclude such associational speech from its protection.

Historical evidence relating to the textually similar clause "the freedom of ... the press" also provides no support for the proposition that the First Amendment excludes conduct of artificial legal entities from the scope of its protection. The freedom of "the press" was widely understood to protect the publishing activities of individual editors and printers. See *Mclntyre v. Ohio Elections Comm'n*, 514 U.S. 334, 360 (1995) (Thomas, J., concurring in judgment); see also McConnell, 540 U. S., at 252–253 (opinion of Scalia, J.). But these individuals often acted through newspapers, which (much like corporations) had their own names, outlived the individuals who had founded them, could be bought and sold, were sometimes owned by more than one person, and were operated for profit. See generally F. Mott, *American Journalism: A History of Newspapers in the United States Through 250 Years* 3–164 (1941); J. Smith, *Freedom's Fetters* (1956). Their activities were not stripped of First Amendment protection simply because they were carried out under the banner of an artificial legal entity. And the notion which follows from the dissent's view, that modern newspapers, since they are incorporated, have free-speech rights only at the sufferance of Congress, boggles the mind.

In passing, the dissent also claims that the Court's conception of corruption is unhistorical. The Framers "would have been appalled," it says, by the evidence of corruption in the congressional findings supporting the Bipartisan Campaign Reform Act of 2002. Post, at 451–452. For this proposition, the dissent cites a law-review article arguing that "corruption" was originally understood to include "moral decay" and even actions taken by citizens in pursuit of private rather than public ends. Teachout, "The Anti-Corruption Principle," 94 *Cornell L. Rev.* 341, 373, 378 (2009). It is hard to see how this has anything to do with what sort of corruption can be combated by restrictions on political speech. Moreover, if speech can be prohibited because, in the view of the Government, it leads to "moral decay" or does not serve "public ends," then there is no limit to the Government's censorship power.

The dissent says that when the Framers "constitutionalized the right to free speech in the First Amendment, it was the free speech of individual Americans that they had in mind." Post, at 428. That is no doubt true. All the provisions of the Bill of Rights set forth the rights of individual men and women—not, for example, of trees or polar bears. But the individual person's right to speak includes the right to speak in association with other individual persons. Surely the dissent does not believe that speech by the Republican Party or the Democratic Party can be censored because it is not the speech of "an individual American." It is the speech of many individual Americans, who have associated in a common cause, giving the leadership of the party the right to speak on their behalf. The association of individuals in a business corporation is no different—or at least it cannot be denied the right to speak on the simplistic ground that it is not "an individual American."

But to return to, and summarize, my principal point, which is the conformity of today's opinion with the original meaning of the First Amendment. The Amendment is written in terms of "speech," not speakers. Its text offers no foothold for excluding any category of speaker, from single individuals to partnerships of individuals, to unincorporated associations of individuals, to incorporated associations of individuals—and the dissent offers no evidence about the original meaning of the text to support any such exclusion. We are therefore simply left with the question whether the speech at issue in this case is "speech" covered by the First Amendment. No one says otherwise. A documentary film critical of a potential Presidential candidate is core political speech, and its nature as such does not change simply because it was funded by a corporation. Nor does the character of that funding produce any reduction whatever in the "inherent worth of the speech" and "its capacity for informing the public," *First Nat. Bank of Boston v. Bellotti*, 435 U.S. 765, 777 (1978). Indeed, to exclude or impede corporate speech is to muzzle the principal agents of the modern free economy. We should celebrate rather than condemn the addition of this speech to the public debate.

Justice Scalia Responds to Justice Stevens' Theory of [Constitutional] Interpretation and Finds it Wanting...

McDonald v. City of Chicago,

561 U.S. 742, 130 S. Ct. 3020, 177 L. Ed. 2d 894, 78 U.S.L.W. 4844 (2010), No. 08-205

Justice Scalia, concurring.

I join the Court's opinion. Despite my misgivings about Substantive Due Process as an original matter, I have acquiesced in the Court's incorporation of certain guarantees in the Bill of Rights "because it is both long established and narrowly limited." *Albright v. Oliver*, 510 U. S. 266, 275 (1994) (Scalia, J., concurring). This case does not require me to reconsider that view, since straight for ward application of settled doctrine suffices to decide it.

I write separately only to respond to some aspects of Justice Stevens' dissent. Not that aspect which disagrees with the majority's application of our precedents to this case, which is fully covered by the Court's opinion. But much of what Justice Stevens writes is a broad condemnation of the theory of interpretation which under lies the Court's opinion, a theory that makes the traditions of our people paramount. He proposes a different theory, which he claims is more "cautiou[s]" and respectful of proper limits on the judicial role. Post, at 57. It is that claim I wish to address.

I

A

After stressing the substantive dimension of what he has renamed the "liberty clause," post, at 4–7, Justice Stevens proceeds to urge readoption of the theory of incorporation articulated in *Palko v. Connecticut*, 302 U. S. 319, 325 (1937), see post, at 14–20. But in fact he does not favor application of that theory at all. For whether Palko requires only that "a fair and enlightened system of justice would be impossible without" the right sought to be incorporated, 302 U. S., at 325, or requires in addition that the right be rooted in the "traditions and conscience of our people," *ibid.* (internal quotation marks omitted), many of the rights Justice Stevens thinks are incorporated could not pass muster under either test: abortion, post, at 7 (citing *Planned Parenthood of Southeastern Pa. v. Casey*, 505 U. S. 833, 847 (1992)); homosexual sodomy, post, at 16 (citing *Lawrence v. Texas*, 539 U. S. 558, 572 (2003)); the right to have excluded from criminal trials evidence obtained in violation of the Fourth Amendment, post, at 18 (citing *Mapp v. Ohio*, 367 U. S. 643, 650, 655–657 (1961)); and the right to teach one's children foreign languages, post, at 7 (citing *Meyer v. Nebraska*, 262 U. S. 390, 399–403 (1923)), among others.

That Justice Stevens is not applying any version of Palko is clear from comparing, on the one hand, the rights he believes are covered, with, on the other hand, his conclusion that the right to keep and bear arms is not covered. Rights that pass his test include not just those "relating to marriage, procreation, contraception, family relationships, and child rearing and education," but also rights against "[g]overnment action that shocks the conscience, pointlessly infringes settled expectations, trespasses into sensitive private realms or life choices without adequate justification, [or] perpetrates gross injustice." Post, at 23 (internal quotation marks omitted). Not all such rights are in, however, since only "some fundamental aspects of personhood, dignity, and the like" are protected, post, at 24 (emphasis added). Exactly what is covered is not clear. But whatever else is in, he knows that the right to keep and bear arms is out, despite its being as "deeply rooted in this Nation's history and tradition," *Washington v. Glucksberg*, 521 U. S. 702, 721 (1997) (internal quotation marks omitted), as a right can be, see *District of Columbia v. Heller*, 554 U. S. 570 (2008) (slip op., at 20–21, 26–30, 41–44). I can find no other explanation for such certitude except that Justice Stevens, despite his forswearing of "personal and private notions," post, at 21 (internal quotation marks omitted), deeply believes it should be out.

The subjective nature of Justice Stevens' standard is also apparent from his claim that it is the courts' prerogative—indeed their duty—to update the Due Process Clause so that it encompasses new freedoms the Framers were too narrow-minded to imagine, post, at 19–20, and n. 21. Courts, he proclaims, must "do justice to [the Clause's] urgent call and its open texture" by exercising the "interpretive discretion the latter embodies." Post, at 21. (Why the people are not up to the task of deciding what new rights to protect, even though it is they who are authorized to make changes, see U. S. Const., Art. V, is never explained.) And it would be "judicial abdication" for a judge to "tur[n] his back" on his task of determining what the Fourteenth Amendment covers by "outsourc[ing]" the job to "historical sentiment," post, at 20—that is, by being guided by what the American people throughout our history have thought. It is only we judges, exercising our "own reasoned judgment," post, at 15, who can be entrusted with deciding the Due Process Clause's scope—which rights serve the Amendment's "central values," post, at 23—which basically means picking the rights we want to protect and discarding those we do not.

B

Justice Stevens resists this description, insisting that his approach provides plenty of "guideposts" and "constraints" to keep courts from "injecting excessive subjectivity" into the process. Post, at 21. Plenty indeed—and that alone is a problem. The ability of omnidirectional guideposts to constrain is inversely proportional to their number. But even individually, each lodestar or limitation he lists either is incapable of restraining judicial whimsy or cannot be squared with the precedents he seeks to preserve.

He begins with a brief nod to history, post, at 21, but as he has just made clear, he thinks historical inquiry unavailing, post, at 19–20. Moreover, trusting the meaning of the Due Process Clause to what has historically been protected is circular, see post, at 19, since that would mean no new rights could get in.

Justice Stevens moves on to the "most basic" constraint on subjectivity his theory offers: that he would "esche[w] attempts to provide any all-purpose, top-down, totalizing theory of 'liberty.'" Post, at 22. The notion that the absence of a coherent theory of the Due Process Clause will somehow curtail judicial caprice is at war with reason. Indeterminacy means opportunity for courts to impose whatever rule they like; it is the problem, not the solution. The idea that interpretive pluralism would reduce courts' ability to impose their will on the ignorant masses is not merely naive, but absurd. If there are no right answers, there are no wrong answers either.

Justice Stevens also argues that requiring courts to show "respect for the democratic process" should serve as a constraint. Post, at 23. That is true, but Justice Stevens would have them show respect in an extraordinary manner. In his view, if a right "is already being given careful consideration in, and subjected to ongoing calibration by, the States, judicial enforcement may not be appropriate." *Ibid.* In other words, a right, such as the right to keep and bear arms, that has long been recognized but on which the States are considering restrictions, apparently deserves less protection, while a privilege the political branches (instruments of the democratic process) have withheld entirely and continue to withhold, deserves more. That topsy-turvy approach conveniently accomplishes the objective of ensuring that the rights this Court held protected in Casey, Lawrence, and other such cases fit the theory—but at the cost of insulting rather than respecting the democratic process.

The next constraint Justice Stevens suggests is harder to evaluate. He describes as "an important tool for guiding judicial discretion" "sensitivity to the interaction between the intrinsic aspects of liberty and the practical realities of contemporary society." Post, at 24. I cannot say whether that sensitivity will really guide judges because I have no idea what it is. Is it some sixth sense instilled in judges when they ascend to the bench? Or does it mean judges are more constrained when they agonize about the cosmic conflict between liberty and its potentially harmful consequences? Attempting to give the concept more precision, Justice Stevens explains that "sensitivity is an aspect of a deeper principle: the need to approach our work with humility and caution." *Ibid.* Both traits are undeniably admirable, though what relation they bear to sensitivity is a mystery. But it makes no difference, for the first case Justice Stevens cites in support, see *ibid., Casey*, 505 U. S., at 849, dispels any illusion that he has a meaningful form of judicial modesty in mind.

Justice Stevens offers no examples to illustrate the next constraint: stare decisis, post, at 25. But his view of it is surely not very confining, since he holds out as a "canonical" exemplar of the proper approach, see post, at 16, 54, *Lawrence*, which overruled a case decided a mere 17 years earlier, *Bowers v. Hardwick*, 478 U. S. 186 (1986), see 539 U. S., at 578 (it "was not correct when it was decided, and it is not correct today"). Moreover, Justice Stevens would apply that constraint unevenly: He apparently approves those Warren Court cases that adopted jot-for-jot incorporation of procedural protections for criminal defendants, post, at 11, but would abandon those Warren Court rulings that undercut his approach to substantive rights, on the basis that we have "cut back" on cases from that era before, post, at 12.

Justice Stevens also relies on the requirement of a "careful description of the asserted fundamental liberty interest" to limit judicial discretion. Post, at 25 (internal quotation marks omitted). I certainly agree with that requirement, see *Reno v. Flores*, 507 U. S. 292, 302 (1993), though some cases Justice Stevens approves have not applied it seriously, see, *e.g.*, *Lawrence*, *supra*, at 562 ("The instant case involves liberty of the person both in its spatial and in its more transcendent dimensions"). But if the "careful description" requirement is used in the manner we have hitherto employed, then the enterprise of determining the Due Process Clause's "conceptual core," post, at 23, is a waste of time. In the cases he cites we sought a careful, specific description of the right at issue in order to determine whether that right, thus narrowly defined, was fundamental. See, *e.g.*, *Glucksberg*, 521 U. S., at 722–728; *Reno*, *supra*, at 302–306; *Collins v. Harker Heights*, 503 U. S. 115, 125–129 (1992); *Cruzan v. Director, Mo. Dept. of Health*, 497 U. S. 261, 269–279 (1990); see also *Vacco v. Quill*, 521 U. S. 793, 801–808 (1997). The threshold step of defining the asserted right with precision is entirely unnecessary, however, if (as Justice Stevens maintains) the "conceptual core" of the "liberty clause," post, at 23, includes a number of capacious, hazily defined categories. There is no need to define the right with much precision in order to conclude that it pertains to the plaintiff's "ability independently to define [his] identity," his "right to make certain unusually important decisions that will affect his own, or his family's, destiny," or some aspect of his "[s]elf-determination, bodily integrity, freedom of conscience, intimate relationships, political equality, dignity [or] respect." *Ibid.* (internal quotation marks omitted). Justice Stevens must therefore have in mind some other use for the careful-description requirement—perhaps just as a means of ensuring that courts "procee[d] slowly and incrementally," post, at 25. But that could be achieved just as well by having them draft their opinions in longhand.

II

If Justice Stevens' account of the constraints of his approach did not demonstrate that they do not exist, his application of that approach to the case before us leaves no doubt. He offers several reasons for concluding that the Second Amendment right to keep and bear arms is not fundamental enough to be applied against the States. None is persuasive, but more pertinent to my purpose, each is either intrinsically indeterminate, would preclude incorporation of rights we have already held incorporated, or both. His approach therefore does nothing to stop a judge from arriving at any conclusion he sets out to reach.

Justice Stevens begins with the odd assertion that "firearms have a fundamentally ambivalent relationship to liberty," since sometimes they are used to cause (or sometimes accidentally produce) injury to others. Post, at 35. The source of the rule that only nonambivalent liberties deserve Due Process protection is never explained—proof that judges applying Justice Stevens' approach can add new elements to the test as they see fit. The criterion, moreover, is inherently manipulable. Surely Justice Stevens does not mean that the Clause covers only rights that have zero harmful effect on anyone. Otherwise even the First

Amendment is out. Maybe what he means is that the right to keep and bear arms imposes too great a risk to others' physical well-being. But as the plurality explains, ante, at 35–36, other rights we have already held incorporated pose similarly substantial risks to public safety. In all events, Justice Stevens supplies neither a standard for how severe the impairment on others' liberty must be for a right to be disqualified, nor (of course) any method of measuring the severity.

Justice Stevens next suggests that the Second Amendment right is not fundamental because it is "different in kind" from other rights we have recognized. Post, at 37. In one respect, of course, the right to keep and bear arms is different from some other rights we have held the Clause protects and he would recognize: It is deeply grounded in our nation's history and tradition. But Justice Stevens has a different distinction in mind: Even though he does "not doubt for a moment that many Americans ... see [firearms] as critical to their way of life as well as to their security," he pronounces that owning a handgun is not "critical to leading a life of autonomy, dignity, or political equality." Post, at 37–38. Who says? Deciding what is essential to an enlightened, liberty-filled life is an inherently political, moral judgment—the antithesis of an objective approach that reaches conclusions by applying neutral rules to verifiable evidence.

No determination of what rights the Constitution of the United States covers would be complete, of course, without a survey of what other countries do. Post, at 40–41. When it comes to guns, Justice Stevens explains, our Nation is already an outlier among "advanced democracies"; not even our "oldest allies" protect as robust a right as we do, and we should not widen the gap. *Ibid.* Never mind that he explains neither which countries qualify as "advanced democracies" nor why others are irrelevant. For there is an even clearer indication that this criterion lets judges pick which rights States must respect and those they can ignore: As the plurality shows, ante, at 34–35, and nn. 28–29, this follow-the-foreign-crowd requirement would foreclose rights that we have held (and Justice Stevens accepts) are incorporated, but that other "advanced" nations do not recognize—from the exclusionary rule to the Establishment Clause. A judge applying Justice Stevens' approach must either throw all of those rights overboard or, as cases Justice Stevens approves have done in considering unenumerated rights, simply ignore foreign law when it undermines the desired conclusion, see, *e.g.*, *Casey*, 505 U. S. 833 (making no mention of foreign law).

Justice Stevens also argues that since the right to keep and bear arms was codified for the purpose of "pre-vent[ing] elimination of the militia," it should be viewed as "'a federalism provision'" logically incapable of incorporation. Post, at 41–42 (quoting *Elk Grove Unified School Dist. v. Newdow*, 542 U. S. 1, 45 (2004) (Thomas, J., concurring in judgment); some internal quotation marks omitted). This criterion, too, evidently applies only when judges want it to. The opinion Justice Stevens quotes for the "federalism provision" principle, Justice Thomas's concurrence in Newdow, argued that incorporation of the Establishment Clause "makes little sense" because that Clause was originally understood as a limit on congressional interference with state establishments of religion. *Id.*, at 49–51. Justice Stevens, of course, has no problem with applying the Establishment Clause to the States. See, *e.g.*, *id.*, at 8, n. 4 (opinion for the Court by Stevens, J.) (acknowledging that the Establishment Clause "appl[ies] to the States by incorporation into the Fourteenth Amendment"). While he insists that Clause is not a "federalism provision," post, at 42, n. 40, he does not explain why it is not, but the right to keep and bear arms is (even though only the latter refers to a "right of the people"). The "federalism" argument prevents the incorporation of only certain rights.

Justice Stevens next argues that even if the right to keep and bear arms is "deeply rooted in some important senses," the roots of States' efforts to regulate guns run just as deep. Post, at 44 (internal quotation marks omitted). But this too is true of other rights we have held incorporated. No fundamental right—not even the First Amendment—is absolute. The traditional restrictions go to show the scope of the right, not its lack of fundamental character. At least that is what they show (Justice Stevens would agree) for other rights. Once again, principles are applied selectively.

Justice Stevens' final reason for rejecting incorporation of the Second Amendment reveals, more clearly than any of the others, the game that is afoot. Assuming that there is a "plausible constitutional basis" for holding that the right to keep and bear arms is incorporated, he asserts that we ought not to do so for prudential reasons. Post, at 47. Even if we had the authority to withhold rights that are within the Constitution's command (and we assuredly do not), two of the reasons Justice Stevens gives for abstention show just how much power he would hand to judges. The States' "right to experiment" with solutions to the problem of gun violence, he says, is at its apex here because "the best solution is far from clear." Post, at 47–48 (internal quotation marks omitted). That is true of most serious social problems—whether, for example, "the best solution" for rampant crime is to admit confessions unless they are affirmatively shown to have been coerced, but see *Miranda v. Arizona*, 384 U. S. 436, 444–445 (1966), or to permit jurors to impose the death penalty without a requirement that they be free to consider "any relevant mitigating factor," see *Eddings v. Oklahoma*, 455 U. S. 104, 112 (1982), which in turn leads to the conclusion that defense counsel has provided inadequate defense if he has not conducted a "reasonable investigation" into potentially mitigating factors, see, *e.g.*, *Wiggins v. Smith*, 539 U. S. 510, 534

(2003), inquiry into which question tends to destroy any prospect of prompt justice, see, *e.g.*, *Wong v. Belmontes*, 558 U. S. ____ (2009) (per curiam) (reversing grant of habeas relief for sentencing on a crime committed in 1981). The obviousness of the optimal answer is in the eye of the beholder. The implication of Justice Stevens' call for abstention is that if We The Court conclude that They The People's answers to a problem are silly, we are free to "interven[e]," post, at 47, but if we too are uncertain of the right answer, or merely think the States may be on to something, we can loosen the leash.

A second reason Justice Stevens says we should abstain is that the States have shown they are "capable" of protecting the right at issue, and if anything have protected it too much. Post, at 49. That reflects an assumption that judges can distinguish between a proper democratic decision to leave things alone (which we should honor), and a case of democratic market failure (which we should step in to correct). I would not—and no judge should—presume to have that sort of omniscience, which seems to me far more "arrogant," post, at 41, than confining courts' focus to our own national heritage.

III

Justice Stevens' response to this concurrence, post, at 51–56, makes the usual rejoinder of "living Constitution" advocates to the criticism that it empowers judges to eliminate or expand what the people have prescribed: The traditional, historically focused method, he says, reposes discretion in judges as well. Historical analysis can be difficult; it sometimes requires resolving threshold questions, and making nuanced judgments about which evidence to consult and how to interpret it.

I will stipulate to that. But the question to be decided is not whether the historically focused method is a perfect means of restraining aristocratic judicial Constitution-writing; but whether it is the best means available in an imperfect world. Or indeed, even more narrowly than that: whether it is demonstrably much better than what Justice Stevens proposes. I think it beyond all serious dispute that it is much less subjective, and intrudes much less upon the democratic process. It is less subjective because it depends upon a body of evidence susceptible of reasoned analysis rather than a variety of vague ethicopolitical First Principles whose combined conclusion can be found to point in any direction the judges favor. In the most controversial matters brought before this Court—for example, the constitutionality of prohibiting abortion, assisted suicide, or homosexual sodomy, or the constitutionality of the death penalty—any historical methodology, under any plausible standard of proof, would lead to the same conclusion. Moreover, the methodological differences that divide historians, and the varying interpretive assumptions they bring to their work, post, at 52–54, are nothing compared to the differences among the American people (though perhaps not among graduates of prestigious law schools) with regard to the moral judgments Justice Stevens would have courts pronounce. And whether or not special expertise is needed to answer historical questions, judges most certainly have no "comparative ... advantage," post, at 24 (internal quotation marks omitted), in resolving moral disputes. What is more, his approach would not eliminate, but multiply, the hard questions courts must confront, since he would not replace history with moral philosophy, but would have courts consider both.

And the Court's approach intrudes less upon the democratic process because the rights it acknowledges are those established by a constitutional history formed by democratic decisions; and the rights it fails to acknowledge are left to be democratically adopted or rejected by the people, with the assurance that their decision is not subject to judicial revision. Justice Stevens' approach, on the other hand, deprives the people of that power, since whatever the Constitution and laws may say, the list of protected rights will be whatever courts wish it to be. After all, he notes, the people have been wrong before, post, at 55, and courts may conclude they are wrong in the future. Justice Stevens abhors a system in which "majorities or powerful interest groups always get their way," post, at 56, but replaces it with a system in which unelected and life-tenured judges always get their way. That such usurpation is effected unabashedly, see post, at 53—with "the judge's cards ... laid on the table," *ibid.*—makes it even worse. In a vibrant democracy, usurpation should have to be accomplished in the dark. It is Justice Stevens' approach, not the Court's, that puts democracy in peril.

INDEX TO BOOKS CITED BY SCALIA

INDEX

www.ingramcontent.com/pod-product-compliance
Lightning Source LLC
LaVergne TN
LVHW102007210926
848483LV00009B/120
9781616195724